Learning to Use

WINDOWS APPLICATIONS

Microsoft

VISUAL BASIC 3.0 FOR WINDOWS

Gary B. Shelly
Thomas J. Cashman
John F. Repede

Contributing Author

Steven G. Forsythe

boyd & fraser
publishing company

Special thanks go to the following reviewers of the Shelly Cashman Series Windows Applications textbooks:

Susan Conners, Purdue University Calumet; **William Dorin**, Indiana University Northwest; **Robert Erickson**, University of Vermont; **Roger Franklin**, The College of William and Mary; **Roy O. Foreman**, Purdue University Calumet; **Patricia Harris**, Mesa Community College; **Cynthia Kachik**, Santa Fe Community College; **Suzanne Lambert**, Broward Community College; **Karen Meyer**, Wright State University; **Mike Michaelson**, Palomar College; **Michael Mick**, Purdue University Calumet; **Cathy Paprocki**, Harper College; **Jeffrey Quasney**, Educational Consultant; **Denise Rall**, Purdue University; **Sorel Reisman**, California State University, Fullerton; **John Ross**, Fox Valley Technical College; **Lorie Szalapski**, St. Paul Technical College; **Susan Sebok**, South Suburban College; **Betty Svendsen**, Oakton Community College; **Jeanie Thibault**, Educational Dynamics Institute; **Margaret Thomas**, Ohio University; **Carol Turner**, University of Wisconsin; **Diane Vaught**, National Business College; **Dwight Watt**, Swainsboro Technical Institute; **Melinda White**, Santa Fe Community College; **Eileen Zisk**, Community College of Rhode Island; and **Sue Zulauf**, Sinclair Community College.

© 1995 boyd & fraser publishing company
One Corporate Place • Ferncroft Village
Danvers, Massachusetts 01923

International Thomson Publishing
boyd & fraser publishing company is an ITP company.
The ITP trademark is used under license.

Manufactured in the United States of America

ISBN 0-87709-760-7

Library of Congress Cataloging-in-Publication Data

1 2 3 4 5 6 7 8 9 10 BC 9 8 7 6 5

Microsoft
VISUAL BASIC 3.0 FOR WINDOWS

F or the past twenty years, the Shelly Cashman Series has successfully introduced computers to millions of students by providing the highest quality, most up-to-date, and innovative materials in computer education. This Annotated Instructor's Edition (AIE) of Learning to Use Windows Applications is a prime example of innovative materials. It is the first-ever AIE for applications software textbooks.

The AIE version, available only to the instructor, is identical to the student textbook except for the annotations in the margins and on the answer lines in the Student Assignments.

The AIE is designed to assist you with your lectures by suggesting transparencies to use, summarizing key points, proposing pertinent questions, offering important tips, alerting you to pitfalls, and by incorporating the answers to the Student Assignments. There are several hundred annotations throughout the book. The six categories of annotations are illustrated below and on the following page.

TO ADD A LINE CONTROL

TRANSPARENCIES
Figure 3-17 through Figure 3-19

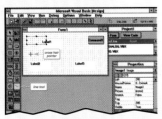

FIGURE 3-17

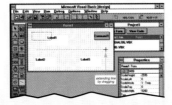

FIGURE 3-18

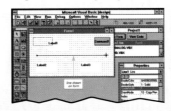

FIGURE 3-19

TRANSPARENCIES
Alerts you to which transparency master to use for the material being presented. All screens, diagrams, and tables shown in the book are available as transparency masters.

Adding Scroll Bar Controls

Scroll bars commonly are used to view the contents of a control when the contents cannot fit within the control's borders. An example is the scroll bar on the Properties list in the Properties window. Visual Basic has two different scroll bar controls; the **horizontal scroll bar** and the **vertical scroll bar**. Their names reflect the orientation of the control on the form, not its use. You control its use. For example, you can use a vertical scroll bar to control the horizontal scrolling of a control on a form.

Another use of the scroll bar control is to give a value to an input. One benefit of using a scroll bar for input is that it prevents you from entering an improper value by mistake, such as a letter instead of a number. The two horizontal scroll bar controls shown in Figure 3-56 are used as input controls for the number of years of the loan and for the annual interest rate.

LECTURE NOTES
■ Ask students to describe how scroll bars are used in applications with which they are familiar.
■ Ask students to identify the scroll bar controls in the Loan application.
■ Discuss the two types of scroll bar controls.
■ Discuss the use of scroll bars in the Loan application.

LECTURE NOTES
Summarizes the key points on the page, helps you to better explain a topic, and includes questions to stimulate class discussion.

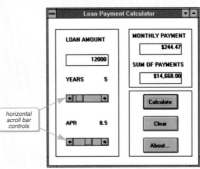

FIGURE 3-56

VB TIPS
■ Setting the BorderStyle to Fixed and the stretch property to True will cause the icon to be elongated to fill the size of an image control.

When Visual Basic loaded the icon, the size of the image control was adjusted automati-cally to the size of its contents (the house icon). This auto-matic sizing occurred because the default value of the image control's BorderStyle property is 0-None. If you set the Border-Style of the image control to 1-Fixed single, Visual Basic does not adjust its size automat-ically.

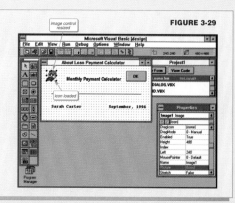

FIGURE 3-29

CAUTION
■ The font names available are only those installed in Win-dows on the PC that you are working with. If you want to run an application whose fonts are different from the default on another PC, you must insure that the second PC has those fonts installed prior to run-ning the application.

Font Properties

Project 2 showed how to change the size of text characters on controls by using the FontSize prop-erty. The Visual Basic con-trols containing text have sev-eral properties that affect the way text appears. For a detailed description of all the properties, use Visual Basic's online Help to search on the word *font*.

Four major font properties are described in Table 3-3. As you can see in Figure 3-24, the labels and captions of controls on the frmLoanabt form have different font properties.

▶ **TABLE 3-3 FONT PROPERTIES**

PROPERTY	DESCRIPTION
FontName	the name of the selected font
FontSize	the size (in printer's points)
FontBold	a True value displays the selected font in bold
FontItalic	a True value displays the selected font in italics

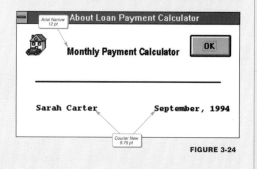

FIGURE 3-24

STUDENT ASSIGNMENT 4
Understanding Controls and Properties

Instructions: Figure SA2-4 lists the controls and properties you used in this project. Place an X in the space provided if the control has the property that follows. Hint: A control may have a property that you haven't used yet. If you're unsure, add the control to a form and look at the drop-down Properties list box in the Properties window or use online Help.

PROPERTIES	CONTROLS								
	Form	Check Box	Combo Box	Command Button	Frame	Label	Option Button	Shape	Text Box
AutoSize	[ ]	[ ]	[ ]	[ ]	[ ]	[X]	[ ]	[ ]	[X]
BorderStyle	[X]	[ ]	[ ]	[ ]	[ ]	[X]	[ ]	[ ]	[X]
Caption	[ ]	[X]	[ ]	[X]	[X]	[X]	[X]	[ ]	[ ]
Default	[ ]	[ ]	[ ]	[X]	[ ]	[ ]	[ ]	[ ]	[ ]
FontSize	[X]	[X]	[X]	[X]	[X]	[X]	[X]	[ ]	[X]
MultiLine	[ ]	[ ]	[ ]	[ ]	[ ]	[ ]	[ ]	[ ]	[X]
Name	[X]	[X]	[X]	[X]	[X]	[X]	[X]	[X]	[X]
ScrollBars	[ ]	[ ]	[ ]	[ ]	[ ]	[ ]	[ ]	[ ]	[X]
Shape	[ ]	[ ]	[ ]	[ ]	[ ]	[ ]	[ ]	[X]	[ ]
Style	[ ]	[ ]	[X]	[ ]	[ ]	[ ]	[ ]	[ ]	[ ]
Text	[ ]	[ ]	[ ]	[ ]	[ ]	[ ]	[ ]	[ ]	[X]
Visible	[X]	[X]	[X]	[X]	[X]	[X]	[X]	[X]	[X]

FIGURE SA2-4

EXERCISE NOTES
■ Exercise 2 builds an application that uses an option button group to control a demon-stration of mathe-matical operations.

COMPUTER LABORATORY EXERCISE 2
Mathematical Operators and Option Groups

Instructions: Start Visual Basic. Open project CLE2-2 from the subdi-rectory VB3 on the Student Diskette that accompanies this book.

Perform the following steps. When you run the completed application, you will enter two numbers and click an option button that designates the operation to perform. The result of the operation then is displayed (Figure CLE2-2).

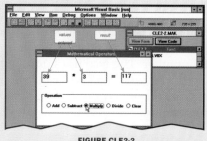

FIGURE CLE2-2

CONTENTS

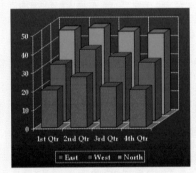

PREFACE

▶ THE WINDOWS ENVIRONMENT

S ince the introduction of Microsoft Windows version 3.1, the personal computing industry has moved rapidly toward establishing Windows as the de facto user interface. The majority of software development funds in software vendor companies are devoted to Windows applications. Virtually all PCs purchased today, at any price, come preloaded with Windows and, often, with one or more Windows applications packages. With an enormous installed base, it is clear that Windows is the operating environment for both now and the future.

The Windows environment places the novice as well as the experienced user in the world of the mouse and a common graphical user interface between all applications. An up-to-date educational institution that teaches applications software to students for their immediate use and as a skill to be used within industry must teach Windows-based applications software.

▶ OBJECTIVES OF THIS TEXTBOOK

L *earning to Use Windows Applications: Microsoft Visual Basic 3.0 for Windows* was specifically developed for a course that covers the essentials of Microsoft Visual Basic. No mathematics beyond the high school freshman level is required. The objectives of this book are as follows:

▶ To teach the fundamentals of Windows and Microsoft Visual Basic 3.0 for Windows
▶ To acquaint the student with the three-step approach to building Windows applications using Visual Basic
▶ To use practical problems to illustrate application-building techniques
▶ To take advantage of the many new capabilities of building applications in a graphical environment (see Figure P-1)

The textbook covers all essential aspects of Visual Basic for Windows. When students complete a course using this book, they will have a firm knowledge of Windows and will be able to develop a wide variety of Windows applications. Further, because they will be learning Windows, students will find the migration to other Windows applications software to be relatively simple and straightforward.

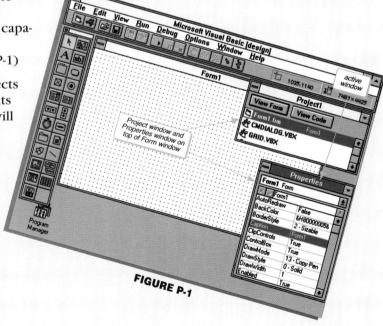

FIGURE P-1

▶ THE SHELLY CASHMAN APPROACH

T he Shelly Cashman Series Windows Applications books present word processing, spreadsheet, database, programming, presentation graphics, and Windows itself by showing the actual screens displayed by Windows and the applications software. Because the student interacts with pictorial displays when using Windows, written words in a textbook does not suffice. For this reason, the Shelly Cashman Series emphasizes screen displays as the primary means of teaching Windows applications software. Every screen shown in the Shelly Cashman Series Windows Applications books appears in color, because the student views color on the screen. In addition, the screens display exactly as the student will see them. The screens in this book were captured while using the software. Nothing has been altered or changed except to highlight portions of the screen when appropriate (see the screens in Figure P-2).

The Shelly Cashman Series Windows Applications books present the material using a unique pedagogy designed specifically for the graphical environment of Windows. The textbooks are primarily designed for a lecture/lab method of presentation, although they are equally suited for a tutorial/hands-on approach wherein the student learns by actually completing each project following the step-by-step instructions. Features of this pedagogy include the following:

▶ **Project Orientation:** Each project in the book solves a complete problem, meaning that the student is introduced to a problem to be solved and is then given the step-by-step process to solve the problem.

▶ **Step-by-Step Instructions:** Each of the tasks required to complete a project is identified throughout the development of the project. For example, a task might be to add a control to a form or change a control's properties using Visual Basic. Then, each step to accomplish the task is specified. The steps are accompanied by screens (see Figure P-2). The student is not told to perform a step without seeing the result of the step on a color screen. Hence, students learn from this book the same as if they were using the computer. This attention to detail in accomplishing a task and showing the resulting screen makes the Shelly Cashman Series Windows Applications textbooks unique.

▶ **Multiple Ways to Use the Book:** Because each step to accomplish a task is illustrated with a screen, the book can be used in a number of ways, including: (a) Lecture and textbook approach — The instructor lectures on the material in the book. The student reads and studies the material and then applies the knowledge to an application on a computer; (b) Tutorial approach — The student performs each specified step on a computer. At the end of the project, the student has solved the problem and is ready to solve comparable student assignments; (c) Reference — Each task in a project is clearly identified. Therefore, the material serves as a complete reference because the student can refer to any task to determine how to accomplish it.

▶ **Windows/Graphical User Interface Approach:** Windows provides a graphical user interface. All of the examples in the book use this interface. Thus, the mouse is used for the majority of control functions and is the preferred user communication tool. When specifying a command to be executed, the sequence is as follows: (a) If a button invokes the command, use the button; (b) If a button is not available, use the command from a menu; (c) If a button or a menu cannot be used, only then is the keyboard used to implement a Windows command.

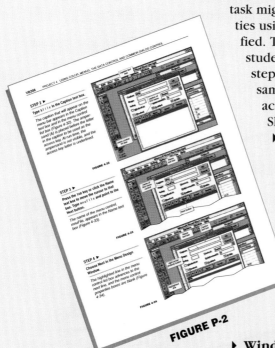

FIGURE P-2

▸ **Emphasis on Windows Techniques:** The most general techniques to implement commands, enter information, and generally interface with Windows are presented. This approach allows the student to move from one application software package to another under Windows with a minimum amount of relearning with respect to interfacing with the software. An application-specific method is taught only when no other option is available.

▸ **Reference for All Techniques:** Even though general Windows techniques are used in all examples, a Quick Reference chart (see Figure P-3) at the end of each project details not only the mouse and menu methods for implementing a command, but also contains the keyboard shortcuts for the commands presented in the project. Therefore, students are exposed to all means for implementing a command.

▶ ORGANIZATION OF THIS TEXTBOOK

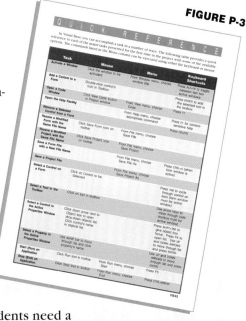

FIGURE P-3

L earning to Use Windows Applications: Microsoft Visual Basic 3.0 for Windows consists of an introduction to computers, two projects on Microsoft Windows 3.1, and five projects on Microsoft Visual Basic 3.0 for Windows.

An Introduction to Computers

Many students taking a course in the use of Visual Basic will have little previous experience using computers. For this reason, the textbook begins with a section titled *Introduction to Computers* that covers computer hardware and software concepts important to first-time computer users.

Using Microsoft Windows 3.1

To effectively use Microsoft Visual Basic 3.0 for Windows, students need a practical knowledge of the Microsoft Windows graphical user interface. Thus, two Microsoft Windows projects are included prior to the Visual Basic projects.

Project 1 – An Introduction to Windows   The first project introduces the students to Windows concepts, Windows terminology, and how to communicate with Windows using the mouse and keyboard. Topics include starting and exiting Windows; opening group windows; maximizing windows; scrolling; selecting menus; choosing a command from a menu; starting and exiting Windows applications; obtaining online Help; and responding to dialog boxes.

Project 2 – Disk and File Management   The second project introduces the students to File Manager. Topics include formatting a diskette; copying a group of files; renaming and deleting files; searching for help topics; activating, resizing, and closing a group window; switching between applications; and minimizing an application window to an application icon.

Building Windows Applications Using Microsoft Visual Basic 3.0 for Windows

After presenting the basic computer and Windows concepts, this textbook provides detailed instruction on how to use Microsoft Visual Basic 3.0 for Windows. The material is divided into five projects as follows:

Project 1 – Building an Application   In Project 1, students are introduced to the major elements of Visual Basic by developing a currency conversion application. The process of building the application consists of three steps: Create the User Interface, Set Properties, and Write Code. Topics include starting Visual Basic; designing a form and adding labels, text boxes, and command buttons; changing the properties of controls; specifying an event procedure; running and saving applications; starting a new project or opening an existing project; and accessing information about Visual Basic through the Help facility and online tutorial.

Project 2 – Working with Controls   Project 2 introduces students to building more complex applications than the one in Project 1. Additional properties of the controls used in Project 1, as well as several new controls, are used to create the movie box office application. Students learn more about writing code by writing six event subroutines and a declaration procedure. Topics include copying controls; copying code between subroutines; using variables in code statements; and using code statements to concatenate string data.

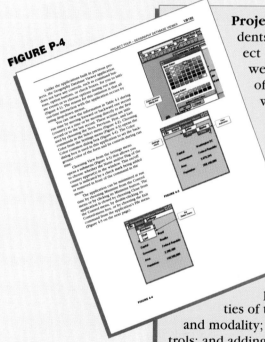

FIGURE P-4

Project 3 – Applications with Multiple Forms and Executable Files   Project 3 extends the basics of building applications that were presented in Project 1 and Project 2. The loan payment calculator application in this project consists of multiple forms and dialog boxes. After building the application, the students compile it into an executable file. Topics include additional properties of the controls presented in Project 1 and Project 2; WindowState and modality; adding an icon to a form; using image, line, and scroll bar controls; and adding and removing program items from program groups.

Project 4 – Using Color, Menus, the Data Control and Common Dialog Control   Project 4 further extends the basics of building applications presented in the first three projects. The geography database viewer interface is made more sophisticated through the use of menus and the Color dialog box (Figure P-4). The Data control is introduced to link the application to a database file. Topics include using color within applications; creating menus; using a control array; writing code that uses the For...Next statement; and using the common dialog control.

Project 5 – Building Applications with Drag-and-Drop Functionality   In Project 5, students use the three-step approach to build the traffic sign tutorial application. The application introduces students to incorporating dragging and dropping of objects within applications. More complex code is written using nested structures, the Select Case structure, and the Do..Loop structure. Students are also introduced to file management issues involved in distributing their applications. Topics include adding and removing custom controls; using the InputBox and UCase$ functions; adding remark statements to code; and printing a record of the application.

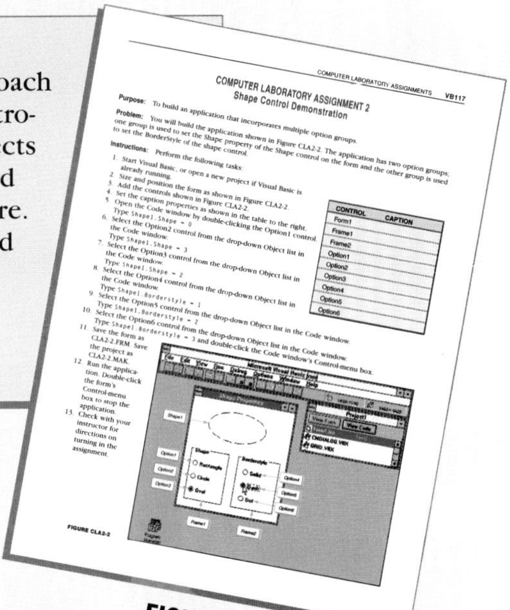

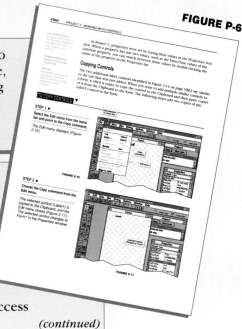

FIGURE P-5

▶ END-OF-PROJECT STUDENT ACTIVITIES

E ach project ends with a wealth of student activities including these notable features:

- ▶ A list of key terms for review
- ▶ A Quick Reference that lists the ways to carry out a task using the mouse, menu, or keyboard shortcuts
- ▶ Six Student Assignments for homework and classroom discussion
- ▶ Three Computer Laboratory Exercises that usually require the student to load and manipulate a Visual Basic program from the Student Diskette that accompanies this book
- ▶ Four Computer Laboratory Assignments (see Figure P-5) that require the student to develop a complete project assignment; the assignments increase in difficulty from a relatively easy assignment to a case study

▶ ANCILLARY MATERIALS FOR TEACHING FROM THE SHELLY CASHMAN SERIES WINDOWS APPLICATIONS TEXTBOOKS

A comprehensive instructor's support package accompanies all textbooks in the Shelly Cashman Series.

FIGURE P-6

Annotated Instructor's Edition (AIE)   The AIE is designed to assist you with your lectures by suggesting transparencies to use, summarizing key points, proposing pertinent questions, offering important tips, alerting you to pitfalls, and by incorporating the answers to the Student Assignments. There are several hundred annotations throughout the textbook (see Figure P-6).

Computer-Based LCD Lecture Success System   The Shelly Cashman Series proudly presents the finest LCD learning material available in textbook publishing. The Lecture Success System diskette, together with a personal computer and LCD technology, are used in lieu of transparencies. The system enables you to explain and illustrate the step-by-step, screen-by-screen development of a project in the textbook without entering large amounts of data, thereby improving your students' grasp of the material. The Lecture Success System leads to a smooth, easy error-free lecture.

(continued)

The Lecture Success System diskette comes with files that correspond to key figures in the book. You load the files that pertain to a project and display them as needed. If the students want to see a series of steps a second time, simply reopen the file you want to start with and redo the steps. This presentation system is available to adopters without charge.

Instructor's Materials   This instructor's ancillary (Figure P-7) contains the following:

▸ Detailed lesson plans including project objectives, project overview, and a three-column outline of each project that includes page references and transparency references
▸ Answers to all student assignments at the end of the projects
▸ A text bank of more than 600 True/False, Multiple Choice, and Fill-In questions
▸ Transparency masters for every screen, diagram, and table in the textbook
▸ An Instructor's Diskette that includes the projects and solutions to the Computer Laboratory Assignments at the end of each project

MicroExam IV   MicroExam IV, a computerized test-generating system, is available free to adopters of any Shelly Cashman Series textbooks. It includes all of the questions from the test bank just described. MicroExam IV is an easy-to-use, menu-driven software package that provides instructors with testing flexibility and allows customizing of testing documents.

FIGURE P-7

▸ ACKNOWLEDGMENTS

The Shelly Cashman Series would not be the success it is without the contributions of outstanding publishing professionals. First, and foremost, among them is Becky Herrington, director of production and designer. She is the heart and soul of the Shelly Cashman Series, and it is only through her leadership, dedication, and untiring efforts that superior products are produced.

Under Becky's direction, the following individuals made significant contributions to these books: Ginny Harvey, series administrator and manuscript editor; Ken Russo, senior illustrator; Anne Craig, Mike Bodnar, Greg Herrington, Dave Bonnewitz, and Dave Wyer, illustrators; Jeanne Black, Betty Hopkins, Rebecca Evans, and Winifred Porter, typographers; Tracy Murphy, series coordinator; Sue Sebok and Melissa Dowling LaRoe, copy editors; Marilyn Martin and Nancy Lamm, proofreaders; Henry Blackham, cover and opener photography; and Dennis Woelky, glass etchings.

Special recognition for a job well done must go to James Quasney, who, together with writing, assumed the responsibilities as series editor. Particular thanks go to Thomas Walker, president and CEO of boyd & fraser publishing company, who recognized the need, and provided the support, to produce the full-color Shelly Cashman Series Windows Applications textbooks.

We hope you will find using the book an enriching and rewarding experience.

Gary B. Shelly
Thomas J. Cashman

▶ SHELLY CASHMAN SERIES – TRADITIONALLY BOUND TEXTBOOKS

T he Shelly Cashman Series presents both Windows- and DOS-based personal computer applications in a variety of traditionally bound textbooks, as shown in the table below. For more information, see your boyd & fraser representative or call 1-800-225-3782.

COMPUTER CONCEPTS	
Computer Concepts	Complete Computer Concepts
	Essential Computer Concepts, Second Edition
Computer Concepts Workbook and Study Guide	Workbook and Study Guide with Computer Lab Software Projects to accompany Complete Computer Concepts
Computer Concepts and Windows Applications	Complete Computer Concepts and Microsoft Works 3.0 for Windows (also available in spiral bound)
	Complete Computer Concepts and Microsoft Works 2.0 for Windows (also available in spiral bound)
	Complete Computer Concepts and Microsoft Word 2.0 for Windows, Microsoft Excel 4 for Windows, and Paradox 1.0 for Windows (also available in spiral bound)
Computer Concepts and DOS Applications	Complete Computer Concepts and WordPerfect 5.1, Lotus 1-2-3 Release 2.2, and dBASE IV Version 1.1 (also available in spiral bound)
	Complete Computer Concepts and WordPerfect 5.1, Lotus 1-2-3 Release 2.2, and dBASE III PLUS (also available in spiral bound)
Computer Concepts and Programming	Complete Computer Concepts and Programming in QuickBASIC
	Complete Computer Concepts and Programming in Microsoft BASIC
WINDOWS APPLICATIONS	
Integrated Package	Microsoft Works 3.0 for Windows (also available in spiral bound)
	Microsoft Works 2.0 for Windows (also available in spiral bound)
Graphical User Interface	Microsoft Windows 3.1 Introductory Concepts and Techniques
	Microsoft Windows 3.1 Complete Concepts and Techniques
Windows Applications	Microsoft Word 2.0 for Windows, Microsoft Excel 4 for Windows, and Paradox 1.0 for Windows (also available in spiral bound)
Word Processing	Microsoft Word 6.0 for Windows
	Microsoft Word 2.0 for Windows
	WordPerfect 6.0 for Windows
	WordPerfect 5.2 for Windows
Spreadsheets	Microsoft Excel 5 for Windows
	Microsoft Excel 4 for Windows
	Lotus 1-2-3 Release 4 for Windows
	Quattro Pro 5.0 for Windows
Database Management	Paradox 4.5 for Windows
	Paradox 1.0 for Windows
	Microsoft Access 2.0 for Windows
Presentation Graphics	Microsoft PowerPoint 4.0 for Windows
DOS APPLICATIONS	
Operating Systems	DOS 6 Introductory Concepts and Techniques
	DOS 6 and Microsoft Windows 3.1 Introductory Concepts and Techniques
Integrated Package	Microsoft Works 3.0 (also available in spiral bound)
DOS Applications	WordPerfect 5.1, Lotus 1-2-3 Release 2.2, and dBASE IV Version 1.1 (also available in spiral bound)
	WordPerfect 5.1, Lotus 1-2-3 Release 2.2, and dBASE III PLUS (also available in spiral bound)
Word Processing	WordPerfect 6.0
	WordPerfect 5.1
	WordPerfect 5.1, Function Key Edition
	WordPerfect 4.2 (with Educational Software)
	Microsoft Word 5.0
	WordStar 6.0 (with Educational Software)
Speadsheets	Lotus 1-2-3 Release 2.4
	Lotus 1-2-3 Release 2.3
	Lotus 1-2-3 Release 2.2
	Lotus 1-2-3 Release 2.01
	Quattro Pro 3.0
	Quattro with 1-2-3 Menus (with Educational Software)
Database Management	dBASE IV Version 1.1
	dBASE III PLUS (with Educational Software)
	Paradox 4.5
	Paradox 3.5 (with Educational Software)
PROGRAMMING	
Programming	Microsoft BASIC
	QuickBASIC
	Microsoft Visual Basic 3.0 for Windows

▶ SHELLY CASHMAN SERIES – **Custom Edition**™ PROGRAM

If you do not find a Shelly Cashman Series traditionally bound textbook to fit your needs, boyd & fraser's unique **Custom Edition** program allows you to choose from a number of options and create a textbook perfectly suited to your course. The customized materials are available in a variety of binding styles, including boyd & fraser's patented **Custom Edition** kit, spiral bound, and notebook bound. Features of the **Custom Edition** program are:

▶ Textbooks that match the content of your course

▶ Windows- and DOS-based materials for the latest versions of personal computer applications software

▶ Shelly Cashman Series quality, with the same full-color materials and Shelly Cashman Series pedagogy found in the traditionally bound books

▶ Affordable pricing so your students receive the **Custom Edition** at a cost similar to that of traditionally bound books

The table on the right summarizes the available materials. For more information, see your boyd & fraser representative or call 1-800-225-3782.

COMPUTER CONCEPTS	
Computer Concepts	Complete Computer Concepts
	Essential Computer Concepts, Second Edition
	Introduction to Computers
OPERATING SYSTEMS	
Graphical User Interface	Microsoft Windows 3.1 Introductory Concepts and Techniques
	Microsoft Windows 3.1 Complete Concepts and Techniques
	DOS 6 and Microsoft Windows 3.1 Introductory Concepts and Techniques
Operating Systems	Introduction to DOS 6 (using DOS prompt)
	Introduction to DOS 5.0 (using DOS shell)
	Introduction to DOS 5.0 or earlier (using DOS prompt)
WINDOWS APPLICATIONS	
Integrated Package	Microsoft Works 3.0 for Windows
	Microsoft Works 2.0 for Windows
Word Processing	Microsoft Word 6.0 for Windows*
	Microsoft Word 2.0 for Windows
	WordPerfect 6.0 for Windows*
	WordPerfect 5.2 for Windows
Spreadsheets	Microsoft Excel 5 for Windows*
	Microsoft Excel 4 for Windows
	Lotus 1-2-3 Release 4 for Windows*
	Quattro Pro 5.0 for Windows
Database Management	Paradox 4.5 for Windows
	Paradox 1.0 for Windows
	Microsoft Access 2.0 for Windows*
Presentation Graphics	Microsoft PowerPoint 4.0 for Windows
DOS APPLICATIONS	
Integrated Package	Microsoft Works 3.0
Word Processing	WordPerfect 6.0
	WordPerfect 5.1
	WordPerfect 5.1, Function Key Edition
	Microsoft Word 5.0
	WordPerfect 4.2
	WordStar 6.0
Speadsheets	Lotus 1-2-3 Release 2.4
	Lotus 1-2-3 Release 2.3
	Lotus 1-2-3 Release 2.2
	Lotus 1-2-3 Release 2.01
	Quattro Pro 3.0
	Quattro with 1-2-3 Menus
Database Management	dBASE IV Version 1.1
	dBASE III PLUS
	Paradox 4.5
	Paradox 3.5
PROGRAMMING	
Programming	Microsoft BASIC
	QuickBASIC
	Microsoft Visual Basic 3.0 for Windows*

* Also available as a mini-module

Introduction to Computers

Objectives

After completing this chapter, you will be able to:

▶ Define the term computer and discuss the four basic computer operations: input, processing, output, and storage
▶ Define data and information
▶ Explain the principal components of the computer and their use
▶ Describe the use and handling of diskettes and hard disks
▶ Discuss computer software and explain the difference between system software and application software
▶ Describe several types of personal computer applications software
▶ Discuss computer communications channels and equipment and LAN and WAN computer networks
▶ Explain how to purchase, install, and maintain a personal computer system

Every day, computers impact how individuals work and how they live. The use of small computers, called personal computers or microcomputers , continues to increase and has made computing available to almost anyone. In addition, advances in communication technology allow people to use personal computer systems to easily and quickly access and send information to other computers and computer users. At home, at work, and in the field, computers are helping people to do their work faster, more accurately, and in some cases, in ways that previously would not have been possible.

Why Study Computers and Application Software?

*T*oday, many people believe that knowing how to use a computer, especially a personal computer, is a basic skill necessary to succeed in business or to function effectively in society. As you can see in Figure 1, the use of computer technology is widespread in the world. It is important to understand that while computers are used in many different ways, there are certain types of common applications computer users need to know. It is this type of software that you will learn as you use this book. Given the widespread use and availability of computer systems, knowing how to use common application software on a computer system is an essential skill for practically everyone.

FIGURE 1
Computers in use in a wide variety of applications and professions. New applications are being developed every day.

Before you learn about application software, however, it will help if you understand what a computer is, the components of a computer, and the types of software used on computers. These topics are explained in this introduction. Also included is information that describes computer networks and a list of guidelines for purchasing, installing, and maintaining a personal computer.

What Is a Computer?

*T*he most obvious question related to understanding computers is, "What is a computer?" A computer is an electronic device, operating under the control of instructions stored in its own memory unit, that can accept data (input), process data arithmetically and logically, produce output from the processing, and store the results for future use. Generally the term is used to describe a collection of devices that function together as a system. An example of the devices that make up a personal computer, or microcomputer, is shown in Figure 2.

FIGURE 2
Devices that comprise a personal computer.

What Does a Computer Do?

*W*hether small or large, computers can perform four general operations. These operations comprise the information processing cycle and are: input, process, output, and storage. Collectively, these operations describe the procedures a computer performs to process data into information and store it for future use.

All computer processing requires data. Data refers to the raw facts, including numbers, words, images, and sounds, given to a computer during the input operation. In the processing phase, the computer manipulates the data to create information. Information refers to data processed into a form that has meaning and is useful. During the output operation, the information that has been created is put into some form, such as a printed report, that people can use. The information can also be placed in computer storage for future use.

These operations occur through the use of electronic circuits contained on small silicon chips inside the computer (Figure 3). Because these electronic circuits rarely fail and the data flows along these circuits at close to the speed of light, processing can be accomplished in billionths of a second. Thus, the computer is a powerful tool because it can perform these four operations reliably and quickly.

The people who either use the computer directly or use the information it provides are called computer users, end users, or sometimes, just users.

FIGURE 3
Inside a computer are chips and other electronic components that process data in billionths of a second.

How Does a Computer Know What to Do?

For a computer to perform the operations in the information processing cycle, it must be given a detailed set of instructions that tell it exactly what to do. These instructions are called a computer program, or software. Before processing for a specific job begins, the computer program corresponding to that job is stored in the computer. Once the program is stored, the computer can begin to operate by executing the program's first instruction. The computer executes one program instruction after another until the job is complete.

What Are the Components of a Computer?

To understand how computers process data into information, you need to examine the primary components of the computer. The four primary components of a computer are: input devices, the processor unit, output devices, and auxiliary storage units (Figure 4).

Input Devices

Input devices enter data into main memory. Many input devices exist. The two most commonly used are the keyboard and the mouse.

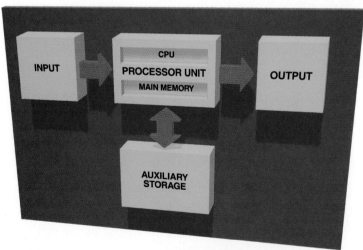

FIGURE 4
A computer is composed of input devices through which data is entered into the computer; the processor that processes data stored in main memory; output devices on which the results of the processing are made available; and auxiliary storage units that store data for future processing.

The Keyboard   The most commonly used input device is the keyboard, on which
data is entered by manually keying in or typing. The keyboard on most computers is
laid out in much the same manner as the one shown in Figure 5. The alphabetic keys
are arranged like those on a typewriter.

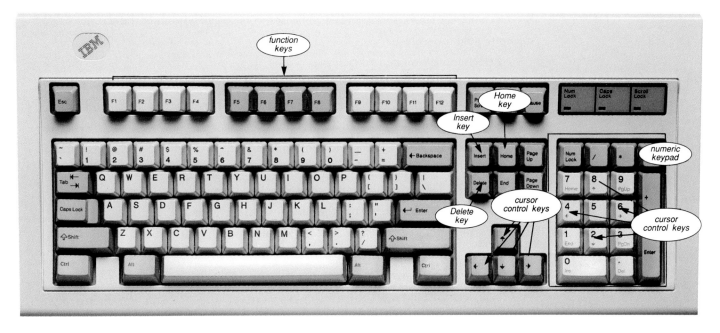

A **numeric keypad** is located on the right side of most keyboards. This arrangement of keys allows you to enter numeric data rapidly. To activate the numeric keypad
you press and engage the NUMLOCK key located above the numeric keypad. The
NUMLOCK key activates the numeric keypad so when the keys are pressed, numeric
characters are entered into the computer memory and appear on the screen. A light
turns on at the top right of the keyboard to indicate that the numeric keys are in use.

The **cursor** is a symbol, such as an underline character, which indicates where you
are working on the screen. The **cursor control keys**, or **arrow keys**, allow you to move
the cursor around the screen. Pressing the UP ARROW (↑) key causes the cursor to
move upward on the screen. The DOWN ARROW (↓) key causes the cursor to move
down; the LEFT ARROW (←) and RIGHT ARROW (→) keys cause the cursor to
move left and right on the screen. On the keyboard in Figure 5, there are two sets of
cursor control keys. One set is included as part of the numeric keypad. The second set
of cursor control keys is located between the typewriter keys and the numeric keypad.
To use the numeric keypad for cursor control, the NUMLOCK key must be disengaged.
If the NUMLOCK key is engaged (indicated by the fact that as you press any numeric
keypad key, a number appears on the screen), you can return to the cursor mode by
pressing the NUMLOCK key. On most keyboards, a NUMLOCK light will indicate when
the numeric keypad is in the numeric mode or the cursor mode.

FIGURE 5
This keyboard represents
most desktop personal
computer keyboards.

The other keys on the keypad—PAGE UP, PAGE DOWN, HOME, and END—have various functions depending on the software you use. Some programs make no use of these keys; others use the PAGE UP and PAGE DOWN keys, for example, to display previous or following pages of data on the screen. Some software uses the HOME key to move the cursor to the upper left corner of the screen. Likewise, the END key may be used to move the cursor to the end of a line of text or to the bottom of the screen, depending on the software.

Function keys on many keyboards can be programmed to accomplish specific tasks. For example, a function key might be used as a help key. Whenever that key is pressed, messages display that give instructions to help the user. The keyboard in Figure 5 has twelve function keys located across the top of the keyboard.

Other keys have special uses in some applications. The SHIFT keys have several functions. They work as they do on a typewriter, allowing you to type capital letters. The SHIFT key is always used to type the symbol on the upper portion of any key on the keyboard. Also, to temporarily use the cursor control keys on the numeric keypad as numeric entry keys, you can press the SHIFT key to switch into numeric mode. If you have instead pressed the NUMLOCK key to use the numeric keys, you can press the SHIFT key to shift temporarily back to the cursor mode.

The keyboard has a BACKSPACE key, a TAB key, an INSERT key and a DELETE key that perform the functions their names indicate.

The ESCAPE (ESC) key is generally used by computer software to cancel an instruction or exit from a situation. The use of the ESC key varies between software packages.

As with the ESC key, many keys are assigned special meaning by the computer software. Certain keys may be used more frequently than others by one piece of software but rarely used by another. It is this flexibility that allows you to use the computer in so many different applications.

The Mouse   A mouse (Figure 6) is a pointing device you can use instead of the cursor control keys. You lay the palm of your hand over the mouse and move it across the surface of a pad that provides traction for a rolling ball on the bottom of the mouse. The mouse detects the direction of the ball movement and sends this information to the screen to move the cursor. You push buttons on top of the mouse to indicate your choices of actions from lists or icons displayed on the screen.

FIGURE 6
The mouse input device is used to move the cursor and choose selections on the computer screen.

The Processor Unit

The **processor unit** is composed of the central processing unit and main memory. The **central processing unit (CPU)** contains the electronic circuits that cause processing to occur. The CPU interprets instructions to the computer, performs the logical and arithmetic processing operations, and causes the input and output operations to occur. On personal computers, the CPU is designed into a chip called a **microprocessor** (Figure 7).

Main memory, also called **random access memory**, or **RAM**, consists of electronic components that store data including numbers, letters of the alphabet, graphics, and sound. Any data to be processed must be stored in main memory. The amount of main memory in computers is typically measured in kilobytes or megabytes. One **kilobyte (K or KB)** equals 1,024 memory locations and one **megabyte (M or MB)** equals approximately 1 million memory locations. A memory location, or **byte**, usually stores one character. Therefore, a computer with 4MB can store approximately 4 million characters. One megabyte of memory can hold approximately 500 pages of text information.

FIGURE 7
A Pentium microprocessor from Intel Corporation. The microprocessor circuits are located in the center. Small gold wires lead from the circuits to the pins that fit in the microprocessor socket on the main circuit board of the computer. The pins provide an electronic connection to different parts of the computer.

Output Devices

Output devices make the information resulting from processing available for use. The output from computers can be presented in many forms, such as a printed report or color graphics. When a computer is used for processing tasks, such as word processing, spreadsheets, or database management, the two output devices most commonly used are the printer and the television-like display device called a screen, monitor, or CRT (cathode ray tube).

Printers   Printers used with computers can be either impact printers or nonimpact printers. An **impact printer** prints by striking an inked ribbon against the paper. One type of impact printer often used with personal computers is the dot matrix printer (Figure 8).

FIGURE 8
Dot matrix are the least expensive of the personal computer printers. Some can be purchased for less than $200. Advantages of dot matrix printers include the capability to handle wide paper and to print multipart forms.

FIGURE 9
On a dot matrix printer with a nine-pin print head, the letter E is formed with seven vertical and five horizontal dots. As the nine-pin print head moves from left to right, it fires one or more pins into the ribbon, making a dot on the paper. At the first print position, it fires pins 1 through 7. At print positions 2 through 4, it fires pins 1,4, and 7. At print position 5, it fires pins 1 and 7. Pins 8 and 9 are used for lowercase characters such as g, j, p, q, and y that extend below the line.

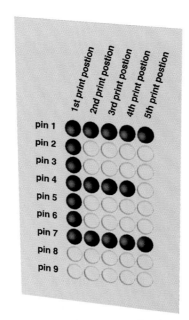

FIGURE 10 ▲
Two types of nonimpact printers are the laser printer (top) and the ink jet printer. Nonimpact printers are excellent for printing work that includes graphics.

FIGURE 11 ▶
Nonimpact printers do an excellent job of printing text in different typefaces, usually referred to as fonts. Technically, a font is a typeface in a particular size. It is common, however, to refer to the different typefaces as fonts. Dot matrix printers can print some fonts but usually at a slower rate and quality than nonimpact printers. The names of four different typefaces (fonts) are shown.

To print a character, a **dot matrix printer** generates a dot pattern representing a particular character. The printer then activates wires in a print head contained on the printer, so selected wires press against the ribbon and paper, creating a character. As you see in Figure 9, the character consists of a series of dots produced by the print head wires. In the actual size created by the printer, the characters are clear and easy to read.

Dot matrix printers vary in the speed with which they can print characters. These speeds range from 50 to more than 300 characters per second. Generally, the higher the speed, the higher the cost of the printer. Compared to other printers, dot matrix offer the lowest initial cost and the lowest per-page operating costs. Other advantages of dot matrix printers are that they can print on multipart forms and they can be purchased with wide carriages that can handle paper larger than 8 1/2 by 11 inches.

Nonimpact printers, such as ink jet printers and laser printers, form characters by means other than striking a ribbon against paper (Figure 10). Advantages of using a nonimpact printer are that it can print graphics and it can print in varying type sizes and styles called **fonts** (Figure 11). An **ink jet printer** forms a character by using a nozzle that sprays drops of ink onto the page. Ink jet printers produce relatively high-quality images and print between 30 and 150 characters per second in text mode and one to two pages per minute in graphics mode.

Laser printers work similar to a copying machine by converting data from the computer into a beam of light that is focused on a photoconductor drum, forming the images to be printed. The photoconductor attracts particles of toner that are fused by heat and pressure onto paper to produce an image. Laser printers produce high-quality output and are used for applications that combine text and graphics such as **desktop publishing** (Figure 12). Laser printers for personal computers can cost from $500 to more than $10,000. They can print four to sixteen pages of text and graphics per minute.

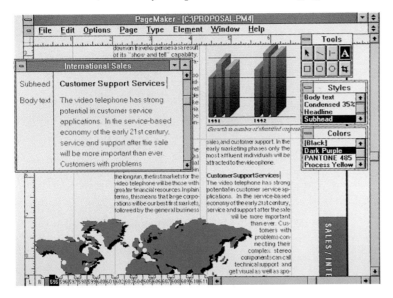

FIGURE 12
High-quality printed documents can be produced with laser printers and desktop publishing software.

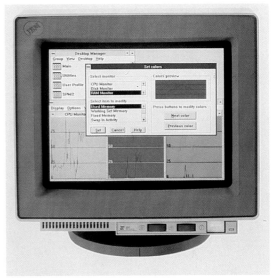

FIGURE 13
Many personal computer systems now come with color screens. Color can be used to enhance the information displayed so the user can understand it more quickly.

Computer Screens   Most full-size personal computers use a TV-like display device called a **screen, monitor,** or **CRT** (cathode ray tube) (Figure 13). Portable computers use a flat panel display that uses **liquid crystal display (LCD)** technology similar to a digital watch. The surface of the screen is made up of individual picture elements called **pixels**. Each pixel can be illuminated to form characters and graphic shapes (Figure 14). Color screens have three colored dots (red, green, and blue) for each pixel. These dots can be turned on to display different colors. Most color monitors today use super VGA (video graphics array) technology that can display 800 × 600 (width × height) pixels.

FIGURE 14
Pixel is an abreviation of the words picture element, one of thousands of spots on a computer screen that can be turned on and off to form text and graphics.

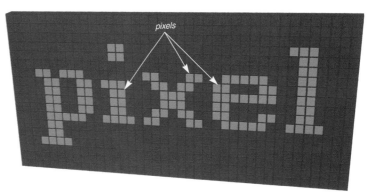

Auxiliary Storage

Auxiliary storage devices are used to store instructions and data when they are not being used in main memory. Two types of auxiliary storage most often used on personal computers are diskettes and hard disks. CD-ROM disk drives are also becoming common.

Diskettes   A **diskette** is a circular piece of oxide-coated plastic that stores data as magnetic spots. Diskettes are available in various sizes and storage capacities. Personal computers most commonly use diskettes that are 5 1/4 inches or 3 1/2 inches in diameter (Figure 15).

FIGURE 15
The most commonly used diskettes for personal computers are the 5 1/4-inch size on the left and the 3 1/2-inch size on the right. Although they are smaller in size, the 3 1/2-inch diskettes can store more data.

To read data stored on a diskette or to store data on a diskette, you insert the diskette in a disk drive (Figure 16). You can tell that the computer is reading data on the diskette or writing data on it because a light on the disk drive will come on while read/write operations are taking place. Do not try to insert or remove a diskette when the light is on as you could cause permanent damage to the data stored on it.

The storage capacities of disk drives and the related diskettes can vary widely (Figure 17). The number of characters that can be stored on a diskette by a disk drive depends on two factors: (1) the recording density of the bits on a track; and (2) the number of tracks on the diskette.

FIGURE 16
A user inserts a 3 1/2-inch diskette into the disk drive of a personal computer.

DIAMETER (INCHES)	DESCRIPTION	CAPACITY (BYTES)
5.25	Double-sided, double-density	360KB
5.25	Double-sided high-density	1.25MB
3.5	Double-sided double-density	720KB
3.5	Double-sided high-density	1.44MB

FIGURE 17
Storage capacities of different size and type diskettes.

Disk drives found on many personal computers are 5 1/4-inch, double-sided disk drives that can store from 360,000 bytes to 1.25 million bytes on the diskette. Another popular type is the 3 1/2-inch diskette, which, although physically smaller, stores from 720,000 bytes to 1.44 million bytes. An added benefit of the 3 1/2-inch diskette is its rigid plastic housing that protects the magnetic surface of the diskette.

The recording density is stated in bits per inch (bpi)—the number of magnetic spots that can be recorded on a diskette in a one-inch circumference of the innermost track on the diskette. Diskettes and disk drives used today are identified as being double-density or high-density. You need to be aware of the density of diskettes used by your system because data stored on high-density diskettes, for example, cannot be processed by a computer that has only double-density disk drives.

The second factor that influences the number of characters that can be stored on a diskette is the number of tracks on the diskette. A **track** is a very narrow recording band forming a full circle around the diskette (Figure 18).

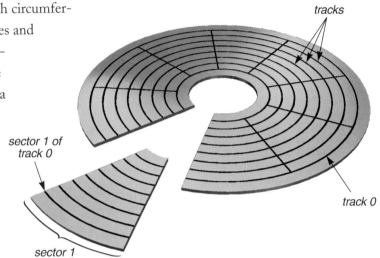

FIGURE 18
Each track on a diskette is a narrow, circular band. On a diskette containing 80 tracks, the outside track is called track 0 and the inside track is called track 79. The disk surface is divided into sectors.

tracks

sector 1 of track 0

track 0

sector 1

The tracks are separated from each other by a very narrow blank gap. Each track on a diskette is divided into sectors. The term sector is used to refer to a pie-shaped section of the disk. It is also used to refer to a section of track. Sectors are the basic units for diskette storage. When data is read from a diskette, it reads a minimum of one full sector from a track. When data is stored on a diskette, it writes one full sector on a track at a time. The tracks and sectors on the diskette and the number of characters that can be stored in each sector are defined by a special formatting program that is used with the computer.

Data stored in sectors on a diskette must be retrieved and placed into main memory to be processed. The time required to access and retrieve data, called the **access time**, can be important in some applications. The access time for diskettes varies from about 175 milliseconds (one millisecond equals 1/1000 of a second) to approximately 300 milliseconds. On average, data stored in a single sector on a diskette can be retrieved in approximately 1/15 to 1/3 of a second.

Diskette care is important to preserve stored data. Properly handled, diskettes can store data indefinitely. However, the surface of the diskette can be damaged and the data stored can be lost if the diskette is handled improperly.

A diskette will give you very good service if you follow a few simple procedures:

1. Keep diskettes in their original box or in a special diskette storage box to protect them from dirt and dust and prevent them from being accidentally bent. Store 5 1/4-inch diskettes in their protective envelopes. Store the container away from heat and direct sunlight. Magnetic and electrical equipment, including telephones, radios, and televisions, can erase the data on a diskette, so do not place diskettes near such devices. Do not place heavy objects on a diskette, because the weight can pinch the covering, causing damage when the disk drive attempts to rotate.

2. To affix one of the self-adhesive labels supplied with most diskettes, it is best to write or type the information on the label before you place the label on the diskette. If the label is already on the diskette, use only a felt-tip pen to write on the label, and press lightly. Do not use ball point pens, pencils, or erasers on lables that are already on diskettes.

3. To use the diskette, grasp the diskette on the side away from the side to be inserted into the disk drive. Slide the diskette carefully into the slot on the disk drive. If the disk drive has a latch or door, close it. If it is difficult to close the disk drive door, do not force it—the diskette may not be inserted fully, and forcing the door closed may damage the diskette. Reinsert the diskette if necessary, and try again to close the door.

The diskette write-protect feature (Figure 19) prevents the accidental erasure of the data stored on a diskette by preventing the disk drive from writing new data or erasing existing data. On a 5 1/4-inch diskette, a write-protect notch is located on the side of the diskette. A special write-protect label is placed over this notch whenever you want to protect the data. On the 3 1/2-inch diskette, a small switch can slide to cover and uncover the write-protection window. On a 3 1/2-inch diskette, when the window is uncovered the data is protected.

FIGURE 19
Data cannot be written on the 3 1/2-inch diskette on the top left because the window in the corner of the diskette is open. A small piece of plastic covers the window of the 3 1/2-inch diskette on the top right, so data can be written on this diskette. The reverse situation is true for the 5 1/4-inch diskettes. The write-protect notch of the 5 1/4-inch diskette on the bottom left is covered and, therefore, data cannot be written to the diskette. The notch of the 5 1/4-inch diskette on the bottom right, however, is open. Data can be written to this diskette.

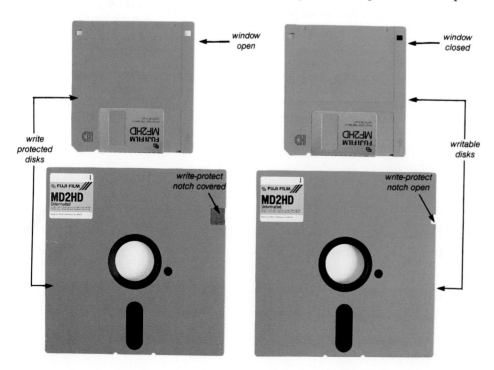

Hard Disk   Another form of auxiliary storage is a hard disk. A hard disk consists of one or more rigid metal platters coated with a metal oxide material that allows data to be magnetically recorded on the surface of the platters (Figure 20). Although hard disks are available in removable cartridge form, most disks cannot be removed from the computer. As with diskettes, the data is recorded on hard disks on a series of tracks. The tracks are divided into sectors when the disk is formatted

The hard disk platters spin at a high rate of speed, typically 3,600 revolutions per minute. When reading data from the disk, the read head senses the magnetic spots that are recorded on the disk along the various tracks and transfers that data to main memory. When writing, the data is transferred from main memory and is stored as magnetic spots on the tracks on the recording surface of one or more of the disk platters. Unlike diskette drives, the read/write heads on a hard disk drive do not actually touch the surface of the disk.

The number of platters permanently mounted on the spindle of a hard disk varies. On most drives, each surface of the platter can be used to store data. Thus, if a hard disk drive uses one platter, two surfaces are available for data. If the drive uses two platters, four sets of read/write heads read and record data from the four surfaces. Storage capacities of internally mounted fixed disks for personal computers range from 80 million characters to more than 500 million characters. Larger capacity, stand-alone hard disk units are also available that can store more than one billion bytes of information. One billion bytes is called a gigabyte.

The amount of effective storage on both hard disks and diskettes can be increased by the use of compression programs. Compression programs use sophisticated formulas to replace spaces and repeated text and graphics patterns with codes that can later be used to recreate the compressed data. Text files can be compressed the most; as much as an eighth of their original volume. Graphics files can be compressed the least. Overall, a 2-to-1 compression ratio is average.

CD-ROM   Compact disk read-only memory (CD-ROM) disks are increasingly used to store large amounts of prerecorded information (Figure 21). Each CD-ROM disk can store more than 600 million bytes of data—the equivalent of 300,000 pages of text. Because of their large storage capacity, CD-ROM is often used for multimedia material. Multimedia combines text, graphics, video (pictures), and audio (sound) (Figure 22 on the next page).

spindle

disk surface

read/write head

access arm

FIGURE 20
The protective cover of this hard disk drive has been removed. A read/write head is at the end of the access arm that extends over the recording surface, called a platter.

FIGURE 21
CD-ROM disk drives allow the user to access tremendous amounts of prerecorded information — more than 600MB of data can be stored on one CD-ROM disk.

Computer Software

C omputer software is the key to productive use of computers. With the correct software, a computer can become a valuable tool. Software can be categorized into two types: system software and application software.

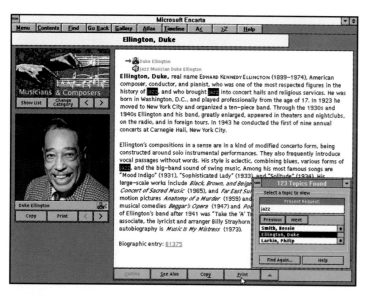

FIGURE 22
Microsoft Encarta is a multimedia encyclopedia available on a CDROM disk. Text, graphics, sound, and animation are all available. The photo-shaped icon at the top of the text indicates that a photograph is available for viewing. The speaker-shaped icon just below the camera indicates that a sound item is available. In this topic, if the user chooses the speaker icon with the mouse, a portion of Duke Ellington's music is played.

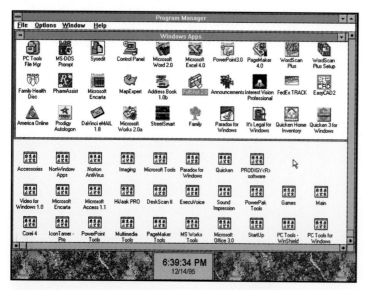

FIGURE 23
Microsoft Windows is a graphical user interface that works with the DOS operating system to make the computer easier to use. The small pictures or symbols on the main part of the screen are called icons. The icons represent different processing options, such as word processing or electronic spreadsheet applications, the user can choose.

System Software

System software consists of programs to control the operations of computer equipment. An important part of system software is a set of programs called the **operating system**. Instructions in the operating system tell the computer how to perform the functions of loading, storing, and executing an application and how to transfer data. For a computer to operate, an operating system must be stored in the computer's main memory. When a computer is started, the operating system is loaded into the computer and stored in main memory. This process is called **booting**. The most commonly used operating system on personal computers is **DOS (Disk Operating System)**.

Many computers use an **operating environment** that works with the operating system to make the computer system easier to use. Operating environments have a **graphical user interface (GUI)** displaying visual clues such as icon symbols to help the user. Each **icon** represents an application software package, such as word processing or a file or document where data is stored. **Microsoft Windows** (Figure 23) is a graphical user interface that works with DOS. Apple Macintosh computers also have a built in graphical user interface in the operating system.

Application Software

Application software consists of programs that tell a computer how to produce information. The different ways people use computers in their careers or in their personal lives, are examples of types of application software. Business, scientific, and educational programs are all examples of application software.

Personal Computer Application Software Packages

Personal computer users often use application software packages. Some of the most commonly used packages are: word processing, electronic spreadsheet, presentation graphics, database, communications, and electronic mail software.

Word processing software (Figure 24) is used to create and print documents. A key advantage of word processing software is its capability to make changes easily in documents, such as correcting spelling, changing margins, and adding, deleting, or relocating entire paragraphs. These changes would be difficult and time consuming to make using manual methods such as a typewriter. With a word processor, documents can be printed quickly and accurately and easily stored on a disk for future use. Word processing software is oriented toward working with text, but most word processing packages can also include numeric and graphic information.

Electronic spreadsheet software (Figure 25) allows the user to add, subtract, and perform user-defined calculations on rows and columns of numbers. These numbers can be changed and the spreadsheet quickly recalculates the new results. Electronic spreadsheet software eliminates the tedious recalculations required with manual methods. Spreadsheet information is frequently converted into a graphic form. Graphics capabilities are now included in most spreadsheet packages.

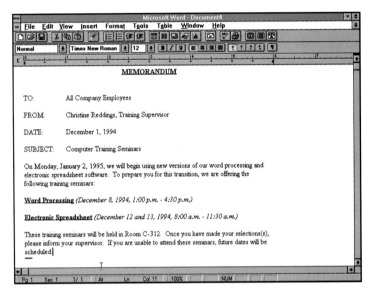

FIGURE 24
Word processing software is used to write letters, memos, and other documents. As the user types words and letters, they display on the screen. The user can easily add, delete, and change any text entered until the document looks exactly as desired. The user can then save the document on auxiliary storage and can also print it on a printer.

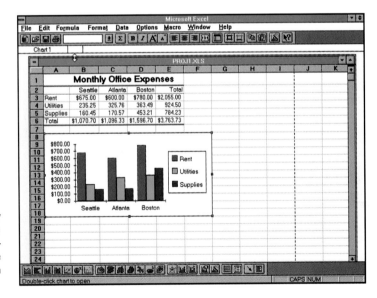

FIGURE 25
Electronic spreadsheet software is frequently used by people who work with numbers. The user enters the data and the formulas to be used on the data and calculates the results. Most spreadsheet programs have the capability to use numeric data to generate charts, such as the bar chart.

Database software (Figure 26) allows the user to enter, retrieve, and update data in an organized and efficient manner. These software packages have flexible inquiry and reporting capabilities that allow users to access the data in different ways and create custom reports that include some or all of the information in the database.

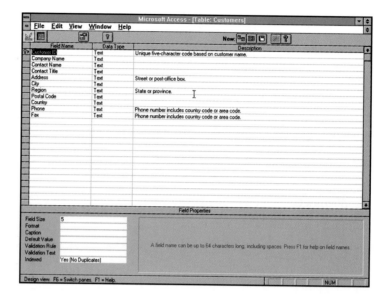

FIGURE 26
Database software allows the user to enter, retrieve, and update data in an organized and efficient manner. This database table illustrates how a business organized customer information. Once the table is defined, the user can add, delete, change, display, print, or reorganize the database records.

Presentation graphics software (Figure 27) allows the user to create documents called slides to be used in making presentations. Using special projection devices, the slides are projected directly from the computer. In addition, the slides can be printed and used as handouts, or converted into transparencies and displayed on overhead projectors. Presentation graphics software includes many special effects, color, and art that enhance information presented on a slide. Because slides frequently include numeric data, presentation graphics software includes the capability to convert the numeric data into many forms of charts.

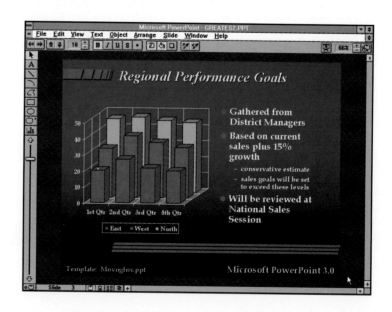

FIGURE 27
Presentation graphics software allows the user to create documents called slides for use in presentations. Using special projection devices, the slides display as they appear on the computer screen. The slides can also be printed and used as handouts or converted into transparencies to be used with overhead projectors.

Communications software (Figure 28) is used to transmit data and information from one computer to another. For the transfer to take place, each computer must have communications software. Organizations use communications software to transfer information from one location to another. Many individuals use communications software to access on-line databases that provide information on current events, airline schedules, finances, weather, and hundreds of other subjects.

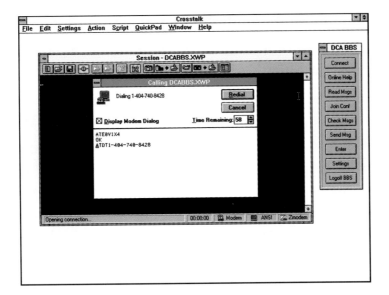

FIGURE 28
Communications software allows users to transmit data from one computer to another. This software enables the user to choose a previusly entered phone number of another computer. Once the number is chosen, the communications software dials the number and establishes a communication link. The user can then transfer data or run programs on the remote computer.

Electronic mail software, also called **e-mail** (Figure 29), allows users to send messages to and receive messages from other computer users. The other users may be on the same computer network or on a separate computer system reached through the use of communications equipment and software.

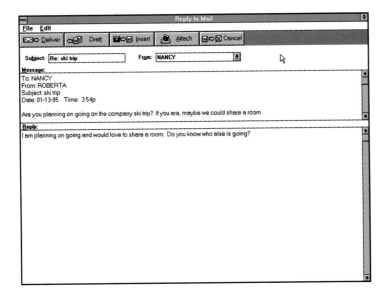

FIGURE 29
Electronic mail software allows users to send and receive messages with other computer users. Each user has an electronic mail box to which messages are sent. This software enables a user to add a reply to a received message and then send the reply back to the person who sent the original message.

What Is Communications?

Communications refers to the transmission of data and information over a communications channel, such as a standard telephone line, between one computer and another computer. Figure 30 shows the basic model for a communications system. This model consists of the following equipment:

1. A computer.
2. Communications equipment that sends (and can usually receive) data.
3. The communications channel over which the data is sent.
4. Communications equipment that receives (and can usually send) data.
5. Another computer.

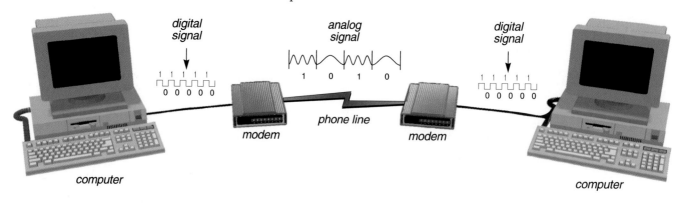

FIGURE 30
The basic model of a communications system. Individual electrical pulses of the digital signal from the computer are converted into analog (electrical wave) signals for transmission over voice telephone lines. At the main computer receiving end, another modem converts the analog signals back into digital signals that can be processed by the computer.

The basic model also includes communications software. When two computers are communicating with each other, compatible communications software is required on each system.

Communications is important to understand because of on-line services and the trend to network computers. With communications equipment and software, access is available to an increasing amount and variety of information and services. **On-line information services** such as Prodigy (Figure 31) and America On-Line offer the latest news, weather, sports, and financial information along with shopping, entertainment, and electronic mail.

International networks such as the Internet allow users to access information at thousands of Internet member organizations around the world. Electronic bulletin boards can be found in most cities with hundreds available in large metropolitan areas. An electronic **bulletin board system (BBS)** is a computer and at least one phone line that allows users to *chat* with the computer operator, called the **system operator (sys op)** or, if more than one phone line is available, with other BBS users. BBS users can also leave messages for other users. BBSs are often devoted to a specific subject area such as games, hobbies, or a specific type of computer or software. Many computer hardware and software companies operate BBSs so users of their products can share information.

Communications Channels

A **communications channel** is the path the data follows as it is transmitted from the sending equipment to the receiving equipment in a communications system. These channels are made up of one or more **transmission media**, including twisted pair wire, coaxial cable, fiber optics, microwave transmission, satellite transmission, and wireless transmission.

Communications Equipment

If a personal computer is within approximately 1,000 feet of another computer, the two devices can usually be directly connected by a cable. If the devices are more than 1,000 feet, however, the electrical signal weakens to the point that some type of special communications equipment is required to increase or change the signal to transmit it farther. A variety of communications equipment exists to perform this task, but the equipment most often used is a modem.

FIGURE 31
Prodigy is one of several on-line service providers offering information on a number of general-interest subjects. The topic areas display on the right. Users access Prodigy and other on-line services by using a modem and special communications software.

Computer equipment is designed to process data as **digital signals**, individual electrical pulses grouped together to represent characters. Telephone equipment was originally designed to carry only voice transmission, which is comprised of a continuous electrical wave called an **analog signal** (see Figure 30). Thus, a special piece of equipment called a modem converts between the digital signals and analog signals so telephone lines can carry data. A **modem** converts the digital signals of a computer to analog signals that are transmitted over a communications channel. A modem also converts analog signals it receives into digital signals used by a computer. The word modem comes from a combination of the words *mo*dulate, which means to change into a sound or analog signal, and *dem*odulate, which means to convert an analog signal into a digital signal. A modem is needed at both the sending and receiving ends of a communications channel. A modem may be an external stand-alone device that is connected to the computer and phone line or an internal circuit board that is installed inside the computer.

Modems can transmit data at rates from 300 to 38,400 bits per second (bps). Most personal computers use a 2,400 bps or higher modem. Business or heavier volume users would use faster and more expensive modems.

Communication Networks

A communication **network** is a collection of computers and other equipment using communications channels to share hardware, software, data, and information. Networks are classified as either local area networks or wide area networks.

Local Area Networks (LANs)

A **local area network,** or LAN, is a privately owned communications network and covers a limited geographic area, such as a school computer laboratory, an office, a building, or a group of buildings.

The LAN consists of a communications channel connecting a group of personal computers to one another. Very sophisticated LANs are capable of connecting a variety of office devices, such as word processing equipment, computer terminals, video equipment, and personal computers.

Three common applications of local area networks are hardware, software, and information resource sharing. **Hardware resource sharing** allows each personal computer in the network to access and use devices that would be too expensive to provide for each user or would not be justified for each user because of only occasional use. For example, when a number of personal computers are used on the network, each may need to use a laser printer. Using a LAN, the purchase of one laser printer serves the entire network. Whenever a personal computer user on the network needs the laser printer, it is accessed over the network. Figure 32 depicts a simple local area network consisting of four personal computers linked together by a cable. Three of the personal computers (computer 1 in the sales and marketing department, computer 2 in the accounting department, and computer 3 in the personnel department) are available for use at all times. Computer 4 is used as a **server,** which is dedicated to handling the communications needs of the other computers in the network. The users of this LAN have connected the laser printer to the server. Using the LAN, all computers and the server can use the printer.

FIGURE 32
A local area network (LAN) consists of multiple personal computers connected to one another. The LAN allows users to share softwre, hardware, and information.

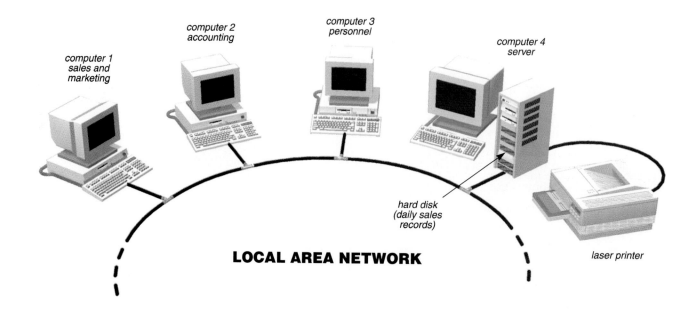

computer 1
sales and
marketing

computer 2
accounting

computer 3
personnel

computer 4
server

hard disk
(daily sales
records)

LOCAL AREA NETWORK

laser printer

Frequently used software is another type of resource sharing that often occurs on a local area network. For example, if all users need access to word processing software, the software can be stored on the hard disk of the server and accessed by all users as needed. This is more convenient and faster than having the software stored on a diskette and available at each computer.

Information resource sharing allows anyone using a personal computer on the local area network to access data stored on any other computer in the network. In actual practice, hardware resource sharing and information resource sharing are often combined. The capability to access and store data on common auxiliary storage is an important feature of many local area networks.

Information resource sharing is usually provided by using either the file-server or client-server method. Using the **file-server** method, the server sends an entire file at a time. The requesting computer then performs the processing. With the **client-server** method, processing tasks are divided between the server computer and the *client* computer requesting the information. Figure 33 illustrates how the two methods would process a request for information stored on the server system for customers with balances over $1,000. With the file-server method, all customer records would be transferred to the requesting computer. The requesting computer would then process the records to identify the customers with balances over $1,000. With the client-server method, the server system would review the customers' records and only transfer records of customers meeting the criteria. The client-server method greatly reduces the amount of data sent over a network but requires a more powerful server system.

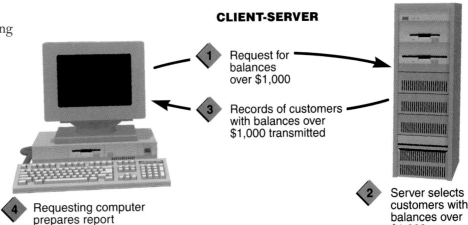

FILE SERVER

1. Request for customer file
3. Entire customer file transmitted
2. Server locates and transmits entire customer file
4. Requesting computer selects customers with balances over $1,000 and prepares report

CLIENT-SERVER

1. Request for balances over $1,000
3. Records of customers with balances over $1,000 transmitted
2. Server selects customers with balances over $1,000
4. Requesting computer prepares report

FIGURE 33
A request for information about customers with balances over $1,000 would be processed differently by the file-server and client-server networks.

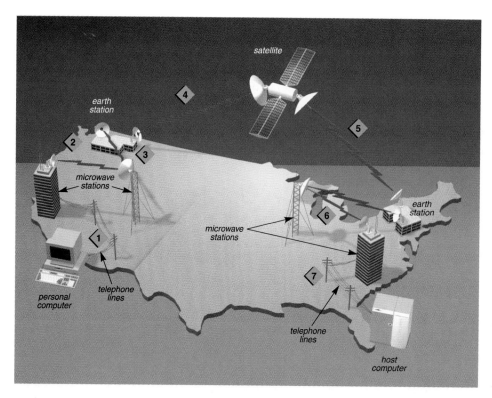

FIGURE 34
A wide area network (WAN) may use a number of different communications channels such as telephone lines, microwaves, and satellites.

Wide Area Networks (WANs)

A wide area network, or WAN, is geographic in scope (as opposed to local) and uses telephone lines, microwaves, satellites, or a combination of communications channels (Figure 34). Public wide area network companies include common carriers such as the telephone companies. Telephone company deregulation has encouraged a number of companies to build their own wide area networks. Communications companies, such as MCI, have built WANs to compete with other communications companies.

How to Purchase a Computer System

The desktop personal computer (PC) is the most widely purchased type of system. The following guidelines assume you are purchasing a desktop IBM-compatible PC, to be used for home or light business use. That is not meant to imply that Macintosh or other non DOS or Windows operating system computers are not worth considering. Software requirements and the need to be compatible with other systems you may work with should determine the type of system you purchase. A portable computer would be an appropriate choice if your situation requires that you have a computer with you when you travel.

1. Determine what applications you will use on your computer. This decision will guide you as to the type and size of computer.

2. Choose your software first. Some packages only run on Macintosh computers, others only on a PC. Some packages only run under the Windows operating system. In addition, some software requires more memory and disk space than other packages.

3. Be aware of hidden costs. Realize that there will be some additional costs associated with buying a computer. Such costs might include; an additional phone line or outlet to use the modem, computer furniture, consumable supplies such as diskettes and paper, diskette holders, reference manuals on specific software packages, and special training classes you may want to take. Depending on where you buy your computer, the seller may be willing to include some or all of these in the system purchase price.

4. **Buy equipment that meets the *Energy Star* power consumption guidelines.** These guidelines require that computer systems, monitors, and printers, reduce electrical consumption if they have not been used for some period of time, usually several minutes. Equipment meeting the guidelines can display the *Energy Star* logo.

5. **Use a spreadsheet like the one shown in Figure 35 to compare purchase alternatives.** Use a separate sheet of paper to take notes on each vendor's system and then summarize the information on the spreadsheet.

6. **Consider buying from local computer dealers and direct mail companies.** Each has certain advantages. The local dealer can more easily provide hands-on support, if necessary. With a mail order company, you are usually limited to speaking to someone over the phone. Mail order companies usually, but not always, offer the lowest prices. The important thing to do when shopping for a system is to make sure you are comparing identical or similar configurations.

System Cost Comparison Worksheet		Desired	#1	#2	#3	#4
Base System	Mfr	—	Delway			
	Model		4500X			
	Processor	486DX	486DX			
	Speed	50MHz	50			
	Pwr Supply	200watts	220			
	Exp Slots	5	5			
	Price		$995			
Memory	8MB Ram		incl			
Disk	Mfr		Conner			
	Size	>300MB	340			
	Price		incl			
Diskette	3 1/2					
	5 1/4					
	Combination		$50			
Monitor	Mfr		NEC			
	Model		5FG			
	Size	15in	15			
	Price		$300			
Sound	Mfr		Media Labs			
	Model		Pro			
	Price		$75			
CDROM	Mfr		NEC			
	Speed		450/200			
	Price		$100			
Mouse	Mfr		Logitech			
	Price		incl			
Modem	Mfr		Boca			
	Mod/fax Speeds	14.4/14.4	14.4/14.4			
	Price		$125			
Printer	Mfr		HP			
	Model		4Z			
	Type		laser			
	Speed	6ppm	8ppm			
	Price		$675			
Surge Protector	Mfr		Brooks			
	Price		$35			
Options	Tape Backup					
	UPS					
Other	Sales Tax		0			
	Shipping		$30			
	1 YR Warranty		incl			
	1 YR On-Site Svc		incl			
	3 YR On-Site Svc		$150			
Software	List free software		Windows			
			MS Works			
			diagnostics			
	TOTAL		$2,535			

FIGURE 35
A spreadsheet is an effective way to summarize and compare the prices and equipment offered by different system vendors.

7. **Consider more than just price.** Don't necessarily buy the lowest cost system. Consider intangibles such as how long the vendor has been in business, its reputation for quality, and reputation for support.

8. **Look for free software.** Many system vendors now include free software with their systems. Some even let you choose which software you want. Such software only has value, however, if you would have purchased it if it had not come with the computer.

9. **Buy a system compatible with the one you use elsewhere.** If you use a personal computer at work or at some other organization, make sure the computer you buy is compatible. That way, if you need or want to, you can work on projects at home.

10. **Consider purchasing an on-site service agreement.** If you use your system for business or otherwise can't afford to be without your computer, consider purchasing an on-site service agreement. Many of the mail order vendors offer such support through third-party companies. Such agreements usually state that a technician will be on-site within 24 hours. Some systems include on-site service for only the first year. It is usually less expensive to extend the service for two or three years when you buy the computer rather than waiting to buy the service agreement later.

11. **Use a credit card to purchase your system.** Many credit cards now have purchase protection benefits that cover you in case of loss or damage to purchased goods. Some also extend the warranty of any products purchased with the card. Paying by credit card also gives you time to install and use the system before you have to pay for it. Finally, if you're dissatisfied with the system and can't reach an agreement with the seller, paying by credit card gives you certain rights regarding withholding payment until the dispute is resolved. Check your credit card agreement for specific details.

12. **Buy a system that will last you for at least three years.** Studies show that many users become dissatisfied because they didn't buy a powerful enough system. Consider the following system configuration guidelines. Each of the components will be discussed separately:

Base System Components:	Optional Equipment:
486SX or 486DX processor, 33 megahertz	5 1/4" diskette drive
150 watt power supply	14.4K fax modem
160 to 300MB hard disk	laser printer
4 to 8MB RAM	sound card and speakers
3 to 5 expansion slots	CD-ROM drive
3 1/2" diskette drive	tape backup
14" or 15" color monitor	uninterruptable power supply (UPS)
mouse or other pointing device	
enhanced keyboard	
ink jet or bubble jet printer	
surge protector	

Processor: A 486SX or 486DX processor with a speed rating of at least 33 mega-hertz is needed for today's more sophisticated software, even word processing soft-ware. Buy a system that can be upgraded to the Pentium processor.

Power Supply: 150 watts. If the power supply is too small, it won't be able to support additional expansion cards that you might want to add in the future.

Hard Disk: 160 to 300 megabytes (MB). Each new release of software requires more hard disk space. Even with disk compression programs, disk space is used up fast. Start with more disk than you ever think you'll need.

Memory (RAM): 4 to 8 megabytes (MB). Like disk space, the new applications are demanding more memory. It's easier and less expensive to obtain the memory when you buy the system than if you wait until later.

Expansion Slots: 3 to 5 open slots on the base system. Expansion slots are needed for scanners, tape drives, video boards, and other equipment you may want to add in the future as your needs change and the price of this equipment becomes lower.

Diskette Drives: Most software is now distributed on 3 1/2-inch disks. Consider adding a 5 1/4-inch diskette to read data and programs that may have been stored on that format. The best way to achieve this is to buy a combination diskette drive which is only slightly more expensive than a single 3 1/2-inch diskette drive. The combination device has both 3 1/2- and 5 1/4-inch diskette drives in a single unit.

Color Monitor: 14 to 15 inch. This is one device where it pays to spend a little more money. A 15-inch super VGA monitor will display graphics better than a 14-inch model. For health reasons, make sure you pick a low radiation model.

Pointing Device: Most systems include a mouse as part of the base package.

Enhanced Keyboard: The keyboard is usually included with the system. Check to make sure the keyboard is the *enhanced* and not the older *standard* model. The enhanced keyboard is sometimes called the *101* keyboard because it has 101 keys.

Printer: The price of nonimpact printers has come within several hundred dollars of the lowest cost dot matrix printers. Unless you need the wide carriage or multi-part form capabilities of a dot matrix, purchase a nonimpact printer.

Surge Protector: A voltage spike can literally destroy your system. It is low-cost insurance to protect yourself with a surge protector. Don't merely buy a fused multi-plug outlet from the local hardware store. Buy a surge protector designed for com-puters with a separate protected jack for your phone (modem) line.

Fax Modem: Volumes of information are available via on-line databases. In addition, many software vendors provide assistance and free software upgrades via bulletin boards. For the speed they provide, 14.4K modems are worth the extra money. Facsimile (fax) capability only costs a few dollars more and gives you more communication options.

Sound Card and Speakers: More and more software and support materials are incorporating sound.

CD-ROM Drive: Multimedia is the wave of the future and it requires a CD-ROM drive. Get a double- or triple-speed model.

Tape Backup: Larger hard disks make backing up data on diskettes impractical. Internal or external tape backup systems are the most common solution. Some portable units, great if you have more than one system, are designed to connect to your printer port. The small cassette tapes can store the equivalent of hundreds of diskettes.

Uninterruptable Power Supply (UPS): A UPS uses batteries to start or keep your system running if the main electrical power is turned off. The length of time they provide depends on the size of the batteries and the electrical requirements of your system but is usually at least 10 minutes. The idea of a UPS is to give you enough time to save your work. Get a UPS that is rated for your size system.

Remember that the types of applications you want to use on your system will guide you as to the type and size of computer that is right for you. The ideal computer system you choose may differ from the general recommendation that is presented here. Determine your needs and buy the best system your budget will allow.

How to Install a Computer System

1. **Allow for adequate workspace around the computer.** A workspace of at least two feet by four feet is recommended.
2. **Install bookshelves.** Bookshelves above and/or to the side of the computer area are useful for keeping manuals and other reference materials handy.
3. **Install your computer in a well-designed work area.** The height of your chair, keyboard, monitor, and work surface is important and can affect your health. See Figure 36 for specific guidelines.
4. **Use a document holder.** To minimize neck and eye strain, obtain a document holder that holds documents at the same height and distance as your computer screen.

5. **Provide adequate lighting.**

6. **While working at your computer, be aware of health issues.** See Figure 37 for a list of computer user health guidelines.

7. **Install or move a phone near the computer.** Having a phone near the computer really helps if you need to call a vendor about a hardware or software problem. Oftentimes the vendor support person can talk you through the correction while you're on the phone. To avoid data loss, however, don't place diskettes on the phone or any other electrical or electronic equipment.

8. **Obtain a computer tool set.** Computer tool sets are available from computer dealers, office supply stores, and mail order companies. These sets will have the right-sized screwdrivers and other tools to work on your system. Get one that comes in a zippered carrying case to keep all the tools together.

9. **Save all the paperwork that comes with your system.** Keep it in an accessible place with the paperwork from your other computer-related purchases. To keep different-sized documents together, consider putting them in a plastic zip-lock bag.

10. **Record the serial numbers of all your equipment and software.** Write the serial numbers on the outside of the manuals that came with the equipment as well as in a single list that contains the serial numbers of all your equipment and software.

11. **Keep the shipping containers and packing materials for all your equipment.** This material will come in handy if you have to return your equipment for servicing or have to move it to another location.

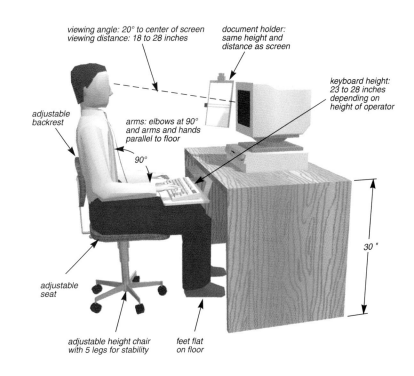

FIGURE 36
More than anything else, a well-designed work area should be flexible to allow adjustment to the height and build of different individuals. Good lighting and air quality should also be considered.

COMPUTER USER HEALTH GUIDELINES
1. Work in a well-designed work area. Figure 36 illustrates the guidelines.
2. Alternate work activities to prevent physical and mental fatigue. If possible, change the order of your work to provide some variety.
3. Take frequent breaks. At least once per hour, get out of your chair and move around. Every two hours, take at least a 15 minute break.
4. Incorporate hand, arm, and body stretching exercises into your breaks. At lunch, try to get outside and walk.
5. Make sure your computer monitor is designed to minimize electromagnetic radiation
6. Try to eliminate or minimize surrounding noise. Noisy environments contribute to stress and tension.
7. If you frequently have to use the phone and the computer at the same time, consider using a telephone headset. Cradling the phone between your head and shoulder can cause muscle strain.
8. Be aware of symptoms of repetitive strain injuries; soreness, pain, numbness, or weakness in neck, shoulders, arms, wrists, and hands. Don't ignore early signs; seek medical advice.

FIGURE 37
All computer users should follow the Computer User Health Guidelines to maintain their health.

12. **Look at the inside of your computer.** Before you connect power to your system, remove the computer case cover and visually inspect the internal components. The user manual usually identifies what each component does. Look for any disconnected wires, loose screws or washers, or any other obvious signs of trouble. Be careful not to touch anything inside the case unless you are grounded. Static electricity can permanently damage the microprocessor chips on the circuit boards. Before you replace the cover, take several photographs of the computer showing the location of the circuit boards. These photos may save you from taking the cover off in the future if you or a vendor has a question about what equipment controller card is installed in what expansion slot.

13. **Identify device connectors.** At the back of your system there are a number of connectors for the printer, the monitor, the mouse, a phone line, etc. If they aren't already identified by the manufacturer, use a marking pen to write the purpose of each connector on the back of the computer case.

14. **Complete and send in your equipment and software registration cards right away.** If you're already entered in the vendors user database, it can save you time when you call in with a support question. Being a registered user also makes you eligible for special pricing on software upgrades.

15. **Install your system in an area where the temperature and humidity can be maintained.** Try to maintain a constant temperature between 60 and 80 degrees farenheight when the computer is operating. High temperatures and humidity can damage electronic components. Be careful when using space heaters; their hot, dry air has been known to cause disk problems.

16. **Keep your computer area clean.** Avoid eating and drinking around the computer. Smoking should be avoided also. Cigarette smoke can quickly cause damage to the diskette drives and diskette surfaces.

17. **Check your insurance.** Some policies have limits on the amount of computer equipment they cover. Other policies don't cover computer equipment at all if it is used for a business (a separate policy is required).

How to Maintain Your Computer System

1. **Learn to use system diagnostic programs.** If a set didn't come with your system, obtain one. These programs help you identify and possibly solve problems before you call for technical assistance. Some system manufacturers now include diagnostic programs with their systems and ask that you run the programs before you call for help.

2. **Start a notebook that includes information on your system.** This notebook should be a single source of information about your entire system, both hardware and software. Each time you make a change to your system, adding or removing hardware or software, or when you change system parameters, you should record the change in the notebook. Items to include in the notebook are the following:

✓ Serial numbers of all equipment and software.

✓ Vendor support phone numbers. These numbers are often buried in user manuals. Look up these numbers once and record all of them on a single sheet of paper at the front of your notebook.

✓ Date and vendor for each equipment and software purchase.

✓ File listings for key system files (e.g., autoexec.bat and config.sys).

✓ Notes on discussions with vendor support personnel.

✓ A chronological history of any equipment or software problems. This history can be helpful if the problem persists and you have to call several times.

3. **Periodically review disk directories and delete unneeded files.** Files have a way of building up and can quickly use up your disk space. If you think you may need a file in the future, back it up to a diskette.

4. **Any time you work inside your computer turn the power off and disconnect the equipment from the power source.** In addition, before you touch anything inside the computer, touch an unpainted metal surface such as the power supply. This will discharge any static electricity that could damage internal components.

5. **Reduce the need to clean the inside of your system by keeping the surrounding area dirt and dust free.** Diskette cleaners are available but should be used sparingly (some owners never use them unless they experience diskette problems). If dust builds up inside the computer it should be carefully removed with compressed air and a small vacuum. Don't touch the components with the vacuum.

6. **Back up key files and data.** At a minimum, you should have a diskette with your **command.com, autoexec.bat,** and **config.sys** files. If your system crashes, these files will help you get going again. In addition, backup any files with a file extension of **.sys.** For Windows systems, all files with a file extension of **.ini** and **.grp** should be backed up.

7. **Protect your system from computer viruses.** Computer viruses are programs designed to *infect* computer systems by copying themselves into other computer files (Figure 38). The virus program spreads when the infected files are used by or copied to another system.

FIGURE 38
How a virus program can be transmitted from one computer to another.

A COMPUTER VIRUS: WHAT IT IS AND HOW IT SPREADS

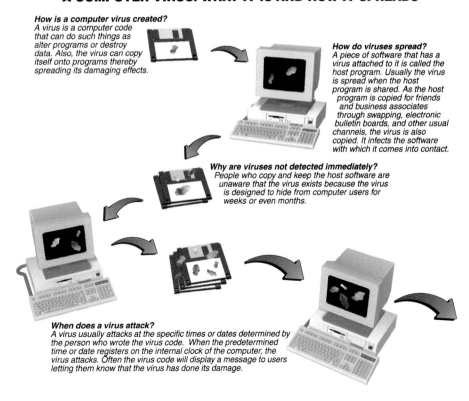

How is a computer virus created?
A virus is a computer code that can do such things as alter programs or destroy data. Also, the virus can copy itself onto programs thereby spreading its damaging effects.

How do viruses spread?
A piece of software that has a virus attached to it is called the host program. Usually the virus is spread when the host program is shared. As the host program is copied for friends and business associates through swapping, electronic bulletin boards, and other usual channels, the virus is also copied. It infects the software with which it comes into contact.

Why are viruses not detected immediately?
People who copy and keep the host software are unaware that the virus exists because the virus is designed to hide from computer users for weeks or even months.

When does a virus attack?
A virus usually attacks at the specific times or dates determined by the person who wrote the virus code. When the predetermined time or date registers on the internal clock of the computer, the virus attacks. Often the virus code will display a message to users letting them know that the virus has done its damage.

Virus programs are dangerous because they are often designed to damage the files of the infected system. Protect yourself from viruses by installing an anti-virus program on your computer.

Summary of Introduction to Computers

*A*s you learn to use the software taught in this book, you will also become familiar with the components and operation of your computer system. When you need help understanding how the components of your system function, refer to this introduction. You can also refer to this section for information on computer communications and for guidelines when you decide to purchase a computer system of your own.

Student Assignments

Student Assignment 1: True/False

Instructions: Circle T if the statement is true or F if the statement is false.

T F   1. A computer is an electronic device, operating under the control of instructions stored in its own memory unit, that can accept data (input), process data arithmetically and logically, produce output from the processing, and store the results for future use.

T F   2. Information refers to data processed into a form that has meaning and is useful.

T F   3. A computer program is a detailed set of instructions that tells a computer exactly what to do.

T F   4. A mouse is a communications device used to convert between digital and analog signals so telephone lines can carry data.

T F   5. The central processing unit contains the processor unit and main memory.

T F   6. A laser printer is an impact printer that provides high-quality output.

T F   7. Auxiliary storage is used to store instructions and data when they are not being used in main memory.

T F   8. A diskette is considered to be a form of main memory.

T F   9. CD-ROM is often used for multimedia material that combines text, graphics, video, and sound.

T F   10. The operating system tells the computer how to perform functions such as how to load, store, and execute an application program and how to transfer data between the input/output devices and main memory.

T F   11. Programs such as database management, spreadsheet, and word processing software are called system software.

T F   12. For data to be transferred from one computer to another over communications lines, communications software is required only on the sending computer.

T F   13. A communications network is a collection of computers and other equipment that use communications channels to share hardware, software, data, and information.

T F 14. Determining what applications you will use on your computer will help you to purchase a computer that is the type and size that meets your needs.

T F 15. The path the data follows as it is transmitted from the sending equipment to the receiving equipment in a communications system is called a modem.

T F 16. Computer equipment that meets the power consumption guidelines can display the *Energy Star* logo.

T F 17. An on-site maintenance agreement is important if you cannot be without the use of your computer.

T F 18. An anit-virus program is used to protect your computer equipment and software.

T F 19. When purchasing a computer, consider only the price because one computer is no different from another.

T F 20. A LAN allows you to share software but not hardware.

Student Assignments 2: Multiple Choice

Instructions: Circle the correct response.

1. The four operations performed by a computer include _____ .
   a. input, control, output, and storage
   b. interface, processing, output, and memory
   c. input, output, processing, and storage
   d. input, logical/rational, arithmetic, and output

2. A hand-held input device that controls the cursor location is _____ .
   a. the cursor control keyboard
   b. a mouse
   c. a modem
   d. the CRT

3. A printer that forms images without striking the paper is _____ .
   a. an impact printer   b. a nonimpact printer   c. an ink jet printer   d. both b and c

4. The amount of storage provided by a diskette is a function of _____ .
   a. the thickness of the disk
   b. the recording density of bits on the track
   c. the number of recording tracks on the diskette
   d. both b and c

5. Portable computers use a flat panel screen called a _____ .
   a. a multichrome monitor
   b. a cathode ray tube
   c. a liquid crystal display
   d. a monochrome monitor

6. When not in use, diskettes should be _____ .
   a. stored away from magnetic fields
   b. stored away from heat and direct sunlight
   c. stored in a diskette box or cabinet
   d. all of the above

7. CD-ROM is a type of _____ .
   a. main memory
   b. auxiliary storage
   c. communications equipment
   d. system software

8. An operating system is considered part of _____ .
   a. word processing software
   b. database software
   c. system software
   d. spreadsheet software

9. The type of application software most commonly used to create and print documents is _____ .
   a. word processing   b. electronic spreadsheet   c. database   d. none of the above

10. The type of application software most commonly used to send messages to and receive messages from other computer users is _____ .
    a. electronic mail   b. database   c. presentation graphics   d. none of the above

Student Assignment 3: Comparing Personal Computer Advertisements

Instructions: Obtain a copy of a recent computer magazine and review the advertisements for desktop personal computer systems. Compare ads for the least and most expensive desktop systems you can find. Discuss the differences.

Student Assignment 4: Evaluating On-Line Information Services

Instructions: Prodigy and America On-Line both offer consumer oriented on-line information services. Contact each company and request each to send you information on the specific services it offers. Try to talk to someone who actually uses one or both of the services. Discuss how each service is priced and the differences between the two on-line services.

Student Assignment 5: Visiting Local Computer Retail Stores

Instructions: Visit local computer retail stores and compare the various types of computers and support equipment available. Ask about warranties, repair services, hardware setup, training, and related issues. Report on the knowledge of the sales staff assisting you and their willingness to answer your questions. Does the store have standard hardware packages, or are they willing to configure a system to your specific needs? Would you feel confident buying a computer from this store?

Index

Photo Credits

Figure 1, (1) Compaq Computer Corp. All rights reserved.; (2) International Business Machines Corp.; (3) UNISYS Corp.; (4) Compaq Computer Corp. All rights reserved.; (5) International Business Machines Corp.; (6) Zenith Data Systems; (7) International Business Machines Corp.; (8) International Business Machines Corp.; (9) Hewlett-Packard Co.; Figure 2, International Business Machines Corp.; Figure 3, Compaq Computer Corp. All rights reserved.; Figure 5, International Business Machines Corp.; Figure 6, Logitech, Inc.; Figure 7, Intel Corp.; Figure 8, Epson America, Inc.; Figure 10 (top), Hewlett-Packard Co.; Figure 10 (bottom), Epson America, Inc.; Figure 12, Aldus Corp.; Figure 13, International Business Machines Corp.; Figure 15, Jerry Spagnoli; Figure 16, Greg Hadel; Figure 19, Jerry Spagnoli; Figure 20, Microscience International Corp.; Figure 21, 3M Corp.; Illustrations, Dave Wyer.

W I N D O W S

USING *M*ICROSOFT *W*INDOWS 3.1

MICROSOFT WINDOWS 3.1

PROJECT ONE

AN INTRODUCTION TO WINDOWS

OBJECTIVES You will have mastered the material in this project when you can:

- ▶ Describe a user interface
- ▶ Describe Microsoft Windows
- ▶ Identify the elements of a window
- ▶ Perform the four basic mouse operations of pointing, clicking, double-clicking, and dragging
- ▶ Correct errors made while performing mouse operations
- ▶ Understand the keyboard shortcut notation
- ▶ Select a menu
- ▶ Choose a command from a menu

- ▶ Respond to dialog boxes
- ▶ Start and exit an application
- ▶ Name a file
- ▶ Understand directories and subdirectories
- ▶ Understand directory structures and directory paths
- ▶ Create, save, open, and print a document
- ▶ Open, enlarge, and scroll a window
- ▶ Obtain online Help while using an application

▶ INTRODUCTION

T he most popular and widely used graphical user interface available today is **Microsoft Windows**, or **Windows**. Microsoft Windows allows you to easily communicate with and control your computer. In addition, Microsoft Windows makes it easy to learn the application software installed on your computer, transfer data between the applications, and manage the data created while using an application.

In this project, you learn about user interfaces, the computer hardware and computer software that comprise a user interface, and Microsoft Windows. You use Microsoft Windows to perform the operations of opening a group window, starting and exiting an application, enlarging an application window, entering and editing data within an application, printing a document on the printer, saving a document on disk, opening a document, and obtaining online Help while using an application.

What Is a User Interface?

A **user interface** is the combination of hardware and software that allows the computer user to communicate with and control the computer. Through the user interface, you are able to control the computer, request information from the computer, and respond to messages displayed by the computer. Thus, a user interface provides the means for dialogue between you and the computer.

Hardware and software together form the user interface. Among the hardware associated with a user interface are the CRT screen, keyboard, and mouse (Figure 1-1). The CRT screen displays messages and provides information. You respond by entering data in the form of a command or other response using the keyboard or mouse. Among the responses available to you are responses that specify what application software to run, when to print, and where to store the data for future use.

FIGURE 1-1

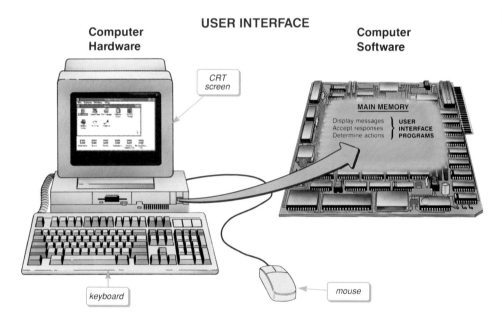

USER INTERFACE

Computer Hardware

Computer Software

CRT screen

MAIN MEMORY

Display messages
Accept responses
Determine actions
} USER INTERFACE PROGRAMS

keyboard

mouse

The computer software associated with the user interface are the programs that engage you in dialogue (Figure 1-1). The computer software determines the messages you receive, the manner in which you should respond, and the actions that occur based on your responses. The goal of an effective user interface is to be **user friendly**, meaning the software can be easily used by individuals with limited training. Research studies have indicated that the use of graphics can play an important role in aiding users to effectively interact with a computer. A **graphical user interface**, or **GUI**, is a user interface that displays graphics in addition to text when it communicates with the user.

▶ MICROSOFT WINDOWS

Microsoft Windows, or Windows, the most popular graphical user interface, makes it easy to learn and work with **application software**, which is software that performs an application-related function, such as word processing. Numerous application software packages are available for purchase from retail computer stores, and several applications are included with the Windows interface software. In Windows terminology, these application software packages are referred to as **applications**.

Starting Microsoft Windows

When you turn on the computer, an introductory screen consisting of the Windows logo, Windows name, version number (3.1), and copyright notices displays momentarily (Figure 1-2). Next, a blank screen containing an hourglass icon (⧗) displays (Figure 1-3). The **hourglass icon** indicates that Windows requires a brief interval of time to change the display on the screen, and you should wait until the hourglass icon disappears.

FIGURE 1-2

FIGURE 1-3

FIGURE 1-4

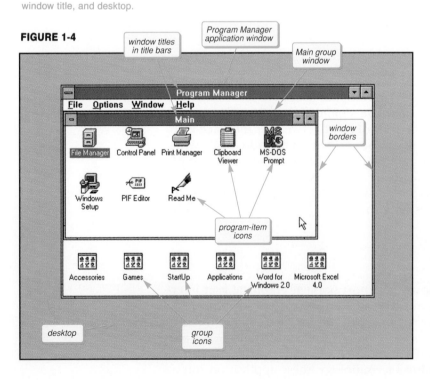

Finally, two rectangular areas, or **windows**, display (Figure 1-4). The double-line, or **window border**, surrounding each window determines their shape and size. The horizontal bar at the top of each window, called the **title bar**, contains a **window title** that identifies each window. In Figure 1-4, the Program Manager and Main titles identify each window.

The screen background on which the windows display is called the **desktop**. If your desktop does not look similar to the desktop in Figure 1-4, your instructor will inform you of the modifications necessary to change your desktop.

The Program Manager window represents the **Program Manager** application. The Program Manager application starts when you start Windows and is central to the operation of Windows. Program Manager organizes related applications into groups and displays the groups in the Program Manager window. A window that represents an application, such as the Program Manager window, is called an **application window**.

Small pictures, or **icons**, represent an individual application or groups of applications. In Figure 1-4 on the previous page, the Main window contains a group of eight icons (File Manager, Control Panel, Print Manager, Clipboard Viewer, MS-DOS Prompt, Windows Setup, PIF Editor, and Read Me). A window that contains a group of icons, such as the Main window, is called a **group window**. The icons in a group window, called **program-item icons**, each represent an individual application. A name below each program-item icon identifies the application. The program-item icons are unique and, therefore, easily distinguished from each other.

The six icons at the bottom of the Program Manager window in Figure 1-4 on the previous page, (Accessories, Games, StartUp, Applications, Word for Windows 2.0, and Microsoft Excel 4.0), called **group icons**, each represent a group of applications. Group icons are similar in appearance and only the name below the icon distinguishes one icon from another icon. Although the program-item icons of the individual applications in these groups are not visible in Figure 1-4, a method to view these icons will be demonstrated later in this project.

▶ COMMUNICATING WITH MICROSOFT WINDOWS

The Windows interface software provides the means for dialogue between you and the computer. Part of this dialogue involves requesting information from the computer and responding to messages displayed by the computer. You can request information and respond to messages using either the mouse or keyboard.

The Mouse and Mouse Pointer

A **mouse** is a pointing device commonly used with Windows that is attached to the computer by a cable and contains one or more buttons. The mouse in Figure 1-5 contains two buttons, the left mouse button and the right mouse button. On the bottom of this mouse is a ball (Figure 1-6).

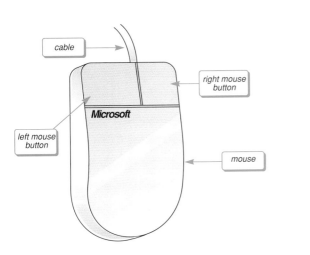

FIGURE 1-5

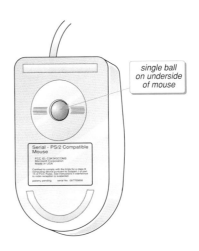

FIGURE 1-6

LECTURE NOTES
▪ Describe the Program Manager application.
▪ Define application window, icon, group window, program-item icon, and group icon.

CAUTION
▪ The group icons in the Program Manager window may be different from those in Figure 1-4.

TRANSPARENCIES
WIN1-5 through WIN1-7

LECTURE NOTES
▪ Emphasize that you communicate by requesting information from the computer and responding to messages using either the mouse or keyboard.
▪ Define mouse and describe the parts of the mouse (buttons, cable, and ball).

LECTURE NOTES
- Define mouse pointer. Show the block arrow mouse pointer.
- Demonstrate how the mouse pointer moves when you move the mouse.

As you move the mouse across a flat surface (Figure 1-7), the movement of the ball is electronically sensed, and a **mouse pointer** in the shape of a block arrow (↖) moves across the desktop in the same direction.

Mouse moves diagonally across flat surface

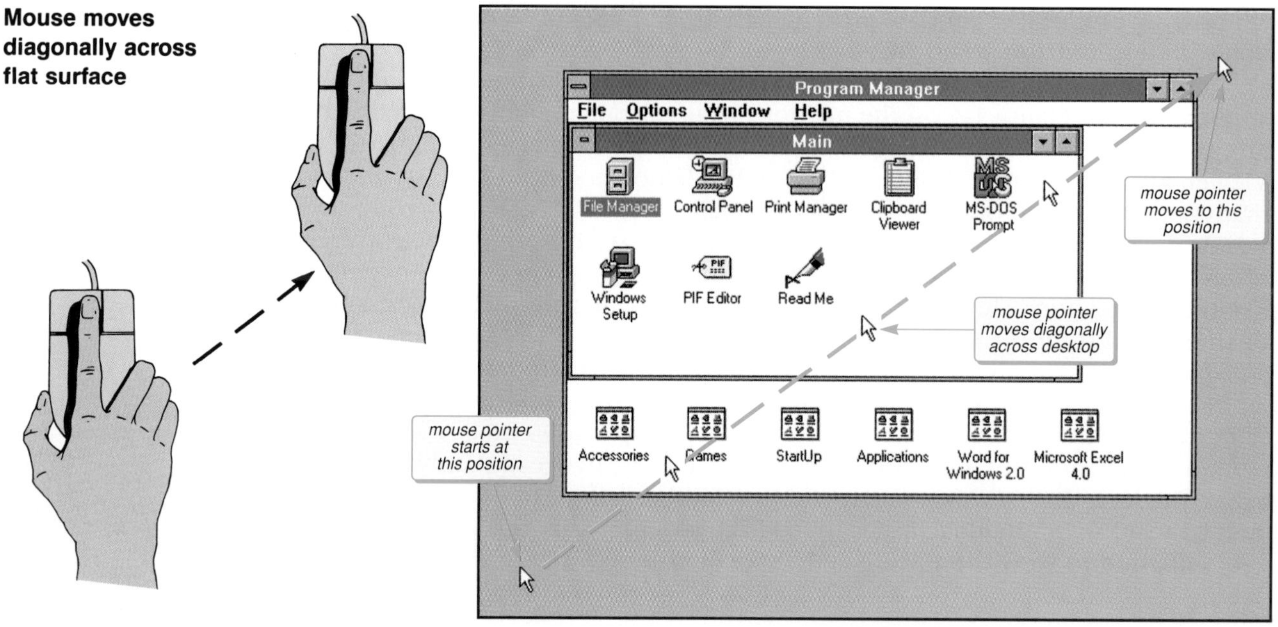

FIGURE 1-7

TRANSPARENCY WIN1-8

Mouse Operations

LECTURE NOTES
- List the four basic mouse operations.
- Define pointing.
- Demonstrate how to point using the mouse.

You use the mouse to perform four basic operations: (1) pointing; (2) clicking; (3) double-clicking; and (4) dragging. **Pointing** means moving the mouse across a flat surface until the mouse pointer rests on the item of choice on the desktop. In Figure 1-8, you move the mouse diagonally across a flat surface until the tip of the mouse pointer rests on the Print Manager icon.

Mouse moves diagonally

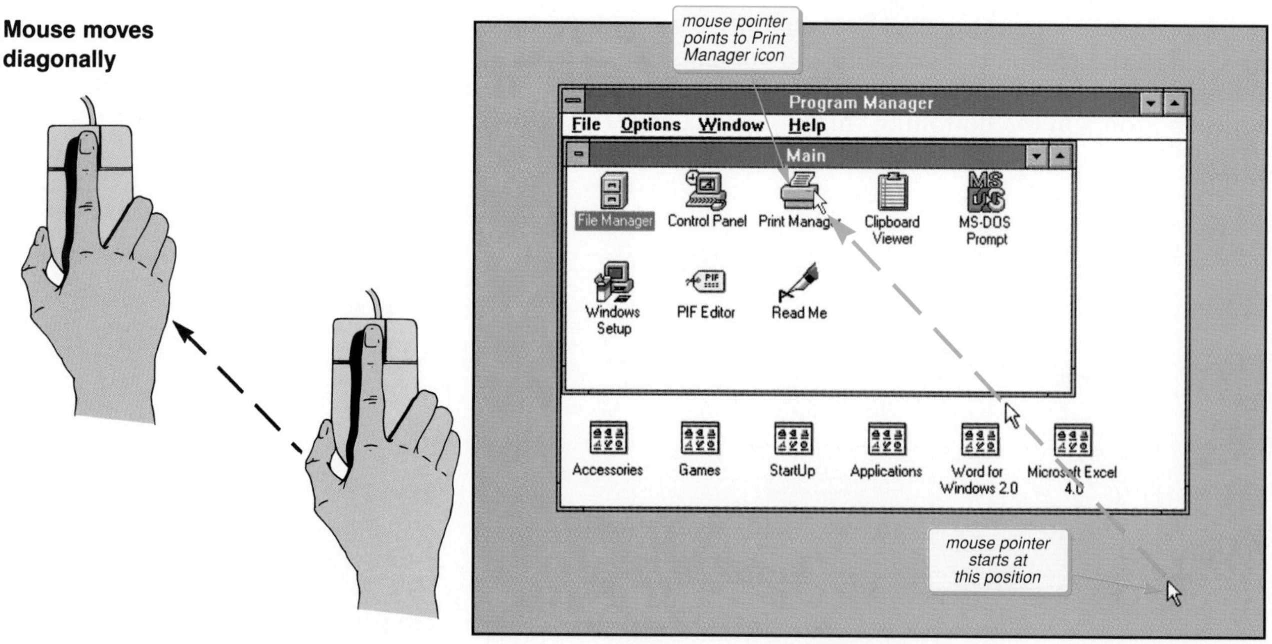

FIGURE 1-8

Clicking means pressing and releasing a mouse button. In most cases, you must point to an item before pressing and releasing a mouse button. In Figure 1-9, you highlight the Print Manager icon by pointing to the Print Manager icon (Step 1) and pressing and releasing the left mouse button (Step 2). These steps are commonly referred to as clicking the Print Manager icon. When you click the Print Manager icon, Windows highlights, or places color behind, the name below the Print Manager icon (Step 3).

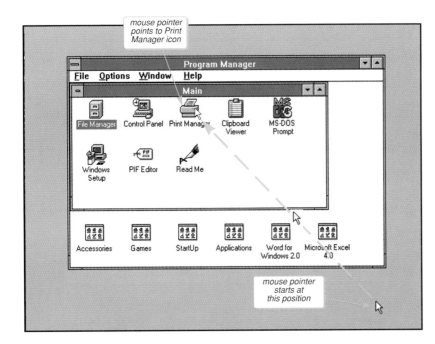

mouse pointer points to Print Manager icon

mouse pointer starts at this position

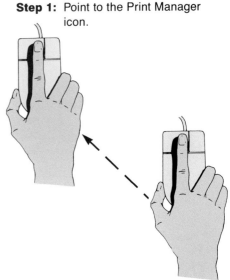

Step 1: Point to the Print Manager icon.

Step 2: Press and release the left mouse button.

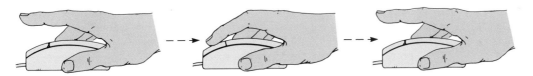

Step 3: Windows highlights the Print Manager name.

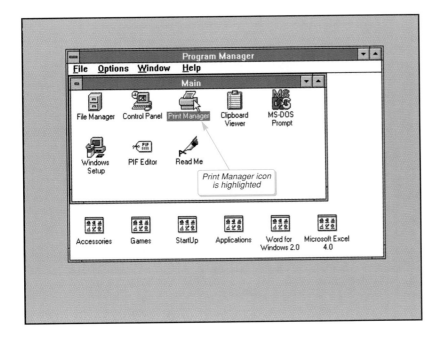

Print Manager icon is highlighted

FIGURE 1-9

Double-clicking means quickly pressing and releasing a mouse button twice without moving the mouse. In most cases, you must point to an item before quickly pressing and releasing a mouse button twice. In Figure 1-10, to open the Accessories group window, point to the Accessories icon (Step 1), and quickly press and release the left mouse button twice (Step 2). These steps are commonly referred to as double-clicking the Accessories icon. When you double-click the Accessories icon, Windows opens a group window with the same name (Step 3).

Step 1: Point to the Accessories icon.

Step 2: Quickly press and release
the left mouse button twice.

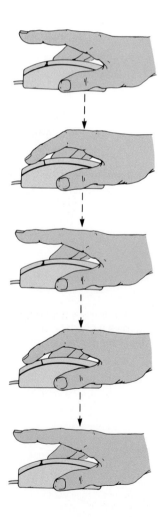

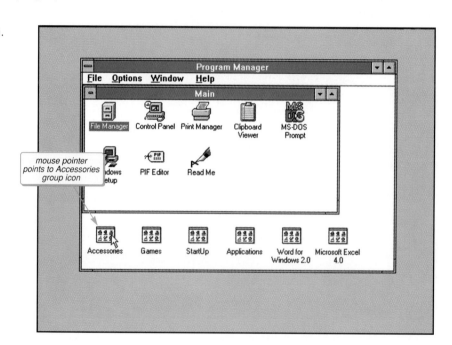

Step 3: Windows opens the
Accessories group
window.

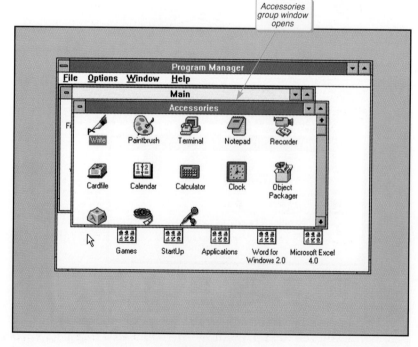

FIGURE 1-10

Dragging means holding down the left mouse button, moving an item to the desired location, and then releasing the left mouse button. In most cases, you must point to an item before doing this. In Figure 1-11, you move the Control Panel program-item icon by pointing to the Control Panel icon (Step 1), holding down the left mouse button while moving the icon to its new location (Step 2), and releasing the left mouse button (Step 3). These steps are commonly referred to as dragging the Control Panel icon.

In Figure 1-11, the location of the Control Panel program-item icon was moved to rearrange the icons in the Main group window. Dragging has many uses in Windows, as you will see in subsequent examples.

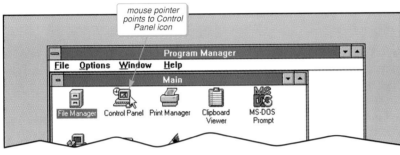
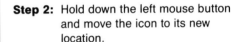

Step 1: Point to the Control Panel icon.

Step 2: Hold down the left mouse button and move the icon to its new location.

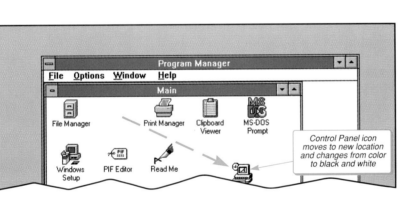
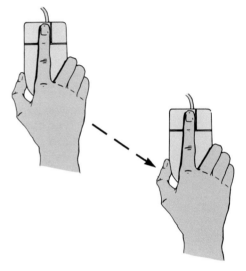

Step 3: Release the left mouse button.

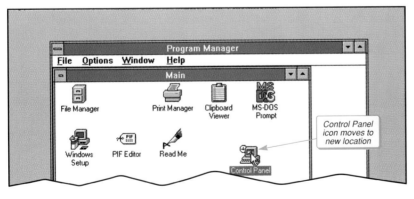
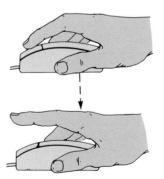

FIGURE 1-11

The Keyboard and Keyboard Shortcuts

The **keyboard** is an input device on which you manually key, or type, data. Figure 1-12 on the next page shows the enhanced IBM PS/2 keyboard. Any task you accomplish with a mouse you can also accomplish with the keyboard. Although the choice of whether you use the mouse or keyboard is a matter of personal preference, the mouse is strongly recommended.

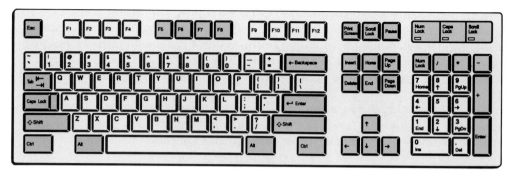

FIGURE 1-12

The Quick Reference at the end of each project provides a list of tasks presented and the manner in which to complete them using a mouse, menu, or keyboard.

To perform tasks using the keyboard, you must understand the notation used to identify which keys to press. This notation is used throughout Windows to identify **keyboard shortcuts** and in the Quick Reference at the end of each project. Keyboard shortcuts can consist of pressing a single key (RIGHT ARROW), pressing two keys simultaneously as shown by two key names separated by a plus sign (CTRL + F6), or pressing three keys simultaneously as shown by three key names separated by plus signs (CTRL + SHIFT + LEFT ARROW).

For example, to move the highlight from one program-item icon to the next you can press the RIGHT ARROW key (RIGHT ARROW). To move the highlight from the Main window to a group icon, hold down the CTRL key and press the F6 key (CTRL + F6). To move to the previous word in certain Windows applications, hold down the CTRL and SHIFT keys and press the LEFT ARROW key (CTRL + SHIFT + LEFT ARROW).

Menus and Commands

A **command** directs the software to perform a specific action, such as printing on the printer or saving data for use at a future time. One method in which you carry out a command is by choosing the command from a list of available commands, called a menu.

Windows organizes related groups of commands into **menus** and assigns a menu name to each menu. The **menu bar**, a horizontal bar below the title bar of an application window, contains a list of the menu names for that application. The menu bar for the Program Manager window in Figure 1-13 contains the following menu names: File, Options, Window, and Help. One letter in each name is underlined.

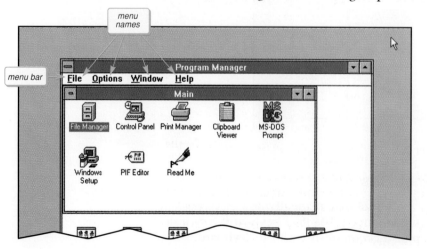

FIGURE 1-13

Selecting a Menu

To display a menu, you select the menu name. **Selecting** means marking an item. In some cases, when you select an item, Windows marks the item with a highlight by placing color behind the item. You select a menu name by pointing to the menu name in the menu bar and pressing the left mouse button (called clicking) or by using the keyboard to press the ALT key and then the keyboard key of the underlined letter in the menu name. Clicking the menu name File in the menu bar or pressing the ALT key and then the F key opens the File menu (Figure 1-14).

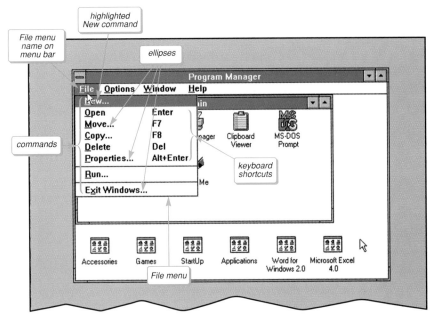

FIGURE 1-14

The File menu in Figure 1-14 contains the following commands: New, Open, Move, Copy, Delete, Properties, Run, and Exit Windows. The first command in the menu (New) is highlighted and a single character in each command is underlined. Some commands (New, Move, Copy, Properties, Run, and Exit Windows) are followed by an ellipsis (...). An **ellipsis** indicates Windows requires more information before executing the command. Commands without an ellipsis, such as the Open command, execute immediately.

Choosing a Command

You **choose** an item to carry out an action. You can choose using a mouse or keyboard. For example, to choose a command using a mouse, either click the command name in the menu or drag the highlight to the command name. To choose a command using the keyboard, either press the keyboard key of the underlined character in the command name or use the Arrow keys to move the highlight to the command name and press the ENTER key.

Some command names are followed by a keyboard shortcut. In Figure 1-14, the Open, Move, Copy, Delete, and Properties command names have keyboard shortcuts. The keyboard shortcut for the Properties command is ALT + ENTER. Holding down the ALT key and then pressing the ENTER key chooses the Properties command without selecting the File menu.

Dialog Boxes

When you choose a command whose command name is followed by an ellipsis (...), Windows opens a dialog box. A **dialog box** is a window that appears when Windows needs to supply information to you or wants you to enter information or select among options.

For example, Windows may inform you that a document is printing on the printer through the use of dialog box; or Windows may ask you whether you want to print all the pages in a printed report or just certain pages in the report.

A dialog box contains a title bar that identifies the name of the dialog box. In Figure 1-15, the name of the dialog box is Print.

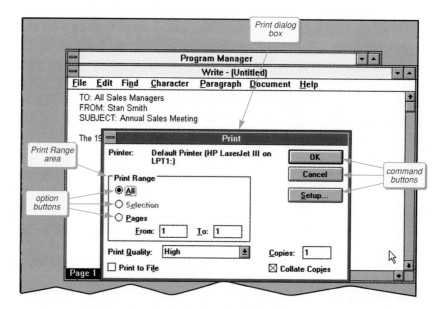

FIGURE 1-15

The types of responses Windows will ask for when working with dialog boxes fall into five categories: (1) Selecting mutually exclusive options; (2) Selecting one or more multiple options; (3) Entering specific information from the keyboard; (4) Selecting one item from a list of items; (5) Choosing a command to be implemented from the dialog box.

Each of these types of responses is discussed in the following paragraphs, together with the method for specifying them.

The Print dialog box in Figure 1-15 opens when you choose the Print command from the File menu of some windows. The Print Range area, defined by the name Print Range and a rectangular box, contains three option buttons.

The **option buttons** give you the choice of printing all pages of a report (All), selected parts of a report (Selection), or certain pages of a report (Pages). The option button containing the black dot (All) is the **selected button**. You can select only one option button at a time. A dimmed option, such as the Selection button, cannot be selected. To select an option button, use the mouse to click the option button or press the TAB key until the area containing the option button is selected and press the Arrow keys to highlight the option button.

The Print dialog box in Figure 1-15 on the previous page also contains the OK, Cancel, and Setup command buttons. **Command buttons** execute an action. The OK button executes the Print command, and the Cancel button cancels the Print command. The Setup button changes the setup of the printer by allowing you to select a printer from a list of printers, select the paper size, etc.

Figure 1-16 illustrates text boxes and check boxes. A **text box** is a rectangular area in which Windows displays text or you enter text. In the Print dialog box in Figure 1-16, the Pages option button is selected, which means only certain pages of a report are to print. You select which pages by entering the first page in the From text box (1) and the last page in the To text box (4). To enter text into a text box, select the text box by clicking it or by pressing the TAB key until the text in the text box is highlighted, and then type the text using the keyboard. The Copies text box in Figure 1-16 contains the number of copies to be printed (3).

Check boxes represent options you can turn on or off. An X in a check box indicates the option is turned on. To place an X in the box, click the box, or press the TAB key until the Print To File check box is highlighted, and then press SPACEBAR. In Figure 1-16, the Print to File check box, which does not contain an X, indicates the Print to File option is turned off and the pages will print on the printer. The Collate Copies check box, which contains an X, indicates the Collate Copies feature is turned on and the pages will print in collated order.

The Print dialog boxes in Figure 1-17 and Figure 1-18 on the next page, illustrate the Print Quality drop-down list box. When first selected, a **drop-down list box** is a rectangular box containing highlighted text and a down arrow box on the right. In Figure 1-17, the highlighted text, or **current selection**, is High.

FIGURE 1-16

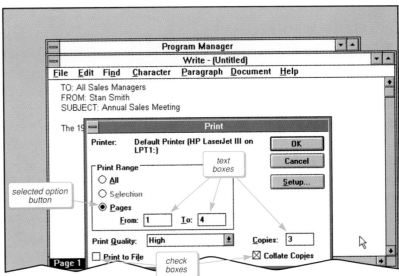

FIGURE 1-17

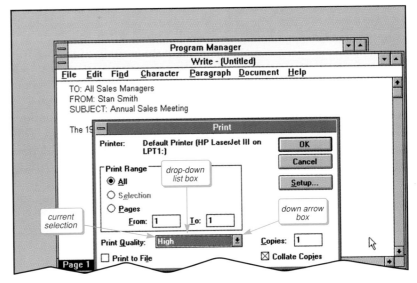

When you click the down arrow button, the drop-down list in Figure 1-18 appears. The list contains three choices (High, Medium, and Low). The current selection, High, is highlighted. To select from the list, use the mouse to click the selection or press the TAB key until the Print Quality drop-down list box is highlighted, press the DOWN ARROW key to highlight the selection, and then press ALT + UP ARROW or ALT + DOWN ARROW to make the selection.

Windows uses drop-down list boxes when a list of options must be presented but the dialog box is too crowded to contain the entire list. After you make your selection, the list disappears and only the current selection displays.

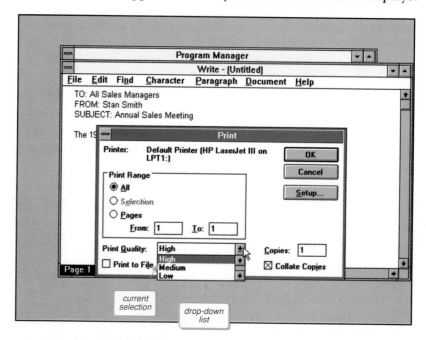

FIGURE 1-18

▶ USING MICROSOFT WINDOWS

The remainder of this project illustrates how to use Windows to perform the operations of starting and quitting an application, creating a document, saving a document on disk, opening a document, editing a document, printing a document and using the Windows help facility. Understanding how to perform these operations will make completing the remainder of the projects in this book easier. These operations are illustrated by the use of the Notepad and Paintbrush applications.

One of the many applications included with Windows is the Notepad application. **Notepad** allows you to enter, edit, save, and print notes. Items that you create while using an application, such as a note, are called **documents**. In the following section, you will use the Notepad application to learn to (1) open a group window, (2) start an application from a group window, (3) maximize an application window, (4) create a document, (5) select a menu, (6) choose a command from a menu, (7) print a document, and (8) quit an application. In the process, you will enter and print a note.

Opening a Group Window

Each group icon at the bottom of the Program Manager window represents a group window that may contain program-item icons. To open the group window and view the program-item icons in that window use the mouse to point to the group icon and then double-click the left mouse button, as shown in the steps on the next page.

TO OPEN A GROUP WINDOW ▼

STEP 1 ►

Point to the Accessories group icon at the bottom of the Program Manager window.

The mouse pointer points to the Accessories icon (Figure 1-19).

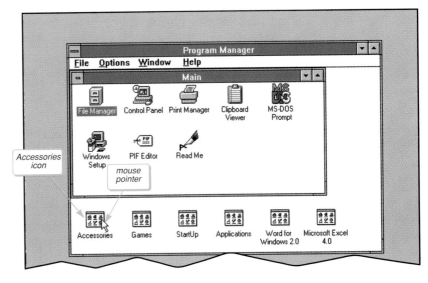

FIGURE 1-19

STEP 2 ►

Double-click the left mouse button.

Windows removes the Accessories icon from the Program Manager window and opens the Accessories group window on top of the Program Manager and Main windows (Figure 1-20). The Accessories window contains the Notepad icon.

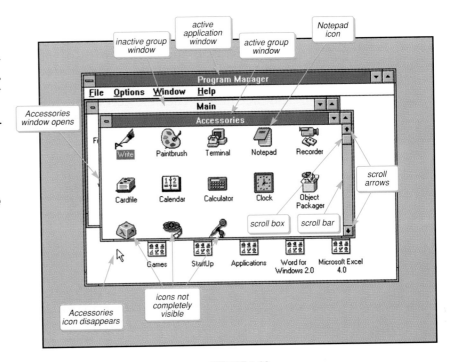

FIGURE 1-20

Opening a group window when one or more group windows are already open in the Program Manager window causes the new group window to display on top of the other group windows. The title bar of the newly opened group window is a different color or intensity than the title bars of the other group windows. This indicates the new group window is the active window. The **active window** is the window currently being used. Only one application window and

CAUTION
■ The colors of the active and inactive window title bars may be different on some computers.

LECTURE NOTES
■ Demonstrate how to use the scroll bar.

WINDOWS TIPS
■ Another method to view the partially hidden row of program-item icons is to resize the Accessories window by pointing to the bottom border and dragging the border toward the top of the window.

TRANSPARENCY
WIN1-21

LECTURE NOTES
■ Explain the Control menu and the commands on the Control menu.
■ Demonstrate how to correct an error made while double-clicking a group icon.

one group window can be active at the same time. In Figure 1-20 on the previous page, the colors of the title bars indicate that Program Manager is the active application window (green title bar) and the Accessories group window is the active group window (green title bar). The color of the Main window title bar (yellow) indicates the Main window is inactive. The colors may not be the same on the computer you use.

A scroll bar appears on the right edge of the Accessories window. A **scroll bar** is a bar that appears at the right and/or bottom edge of a window whose contents are not completely visible. In Figure 1-20 on the previous page, the third row of program-item icons in the Accessories window is not completely visible. A scroll bar contains two **scroll arrows** and a **scroll box** which enable you to view areas of the window not currently visible. To view areas of the Accessories window not currently visible, you can click the down scroll arrow repeatedly, click the scroll bar between the down scroll arrow and the scroll box, or drag the scroll box toward the down scroll arrow until the area you want to view is visible in the window.

Correcting an Error While Double-Clicking a Group Icon

While double-clicking, it is easy to mistakenly click once instead of double-clicking. When you click a group icon such as the Accessories icon once, the **Control menu** for that icon opens (Figure 1-21). The Control menu contains the following seven commands: Restore, Move, Size, Minimize, Maximize, Close, and Next. You choose one of these commands to carry out an action associated with the Accessories icon. To remove the Control menu and open the Accessories window after clicking the Accessories icon once, you can choose the Restore command; or click any open area outside the menu to remove the Control menu and then double-click the Accessories icon; or simply double-click the Accessories icon as if you had not clicked the icon at all.

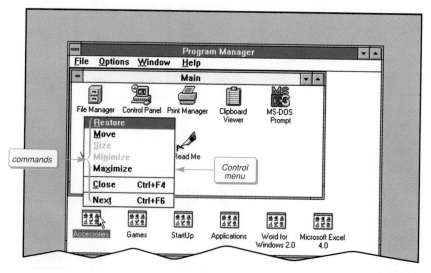

FIGURE 1-21

TRANSPARENCIES
WIN1-22 and WIN1-23

LECTURE NOTES
■ Demonstrate how to start an application from a group window.
■ Discuss active and inactive application windows.
■ Define insertion point.

Starting an Application

Each program-item icon in a group window represents an application. To start an application, double-click the program-item icon. In this project, you want to start the Notepad application. To start the Notepad application, perform the steps on the next page.

TO START AN APPLICATION ▼

STEP 1 ▶

Point to the Notepad icon (Figure 1-22).

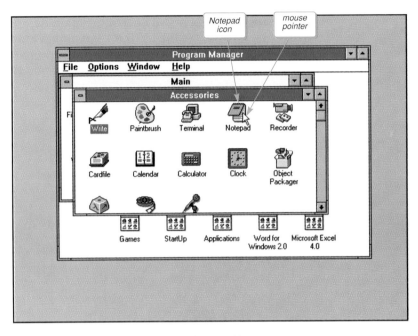

FIGURE 1-22

STEP 2 ▶

Double-click the left mouse button.

*Windows opens the Notepad window on the desktop (Figure 1-23). Program Manager becomes the inactive application (yellow title bar) and Notepad is the active application (green title bar). The word Untitled in the window title (Notepad — [Untitled]) indicates a document has not been created and saved on disk. The menu bar contains the following menus: File, Edit, Search, and Help. The area below the menu bar contains an insertion point, mouse pointer, and two scroll bars. The **insertion point** is a flashing vertical line that indicates the point at which text entered from the keyboard will be displayed. When you point to the interior of the Notepad window, the mouse pointer changes from a block arrow to an I-beam (I).*

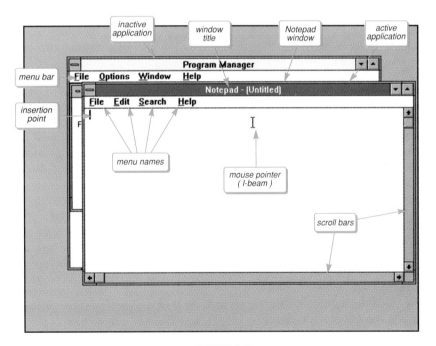

FIGURE 1-23

Correcting an Error While Double-Clicking a Program-Item Icon

While double-clicking a program-item icon you can easily click once instead. When you click a program-item icon such as the Notepad icon once, the icon becomes the **active icon** and Windows highlights the icon name (Figure 1-24). To start the Notepad application after clicking the Notepad icon once, double-click the Notepad icon as if you had not clicked the icon at all.

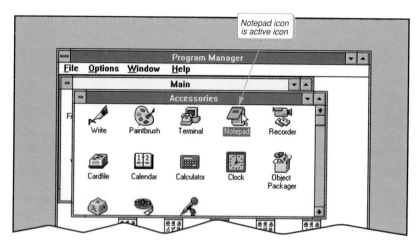

FIGURE 1-24

Maximizing an Application Window

Before you work with an application, maximizing the application window makes it easier to see the contents of the window. You can maximize an application window so the window fills the entire desktop. To maximize an application window to its maximum size, choose the **Maximize button** (▲) by pointing to the Maximize button and clicking the left mouse button. Complete the following steps to maximize the Notepad window.

TO MAXIMIZE AN APPLICATION WINDOW ▼

STEP 1 ▶

Point to the Maximize button in the upper right corner of the Notepad window.

The mouse pointer becomes a block arrow and points to the Maximize button (Figure 1-25).

FIGURE 1-25

STEP 2 ▶

Click the left mouse button.

The Notepad window fills the desktop (Figure 1-26). The **Restore button** *(▼) replaces the Maximize button at the right side of the title bar. Clicking the Restore button will return the window to its size before maximizing.*

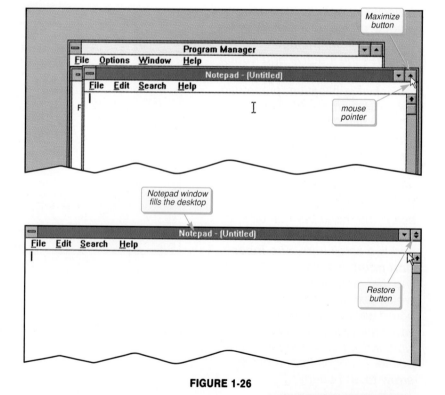

FIGURE 1-26

Creating a Document

To create a document in Notepad, type the text you want to display in the document. After typing a line of text, press the ENTER key to terminate the entry of the line. To create a document, enter the note to the right by performing the steps below.

Things to do today —
1) Take fax\phone to Conway Service Center
2) Pick up payroll checks from ADM
3) Order 3 boxes of copier paper

TO CREATE A NOTEPAD DOCUMENT ▼

STEP 1 ▶

Type Things to do today — **and press the ENTER key.**

The first line of the note is entered and the insertion point appears at the beginning of the next line (Figure 1-27).

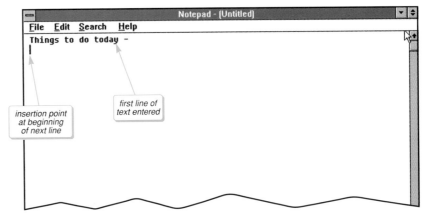

FIGURE 1-27

STEP 2 ▶

Type the remaining lines of the note. Press the ENTER key after typing each line.

The remaining lines in the note are entered and the insertion point is located at the beginning of the line following the note (Figure 1-28).

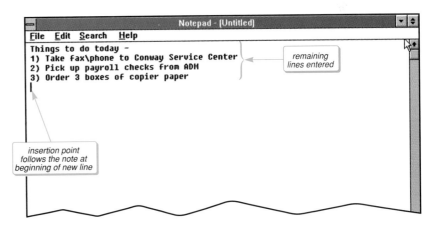

FIGURE 1-28

TRANSPARENCIES
WIN1-29 through
WIN1-33

LECTURE NOTES
■ Demonstrate how to print a document.
■ Explain the Notepad dialog box.

Printing a Document by Choosing a Command from a Menu

After creating a document, you often print the document on the printer. To print the note, complete the following steps.

TO PRINT A DOCUMENT ▼

STEP 1 ►

Point to File on the Notepad menu bar (Figure 1-29).

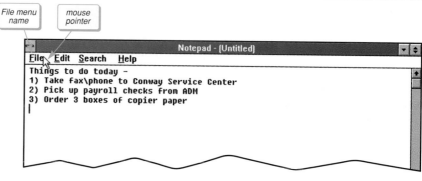

FIGURE 1-29

STEP 2 ►

Select File by clicking the left mouse button.

Windows opens the File menu in the Notepad window (Figure 1-30). The File menu name is high-lighted and the File menu con-tains the following commands: New, Open, Save, Save As, Print, Page Setup, Print Setup, and Exit. Windows highlights the first command in the menu (New). Notice the commands in the Notepad File menu are different than those in the Program Man-ager File menu (see Figure 1-14 on page WIN11). The commands in the File menu will vary depend-ing on the application you are using.

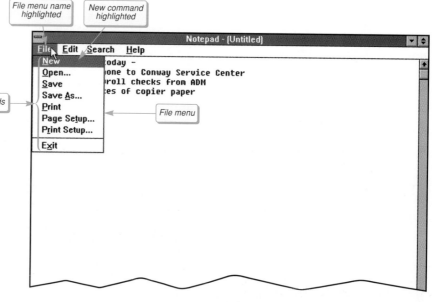

FIGURE 1-30

STEP 3 ►

Point to the Print command.

The mouse pointer points to the Print command (Figure 1-31).

FIGURE 1-31

STEP 4 ▶

Choose the Print command from the File menu by clicking the left mouse button.

Windows momentarily opens the Notepad dialog box (Figure 1-32). The dialog box contains the Now Printing text message and the Cancel command button (⬚Cancel⬚). When the Notepad dialog box closes, Windows prints the document on the printer (Figure 1-33).

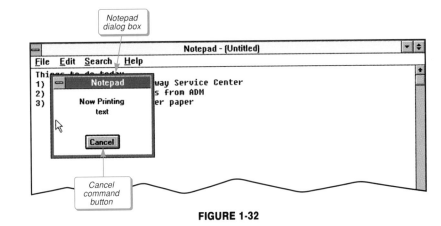

FIGURE 1-32

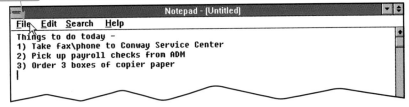

FIGURE 1-33

Quitting an Application

When you have finished creating and printing the document, quit the application by following the steps below and on the next page.

TO QUIT AN APPLICATION ▼

STEP 1 ▶

Point to File on the Notepad menu bar (Figure 1-34).

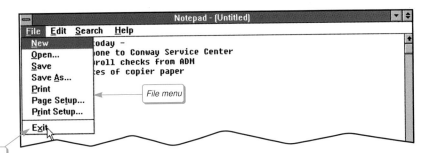

FIGURE 1-34

STEP 2 ▶

Select File by clicking the left mouse button, and then point to the Exit command.

Windows opens the File menu and the mouse pointer points to the Exit command (Figure 1-35).

FIGURE 1-35

STEP 3 ►

Choose the Exit command from the File menu by clicking the left mouse button, and then point to the No button.

Windows opens the Notepad dialog box (Figure 1-36). The dialog box contains the following: The message, The text in the [Untitled] file has changed., the question, Do you want to save the changes?, and the Yes, No, and Cancel command buttons. The mouse pointer points to the No button (Yes). You choose the Yes button (No) to save the document on disk and exit Notepad. You choose the No button if you do not want to save the document and want to exit Notepad. You choose the Cancel button to cancel the Exit command.

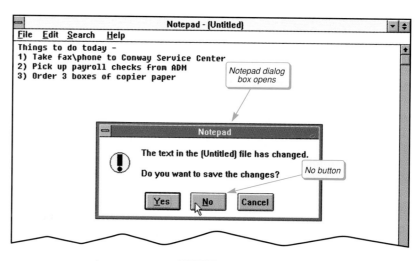

FIGURE 1-36

STEP 4 ►

Choose the No button by clicking the left mouse button.

Windows closes the Notepad dialog box and Notepad window and exits the Notepad application (Figure 1-37).

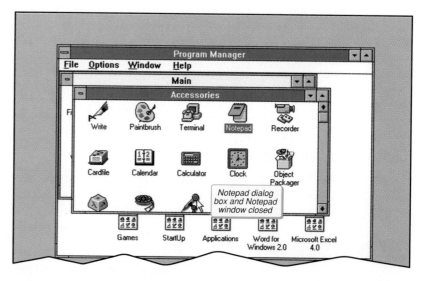

FIGURE 1-37

WINDOWS TIPS
■ Another method to quit an application is to double-click the Control menu box in the upper left corner of the application window.

In the preceding example, you used the Microsoft Windows graphical user interface to accomplish the tasks of opening the Accessories group window, starting the Notepad application from the Accessories group window, maximizing the Notepad application window, creating a document in the Notepad application window, printing the document on the printer, and quitting the Notepad application.

▶ FILE AND DISK CONCEPTS

LECTURE NOTES
■ Emphasize the importance of saving a document to disk.

To protect against the accidental loss of a document and to save a document for use in the future, you should save a document on disk. Before saving a document on disk, however, you must understand the concepts of naming a file, directories, subdirectories, directory structures, and directory paths. The following section explains these concepts.

Naming a File

When you create a document using an application, the document is stored in main memory. If you quit the application without saving the document on disk, the document is lost. To save the document for future use, you must store the document in a **document file** on the hard disk or on a diskette before quitting the application. Before saving a document, you must assign a name to the document file.

All files are identified on disk by a **filename** and an **extension**. For example, the name SALES.TXT consists of a filename (SALES) and an extension (.TXT). A filename can contain from one to eight characters and the extension begins with a period and can contain from one to three characters. Filenames must start with a letter or number. Any uppercase or lowercase character is valid except a period (.), quotation mark (''), slash (/), backslash (\), brackets ([]), colon (:), semicolon (;), vertical bar (|), equal sign (=), comma (,), or blank space. Filenames cannot be CON, AUX, COM1, COM2, COM3, COM4, LPT1, LPT2, LPT3, PRN, and NUL.

To more easily identify document files on disk, it is convenient to assign the same extension to document files you create with a given application. The Notepad application, for instance, automatically uses the .TXT extension for each document file saved on disk. Typical filenames and extensions of document files saved using Notepad are: SHOPPING.TXT, MECHANIC.TXT, and 1994.TXT.

You can use the asterisk character (*) in place of a filename or extension to refer to a group of files. For example, the asterisk in the expression *.TXT tells Windows to reference any file that contains the .TXT extension, regardless of the filename. This group of files might consist of the HOME.TXT, AUTOPART.TXT, MARKET.TXT, JONES.TXT, and FRANK.TXT files.

The asterisk in MONTHLY.* tells Windows to reference any file that contains the filename MONTHLY, regardless of the extension. Files in this group might consist of the MONTHLY.TXT, MONTHLY.CAL, and MONTHLY.CRD files.

Directory Structures and Directory Paths

After selecting a name and extension for a file, you must decide which auxiliary storage device (hard disk or diskette) to use and in which directory you want to save the file. A **directory** is an area of a disk created to store related groups of files. When you first prepare a disk for use on a computer, a single directory, called the **root directory**, is created on the disk. You can create **subdirectories** in the root directory to store additional groups of related files. The hard disk in Figure 1-38 contains the root directory and the WINDOWS, MSAPPS, and SYSTEM subdirectories. The WINDOWS, MSAPPS, and SYSTEM subdirectories are created when Windows is installed and contain files related to Windows.

HARD DISK

FIGURE 1-38

Directory Structure	Directory Path
📂 c:\	C:\
📂 windows	C:\WINDOWS
📁 msapps	C:\WINDOWS\MSAPPS
📁 system	C:\WINDOWS\SYSTEM

▶ **TABLE 1-1**

LECTURE NOTES
■ Define directory struc-
ture and directory path.
■ Discuss the directory
structures and directory
paths in Table 1-1.

TRANSPARENCIES
WIN1-39 through
WIN1-46

LECTURE NOTES
■ Explain why you must
format a disk before sav-
ing a file to the disk.
■ Point out the Save As
command and dialog box.
■ Point out the drive icons
in the Drives drop-down
list box.

WINDOWS TIPS
■ The .TXT extension is
added automatically when
saving a Notepad docu-
ment.

FIGURE 1-39

The relationship between the root directory and any subdirectories is called the **directory structure**. Each directory or subdirectory in the directory structure has an associated directory path. The **directory path** is the path Windows follows to find a file in a directory. Table 1-1 contains a graphic representation of the directory structure and the associated paths of drive C.

Each directory and subdirectory on drive C is represented by a file folder icon in the directory structure. The first file folder icon, an unshaded open file folder (📂), represents the root directory of the current drive (drive C). The c:\ entry to the right of the icon symbolizes the root directory (identified by the \ character) of drive C (c:). The path is C:\. Thus, to find a file in this directory, Windows locates drive C (C:) and the root directory (\) on drive C.

The second icon, a shaded open file folder (📂), represents the current subdirectory. This icon is indented below the first file folder icon because it is a subdirectory. The name of the subdirectory (windows) appears to the right of the shaded file folder icon. Because the WINDOWS subdirectory was created in the root directory, the path for the WINDOWS subdirectory is C:\WINDOWS. To find a file in this subdirectory, Windows locates drive C, locates the root directory on drive C, and then locates the WINDOWS subdirectory in the root directory.

Because the current path is C:\WINDOWS, the file folder icons for both the root directory and WINDOWS subdirectory are open file folders. An open file folder indicates the directory or subdirectory is in the current path. Unopened file folders represent subdirectories not in the current path.

The third and fourth icons in Table 1-1, unopened file folders (📁), represent the MSAPPS and SYSTEM subdirectories. The unopened file folders indicate these subdirectories are not part of the current path. These file folder icons are indented below the file folder for the WINDOWS subdirectory which means they were created in the WINDOWS subdirectory. The subdirectory names (msapps and system) appear to the right of the file folder icons.

Since the MSAPPS and SYSTEM subdirectories were created in the WINDOWS subdirectory, the paths for these subdirectories are C:\WINDOWS\MSAPPS and C:\WINDOWS\SYSTEM. The second backslash (\) in these paths separates the two subdirectory names. To find a file in these subdirectories, Windows locates drive C, locates the root directory on drive C, then locates the WINDOWS subdirectory in the root directory, and finally locates the MSAPPS or SYSTEM subdirectory in the WINDOWS subdirectory.

Saving a Document on Disk

After entering data into a document, you will often save it on the hard disk or a diskette to protect against accidental loss and to make the document available for use later. In the previous example using the Notepad application, the note was not saved prior to exiting Notepad. Instead of exiting, assume you want to save the document you created. The screen before you begin to save the document is shown in Figure 1-39. To save the document on a diskette in drive A using the filename, agenda, perform the steps that begin at the top of the next page.

```
━  Notepad - [Untitled]                    ▼ ▲
File  Edit  Search  Help
Things to do today -
1) Take fax\phone to Conway Service Center
2) Pick up payroll checks from ADM
3) Order 3 boxes of copier paper
│
```

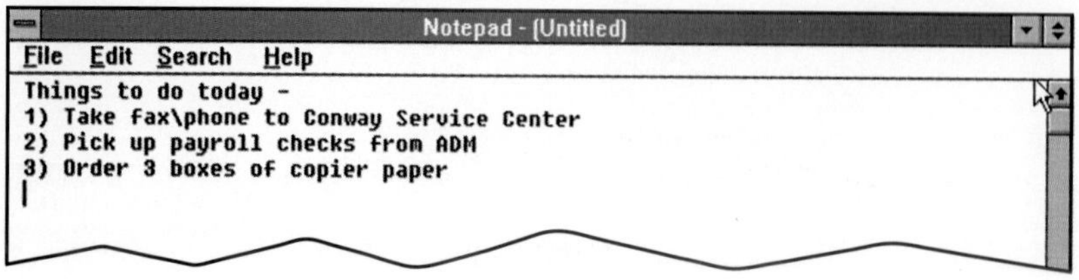

TO SAVE A FILE ▼

STEP 1 ▶

Insert a formatted diskette into drive A (Figure 1-40).

The diskette must be properly formatted before being used to save data. To learn the technique for formatting a diskette see Project 2.

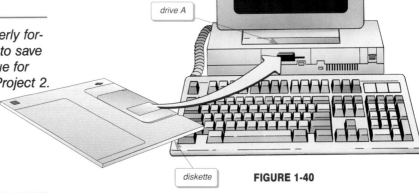

FIGURE 1-40

STEP 2 ▶

Select File on the Notepad menu bar, and then point to the Save As command.

Windows opens the File menu in the Notepad window and the mouse pointer points to the Save As command (Figure 1-41). The ellipsis (...) following the Save As command indicates Windows will open a dialog box when you choose this command.

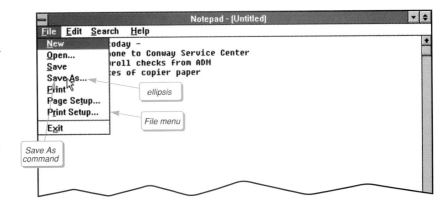

FIGURE 1-41

STEP 3 ▶

Choose the Save As command from the File menu by clicking the left mouse button.

The Save As dialog box opens (Figure 1-42). The File Name text box contains the highlighted *.txt entry. Typing a filename from the keyboard will replace the entire *.txt entry with the filename entered from the keyboard. The current path is c:\windows and the Directories list box contains the directory structure of the current subdirectory (windows). The drive selection in the Drives drop-down list box is c:. The dialog box contains the OK (OK) and Cancel (Cancel) command buttons.

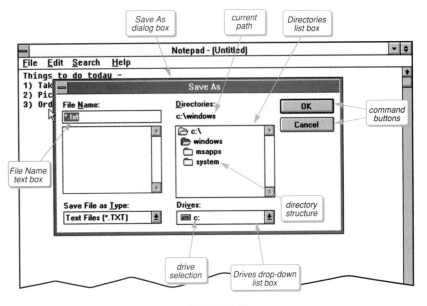

FIGURE 1-42

STEP 4 ▶

Type agenda **in the File Name text box, and then point to the Drives drop-down list box arrow.**

The filename, agenda, and an insertion point display in the File Name text box (Figure 1-43). When you save this document, Notepad will automatically add the .TXT extension to the agenda filename and save the file on disk using the name AGENDA.TXT. The mouse pointer points to the Drives drop-down list box arrow.

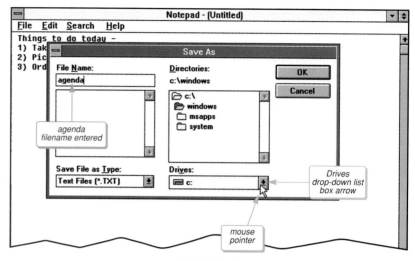

FIGURE 1-43

STEP 5 ▶

Choose the Drives drop-down list box arrow by clicking the left mouse button, and then point to the drive a: icon (🖫) in the Drives drop-down list.

Windows displays the Drives drop-down list (Figure 1-44). The drive a: icon and drive c: icon appear in the drop-down list. The mouse pointer points to the drive a: icon.

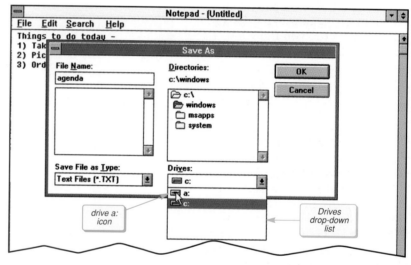

FIGURE 1-44

STEP 6 ▶

Select the drive a: icon by clicking the left mouse button, and then point to the OK button.

The selection is highlighted and the light on drive A turns on while Windows checks for a diskette in drive A (Figure 1-45). The current path changes to a:\ and the Directories list box contains the directory structure of the diskette in drive A.

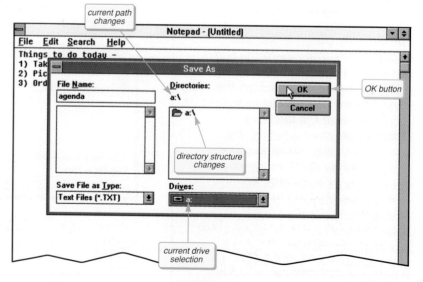

FIGURE 1-45

STEP 7 ▶

Choose the OK button in the Save As dialog box by clicking the left mouse button.

Windows closes the Save As dialog box and displays an hourglass icon while saving the AGENDA.TXT document file on the diskette in drive A. After the file is saved, Windows changes the window title of the Notepad window to reflect the name of the AGENDA.TXT file (Figure 1-46).

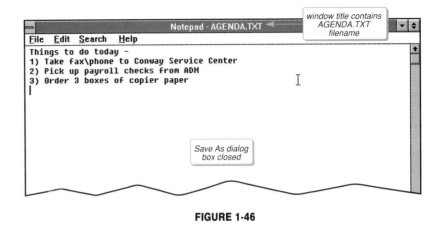

FIGURE 1-46

Correcting Errors Encountered While Saving a Document File

Before you can save a document file on a diskette, you must insert a formatted diskette into the diskette drive. **Formatting** is the process of preparing a diskette for use on a computer by establishing the sectors and cylinders on a disk, analyzing the diskette for defective cylinders, and establishing the root directory. The technique for formatting a diskette is shown in Project 2. If you try to save a file on a diskette and forget to insert a diskette, forget to close the diskette drive door after inserting a diskette, insert an unformatted diskette, or insert a damaged diskette, Windows opens the Save As dialog box in Figure 1-47.

The dialog box contains the messages telling you the condition found and the Retry (Retry) and Cancel buttons. To save a file on the diskette in drive A after receiving this message, insert a formatted diskette into the diskette drive, point to the Retry button, and click the left mouse button.

In addition, you cannot save a document file on a write-protected diskette. A **write-protected diskette** prevents accidentally erasing data stored on the diskette by not letting the disk drive write new data or erase existing data on the diskette. If you try to save a file on a write-protected diskette, Windows opens the Save As dialog box shown in Figure 1-48.

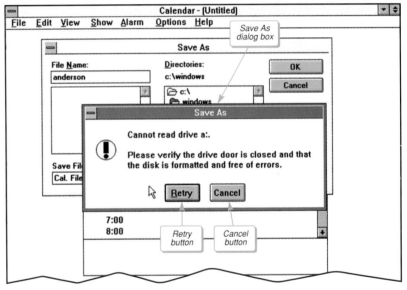

FIGURE 1-47

TRANSPARENCIES
WIN1-47 and WIN1-48

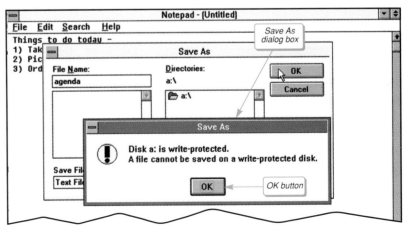

FIGURE 1-48

The Save As dialog box in Figure 1-48 on the previous page contains the messages, Disk a: is write-protected., and, A file cannot be saved on a write-protected disk., and the OK button. To save a file on diskette after inserting a write-protected diskette into drive A, remove the diskette from the diskette drive, remove the write-protection from the diskette, insert the diskette into the diskette drive, point to the OK button, and click the left mouse button.

Quitting an Application

When you have finished saving the AGENDA.TXT file on disk, you can quit the Notepad application as shown in Figure 1-34 through Figure 1-37 on pages WIN21 and WIN22. The steps are summarized below.

TO QUIT AN APPLICATION

Step 1: Point to File on the Notepad menu bar.
Step 2: Select File by clicking the left mouse button, and then point to the Exit command.
Step 3: Choose the Exit command by clicking the left mouse button.

If you have made changes to the document since saving it on the diskette, Notepad will ask if you want to save the changes. If so, choose the Yes button in the dialog box; otherwise, choose the No button.

▶ OPENING A DOCUMENT FILE

C hanges are frequently made to a document saved on disk. To make these changes, you must first open the document file by retrieving the file from disk using the Open command. After modifying the document, you save the modified document file on disk using the Save command. Using the Notepad application, you will learn to (1) open a document file and (2) save an edited document file on diskette. In the process, you will add the following line to the AGENDA.TXT file: 4) Buy copier toner.

Starting the Notepad Application and Maximizing the Notepad Window

To start the Notepad application and maximize the Notepad window, perform the following step.

TO START AN APPLICATION AND MAXIMIZE ITS WINDOW ▼

STEP 1 ▶

Double-click the Notepad icon in the Accessories group window. When the Notepad window opens, click the Maximize button.

Double-clicking the Notepad icon opens the Notepad window. Clicking the Maximize button maximizes the Notepad window (Figure 1-49).

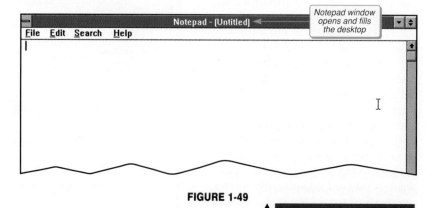

FIGURE 1-49

Opening a Document File

Before you can modify the AGENDA.TXT document, you must open the file from the diskette on which it was stored. To do so, ensure the diskette containing the file is inserted into drive A, then perform the following steps.

TO OPEN A DOCUMENT FILE ▼

STEP 1 ►

Select File on the menu bar, and then point to the Open command.

Windows opens the File menu and the mouse pointer points to the Open command (Figure 1-50).

STEP 2 ►

Choose the Open command from the File menu by clicking the left mouse button, and then point to the Drives drop-down list box arrow.

*The Open dialog box opens (Figure 1-51). The File Name text box contains the *.txt entry and the File Name list box is empty because no files with the .TXT extension appear in the current directory. The current path is c:\windows. The Directories list box contains the directory struc- ture of the current subdirectory (WINDOWS). The selected drive in the Drives drop-down list box is c:. The mouse pointer points to the Drives drop-down list box arrow.*

STEP 3 ►

Choose the Drives drop-down list box arrow by clicking the left mouse button, and then point to the drive a: icon.

Windows displays the Drives drop-down list (Figure 1-52). The drive a: icon and drive c: icon appear in the drop-down list. The current selection is c:. The mouse pointer points to the drive a: icon.

FIGURE 1-50

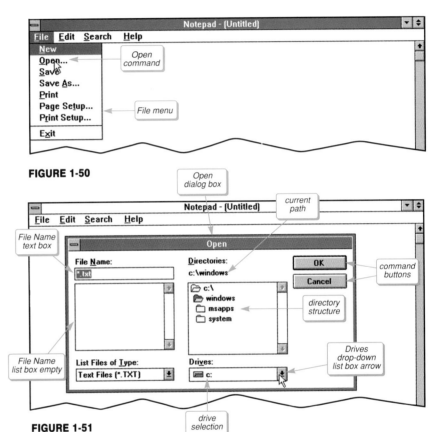

FIGURE 1-51

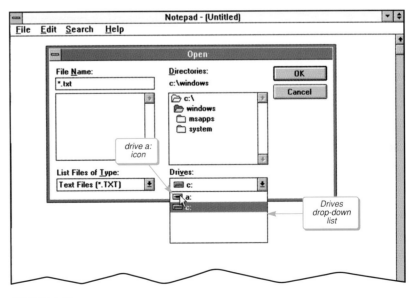

FIGURE 1-52

STEP 4 ▶

Select the drive a: icon by clicking the left mouse button, and then point to the agenda.txt entry in the File Name list box.

The light on drive A turns on, and Windows checks for a diskette in drive A. If there is no diskette in drive A, a dialog box opens to indicate this fact. The current selection in the Drives drop-down list box is highlighted (Figure 1-53). The File Name list box contains the filename agenda.txt, the current path is a:\, and the Directories list box contains the directory structure of drive A. The mouse pointer points to the agenda.txt entry.

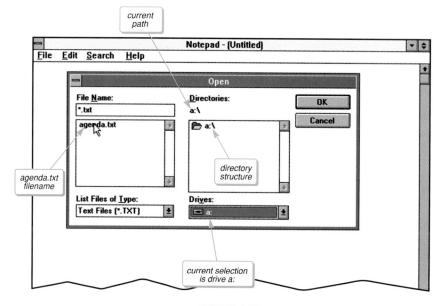

FIGURE 1-53

STEP 5 ▶

Select the agenda.txt file by clicking the left mouse button, and then point to the OK button.

Notepad highlights the agenda.txt entry in the File Name text box, and the agenda.txt filename appears in the File Name text box (Figure 1-54). The mouse pointer points to the OK button.

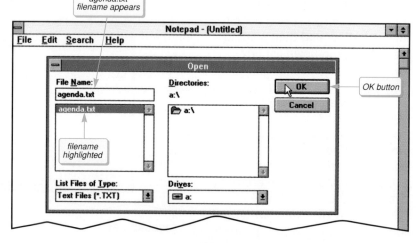

FIGURE 1-54

STEP 6 ▶

Choose the OK button from the Open dialog box by clicking the left mouse button.

Windows retrieves the agenda.txt file from the diskette in drive A and opens the AGENDA.TXT document in the Notepad window (Figure 1-55).

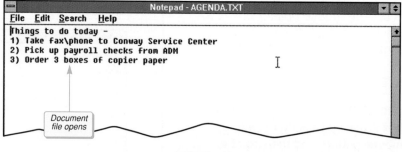

FIGURE 1-55

Editing the Document File

You edit the AGENDA.TXT document file by entering the fourth line of text.

TO EDIT THE DOCUMENT ▼

STEP 1 ►

Press the DOWN ARROW key four times to position the insertion point, and then type the new line, 4) Buy Copier toner.

The new line appears in the Note-pad document (Figure 1-56).

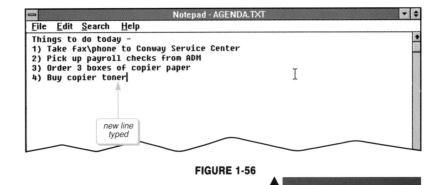

FIGURE 1-56

Saving the Modified Document File

After modifying the AGENDA.TXT document, you should save the modified document on disk using the same AGENDA.TXT filename. To save a modified file on disk, choose the Save command. The Save command differs from the Save As command in that you choose the Save command to save changes to an existing file while you choose the Save As command to name and save a new file or to save an existing file under a new name.

TO SAVE A MODIFIED DOCUMENT FILE ▼

STEP 1 ►

Select File on the Notepad menu bar, and then point to the Save command.

Windows opens the File menu and the mouse pointer points to the Save command (Figure 1-57).

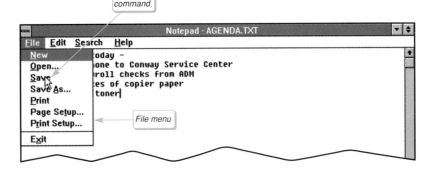

FIGURE 1-57

STEP 2 ►

Choose the Save command from the File menu by clicking the left mouse button.

Windows closes the File menu, displays the hourglass icon momentarily, and saves the AGENDA.TXT document on the diskette in drive A (Figure 1-58).

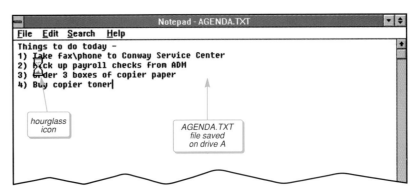

FIGURE 1-58

STEP 3 ▶

Remove the diskette from Drive A (Figure 1-59).

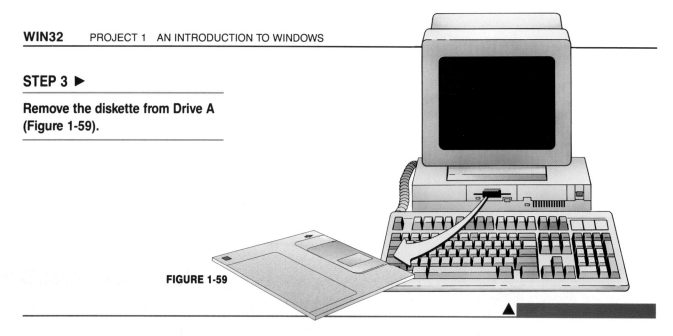

FIGURE 1-59

When you have finished saving the modified AGENDA.TXT file, quit the Notepad application by performing the following steps.

TO QUIT NOTEPAD

Step 1: Select File on the Notepad menu bar.
Step 2: Choose the Exit command.

▶ USING WINDOWS HELP

I f you need help while using an application, you can use Windows online Help. **Online Help** is available for all applications except Clock. To illustrate Windows online Help, you will start the Paintbrush application and obtain help about the commands on the Edit menu. **Paintbrush** is a drawing program that allows you to create, edit, and print full-color illustrations.

TO START AN APPLICATION

STEP 1 ▶

Double-click the Paintbrush icon (🐚) in the Accessories group window in Program Manager, and then click the Maximize button on the Paintbrush — [Untitled] window.

Windows opens and maximizes the Paintbrush window (Figure 1-60).

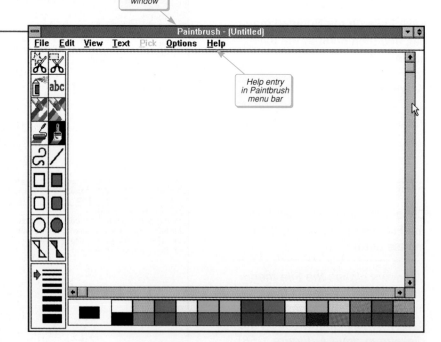

FIGURE 1-60

TO OBTAIN HELP ▼

STEP 1 ►

Select Help on the Paintbrush menu bar, and then point to the Contents command.

Windows opens the Help menu (Figure 1-61). The Help menu contains four commands. The mouse pointer points to the Contents command.

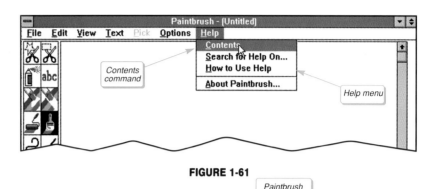

FIGURE 1-61

STEP 2 ►

Choose the Contents command from the Help menu by clicking the left mouse button. Then click the Maximize button on the Paintbrush Help window.

Windows opens the Paintbrush Help window (Figure 1-62), and when you click the Maximize button, it maximizes the window.

FIGURE 1-62

The Contents for Paintbrush Help screen appears in the window. This screen contains information about the Paintbrush application, how to learn to use online Help (press F1), and an alphabetical list of all help topics for the Paintbrush application. Each **help topic** is underlined with a solid line. The solid line indicates additional information relating to the topic is available. Underlined help topics are called jumps. A **jump** provides a link to viewing information about another help topic or more information about the current topic. A jump may be either text or graphics.

Choosing a Help Topic

To choose an underlined help topic, scroll the help topics to make the help topic you want visible, then point to the help topic and click the left mouse button. When you place the mouse pointer on a help topic, the mouse pointer changes to a hand ( ). To obtain help about the Edit menu, perform the steps on the next page.

TO CHOOSE A HELP TOPIC ▼

STEP 1 ▶

Point to the down scroll arrow (Figure 1-63).

FIGURE 1-63

STEP 2 ▶

Hold down the left mouse button (scroll) until the Edit Menu Commands help topic is visible, and then point to the Edit Menu Commands topic.

The Commands heading and the Edit Menu Commands topic are visible (Figure 1-64). The mouse pointer changes to a hand icon and points to the Edit Menu Commands topic.

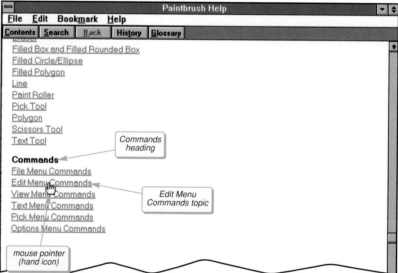

FIGURE 1-64

STEP 3 ▶

Choose the Edit Menu Commands topic by clicking the left mouse button.

The Edit Menu Commands screen contains information about each of the commands in the Edit menu (Figure 1-65). Two terms (scroll bar and cutout) are underlined with a dotted line. Terms underlined with a dotted line have an associated glossary definition. To display a term's glossary definition, point to the term and click the left mouse button.

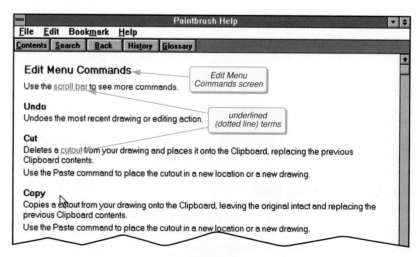

FIGURE 1-65

TO DISPLAY A DEFINITION ▼

STEP 1 ▶

Point to the term, scroll bar.

The mouse pointer changes to a hand and points to the term, scroll bar (Figure 1-66).

TRANSPARENCIES
WIN1-66 through
WIN1-68

```
scroll bar
term
┌─────────────────────────────────────────────┐
│ ═  Paintbrush Help                    ▼ ▲    │
│ File  Edit  Bookmark  Help                   │
│ Contents │ Search │ Back │ History │ Glossary│
│                                              │
│ Edit Menu Commands                           │
│ Use the scroll bar to see more commands.   mouse
│                                            pointer│
│ Undo                                         │
│ Undoes the most recent drawing or editing action.│
└─────────────────────────────────────────────┘
```

FIGURE 1-66

STEP 2 ▶

Choose the term, scroll bar, by clicking the left mouse button.

*Windows opens a **pop-up window** containing the glossary definition of the term, scroll bar (Figure 1-67).*

LECTURE NOTES
▪ Demonstrate how to display a definition.
▪ Point out the pop-up window.

FIGURE 1-67

```
┌──────────────────────────────────────────────────┐
│ ═  Paintbrush Help                         ▼ ▲   │
│ File  Edit  Bookmark  Help          pop-up        │
│ Contents │ Search │ Back │ History │ Glossary window│
│                                                   │
│ Edit Menu Commands                                │
│ Use the scroll bar to see more commands.          │
│ ┌──────────────────────────────────────────────┐ │
│ │ scroll bar                                    │ │
│ │ A bar that appears at the right and/or bottom edge of a window or list box whose contents are │ │
│ │ not completely visible. Each scroll bar contains two scroll arrows and a scroll box, which │ │
│ │ enable you to scroll through the contents of the window or list box. │ │
│ └──────────────────────────────────────────────┘ │
│ Clipboard contents.                               │
│ Use the Paste command to place the cutout in a new location or a new drawing.│
└──────────────────────────────────────────────────┘
```

definition
displayed

STEP 3 ▶

When you have finished reading the definition, close the pop-up window by clicking anywhere on the screen.

Windows closes the pop-up window containing the glossary definition (Figure 1-68).

```
┌──────────────────────────────────────────────────┐
│ ═  Paintbrush Help                         ▼ ▲   │
│ File  Edit  Bookmark  Help                        │
│ Contents │ Search │ Back │ History │ Glossary     │
│                                                   │
│ Edit Menu Commands                                │
│ Use the scroll bar to see more commands.          │
│                                                   │
│ Undo                                 pop-up window│
│ Undoes the most recent drawing or editing action. closed│
│                                                   │
│ Cut                                               │
│ Deletes a cutout from your drawing and places it onto the Clipboard, replacing the previous│
│ Clipboard contents.                               │
│ Use the Paste command to place the cutout in a new location or a new drawing.│
└──────────────────────────────────────────────────┘
```

FIGURE 1-68

Exiting the Online Help and Paintbrush Applications

After obtaining help about the Edit Menu commands, quit Help by choosing the Exit command from the Help File menu. Then, quit Paintbrush by choosing the Exit command from the Paintbrush File menu. The steps are summarized below.

TO QUIT PAINTBRUSH HELP

Step 1: Select File on the Paintbrush Help menu bar.
Step 2: Choose the Exit command.

TO QUIT PAINTBRUSH

Step 1: Select File on the Paintbrush menu bar.
Step 2: Choose the Exit command.

▶ QUITTING WINDOWS

You always want to return the desktop to its original state before beginning your next session with Windows. Therefore, before exiting Windows, you must verify that any changes made to the desktop are not saved when you quit windows.

Verify Changes to the Desktop Will Not be Saved

Because you want to return the desktop to its state before you started Windows, no changes should be saved. The Save Settings on Exit command on the Program Manager Options menu controls whether changes to the desktop are saved or are not saved when you quit Windows. A check mark (✓) preceding the Save Settings on Exit command indicates the command is active and all changes to the layout of the desktop will be saved when you quit Windows. If the command is preceded by a check mark, choose the Save Settings from Exit command by clicking the left mouse button to remove the check mark, so the changes will not be saved. Perform the following steps to verify that changes are not saved to the desktop.

TO VERIFY CHANGES ARE NOT SAVED TO THE DESKTOP ▼

STEP 1 ▶

Select Options on the Program Manager menu bar, and then point to the Save Settings on Exit command.

The Options menu opens (Figure 1-69). A check mark (✓) precedes the Save Settings on Exit command.

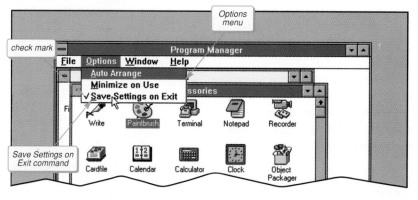

FIGURE 1-69

STEP 2 ▶

To remove the check mark, choose the Save Settings on Exit command from the Options menu by clicking the left mouse button.

Windows closes the Options menu (Figure 1-70). Although not visible in Figure 1-70, the check mark preceding the Save Settings from Exit command has been removed. This means any changes made to the desktop will not be saved when you exit Windows.

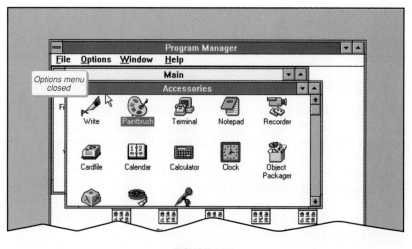

FIGURE 1-70

Quitting Windows Without Saving Changes

After verifying the Save Settings on Exit command is not active, quit Windows by choosing the Exit Windows command from the File menu, as shown below.

TRANSPARENCIES
WIN1-71 and WIN1-72

LECTURE NOTES
■ Explain the Exit
Windows command and
dialog box.

TO QUIT WINDOWS ▼

STEP 1 ▶

Select File on the Program Manager menu bar, and then point to the Exit Windows command.

Windows opens the File menu and the mouse pointer points to the Exit Windows command (Figure 1-71).

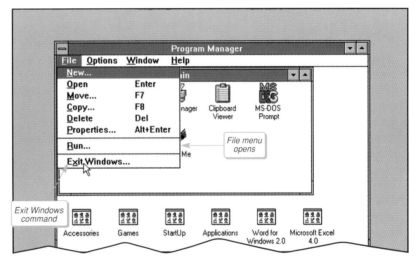

FIGURE 1-71

STEP 2 ▶

Choose the Exit Windows command from the File menu by clicking the left mouse button and point to the OK button.

The Exit Windows dialog box opens and contains the message, This will end your Windows session., and the OK and Cancel buttons (Figure 1-72). Choosing the OK button exits Windows. Choosing the Cancel button cancels the exit from Windows and returns you to the Program Manager window. The mouse pointer points to the OK button.

STEP 3 ▶

Choose the OK button by clicking the left mouse button.

When you quit Windows, all windows are removed from the desktop and control is returned to the DOS operating system.

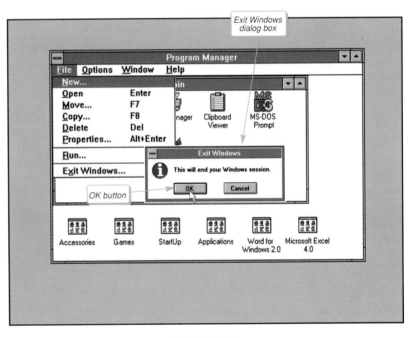

FIGURE 1-72

▶ PROJECT SUMMARY

In this project you learned about user interfaces and the Microsoft Windows graphical user interface. You started and exited Windows and learned the parts of a window. You started Notepad, entered and printed a note, edited the note, opened and saved files, and exited the applications. You opened group windows, maximized application windows, and scrolled the windows. You used the mouse to select a menu, choose a command from a menu, and respond to dialog boxes. You used Windows online Help to obtain help about the Paintbrush application.

▶ KEY TERMS

active icon (*WIN18*)
active window (*WIN15*)
application (*WIN3*)
application software (*WIN3*)
application window (*WIN5*)
check box (*WIN13*)
choosing (*WIN11*)
choosing a command (*WIN11*)
choosing a help topic (*WIN33*)
clicking (*WIN7*)
command (*WIN10*)
command button (*WIN13*)
Control menu (*WIN16*)
creating a document (*WIN19*)
current selection (*WIN13*)
desktop (*WIN4*)
dialog box (*WIN12*)
directory (*WIN23*)
directory path (*WIN24*)
directory structure (*WIN24*)
displaying a definition (*WIN35*)
document (*WIN14*)
document file (*WIN23*)
double-clicking (*WIN8*)
dragging (*WIN9*)
drop-down list box (*WIN13*)
ellipsis (*WIN11*)
edit a document file (*WIN31*)
error correction (*WIN16,*
  WIN18, WIN27)
extension (*WIN23*)
file and disk concepts
  (*WIN22–WIN24*)

filename (*WIN23*)
formatting (*WIN27*)
graphical user interface (GUI)
  (*WIN3*)
group icons (*WIN5*)
group window (*WIN5*)
GUI (*WIN3*)
help topic (*WIN33*)
hourglass icon (*WIN4*)
icons (*WIN5*)
insertion point (*WIN17*)
jump (*WIN33*)
keyboard (*WIN9*)
keyboard shortcuts (*WIN10*)
Maximize button (*WIN18*)
maximizing a window (*WIN18*)
menu (*WIN10*)
menu bar (*WIN10*)
Microsoft Windows (*WIN2*)
mouse (*WIN5*)
mouse operations (*WIN6–WIN9*)
mouse pointer (*WIN6*)
naming a file (*WIN23*)
Notepad (*WIN14*)
online Help (*WIN32*)
opening a document file
  (*WIN28*)
opening a window (*WIN14*)
option button (*WIN12*)
Paintbrush (*WIN32*)
pointing (*WIN6*)
pop-up window (*WIN35*)

printing a document (*WIN20*)
Program Manager (*WIN5*)
program-item icons (*WIN5*)
quitting an application (*WIN21,*
  WIN28)
quitting Windows (*WIN36*)
Restore button (*WIN18*)
root directory (*WIN23*)
saving a document (*WIN24*)
saving a modified document file
  (*WIN31*)
scroll arrows (*WIN16*)
scroll bar (*WIN16*)
scroll box (*WIN16*)
selected button (*WIN12*)
selecting (*WIN11*)
selecting a menu (*WIN11*)
starting an application (*WIN16*)
starting Microsoft Windows
  (*WIN4*)
subdirectory (*WIN23*)
text box (*WIN13*)
title bar (*WIN4*)
user friendly (*WIN3*)
user interface (*WIN3*)
using Windows help (*WIN32*)
window (*WIN4*)
window border (*WIN4*)
window title (*WIN4*)
Windows (*WIN2*)
write-protected diskette
  (*WIN27*)

In Microsoft Windows you can accomplish a task in a number of ways. The following table provides a quick reference to each task presented in this project with it available options. The commands listed in the Menu column can be executed using either the keyboard or mouse.

Task	Mouse	Menu	Keyboard Shortcuts
Choose a Command from a menu	Click command name, or drag highlight to command name and release mouse button		Press underlined character; or press arrow keys to select command, and press ENTER
Choose a Help Topic	Click Help topic		Press TAB, ENTER
Display a Definition	Click definition		Press TAB, ENTER
Enlarge an Application Window	Click Maximize button	From Control menu, choose Maximize	
Obtain Online Help		From Help menu, choose Contents	Press F1
Open a Document		From File menu, choose Open	
Open a Group Window	Double-click group icon	From Window menu, choose group window name	Press CTRL + F6 (or CTRL + TAB) to select group icon, and press ENTER
Print a File		From File menu, choose Print	
Quit an Application	Double-click control menu box, click OK button	From File menu, choose Exit	
Quit Windows	Double-click Control menu box, click OK button	From File menu, choose Exit Windows, choose OK button	
Remove a Definition	Click open space on desktop		Press ENTER
Save a Document on Disk		From File menu, choose Save As	
Save an Edited Document on Disk		From File menu, choose Save	
Save Changes when Quitting Windows		From Options menu, choose Save Settings on Exit if no check mark precedes command	
Save No Changes when Quitting Windows		From Options menu, choose Save Settings on Exit if check mark precedes command	
Scroll a Window	Click up or down arrow, drag scroll box, click scroll bar		Press UP or DOWN ARROW
Select a Menu	Click menu name on menu bar		Press ALT + underlined character (or F10 + underlined character)
Start an Application	Double-click program-item icon	From File menu, choose Open	Press arrow keys to select program-item icon, and press ENTER

STUDENT ASSIGNMENT 1
True/False

Instructions: Circle T if the statement is true or F if the statement is false.

Ⓣ F   1. A user interface is a combination of computer hardware and computer software.
Ⓣ F   2. Microsoft Windows is a graphical user interface.
T Ⓕ   3. The Program Manager window is a group window.
Ⓣ F   4. The desktop is the screen background on which windows are displayed.
T Ⓕ   5. A menu is a small picture that can represent an application or a group of applications.
T Ⓕ   6. Clicking means quickly pressing and releasing a mouse button twice without moving the mouse.
Ⓣ F   7. CTRL + SHIFT + LEFT ARROW is an example of a keyboard shortcut.
Ⓣ F   8. You can carry out an action in an application by choosing a command from a menu.
Ⓣ F   9. Selecting means marking an item.
Ⓣ F 10. Windows opens a dialog box to supply information, allow you to enter information, or select among several options.
T Ⓕ 11. A program-item icon represents a group of applications.
Ⓣ F 12. You open a group window by pointing to its icon and double-clicking the left mouse button.
Ⓣ F 13. A scroll bar allows you to view areas of a window that are not currently visible.
Ⓣ F 14. Notepad and Paintbrush are applications.
T Ⓕ 15. Choosing the Restore button maximizes a window to its maximize size.
T Ⓕ 16. APPLICATION.TXT is a valid name for a document file.
Ⓣ F 17. The directory structure is the relationship between the root directory and any subdirectories.
Ⓣ F 18. You save a new document on disk by choosing the Save As command from the File menu.
T Ⓕ 19. You open a document by choosing the Retrieve command from the File menu.
T Ⓕ 20. Help is available while using Windows only in the *User's Guide* that accompanies the Windows software.

STUDENT ASSIGNMENT 2
Multiple Choice

Instructions: Circle the correct response.

1. Through a user interface, the user is able to _____.
    a. control the computer
    b. request information from the computer
    c. respond to messages displayed by the computer
    ⓓ all of the above
2. _____ is quickly pressing and releasing a mouse button twice without moving the mouse.
    ⓐ Double-clicking
    b. Clicking
    c. Dragging
    d. Pointing

3. To view the commands in a menu, you _____ the menu name.
   a. choose
   b. maximize
   c. close
   (d) select
4. A _____ is a window that displays to supply information, allow you to enter information, or choose among several options.
   a. group window
   (b) dialog box
   c. application window
   d. drop-down list box
5. A _____ is a rectangular area in which Windows displays text or you enter text.
   a. dialog box
   (b) text box
   c. drop-down list box
   d. list box
6. The title bar of one group window that is a different color or intensity than the title bars of the other group windows indicates a(n) _____ window.
   a. inactive
   b. application
   c. group
   (d) active
7. To view an area of a window that is not currently visible in a window, use the _____.
   a. title bar
   (b) scroll bar
   c. menu bar
   d. Restore button
8. The _____ menu in the Notepad application contains the Save, Open, and Print commands.
   a. Window
   b. Options
   c. Help
   (d) File
9. Before exiting Windows, you should check the _____ command to verify that no changes to the desktop will be saved.
   a. Open
   b. Exit Windows
   (c) Save Settings on Exit
   d. Save Changes
10. Online Help is available for all applications except _____.
    a. Program Manager
    b. Calendar
    (c) Clock
    d. File Manager

STUDENT ASSIGNMENT 3
Identifying Items in the Program Manager Window

Instructions: On the desktop in Figure SA1-3, arrows point to several items in the Program Manager window. Identify the items in the space provided.

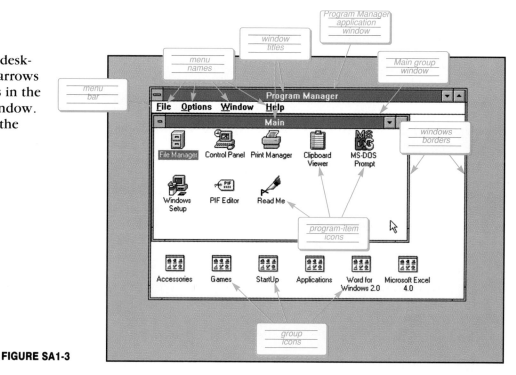

FIGURE SA1-3

STUDENT ASSIGNMENT 4
Starting an Application

Instructions: Using the desktop shown in Figure SA1-4, list the steps in the space provided to open the Accessories window and start the Notepad application.

Step 1: Point to the Accessories group icon in the Program Manager window.

Step 2: Double-click the left mouse button.

Step 3: Point to the Notepad icon in the Accessories group window.

Step 4: Double-click the left mouse button.

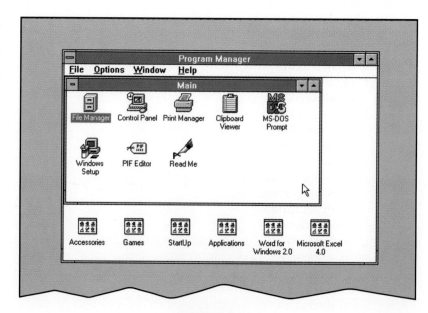

FIGURE SA1-4

COMPUTER LABORATORY EXERCISE 1
Improving Your Mouse Skills

Instructions: Use a computer to perform the following tasks.

1. Start Microsoft Windows.
2. Double-click the Games group icon (🎮) to open the Games window if necessary.
3. Double-click the Solitaire program-item icon (🃏).
4. Click the Maximize button to maximize the Solitaire window.
5. From the Help menu in the Solitaire window (Figure CLE1-1), choose the Contents command. One-by-one click on the help topics in green. Double-click on the Control-menu box in the title bar of the Solitaire Help window to close it.
6. Play the game of Solitaire.
7. To quit Solitaire choose the Exit command from the Game menu.

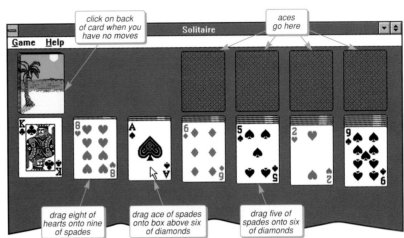

FIGURE CLE1-1

COMPUTER LABORATORY EXERCISE 2
Windows Tutorial

Instructions: Use a computer to perform the following tasks.

1. Start Microsoft Windows.
2. From the Help menu in the Program Manager window, choose the Windows Tutorial command.
3. Type the letter M. Follow the instructions (Figure CLE1-2) to step through the mouse practice lesson. Press the ESC key to exit the tutorial.
4. From the Help menu in the Program Manager window, choose the Windows Tutorial command.

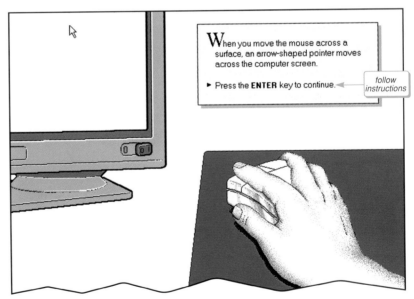

FIGURE CLE1-2

5. Type the letter W. Click the Instructions button (Instructions) and read the information. When you are finished, choose the Return to the Tutorial button (Return to the Tutorial). Next choose the Contents button (Contents) in the lower right corner of the screen.
6. Choose the second item (Starting an Application) from the Contents list. The Windows tutorial will step you through the remaining lessons. Respond as needed to the questions and instructions. Press the ESC key to exit the tutorial.

COMPUTER LABORATORY EXERCISE 3
Creating, Saving, and Printing Documents

EXERCISE NOTES
■ Some computers have multiple diskette drives. Tell your students which drive selection to use in Step 10.

Instructions: Use a computer to perform the following tasks.

1. Start Microsoft Windows if necessary.
2. Double-click the Accessories icon to open the Accessories window.
3. Double-click the Notepad icon to start the Notepad application.
4. Click the Maximize button to maximize the Notepad window.
5. Enter the note shown at the right at the insertion point on the screen.
6. Insert the Student Diskette that accompanies this book into drive A.
7. Select the File menu on the Notepad menu bar.
8. Choose the Save As command.
9. Enter grocery in the File Name text box.
10. Change the current selection in the Drives drop-down list box to a:.
11. Click the OK button to save the document on drive A.
12. Select the File menu on the Notepad menu bar.
13. Choose the Print command to print the document on the printer (Figure CLE1-3).
14. Remove the Student Diskette from drive A.
15. Select the File menu on the Notepad menu bar.
16. Choose the Exit command to quit Notepad.

Grocery List —
1/2 Gallon of Low Fat Milk
1 Dozen Medium Size Eggs
1 Loaf of Wheat Bread

EXERCISE NOTES
■ Remind students that IF they quit Windows after this exercise, no changes to the desktop should be saved. To do this, remove the check mark preceding the Save Settings on Exit command on the Options menu before quitting Windows.
■ Remind students to put their names on the printed grocery list and hand in for grading or credit.

```
                          GROCERY.TXT



        Grocery List -
        1/2 Gallon of Low Fat Milk
        1 Dozen Medium Size Eggs
        1 Loaf of Wheat Bread
```

FIGURE CLE1-3

COMPUTER LABORATORY EXERCISE 4
Opening, Editing, and Saving Documents

Instructions: Use a computer to perform the following tasks. If you have questions on how to procede, use the Calendar Help menu.

1. Start Microsoft Windows if necessary.
2. Double-click the Accessories icon to open the Accessories window.
3. Double-click the Calendar icon (⬛) to start the Calendar application.
4. Click the Maximize button to maximize the Calendar window.
5. Insert the Student Diskette that accompanies this book into drive A.
6. Select the File menu on the Calendar menu bar.

EXERCISE NOTES
■ Remind students to use the Online Help feature if they have questions about the Calendar application.

7. Choose the Open command.
8. Change the current selection in the Drives drop-down list box to a:.
9. Select the thompson.cal filename in the File Name list box. The THOMPSON.CAL file contains the daily appointments for Mr. Thompson.
10. Click the OK button in the Open dialog box to open the THOMPSON.CAL document. The document on your screen is shown in Figure CLE1-4a.
11. Click the Left or Right Scroll arrow repeatedly to locate the appointments for Thursday, September 29, 1994.
12. Make the changes shown below to the document.

TIME	CHANGE
11:00 AM	Stay at Auto Show one more hour
2:00 PM	Change the Designer's Meeting from 2:00 PM to 3:00 PM
4:00 PM	Remove the Quality Control Meeting

13. Select the File menu on the Calendar menu bar.
14. Choose the Save As command to save the document file on drive A. Use the filename PETER.CAL.
15. Select the File menu on the Calendar menu bar.
16. Choose the Print command.
17. Choose the OK button to print the document on the printer (Figure CLE1-4b).
18. Remove the Student Diskette from drive A.
19. Select the File menu on the Calendar menu bar.
20. Choose the Exit command to quit Calendar.

EXERCISE NOTES
- Some computers have multiple diskette drives. Tell your students which drive selection to use in Step 8.
- When you open the THOMPSON.CAL file, the appointment calendar for the current date displays. As suggested in Step 11, you can use the scroll arrows to display the calendar for Thursday, September 29, 1994. An easier method is to choose the Date command from the Show menu, enter 09/29/94 in the Show Date text box, and choose the OK button.
- Use the UP and DOWN ARROW keys to move the insertion point to another time. Use the DELETE or BACKSPACE key to delete an appointment.
- Remind your students that IF they quit Windows after this exercise, no changes to the desktop should be saved. To do this, remove the check mark preceding the Save Settings on Exit command on the Options menu before quitting Windows.
- Remind students to put their names on the printed appointment calendar and hand in for grading or credit.

FIGURE CLE1-4a

```
                    PETER.CAL


Thursday, September 29, 1994

    7:00 AM Mr. Brinks - Breakfast at Canyon Towers
    9:00    Auto Show - Convention Center
    10:00   Auto Show - Convention Center
    12:00 PM Mrs. Fieldstone - Brown's Bar and Grill
    2:00    Designer's Meeting - Room 3457
    4:00    Quality Control Meeting - Room 4758
```

FIGURE CLE1-4b

COMPUTER LABORATORY EXERCISE 5
Using Online Help

EXERCISE NOTES
■ Remind students that IF they quit Windows after this exercise, no changes to the desktop should be saved. To do this, remove the check mark preceding the Save Settings on Exit command on the Options menu before quitting Windows.
■ Remind students to put their names on the printed "Adding More Cards" and "Selecting Cards" help topics and hand in for grading or credit.

Instructions: Use a computer to perform the following tasks.

1. Start Microsoft Windows if necessary.
2. Double-click the Accessories icon to open the Accessories window.
3. Double-click the Cardfile icon (📇) to start the Cardfile application.
4. Select the Help menu.
5. Choose the Contents command.
6. Click the Maximize button to maximize the Cardfile Help window.
7. Choose the Add More Cards help topic.
8. Select the File menu on the Cardfile Help menu bar.
9. Choose the Print Topic command to print the Adding More Cards help topic on the printer (Figure CLE1-5a).
10. Display the definition of the term, index line.
11. Remove the index line definition from the desktop.
12. Choose the Contents button.
13. Choose the Delete Cards help topic.
14. Choose the Selecting Cards help topic at the bottom of the Deleting Cards screen.

Adding More Cards

Cardfile adds new cards in the correct alphabetic order and scrolls to display the new card at the front.

To add a new card to a file
1   From the Card menu, choose Add.
2   Type the text you want to appear on the <u>index line</u>.
3   Choose the OK button.
4   In the <u>information area</u>, type text.

FIGURE CLE1-5a

15. Select the File menu on the Cardfile Help menu bar.
16. Choose the Print Topic command to print the Selecting Cards help topic (Figure CLE 1-5b).
17. Select the File menu on the Cardfile Help menu bar.
18. Choose the Exit command to quit Cardfile Help.
19. Select the File menu on the Cardfile window menu bar.
20. Choose the Exit command to quit Cardfile.

Selecting Cards

To select a card in Card view
▸ Click the card's index line if it is visible.
  Or click the arrows in the status bar until the index line is visible, and then click it.
  If you are using the keyboard, press and hold down CTRL+SHIFT and type the first letter of the <u>index line</u>.

To select a card by using the Go To command
1   From the Search menu, choose Go To.
2   Type text from the card's index line.
3   Choose the OK button.

To select a card in List view
▸ Click the card's index line.
  Or use the arrow keys to move to the card's index line.

See Also
<u>Moving Through a Card File</u>

FIGURE CLE1-5b

MICROSOFT WINDOWS 3.1

DISK AND FILE MANAGEMENT

OBJECTIVES   You will have mastered the material in this project when you can:

▶ Identify the elements of the directory tree window
▶ Understand the concepts of diskette size and capacity
▶ Format and copy a diskette
▶ Select and copy one file or a group of files
▶ Change the current drive
▶ Rename or delete a file

▶ Create a backup diskette
▶ Search for help topics using Windows online Help
▶ Switch between applications
▶ Activate, resize, and close a group window
▶ Arrange the icons in a group window
▶ Minimize an application window to an icon

▶ INTRODUCTION

F **ile Manager** is an application included with Windows that allows you to organize and work with your hard disk and diskettes and the files on those disks. In this project, you will use File Manager to (1) format a diskette; (2) copy files between the hard disk and a diskette; (3) copy a diskette; (4) rename a file on diskette; and (5) delete a file from diskette.

Formatting a diskette and copying files to a diskette are common operations illustrated in this project that you should understand how to perform. While performing the Computer Laboratory Exercises and the Computer Laboratory Assignments at the end of each application project, you will save documents on a diskette that accompanies this textbook. To prevent the accidental loss of stored documents on a diskette, it is important to periodically make a copy of the entire diskette. A copy of a diskette is called a **backup diskette**. In this project, you will learn how to create a backup diskette to protect against the accidental loss of documents on a diskette.

You will also use Windows online Help in this project. In Project 1, you obtained help by choosing a topic from a list of help topics. In this project, you will use the Search feature to search for help topics.

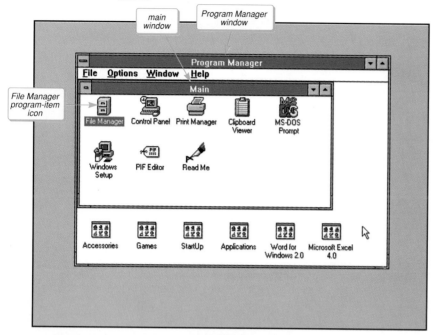

FIGURE 2-1

▶ STARTING WINDOWS

As explained in Project 1, when you turn on the computer, an introductory screen consisting of the Windows logo, Windows name, version number, and copyright notices displays momentarily. Next, a blank screen containing an hourglass icon displays. Finally, the Program Manager and Main windows open on the desktop (Figure 2-1). The File Manager program-item icon displays in the Main window. If your desktop does not look similar to the desktop in Figure 2-1, your instructor will inform you of the modifications necessary to change your desktop.

Starting File Manager and Maximizing the File Manager Window

To start File Manager, double-click the File Manager icon (▤) in the Main window. To maximize the File Manager window, choose the Maximize button on the File Manager window by pointing to the Maximize button and clicking the left mouse button.

TO START AN APPLICATION AND MAXIMIZE ITS WINDOW ▼

STEP 1 ▶

Double-click the File Manager icon in the Main window (see Figure 2-1), then click the Maximize button on the File Manager title bar.

Windows opens and maximizes the File Manager window (Figure 2-2).

FIGURE 2-2

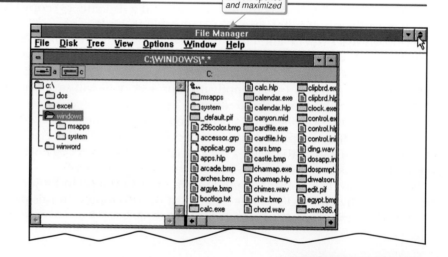

▶ FILE MANAGER

When you start File Manager, Windows opens the File Manager window (Figure 2-3). The menu bar contains the File, Disk, Tree, View, Options, Window, and Help menus. These menus contain the commands to organize and work with the disks and the files on those disks.

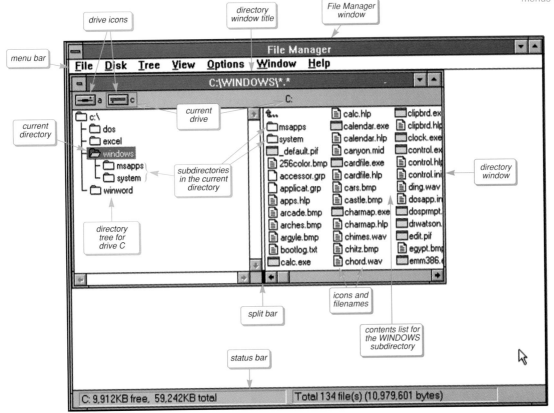

FIGURE 2-3

Below the menu bar is a **directory window** titled C:\WINDOWS*.*. The window title consists of a directory path (C:\WINDOWS), backslash (\), and filename (*.*). The directory path is the path of the current directory on drive C (WINDOWS subdirectory). The backslash separates the path and filename. The filename (*.*) references a group of files whose filename and extension can be any valid filename and extension.

Below the title bar is a horizontal bar that contains two **drive icons**. The drive icons represent the disk drives attached to the computer. The first drive icon (▦ a:) represents drive A (diskette drive) and the second drive icon (▦ c:) represents drive C (hard drive). Depending upon the number of disk drives attached to your computer, there may be more than two drive icons in the horizontal bar. A rectangular box surrounding the drive C icon indicates drive C is the **current drive**. The entry to the right of the icons (C:) also indicates drive C is the current drive.

LECTURE NOTES
■ Show the split bar, directory tree, and directory structure.
■ Explain the difference between shaded open file folders and unopened file folders.
■ Point out the contents list and icons and filenames in the contents list.
■ Explain the entries on the status bar.

The directory window is divided into two equal-sized areas. Each area is separated by a split bar. The **directory tree** in the area on the left contains the directory structure. The **directory tree** in the **directory structure** shows the relationship between the root directory and any subdirectories on the current drive (drive C). You can drag the **split bar** to the left or right to change the size of the two areas.

In the left area, a file folder icon represents each directory or subdirectory in the directory structure (see Figure 2-3). The shaded open file folder (📂) and subdirectory name for the current directory (WINDOWS subdirectory) are highlighted. The unopened file folder icons (📁) for the two subdirectories in the WINDOWS subdirectory (MSAPPS and SYSTEM) are indented below the icon for the WINDOWS subdirectory.

The area on the right contains the contents list. The **contents list** is a list of the files in the current directory (WINDOWS subdirectory). Each entry in the contents list consists of an icon and name. The shaded file folder icons for the two subdirectories in the current directory (MSAPPS and SYSTEM) display at the top of the first column in the list.

The status bar at the bottom of the File Manager window indicates the amount of unused disk space on the current drive (9,912KB free), amount of total disk space on the current drive (59,242KB total), number of files in the current directory (134 files), and the amount of disk space the files occupy (10,979,601 bytes).

▶ FORMATTING A DISKETTE

LECTURE NOTES
■ Point out that a diskette must be formatted prior to being used.
■ Explain what happens when a diskette is formatted.

Before saving a document file on a diskette or copying a file onto a diskette, you must format the diskette. **Formatting** prepares a diskette for use on a computer by establishing the sectors and cylinders on the diskette, analyzing the diskette for defective cylinders, and establishing the root directory. To avoid errors while formatting a diskette, you should understand the concepts of diskette size and capacity that are explained in the following section.

Diskette Size and Capacity

LECTURE NOTES
■ Define diskette size.
■ Mention the common diskette sizes (5 1/4-inch and 3 1/2-inch).
■ Define diskette capacity.
■ Discuss common diskette capacities (360K and 1.2MB for 5 1/4-inch diskettes and 720K and 1.44MB for 3 1/2-inch diskettes).
■ Explain that a diskette drive's capabilities are established by the manufacturer.
■ Mention that when formatting a diskette, the diskette drive used to format a diskette must be capable of formatting the size of diskette to be formatted.

How a diskette is formatted is determined by the size of the diskette, capacity of the diskette as established by the diskette manufacturer, and capabilities of the disk drive you use to format the diskette. **Diskette size** is the physical size of the diskette. Common diskette sizes are 5 1/4-inch and 3 1/2-inch.

Diskette capacity is the amount of space on the disk, measured in kilobytes (K) or megabytes (MB), available to store data. A diskette's capacity is established by the diskette manufacturer. Common diskette capacities are 360K and 1.2MB for a 5 1/4-inch diskette and 720K and 1.44MB for a 3 1/2-inch diskette.

A diskette drive's capability is established by the diskette drive manufacturer. There are 3 1/2-inch diskette drives that are capable of formatting a diskette with a capacity of 720K or 1.44MB and there are 5 1/4-inch diskette drives capable of formatting a diskette with a capacity of 360K or 1.2MB.

Before formatting a diskette, you must consider two things. First, the diskette drive you use to format a diskette must be capable of formatting the size of diskette you want to format. You can use a 3 1/2-inch diskette drive to format a 3 1/2-inch diskette, but you cannot use a 3 1/2-inch diskette drive to format a

5 1/4-inch diskette. Similarly, you can use a 5 1/4-inch diskette drive to format a 5 1/4-inch diskette, but you cannot use a 5 1/4-inch diskette drive to format a 3 1/2-inch diskette.

Second, the diskette drive you use to format a diskette must be capable of formatting the capacity of the diskette you want to format. A 5 1/4-inch diskette drive capable of formatting 1.2MB diskettes can be used to either format a 360K or 1.2MB diskette. However, because of the differences in the diskette manufacturing process, you cannot use a diskette drive capable of formatting 360K diskettes to format a 1.2MB diskette. A 3 1/2-inch diskette drive capable of formatting 1.44MB diskettes can be used to format either a 720K or 1.44MB diskette. Since the 1.44 MB diskette is manufactured with two square holes in the plastic cover and the 720K diskette is manufactured with only one square hole, you cannot use a diskette drive capable of formatting 720K diskette to format a 1.44MB diskette.

The computer you use to complete this project should have a 3 1/2-inch diskette drive capable of formatting a diskette with 1.44MB of disk storage. Trying to format a 3 1/2-inch diskette with any other diskette drive may result in an error. Typical errors encountered because of incorrect diskette capacity and diskette drive capabilities are explained later in this project. For more information about the diskette drive you will use to complete the projects in this textbook, contact your instructor.

Formatting a Diskette

To store a file on a diskette, the diskette must already be formatted. If the diskette is not formatted, you must format the diskette using File Manager. When formatting a diskette, use either an unformatted diskette or a diskette containing files you no longer need. Do not format the Student Diskette that accompanies this book.

To format a diskette using File Manager, you insert the diskette into the diskette drive, and then choose the **Format Disk command** from the Disk menu. Perform the following steps to format a diskette.

TO FORMAT A DISKETTE ▼

STEP 1

Insert an unformatted diskette or a formatted diskette containing files you no longer need into drive A.

STEP 2 ▶

Select the Disk menu, and then point to the Format Disk command.

Windows opens the Disk menu (Figure 2-4). The mouse pointer points to the Format Disk command.

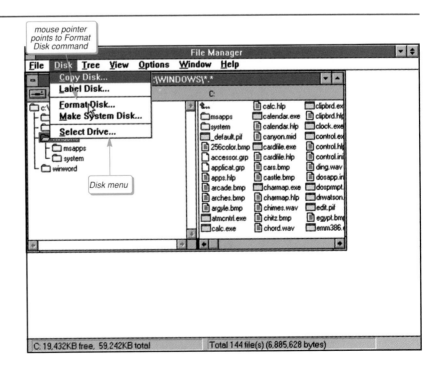

FIGURE 2-4

STEP 3 ▶

Choose the Format Disk command from the Disk menu, and then point to the OK button.

Windows opens the Format Disk dialog box (Figure 2-5). The current selections in the Disk In and Capacity boxes are Drive A: and 1.44 MB, respectively. With these selections, the diskette in drive A will be formatted with a capacity of 1.44MB. The Options list box is not required to format a diskette in this project. The mouse pointer points to the OK button.

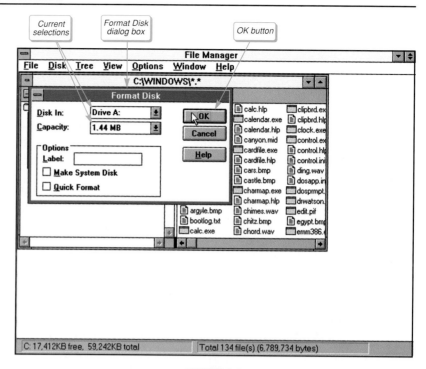

FIGURE 2-5

STEP 4 ▶

Choose the OK button by clicking the left mouse button, and then point to the Yes button.

Windows opens the Confirm Format Disk dialog box (Figure 2-6). This dialog box reminds you that if you continue, Windows will erase all data on the diskette in drive A. The mouse pointer points to the Yes button.

CAUTION
■ Choosing the Yes button will erase all data on the diskette in drive A.

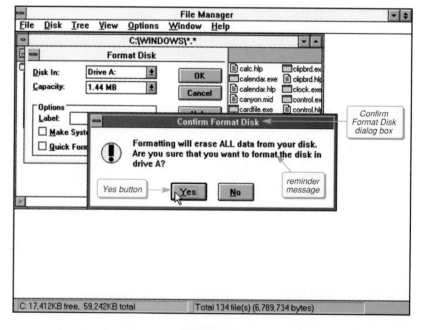

FIGURE 2-6

STEP 5 ▶

Choose the Yes button by clicking the left mouse button.

Windows opens the Formatting Disk dialog box (Figure 2-7). As the formatting process progresses, a value from 1 to 100 indicates what percent of the formatting process is complete. Toward the end of the formatting process, the creating root directory message replaces the 1% completed message to indicate Windows is creating the root directory on the diskette. The formatting process takes approximately two minutes.

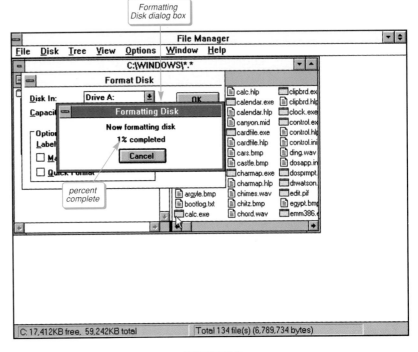

FIGURE 2-7

When the formatting process is complete, Windows opens the Format Complete dialog box (Figure 2-8). The dialog box contains the total disk space (1,457,664 bytes) and available disk space (1,457,664 bytes) of the newly formatted diskette. The values for the total disk space and available disk space in the Format Complete dialog box may be different for your computer.

STEP 6 ▶

Choose the No button by pointing to the No button, and then clicking the left mouse button.

Windows closes the Format Disk and Format Complete dialog boxes.

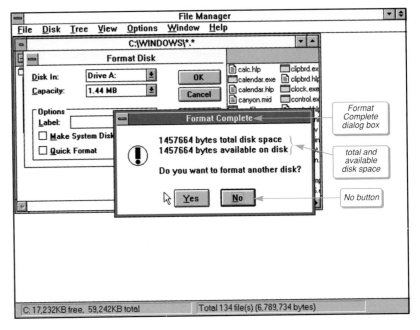

FIGURE 2-8

LECTURE NOTES
■ Mention that the formatting process formatted a
3 1/2-inch diskette with
1.44MB of disk storage.

Correcting Errors Encountered While Formatting a Diskette

When you try to format a diskette but forget to insert a diskette into the diskette drive or the diskette you inserted is write-protected, damaged, or does not
have the correct capacity for the diskette drive, Windows opens the Format Disk
Error dialog box shown in Figure 2-9. The dialog box contains an error message
(Cannot format disk.), a suggested action (Make sure the disk is in the drive and
not write-protected, damaged, or of wrong density rating.), and the OK button.
To format a diskette after forgetting to insert the diskette into the diskette drive,
insert the diskette into the diskette drive, choose the OK button, and format the
diskette.

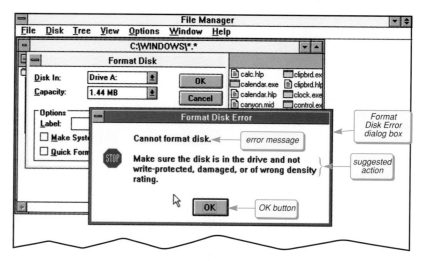

FIGURE 2-9

If the same dialog box opens after inserting a diskette into drive A, remove
the diskette and determine if the diskette is write-protected, not the correct
capacity for the diskette drive, or damaged. If the diskette is write-protected,
remove the write-protection from the diskette, choose the OK button and format
the diskette. If the diskette is not write-protected, check the diskette to determine if the diskette is the same capacity as the diskette drive. If it is not, insert a
diskette with the correct capacity into the diskette drive, choose the OK button
and format the diskette. If the diskette is not write-protected and the correct
capacity, throw the damaged diskette away and insert another diskette into drive
A, choose the OK button, and format the new diskette.

▶ COPYING FILES TO A DISKETTE

A fter formatting a diskette, you can save files on the diskette or copy files
to the diskette from the hard drive or another diskette. You can easily
copy a single file or group of files from one directory to another directory using File Manager. When copying files, the drive and directory containing
the files to be copied are called the **source drive** and **source directory**,
respectively. The drive and directory to which the files are copied are called the
destination drive and **destination directory**, respectively.

To copy a file, select the filename in the contents list and drag the highlighted filename to the destination drive icon or destination directory icon. Groups of files are copied in a similar fashion. You select the filenames in the contents list and drag the highlighted group of filenames to the destination drive or destination directory icon. In this project, you will copy a group of files consisting of the ARCADE.BMP, CARS.BMP, and EGYPT.BMP files from the WINDOWS subdirectory of drive C to the root directory of the diskette that you formatted earlier in this project. Before copying the files, maximize the directory window to make it easier to view the contents of the window.

LECTURE NOTES
- Explain the procedure to copy a file.
- Mention that the ARCADE.BMP, CARS.BMP, and EGYPT.BMP files will be copied from the WINDOWS subdirectory on drive C to the root directory of drive A.

TRANSPARENCY
Figure 2-10

Maximizing the Directory Window

To enlarge the C:\WINDOWS*.* window, click the Maximize button on the right side of the directory window title bar. When you maximize a directory window, the window fills the File Manager window.

LECTURE NOTES
- Explain how to maximize a directory window.
- Explain the changes that take place in the File Manager window.

TO MAXIMIZE A DIRECTORY WINDOW ▼

STEP 1 ►

Click the Maximize button on the right side of the C:\WINDOWS*.* window title bar.

The directory window fills the File Manager window (Figure 2-10). Windows changes the File Manager window title to contain the directory window title (File Manager - [C:\WINDOWS.*]) and removes the title bar of the directory tree window. A Restore button displays at the right side of the File Manager menu bar. Clicking the Restore button returns the directory window to its previous size.*

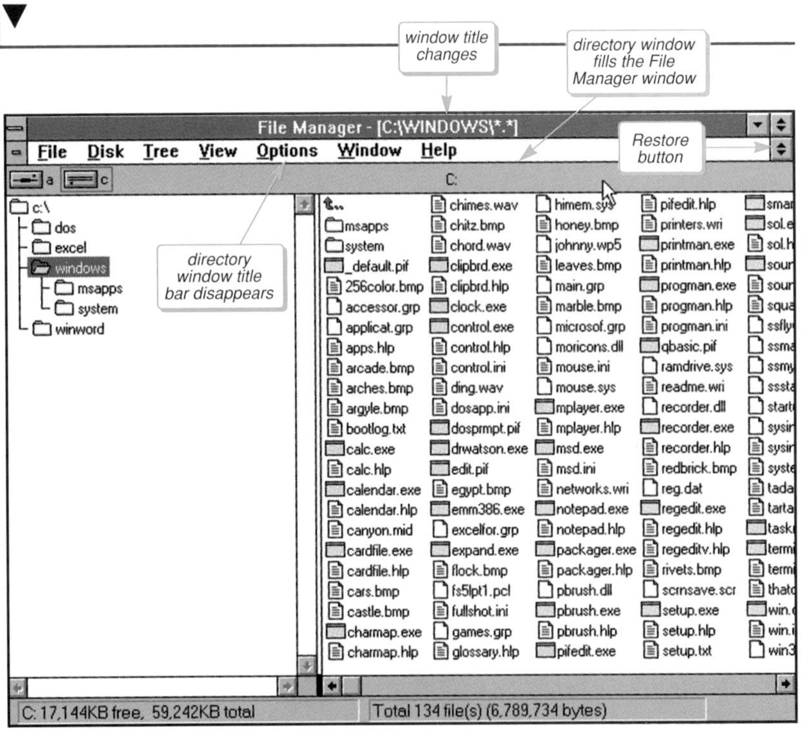

FIGURE 2-10

▲

Selecting a Group of Files

Before copying a group of files, you must select (highlight) each file in the contents list. You select the first file in a group of files by pointing to its icon or filename and clicking the left mouse button. You select the remaining files in the group by pointing to each file icon or filename, holding down the CTRL key, clicking the left mouse button, and releasing the CTRL key. The steps on the following pages show how to select the group of files consisting of the ARCADE.BMP, CARS.BMP, and EGYPT.BMP files.

LECTURE NOTES
- Explain how to select a group of files.

WINDOWS TIPS
- To select all files in the contents list, select one file, then hold down the CTRL key and press the SLASH (/) key.

TRANSPARENCIES
Figures 2-11 through 2-14

TO SELECT A GROUP OF FILES ▼

STEP 1 ▶

Point to the ARCADE.BMP filename in the contents list (Figure
2-11).

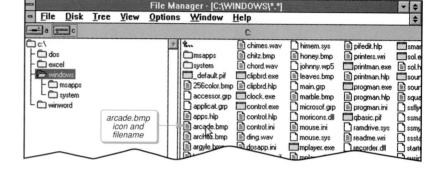

FIGURE 2-11

STEP 2 ▶

Select the ARCADE.BMP file by
clicking the left mouse button, and
then point to the CARS.BMP
filename.

*When you select the first file, the
highlight on the current directory
(WINDOWS) in the directory tree
changes to a rectangular box
(Figure 2-12). The ARCADE.BMP
entry is highlighted, and the
mouse pointer points to the
CARS.BMP filename.*

FIGURE 2-12

STEP 3 ▶

Hold down the CTRL key, click the
left mouse button, release the CTRL
key, and then point to the
EGYPT.BMP filename.

*Two files, ARCADE.BMP and
CARS.BMP are highlighted
(Figure 2-13). The mouse pointer
points to the EGYPT.BMP
filename.*

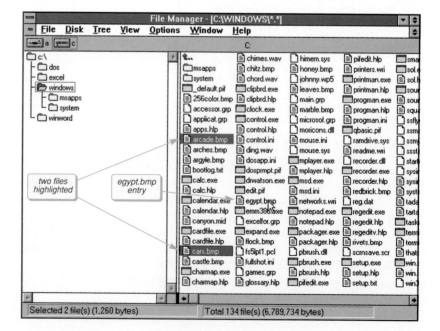

FIGURE 2-13

STEP 4 ▶

Hold down the CTRL key, click the
left mouse button, and then
release the CTRL key.

*The group of files consisting of
the ARCADE.BMP, CARS.BMP,
and EGYPT.BMP files is highlighted (Figure 2-14).*

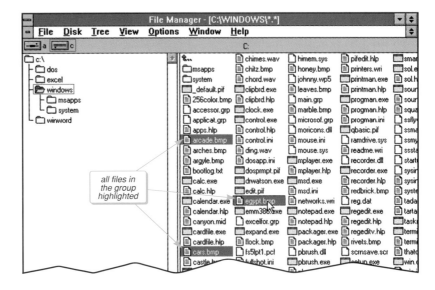

FIGURE 2-14

The ARCADE.BMP, CARS,BMP, and EGYPT.BMP files in Figure 2-14 are not
located next to each other (sequentially) in the contents list. To select this group
of files you selected the first file by pointing to its filename and clicking the left
mouse button. Then, you selected each of the other files by pointing to their
filenames, holding down the CTRL key, and clicking the left mouse button. If a
group of files is located sequentially in the contents list, you select the group by
pointing to the first filename in the list and clicking the left mouse button, and
then hold down the SHIFT key, point to the last filename in the group and click
the left mouse button.

Copying a Group of Files

After selecting each file in the group, insert the formatted diskette into drive
A, and then copy the files to drive A by pointing to any highlighted filename and
dragging the filename to the drive A icon.

TO COPY A GROUP OF FILES ▼

STEP 1

Verify that the formatted diskette is
in drive A.

STEP 2 ▶

Point to the highlighted
ARCADE.BMP entry (Figure 2-15).

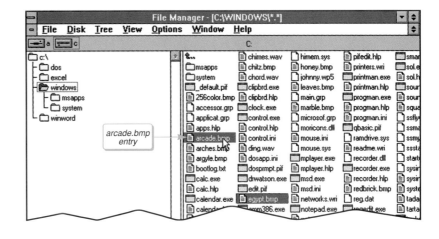

FIGURE 2-15

STEP 3 ▶

Drag the ARCADE.BMP filename over to the drive A icon.

As you drag the entry, the mouse pointer changes to an outline of a group of documents ( ) (Figure 2-16). The outline contains a plus sign to indicate the group of files is being copied, not moved.

LECTURE NOTES
▪ Mention the mouse pointer changes.

FIGURE 2-16

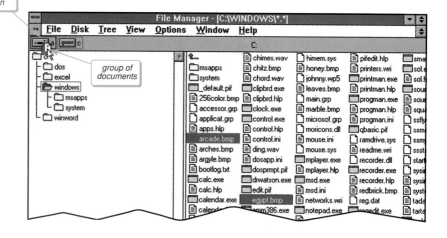

STEP 4 ▶

Release the mouse button, and then point to the Yes button.

Windows opens the Confirm Mouse Operation dialog box (Figure 2-17). The dialog box opens to confirm that you want to copy the files to the root directory of drive A (A:\). The highlight over the CARS.BMP entry is replaced with a dashed rectangular box. The mouse pointer points to the Yes button.

WINDOWS TIPS
▪ To move a file (or group of files), select the file(s), hold down SHIFT, and drag the file(s).
▪ To move a file (or group of files) to a destination on the same disk drive, don't hold down SHIFT.

FIGURE 2-17

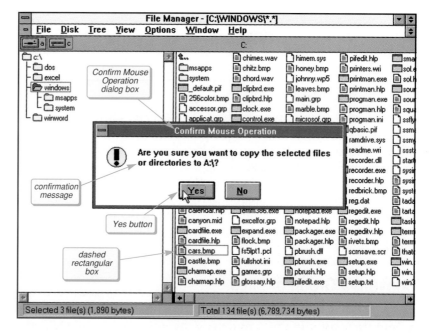

STEP 5 ▶

Choose the Yes button by clicking the left mouse button.

Windows opens the Copying dialog box, and the dialog box remains on the screen while Windows copies each file to the diskette in drive A (Figure 2-18). The dialog box in Figure 2-18 indicates the EGYPT.BMP file is currently being copied.

FIGURE 2-18

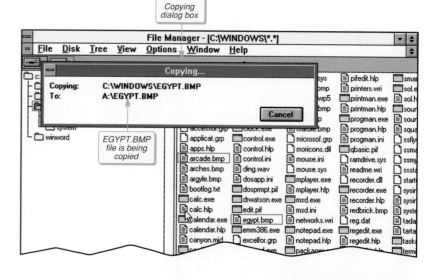

Correcting Errors Encountered While Copying Files

When you try to copy a file to an unformatted diskette, Windows opens the Error Copying File dialog box illustrated in Figure 2-19. The dialog box contains an error message (The disk in drive A is not formatted.), a question (Do you want to format it now?), and the Yes and No buttons. To continue the copy operation, format the diskette by choosing the Yes button. To cancel the copy operation, choose the No button.

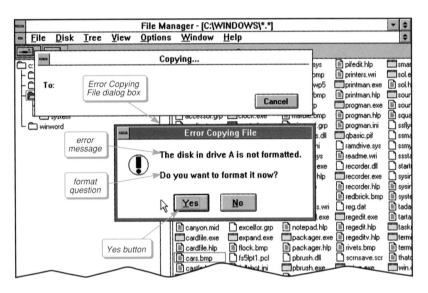

FIGURE 2-19

When you try to copy a file to a diskette but forget to insert a diskette into the diskette drive, Windows opens the Error Copying File dialog box shown in Figure 2-20. The dialog box contains an error message (There is no disk in drive A.), a suggested action (Insert a disk, and then try again.), and the Retry and Cancel buttons. To continue the copy operation, insert a diskette into drive A, and then choose the Retry button.

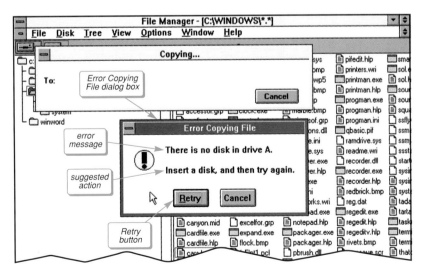

FIGURE 2-20

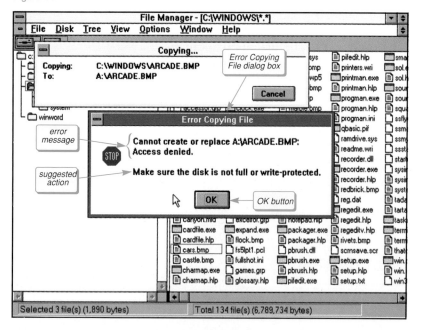

FIGURE 2-21

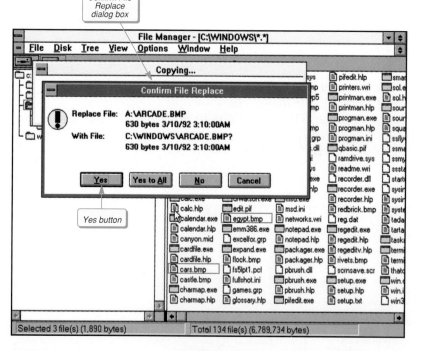

FIGURE 2-22

If you try to copy a file to a diskette that does not have enough room for the file, or you have inserted a write-protected diskette into the diskette drive, Windows opens the Error Copying File dialog box in Figure 2-21. The dialog box contains an error message (Cannot create or replace A:\ARCADE.BMP: Access denied.), a suggested action (Make sure the disk is not full or write-protected.), and the OK button. To continue with the copy operation, first remove the diskette from the diskette drive. Next, determine if the diskette is write-protected. If it is, remove the write-protection from the diskette, insert the diskette into the diskette drive, and then choose the OK button. If you determine the diskette is not write-protected, insert a diskette that is not full into the diskette drive, and then choose the OK button.

Replacing a File on Disk

If you try to copy a file to a diskette that already contains a file with the same filename and extension, Windows opens the Confirm File Replace dialog box (Figure 2-22). The Confirm File Replace dialog box contains information about the file being replaced (A:\ARCADE.BMP), the file being copied (C:\WINDOWS\ARCADE.BMP), and the Yes, Yes to All, No, and Cancel buttons. If you want to replace the file, on the diskette with the file being copied, choose the Yes button. If you do not want to replace the file choose the No button. If you want to cancel the copy operation, choose the Cancel button.

Changing the Current Drive

TRANSPARENCIES
Figures 2-23 through 2-24

LECTURE NOTES
■ Explain how to change
the current drive.

WINDOWS TIPS
■ Change the current
drive by holding down the
CTRL key and typing the
letter of the diskette drive.

After copying a group of files, you should verify the files were copied onto the correct drive and into the correct directory. To view the files on drive A, change the current drive to drive A by pointing to the drive A icon and clicking the left mouse button.

TO CHANGE THE CURRENT DRIVE ▼

STEP 1 ▶

Point to the drive A icon.

The mouse pointer points to the drive A icon and the current drive is drive C (Figure 2-23).

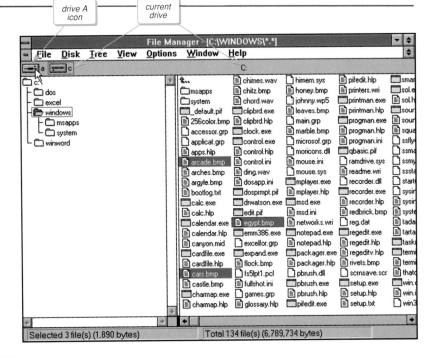

FIGURE 2-23

STEP 2 ▶

Choose the drive A icon by clicking the left mouse button.

A rectangular box surrounds the drive A icon and the current drive entry changes to drive A (Figure 2-24). The directory tree of drive A and the contents list consisting of the files in the root directory of drive A display in the directory window. Another rectangular box surrounds the a:\ entry in the directory tree to indicate the current drive is drive A and the current directory is the root directory (\).

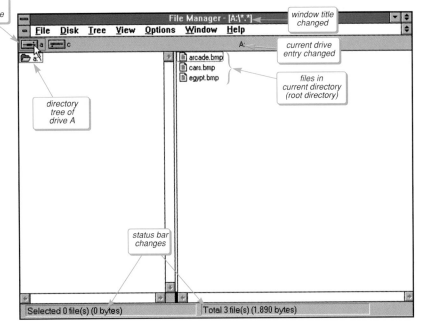

FIGURE 2-24

Correcting Errors Encountered While Changing the Current Drive

When you try to change the current drive before inserting a diskette into the diskette drive, Windows opens the Error Selecting Drive dialog box illustrated in Figure 2-25. The dialog box contains an error message (There is no disk in drive A.), a suggested action (Insert a disk, and then try again.), and the Retry and Cancel buttons. To change the current drive after forgetting to insert a diskette into drive A, insert a diskette into drive A, and choose the Retry button.

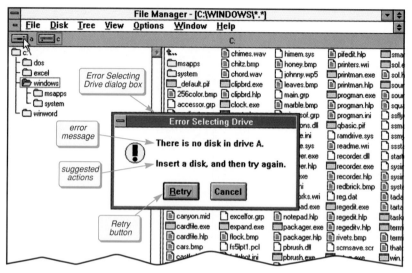

FIGURE 2-25

When you try to change the current drive and there is an unformatted diskette in the diskette drive, Windows opens the Error Selecting Drive dialog box shown in Figure 2-26. The dialog box contains an error message (The disk in drive A is not formatted.), a suggested action (Do you want to format it now?), and the Yes and No buttons. To change the current drive after inserting an unformatted diskette into drive A, choose the Yes button to format the diskette and change the current drive. Choose the No button to cancel the change.

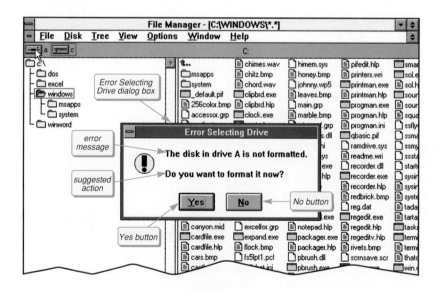

FIGURE 2-26

▶ RENAMING A FILE

S ometimes you may want to rename a file by changing its name or file-name extension. You change the name or extension of a file by selecting the filename in the contents list, choosing the **Rename command** from the File menu, entering the new filename, and choosing the OK button. In this project, you will change the name of the CARS.BMP file on the diskette in drive A to AUTOS.BMP.

TRANSPARENCIES
Figures 2-27 through 2-31

LECTURE NOTES
▪ Explain how to rename
a file using the Rename
command.
▪ Explain that the
CARS.BMP file will be
renamed AUTOS.BMP.

CAUTION
▪ Renaming some files
(i.e., with the .SYS exten-
tion) can cause Windows
to start incorrectly.

TO RENAME A FILE ▼

STEP 1 ▶

Select the CARS.BMP entry by clicking the CARS.BMP filename in the contents list.

The CARS.BMP entry is high-lighted (Figure 2-27).

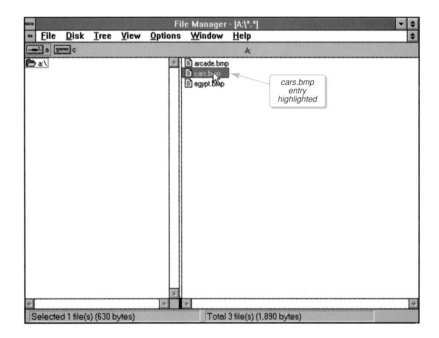

FIGURE 2-27

STEP 2 ▶

Select the File menu, and then point to the Rename command.

Windows opens the File menu (Figure 2-28). The mouse pointer points to the Rename command.

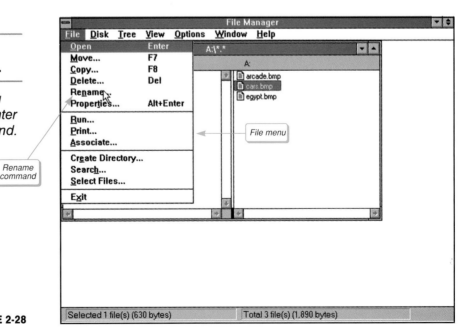

FIGURE 2-28

STEP 3 ▶

Choose the Rename command from the File menu by clicking the left mouse button.

Windows opens the Rename dialog box (Figure 2-29). The dialog box contains the Current Directory : A:\ message, the From and To text boxes, and the OK, Cancel, and Help buttons. The From text box contains the CARS.BMP filename and To text box contains an insertion point.

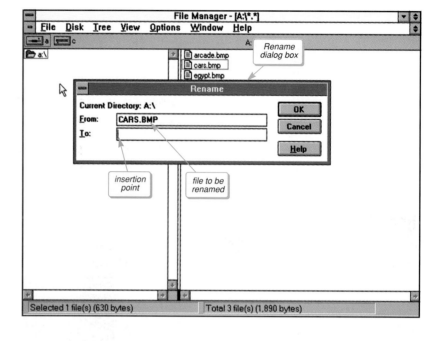

FIGURE 2-29

STEP 4 ▶

Type autos.bmp in the To text box, and then point to the OK button.

The To text box contains the AUTOS.BMP filename and the mouse points to the OK button (Figure 2-30).

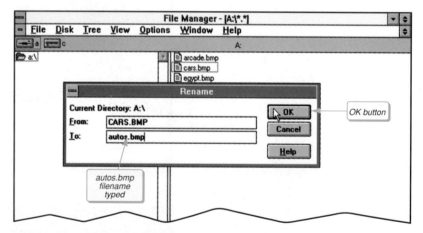

FIGURE 2-30

STEP 5 ▶

Choose the OK button by clicking the left mouse button.

The filename in the cars.bmp entry changes to autos.bmp (Figure 2-31).

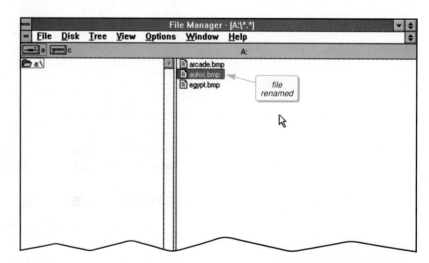

FIGURE 2-31

▶ DELETING A FILE

W hen you no longer need a file, you can delete it by selecting the file-name in the contents list, choosing the **Delete command** from the File menu, choosing the OK button, and then choosing the Yes button. In this project, you will delete the EGYPT.BMP file from the diskette in drive A.

TO DELETE A FILE ▼

STEP 1 ▶

Select the EGYPT.BMP entry.

The EGYPT.BMP entry is high-lighted (Figure 2-32).

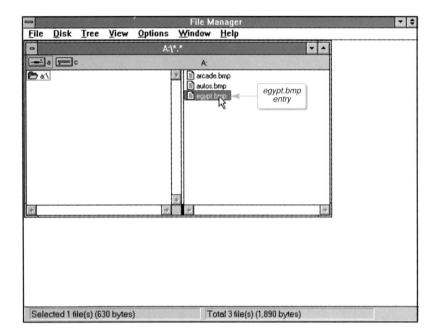

FIGURE 2-32

STEP 2 ▶

Select the File menu from the menu bar, and then point to the Delete command.

Windows opens the File menu (Figure 2-33). The mouse pointer points to the Delete command.

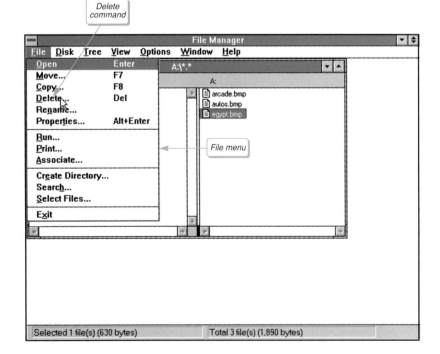

FIGURE 2-33

STEP 3 ▶

Choose the Delete command from the File menu by clicking the left mouse button, and then point to the OK button.

Windows opens the Delete dialog box (Figure 2-34). The dialog box contains the Current Directory: A:\ message, Delete text box, and the OK, Cancel, and Help buttons. The Delete text box contains the name of the file to be deleted (EGYPT.BMP), and the mouse pointer points to the OK button.

FIGURE 2-34

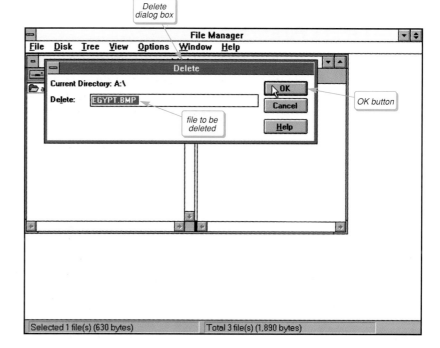

STEP 4 ▶

Choose the OK button by clicking the left mouse button, and then point to the Yes button.

Windows opens the Confirm File Delete dialog box (Figure 2-35). The dialog box contains the Delete File message and the path and filename of the file to delete (A:\EGYPT.BMP). The mouse pointer points to the Yes button.

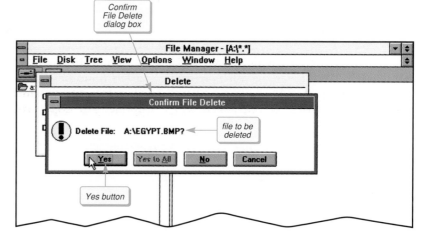

FIGURE 2-35

STEP 5 ▶

Choose the Yes button by clicking the left mouse button.

Windows deletes the EGYPT.BMP file from the diskette on drive A, removes the EGYPT.BMP entry from the contents list, and highlights the AUTOS.BMP file (Figure 2-36).

STEP 6

Remove the diskette from drive A.

FIGURE 2-36

▶ CREATING A BACKUP DISKETTE

T o prevent accidental loss of a file on a diskette, you should make a backup copy of the diskette. A copy of a diskette made to prevent accidental loss of data is called a **backup diskette**. Always be sure to make backup diskettes before installing software stored on diskettes onto the hard drive.

The first step in creating a backup diskette is to protect the diskette to be copied, or **source diskette**, from accidental erasure by write-protecting the diskette. After write-protecting the source diskette, choose the **Copy Disk command** from the Disk menu to copy the contents of the source diskette to another diskette, called the **destination diskette**. After copying the source diskette to the destination diskette, remove the write-protection from the source diskette and identify the destination diskette by writing a name on the paper label supplied with the diskette and affixing the label to the diskette.

In this project, you will use File Manager to create a backup diskette for a diskette labeled Business Documents. The Business Documents diskette contains valuable business documents that should be backed up to prevent accidental loss. The source diskette will be the Business Documents diskette and the destination diskette will be a formatted diskette that will later be labeled Business Documents Backup. To create a backup diskette, both the Business Documents diskette and the formatted diskette must be the same size and capacity.

File Manager copies a diskette by asking you to insert the source diskette into drive A, reading data from the source diskette into main memory, asking you to insert the destination disk, and then copying the data from main memory to the destination disk. Depending on the size of main memory on your computer, you may have to insert and remove the source and destination diskettes several times before the copy process is complete. The copy process takes about three minutes to complete.

TO COPY A DISKETTE ▼

STEP 1 ▶

Write-protect the Business Documents diskette by opening the write-protect window (Figure 2-37).

write-protect window open means diskette is write-protected

FIGURE 2-37

STEP 2 ▶

Select the Disk menu from the menu bar, and then point to the Copy Disk command.

Windows opens the Disk menu (Figure 2-38). The mouse pointer points to the Copy Disk command.

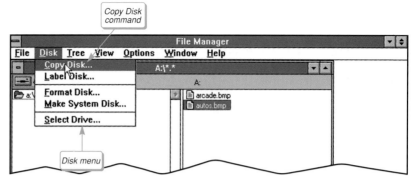

FIGURE 2-38

STEP 3 ▶

Choose the Copy Disk command from the Disk menu by clicking the left mouse button, and then point to the Yes button.

Windows opens the Confirm Copy Disk dialog box (Figure 2-39). The dialog box reminds you that the copy process will erase all data on the destination disk. The mouse pointer points to the Yes button.

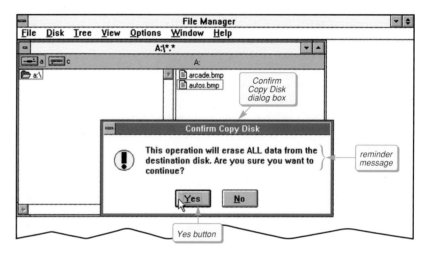

FIGURE 2-39

STEP 4 ▶

Choose the Yes button by clicking the left mouse button, and then point to the OK button.

Windows opens the Copy Disk dialog box (Figure 2-40). The dialog box contains the Insert source disk message and the mouse pointer points to the OK button.

STEP 5 ▶

Insert the source diskette, the Business Documents diskette, into drive A.

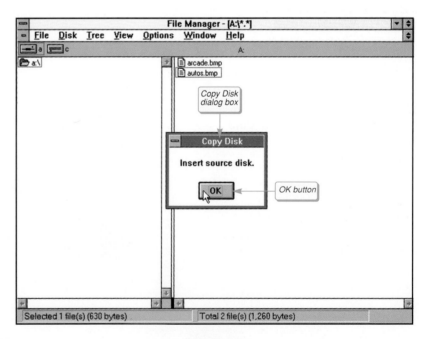

FIGURE 2-40

STEP 6 ▶

Choose the OK button in the Copy Disk dialog box by clicking the left mouse button.

Windows opens the Copying Disk dialog box (Figure 2-41). The dialog box contains the messages, Now Copying disk in Drive A:. and 1% completed. As the copy process progresses, a value from 1 to 100 indicates what percent of the copy process is complete.

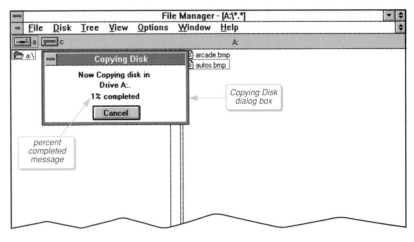

FIGURE 2-41

When as much data from the source diskette as will fit in main memory is copied to main memory, Windows opens the Copy Disk dialog box (Figure 2-42). The dialog box contains the message, Insert destination disk, and the OK button.

STEP 7 ▶

Remove the source diskette (Business Documents diskette) from drive A and insert the destination diskette (Business Documents Backup diskette) into drive A.

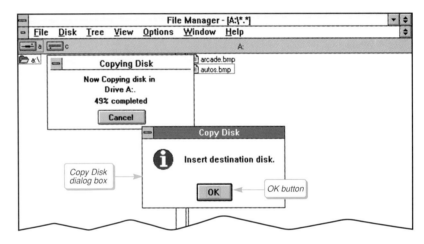

FIGURE 2-42

STEP 8 ▶

Choose the OK button from the Copy Disk dialog box.

Windows opens the Copying Disk dialog box (Figure 2-43). A value from 1 to 100 displays as the data in main memory is copied to the destination disk.

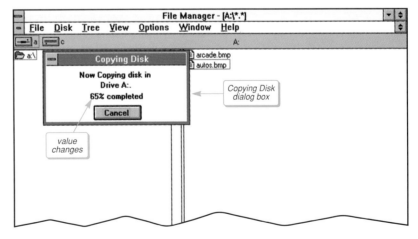

FIGURE 2-43

STEP 9 ▶

**Remove the Business Documents
Backup diskette from drive A and
remove the write-protection from
the Business Documents diskette
by closing the write-protect
window.**

*The write-protection is removed
from the 3 1/2—inch Business
Documents diskette (Figure
2-44).*

write-protect
window closed
means you can write
to this diskette

Business
Documents

FIGURE 2-44

STEP 10 ▶

**Identify the Business Documents
Backup diskette by writing the
words Business Documents
Backup on the paper label supplied with the diskette and then
affix the label to the diskette
(Figure 2-45).**

Business
Documents
Backup

FIGURE 2-45

Depending on the size of main memory on your computer, you may have to
insert and remove the source and destination diskettes several times before the
copy process is complete. If prompted by Windows to insert the source diskette,
remove the destination diskette (Business Documents Backup diskette) from
drive A, insert the source diskette (Business Documents diskette) into drive A,
and then choose the OK button. If prompted to insert the destination diskette,
remove the source diskette (Business Documents diskette) from drive A, insert
the destination diskette (Business Documents Backup diskette) into drive A, and
then choose the OK button.

In the future if you change the contents of the Business Documents diskette,
choose the Copy Disk command to copy the contents of the Business Documents diskette to the Business Documents Backup diskette. If the Business Documents diskette becomes unusable, you can format a diskette, choose the Copy
Disk command to copy the contents of the Business Documents Backup diskette
(source diskette) to the formatted diskette (destination diskette), label the formatted diskette, Business Documents, and use the new Business Documents diskette
in place of the unusable Business Documents diskette.

Correcting Errors Encountered While Copying A Diskette

When you try to copy a disk and forget to insert the source diskette when prompted, insert an unformatted source diskette, forget to insert the destination diskette when prompted, or insert a write-protected destination diskette, Windows opens the Copy Disk Error dialog box illustrated in Figure 2-46. The dialog box contains the Unable to copy disk error message and OK button. To complete the copy process after forgetting to insert a source diskette or inserting an unformatted source diskette, choose the OK button, insert the formatted source diskette into the diskette drive, and choose the **Disk Copy command** to start over the disk copy process. To complete the copy process after forgetting to insert a destination diskette or inserting a write-protected destination diskette, choose the OK button, insert a nonwrite-protected diskette in the diskette drive, and choose the Disk Copy command to start over the disk copy.

TRANSPARENCY
Figure 2-46

LECTURE NOTES
■ Mention that the error in Figure 2-46 is forgetting to insert a source or destination diskette into drive A, inserting an unformatted source diskette, or inserting a write-protected destination diskette.
■ Explain how to recover from the errors.

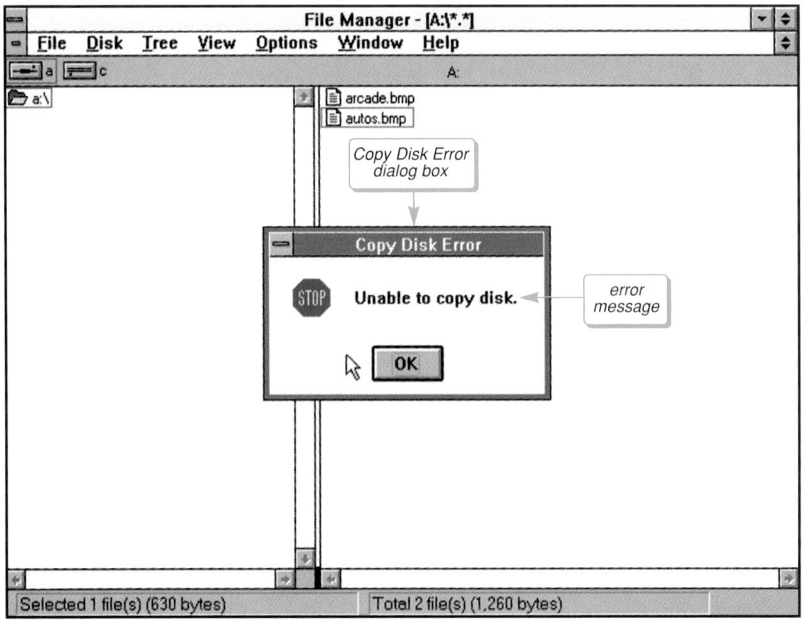

FIGURE 2-46

▶ SEARCHING FOR HELP USING ONLINE HELP

I n Project 1, you obtained help about the Paintbrush application by choosing the Contents command from the Help menu of the Paintbrush window (see pages WIN32 through WIN35). You then chose a topic from a list of help topics on the screen. In addition to choosing a topic from a list of available help topics, you can use the Search feature to search for help topics. In this project, you will use the Search feature to obtain help about copying files and selecting groups of files using the keyboard.

LECTURE NOTES
■ Review how help was obtained in Project 1 by choosing the Contents command.

Searching for a Help Topic

In this project, you used a mouse to select and copy a group of files. If you want to obtain information about how to select a group of files using the key-board instead of the mouse, you can use the Search feature. A search can be per-formed in one of two ways. The first method allows you to select a search topic from a list of search topics. A list of help topics associated with the search topic displays. You then select a help topic from this list. To begin the search, choose the **Search for Help on command** from the Help menu.

TO SEARCH FOR A HELP TOPIC ▼

STEP 1 ►

Select the Help menu from the File Manager window menu bar, and then point to the Search for Help on command.

Windows opens the Help menu (Figure 2-47). The mouse pointer points to the Search for Help on command.

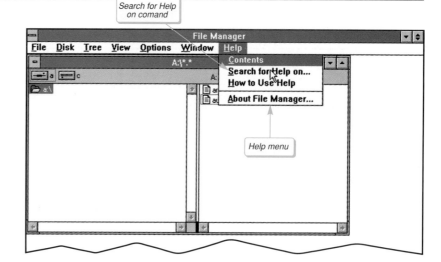

FIGURE 2-47

STEP 2 ►

Choose the Search for Help on command from the Help menu by clicking the left mouse button.

Windows opens the Search dialog box (Figure 2-48). The dialog box consists of two areas separated by a horizontal line. The top area contains the Search For text box, Search For list box, and Cancel and Show Top-ics buttons. The Search For list box contains an alphabetical list of search topics. A vertical scroll bar indicates there are more search topics than appear in the list box. The Cancel button cancels the Search operation. The Show Top-ics button is dimmed and cannot be chosen. The bottom area of the dialog box contains the empty Help Topics list box and the dimmed Go To button.

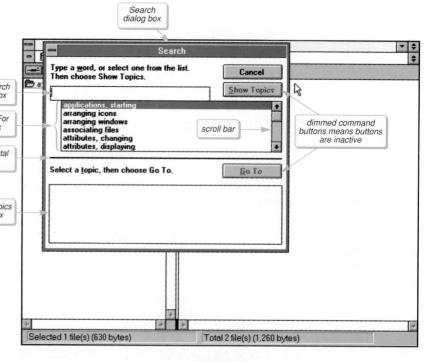

FIGURE 2-48

STEP 3 ▶

Point to the down scroll arrow in the Search For list box (Figure 2-49).

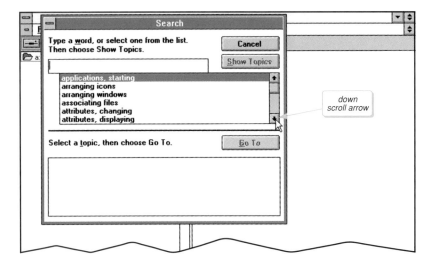

FIGURE 2-49

STEP 4 ▶

Hold down the left mouse button until the selecting files search topic is visible, and then point to the selecting files search topic (Figure 2-50).

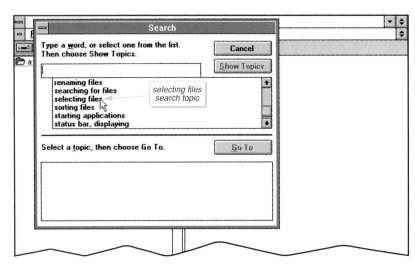

FIGURE 2-50

STEP 5 ▶

Select the selecting files search topic by clicking the left mouse button, and then point to the Show Topics button (Show Topics).

The selecting files search topic is highlighted in the Search For list box and displays in the Search For text box (Figure 2-51). The Show Topics button is no longer dimmed and the mouse pointer points to the Show Topics button.

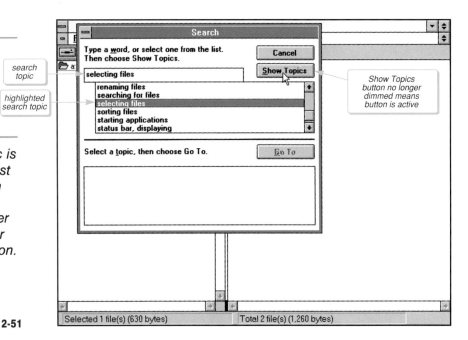

FIGURE 2-51

STEP 6 ▶

Choose the Show Topics button by clicking the left mouse button, and then point to the Using the Keyboard to Select Files help topic.

The Help Topics list box contains four help topics (Figure 2-52). The Go To button (Go To) is no longer dimmed, and the mouse pointer points to the Using the Keyboard to Select Files help topic.

FIGURE 2-52

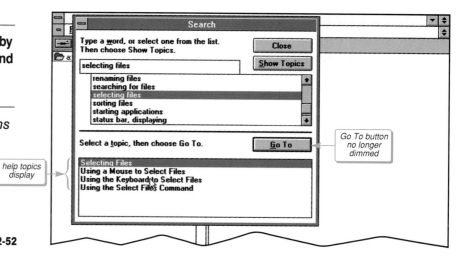

STEP 7 ▶

Select the Using the Keyboard to Select Files help topic by clicking the left mouse button, and then point to the Go To button.

The Using the Keyboard to Select Files help topic is highlighted in the Help Topics list box and the mouse pointer points to the Go To button (Figure 2-53).

FIGURE 2-53

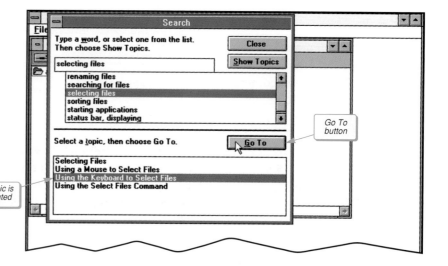

STEP 8 ▶

Choose the Go To button by clicking the left mouse button.

Windows closes the Search dialog box and opens the File Manager Help window (Figure 2-54). The Using the Keyboard to Select Files screen displays in the window.

FIGURE 2-54

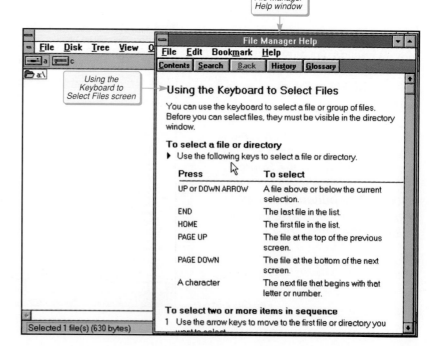

STEP 9 ►

Click the Maximize button (⊕) to maximize the File Manager Help window (Figure 2-55).

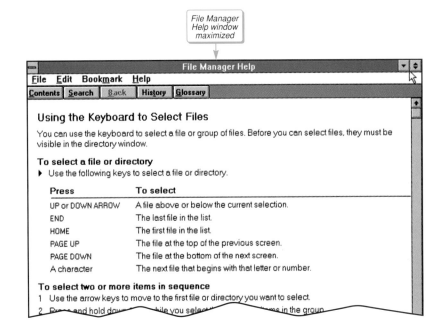

FIGURE 2-55

Searching for Help Using a Word or Phrase

The second method you can use to search for help involves entering a word or phrase to assist the Search feature in finding help related to the word or phrase. In this project, you copied a group of files from the hard disk to a diskette. To obtain additional information about copying files, choose the Search button and type copy from the keyboard.

TO SEARCH FOR A HELP TOPIC ▼

STEP 1 ►

Point to the Search button (Search) (Figure 2-56).

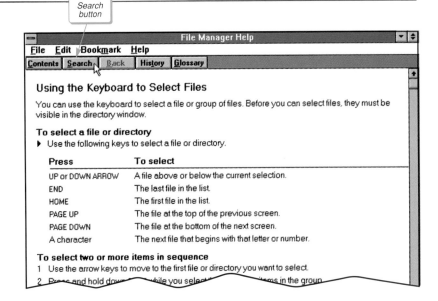

FIGURE 2-56

STEP 2 ▶

Choose the Search button by clicking the left mouse button, and then type `copy`.

Windows opens the Search dialog box (Figure 2-57). As you type the word copy, each letter of the word displays in the Search For text box and the Search For Topics in the Search For Topics list box change. When the entry of the word is complete, the word copy displays in the Search For text box and the Search For topics beginning with the four letters c-o-p-y display first in the Search For list box.

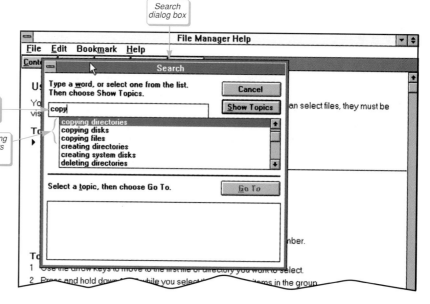

FIGURE 2-57

STEP 3 ▶

Select the copying files search topic by pointing to the topic and clicking the left mouse button, and then point to the Show Topics button.

The copying files search topic is highlighted in the Search For list box and displays in the Search For text box (Figure 2-58).

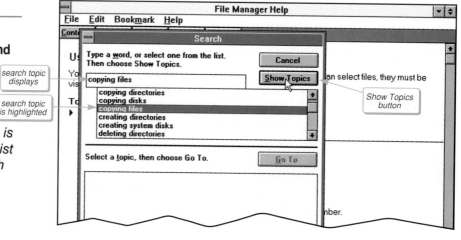

FIGURE 2-58

STEP 4 ▶

Choose the Show Topics button by clicking the left mouse button, and then point to the Go To button.

Only the Copying Files and Directories help topic display in the Help Topic list box (Figure 2-59).

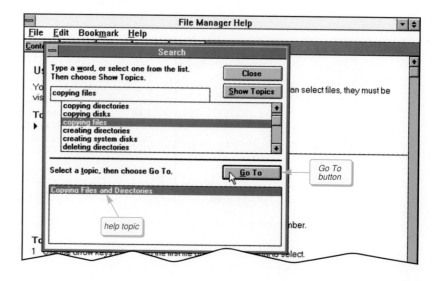

FIGURE 2-59

STEP 5 ▶

Choose the Go To button by clicking the left mouse button.

Windows closes the Search dialog box and displays the Copying Files and Directories help screen (Figure 2-60).

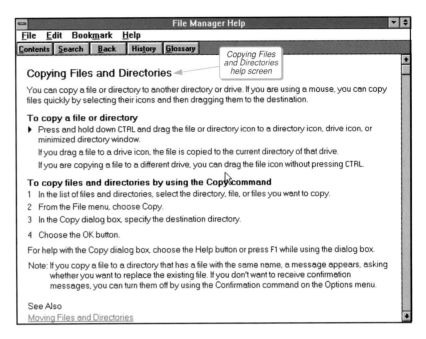

FIGURE 2-60

Quitting File Manager and Online Help

When you finish using File Manager and Windows online Help, you should quit the File Manager Help and File Manager applications. One method of quitting these applications is to first quit the File Manager Help application, and then quit the File Manager application. However, because quitting an application automatically quits the help application associated with that application, you can simply quit the File Manager application to quit both applications. Because the Program Manager and File Manager windows are hidden behind the File Manager Help window (see Figure 2-60), you must move the File Manager window on top of the other windows before quitting File Manager. To do this, you must switch to the File Manager application.

▶ SWITCHING BETWEEN APPLICATIONS

E ach time you start an application and maximize its window, its application window displays on top of the other windows on the desktop. To display a hidden application window, you must switch between applications on the desktop using the ALT and TAB keys. To switch to another application, hold down the ALT key, press the TAB key one or more times, and then release the ALT key. Each time you press the TAB key, a box containing an application icon and application window title opens on the desktop. To display the File Manager window, you will have to press the TAB key only once.

TO SWITCH BETWEEN APPLICATIONS ▼

STEP 1 ▶

Hold down the ALT key, and then press the TAB key.

A box containing the File Manager application icon and window title (File Manager) displays (Figure 2-61).

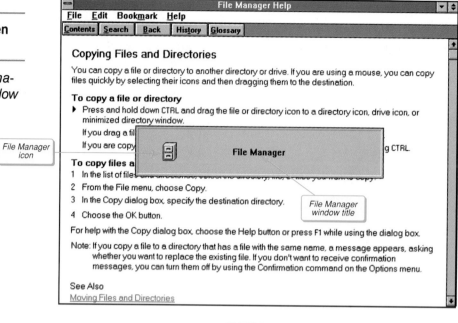

FIGURE 2-61

STEP 2 ▶

Release the ALT key.

The File Manager window moves on top of the other windows on the desktop (Figure 2-62).

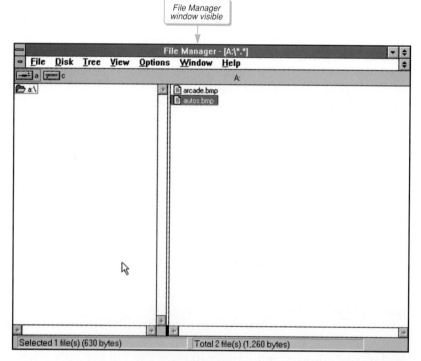

FIGURE 2-62

Verify Changes to the File Manager Window Will Not Be Saved

Because you want to return the File Manager window to its state before you started the application, no changes should be saved. The **Save Settings on Exit command** on the Options menu controls whether changes to the File Manager window are saved or not saved when you quit File Manager. A check mark (✓) preceding the Save Settings on Exit command indicates the command is active and all changes to the layout of the File Manager window will be saved when you quit File Manager. If the command is preceded by a check mark, choose the Save Settings on Exit command by clicking the left mouse button to remove the check mark, so the changes will not be saved. Perform the following steps to verify that changes are not saved to the File Manager window.

TO VERIFY CHANGES WILL NOT BE SAVED ▼

STEP 1 ►

Select the Options menu from the File Manager menu bar.

The Options menu opens (Figure 2-63). A check mark (✓) precedes the Save Settings on Exit command.

STEP 2 ►

To remove the check mark, choose the Save Settings on Exit command from the Options menu by pointing to the Save Settings on Exit command and clicking the left mouse button.

Windows closes the Options menu. Although not visible, the check mark preceding the Save Settings on Exit command has been removed. This means any changes made to the desktop will not be saved when you exit File Manager.

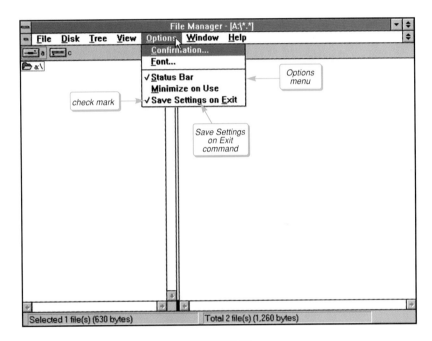

FIGURE 2-63

Quitting File Manager

After verifying no changes to the File Manager window will be saved, the Save Settings on Exit command is not active, so you can quit the File Manager application. In Project 1 you chose the Exit command from the File menu to quit an application. In addition to choosing a command from a menu, you can also quit an application by pointing to the **Control-menu box** in the upper left corner of the application window and double-clicking the left mouse button, as shown in the steps on the next page.

TO QUIT AN APPLICATION ▼

STEP 1 ▶

Point to the Control-menu box in the upper left corner of the File Manager window (Figure 2-64).

STEP 2 ▶

Double-click the left mouse button to exit the File Manager application.

Windows closes the File Manager and File Manager Help windows, causing the Program Manager window to display.

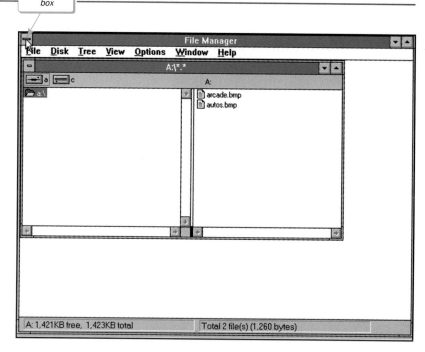

FIGURE 2-64

TO QUIT WINDOWS

Step 1: Select the Options menu from the Program Manager menu bar.
Step 2: If a check mark precedes the Save Settings on Exit command, choose the Save Settings on Exit command.
Step 3: Point to the Control-menu box in the upper left corner of the Program Manager window.
Step 4: Double-click the left mouse button.
Step 5: Choose the OK button to exit Windows.

▶ ADDITIONAL COMMANDS AND CONCEPTS

I n addition to the commands and concepts presented in Project 1 and this project, you should understand how to activate a group window, arrange the program-item icons in a group window, and close a group window. These topics are discussed on the following pages. In addition, methods to resize a window and minimize an application window to an application icon are explained.

Activating a Group Window

Frequently, several group windows are open in the Program Manager window at the same time. In Figure 2-65, two group windows (Main and Accessories) are open. The Accessories window is the active group window, and the inactive Main window is partially hidden behind the Accessories window. To view a group window that is partially hidden, activate the hidden window by selecting the Window menu and then choosing the name of the group window you wish to view.

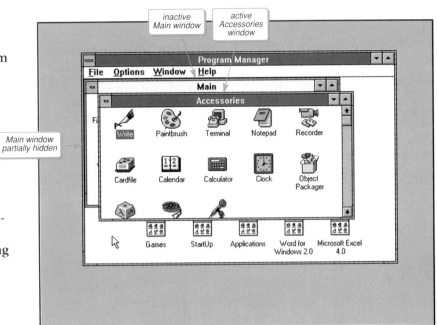

FIGURE 2-65

TO ACTIVATE A GROUP WINDOW ▼

STEP 1 ►

Select the Window menu from the Program Manager menu bar, and then point to the Main group window name.

The Window menu consists of two areas separated by a horizontal line (Figure 2-66). Below the line is a list of the group windows and group icons in the Program Manager window. Each entry in the list is preceded by a value from one to seven. The number of the active window (Accessories) is preceded by a check mark and the mouse pointer points to the Main group window name.

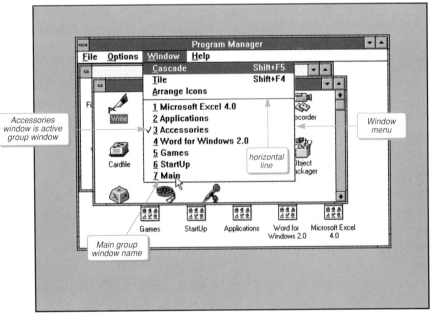

FIGURE 2-66

STEP 2 ▶

Choose the Main group window name by clicking the left mouse button.

The Main window moves on top of the Accessories window (Figure 2-67). The Main window is now the active window.

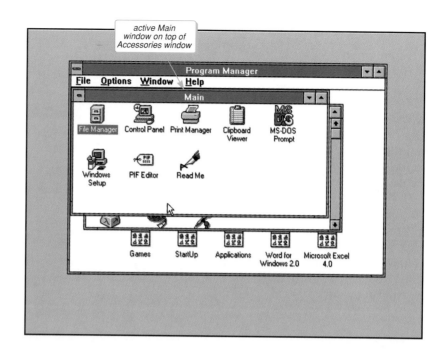

FIGURE 2-67

An alternative method of activating an inactive window is to point to any open area of the window and click the left mouse button. This method cannot be used if the inactive window is completely hidden behind another window.

Closing a Group Window

When several group windows are open in the Program Manager window, you may want to close a group window to reduce the number of open windows. In Figure 2-68, the Main, Accessories, and Games windows are open. To close the Games window, choose the Minimize button on the right side of the Games title bar. Choosing the Minimize button removes the group window from the desktop and displays the Games group icon at the bottom of the Program Manager window.

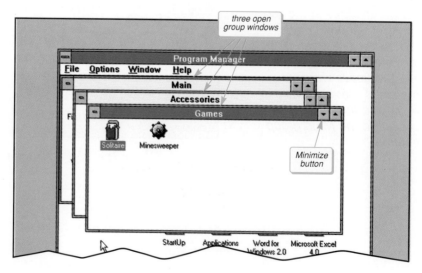

FIGURE 2-68

TO CLOSE A GROUP WINDOW ▼

STEP 1 ▶

Choose the Minimize button (▼) on the Games title bar.

The Games window closes and the Games icon displays at the bottom edge of the Program Manager window (Figure 2-69).

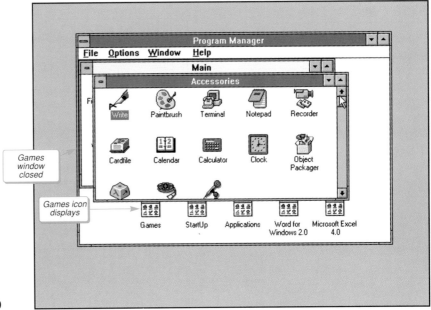

Games window closed

Games icon displays

FIGURE 2-69

Resizing a Group Window

When more than six group icons display at the bottom of the Program Manager window, some group icons may not be completely visible. In Figure 2-70, the name of the Microsoft SolutionsSeries icon is partially visible. To make the icon visible, resize the Main window by dragging the bottom window border toward the window title.

LECTURE NOTES
■ Explain why some group icons may be partially visible at the bottom of the Program Manager window.
■ Indicate how to view a partially visible group icon.

TRANSPARENCIES
Figures 2-70 through 2-72

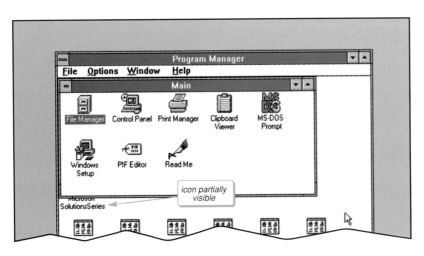

icon partially visible

FIGURE 2-70

TO RESIZE A WINDOW ▼

STEP 1 ▶

Point to the bottom border of the Main window.

As the mouse pointer approaches the window border, the mouse pointer changes to a double-headed arrow icon (⇕) (Figure 2-71).

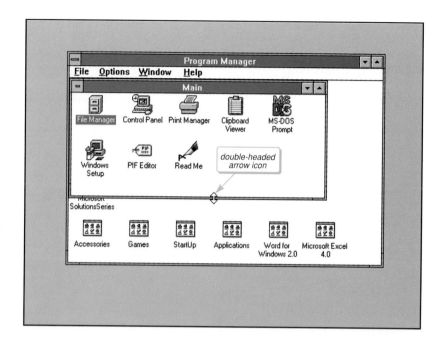

FIGURE 2-71

STEP 2 ▶

Drag the bottom border toward the window title until the Microsoft SolutionsSeries icon is visible.

The Main window changes shape, and the Microsoft SolutionsSeries icon is visible (Figure 2-72).

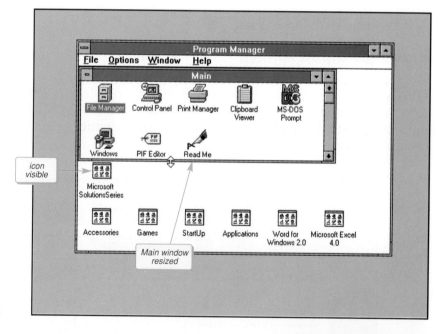

FIGURE 2-72

In addition to dragging a window border to resize a window, you can also drag a window corner to resize the window. By dragging a corner, you can change both the width and length of a window.

WINDOWS TIPS
▪ Change the size of a window by dragging its border or a corner. Move a window by pointing to the title bar and dragging the title bar.

TRANSPARENCY
Figure 2-73

LECTURE NOTES
▪ Explain how program-item icons become unorganized in a group window.
▪ Explain that the Arrange Icons command arranges unorganized icons.

Arranging Icons

Occasionally, a program-item icon is either accidentally or intentionally moved within a group window. The result is that the program-item icons are not arranged in an organized fashion in the window. Figure 2-73 shows the eight program-item icons in the Main window. One icon, the File Manager icon, is not aligned with the other icons. As a result, the icons in the Main window appear unorganized. To arrange the icons in the Main window, choose the **Arrange Icons command** from the Window menu.

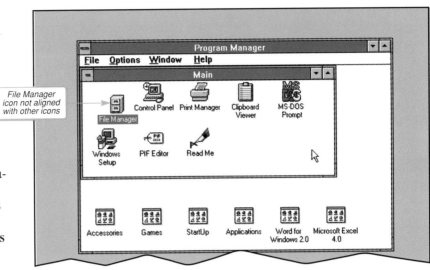

FIGURE 2-73

TRANSPARENCIES
Figures 2-74 and 2-75

TO ARRANGE PROGRAM-ITEM ICONS ▼

STEP 1 ▶

Select the Window menu from the Program Manager menu bar, and then point to the Arrange Icons command.

Windows opens the Window menu (Figure 2-74). The mouse pointer points to the Arrange Icons command.

FIGURE 2-74

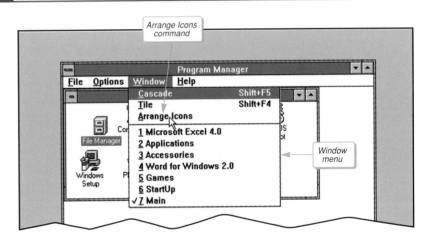

STEP 2 ▶

Choose the Arrange Icons command by clicking the left mouse button.

The icons in the Main window are arranged (Figure 2-75).

FIGURE 2-75

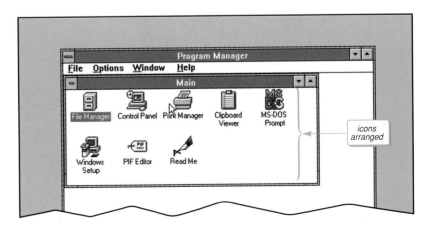

TRANSPARENCY
Figure 2-76

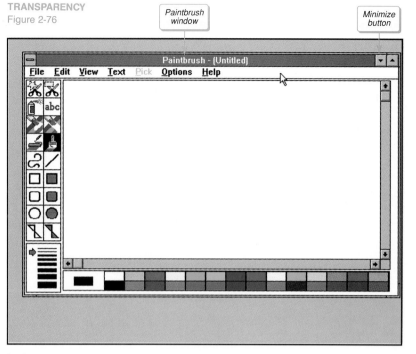

Paintbrush window

Minimize button

FIGURE 2-76

LECTURE NOTES
▪ Define application icon.
▪ Explain when to mini-
mize an application
window.
▪ Identify the benefits of
minimizing an application
window.

TRANSPARENCY
Figure 2-77

Minimizing an Application Window to an Icon

When you finish work in an application and there is a possibility of using the application again before quitting Windows, you should minimize the application window to an application icon instead of quitting the application. An **application icon** represents an application that was started and then minimized. Minimizing a window to an application icon saves you the time of starting the application and maximizing its window if you decide to use the application again. In addition, you free space on the desktop without quitting the application. The desktop in Figure 2-76 contains the Paintbrush window. To minimize the Paintbrush window to an application icon, click the Minimize button on the right side of the Paintbrush title bar.

TO MINIMIZE AN APPLICATION WINDOW TO AN ICON ▼

STEP 1 ▶

Click the Minimize button on the right side of the Paintbrush title bar.

Windows closes the Paintbrush window and displays the Paintbrush application icon at the bottom of the desktop (Figure 2-77).

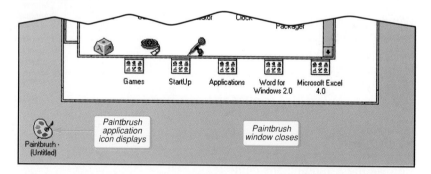

Paintbrush application icon displays

Paintbrush window closes

FIGURE 2-77

After minimizing an application window to an application icon, you can start the application again by double-clicking the application icon.

▶ PROJECT SUMMARY

In this project, you used File Manager to format and copy a diskette, copy a group of files, and rename and delete a file. You searched for help about File Manager using the Search feature of online Help, and you switched between applications on the desktop. In addition, you activated, resized, and closed a group window, arranged the icons in a group window, and minimized an application window to an application icon.

▶ KEY TERMS

application icon (*WIN86*)
Arrange Icons command
    (*WIN85*)
backup diskette (*WIN47*)
Cascade command (*WIN94*)
contents list (*WIN49*)
Control-menu box (*WIN79*)
Copy Disk command (*WIN67*)
current drive (*WIN48*)
Delete command (*WIN65*)
destination directory (*WIN54*)
destination diskette (*WIN67*)
destination drive (*WIN54*)

directory structure (*WIN49*)
directory tree (*WIN49*)
directory window (*WIN48*)
Disk Copy command (*WIN71*)
Disk menu (*WIN51*)
diskette capacity (*WIN50*)
diskette size (*WIN50*)
drive icon (*WIN48*)
File Manager (*WIN48*)
Format Disk command (*WIN51*)
formatting (*WIN50*)
Help menu (*WIN72*)

Options menu (*WIN79*)
Rename command (*WIN63*)
Save Settings on Exit command
    (*WIN79*)
Search for Help on command
    (*WIN72*)
source directory (*WIN54*)
source diskette (*WIN67*)
source drive (*WIN54*)
split bar (*WIN49*)
Tile command (*WIN94*)
Window menu (*WIN81*)

Q U I C K   R E F E R E N C E

In Windows you can accomplish a task in a number of ways. The following table provides a quick reference to each task presented in the project with its available options. The commands listed in the Menu column can be executed using either the keyboard or mouse.

Task	Mouse	Menu	Keyboard Shortcuts
Activate a Group Window	Click group window	From Window menu, choose window title	
Arrange Program-Item Icons in a Group Window		From Window menu, choose Arrange Icons	
Change the Current Drive	Click drive icon		Press TAB to move highlight to drive icon area, press arrow keys to outline drive icon, and press ENTER
Close a Group Window	Click Minimize button or double-click control-menu box	From Control menu, choose Close	Press CTRL + F4
Copy a Diskette		From Disk menu, choose Copy Disk	
Copy a File or Group of Files	Drag highlighted file-name(s) to destination drive or directory icon	From File menu, choose Copy	
Delete a File		From File menu, choose Delete	Press DEL
Format a Diskette		From Disk menu, choose Format Disk	

(continued)

QUICK REFERENCE (continued)

Task	Mouse	Menu	Keyboard Shortcuts
Maximize a Directory Window	Click Maximize button	From Control menu, choose Maximize	
Minimize an Application Window	Click Minimize button	From Control menu, choose Minimize	Press ALT, SPACE BAR, N
Rename a File		From File menu, choose Rename	
Resize a Window	Drag window border or corner	From Control menu, choose Size	
Save Changes when Quitting File Manager		From Options menu, choose Save Settings on Exit if no check mark precedes command	
Save No Changes when Quitting Windows		From Options menu, choose Save Settings on Exit if check mark precedes command	
Search for a Help Topic		From Help menu, choose Search for Help on	
Select a File in the Contents List	Click the filename		Press arrow keys to outline filename, press SHIFT + F8
Select a Group of Files in the Contents List	Select first file, hold down CTRL key and select other files		Press arrow keys to outline first file, press SHIFT + F8, press arrow keys to outline each additional filename, and press SPACEBAR
Switch between Applications	Click application window		Hold down ALT, press TAB (or ESC), release ALT

S T U D E N T   A S S I G N M E N T S

STUDENT ASSIGNMENT 1
True/False

Instructions: Circle T if the statement is true or F if the statement if false.

(T) F   1. Formatting prepares a diskette for use on a computer.

T (F)   2. It is not important to create a backup diskette of the Business Documents diskette.

T (F)   3. Program Manager is an application you can use to organize and work with your hard disk and diskettes and the files on those disks.

(T) F   4. A directory window title bar usually contains the current directory path.

(T) F   5. A directory window consists of a directory tree and contents list.

T (F)   6. The directory tree contains a list of the files in the current directory.

T (F)   7. The disk capacity of a 3 1/2-inch diskette is typically 360K or 1.2MB.

(T) F   8. The source drive is the drive from which files are copied.

(T) F   9. You select a single file in the contents list by pointing to the filename and clicking the left mouse button.

T (F) 10. You select a group of files in the contents list by pointing to each filename and clicking the left mouse button.
(T) F 11. Windows opens the Error Copying File dialog box if you try to copy a file to an unformatted diskette.
T (F) 12. You change the filename or extension of a file using the Change command.
(T) F 13. Windows opens the Confirm File Delete dialog box when you try to delete a file.
T (F) 14. When creating a backup diskette, the disk to receive the copy is the source disk.
T (F) 15. The first step in creating a backup diskette is to choose the Copy Disk command from the Disk menu.
(T) F 16. On some computers, you may have to insert and remove the source and destination diskettes several times to copy a diskette.
(T) F 17. Both the Search for Help on command and the Search button initiate a search for help.
(T) F 18. An application icon represents an application that was started and then minimized.
T (F) 19. You hold down the TAB key, press the ALT key, and then release the TAB key to switch between applications on the desktop.
(T) F 20. An application icon displays on the desktop when you minimize an application window.

STUDENT ASSIGNMENT 2
Multiple Choice

Instructions: Circle the correct response.

1. The _____ application allows you to format a diskette.
   a. Program Manager
   (b.) File Manager
   c. online Help
   d. Paintbrush
2. The _____ contains the directory structure of the current drive.
   a. contents list
   b. status bar
   c. split bar
   (d.) directory tree
3. The _____ key is used when selecting a group of files.
   (a.) CTRL
   b. ALT
   c. TAB
   d. ESC
4. After selecting a group of files, you _____ the group of files to copy the files to a new drive or directory.
   a. click
   b. double-click
   (c.) drag
   d. none of the above
5. The commands to rename and delete a file are located on the _____ menu.
   a. Window
   b. Options
   c. Disk
   (d.) File
6. The first step in creating a backup diskette is to _____.
   a. write-protect the destination diskette
   b. choose the Copy command from the Disk menu
   (c.) write-protect the source diskette
   d. label the destination diskette

STUDENT ASSIGNMENT 2 (continued)

7. When searching for help, the _____ button displays a list of Help topics.
   a. Go To
   b. Topics
   c. Show Topics
   d. Search

8. You use the _____ and _____ keys to switch between applications on the desktop.
   a. ALT, TAB
   b. SHIFT, ALT
   c. ALT, CTRL
   d. ESC, CTRL

9. When you choose a window title from the Window menu, Windows _____ the associated group window.
   a. opens
   b. closes
   c. enlarges
   d. activates

10. To resize a group window, you can use the _____.
    a. title bar
    b. window border
    c. resize command on the Window menu
    d. arrange Icons command on the Options menu

STUDENT ASSIGNMENT 3
Identifying the Parts of a Directory Window

Instructions: On the desktop in Figure SA2-3, arrows point to several items in the C:\WINDOWS*.* directory window. Identify the items in the space provided.

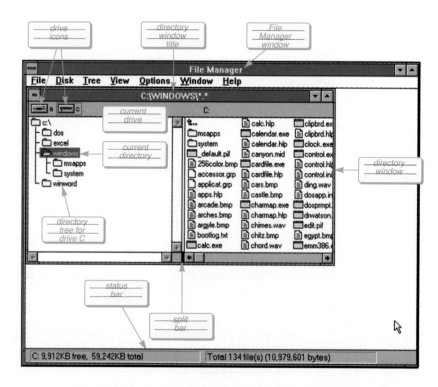

FIGURE SA2-3

STUDENT ASSIGNMENT 4
Selecting a Group of Files

Instructions: Using the desktop in Figure SA2-4, list the steps to select the group of files consisting of the ARCADE.BMP, CARS.BMP, and EGYPT.BMP files in the space provided.

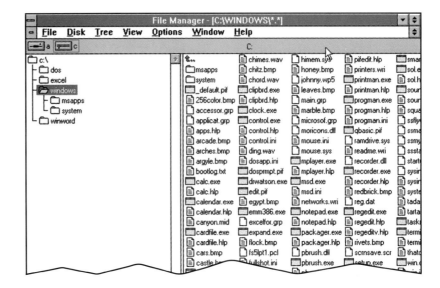

FIGURE SA2-4

Step 1: Point to the ARCADE.BMP filename in the contents list.

Step 2: Select the ARCADE.BMP file by clicking the left mouse button, and then point to the CARS.BMP filename.

Step 3: Hold down the CTRL key, click the left mouse button, release the CTRL key, and then point to the EGYPT.BMP filename.

Step 4: Hold down the CTRL key, click the left mouse button, and then release the CTRL key.

STUDENT ASSIGNMENT 5
Copying a Group of Files

Instructions: Using the desktop in Figure SA2-5, list the steps to copy the group of files selected in Student Assignment 4 to the root directory of drive A. Write the steps in the space provided.

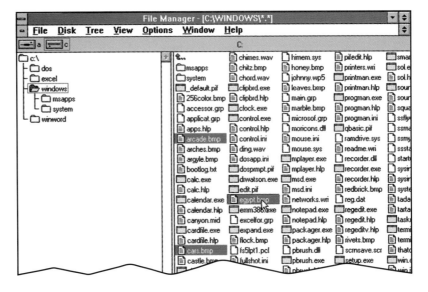

FIGURE SA2-5

Step 1: Verify that the formatted diskette is in drive A. Point to the highlighted ARCADE.BMP entry.

Step 2: Drag the ARCADE.BMP filename over to the drive A icon.

Step 3: Release the mouse button, and then point to the Yes button in the Confirm Mouse Operation dialog box.

Step 4: Choose the Yes button by clicking the left mouse button.

STUDENT ASSIGNMENT 6
Searching for Help

Instructions: Using the desktop in Figure SA2-6, list the steps to complete the search for the Using the Keyboard to Select Files help topic. The mouse pointer points to the down scroll arrow. Write the steps in the space provided.

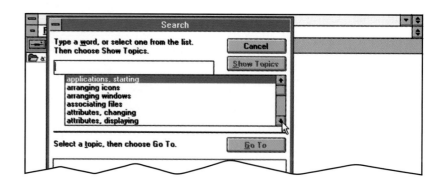

FIGURE SA2-6

Step 1: Hold down left mouse button until the selecting files search topic is visible, then point to the selecting files search topic.

Step 2: Select the selecting files search topic by clicking the left mouse button, and then point to the Show Topics button.

Step 3: Choose Show Topics button by clicking left mouse button, then point to Using the Keyboard to Select Files help topic.

Step 4: Select Using the Keyboard to Select Files help topic by clicking the left mouse button, then point to the Go To button.

Step 5: Choose the Go To button by clicking the left mouse button.

Step 6: Click the Maximize button to maximize the File Manager Help window.

C O M P U T E R   L A B O R A T O R Y   E X E R C I S E S

EXERCISE NOTES
■ Some computers have multiple disk drives. Tell students which diskette drive to use in this exercise.

COMPUTER LABORATORY EXERCISE 1
Selecting and Copying Files

Instructions: Perform the following tasks using a computer.

Part 1:

1. Start Windows.
2. Double-click the File Manager icon to start File Manager.
3. Click the Maximize button on the File Manager window to enlarge the File Manager window.
4. Click the Maximize button on the C:\WINDOWS*.* window to enlarge the C:\WINDOWS*.* window.
5. Select the CHITZ.BMP file.
6. Hold down the CTRL key and click the LEAVES.BMP filename to select the LEAVES.BMP file. The CHITZ.BMP and LEAVES.BMP files should both be highlighted.
7. Insert the Student Diskette into drive A.
8. Drag the group of files to the drive A icon.
9. Choose the Yes button in the Confirm Mouse Operation dialog box.
10. Choose the drive A icon to change the current drive to drive A.
11. Select the CHITZ.BMP file.
12. Choose the Delete command from the File menu.
13. Choose the OK button in the Delete dialog box.
14. Choose the Yes button in the Confirm File Delete dialog box.
15. If the LEAVES.BMP file is not highlighted, select the LEAVES.BMP file.

EXERCISE NOTES
■ Remind students that if they quit Windows after this exercise, no changes to the desktop should be saved.

16. Choose the Rename command from the File menu.
17. Type AUTUMN.BMP in the To text box.
18. Choose the OK button in the Rename dialog box to rename the LEAVES.BMP file.

Part 2:

1. Hold down the ALT key, press the TAB key, and release the ALT key to switch to the Program Manager application.
2. Double-click the Accessories icon to open the Accessories window.
3. Double-click the Paintbrush icon to start Paintbrush.
4. Click the Maximize button on the Paintbrush window to enlarge the Paintbrush window.
5. Choose the Open command from the File menu.
6. Click the Down Arrow button in the Drives drop down list box to display the Drives drop down list.
7. Select the drive A icon.
8. Select the AUTUMN.BMP file in the File Name list box.
9. Choose the OK button to retrieve the AUTUMN.BMP file into Paintbrush.
10. Choose the Print command from the File menu.
11. Click the Draft option button in the Print dialog box.
12. Choose the OK button in the Print dialog box to print the contents of the AUTUMN.BMP file.
13. Remove the Student Diskette from drive A.
14. Choose the Exit command from the File menu to quit Paintbrush.
15. Hold down the ALT key, press the TAB key, and release the ALT key to switch to the File Manager application.
16. Select the Options menu.
17. If a check mark precedes the Save Settings on Exit command, choose the Save Settings on Exit command.
18. Choose the Exit command from the File menu of the File Manager window to quit File Manager.
19. Choose the Exit Windows command from the File menu of the Program Manager window.
20. Click the OK button to quit Windows.

COMPUTER LABORATORY EXERCISE 2
Searching with Online Help

Instructions: Perform the following tasks using a computer.

1. Start Microsoft Windows.
2. Double-click the Accessories icon to open the Accessories window.
3. Double-click the Write icon to start the Write application.
4. Click the Maximize button on the Write window to enlarge the Write window.
5. Choose the Search for Help on command from the Help menu.
6. Scroll the Search For list box to make the cutting text topic visible.
7. Select the cutting text topic.
8. Choose the Show Topics button.
9. Choose the Go To button to display the Copying, Cutting, and Pasting Text topic.
10. Click the Maximize button on the Write Help window to enlarge the window.
11. Choose the Print Topic command from the File menu to print the Copying, Cutting, and Pasting Text topic on the printer.
12. Choose the Search button.
13. Enter the word paste in the Search For list box.
14. Select the Pasting Pictures search topic.
15. Choose the Show Topics button.
16. Choose the Go To button to display the Copying, Cutting, and Pasting Pictures topic.
17. Choose the Print Topic command from the File menu to print the Copying, Cutting, and Pasting Pictures topic on the printer.

COMPUTER LABORATORY EXERCISE 2 (continued)

18. Choose the Exit command from the File menu to quit Write Help.
19. Choose the Exit command from the File menu to quit Write.
20. Select the Options menu.
21. If a check mark precedes the Save Settings on Exit command, choose the Save Settings on Exit command.
22. Choose the Exit Windows command from the File menu.
23. Click the OK button to quit Windows.

COMPUTER LABORATORY EXERCISE 3
Working with Group Windows

Instructions: Perform the following tasks using a computer.

1. Start Windows. The Main window should be open in the Program Manger window.
2. Double-click the Accessories icon to open the Accessories window.
3. Double-click the Games icon to open the Games window.
4. Choose the Accessories window title from the Window menu to activate the Accessories window.
5. Click the Minimize button on the Accessories window to close the Accessories window.
6. Choose the **Tile command** from the Window menu. The Tile command arranges a group of windows so no windows overlap, all windows are visible, and each window occupies an equal portion of the screen.
7. Move and resize the Main and Games windows to resemble the desktop in Figure CLE2-3. To resize a window, drag the window border or corner. To move a group window, drag the window title bar. Choose the Arrange Icons command from the Window menu to arrange the icons in each window.

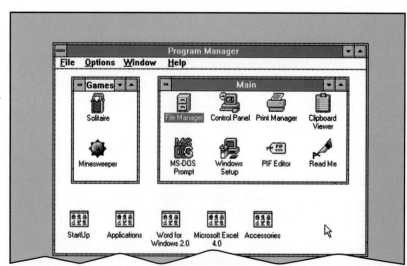

FIGURE CLE2-3

8. Press the PRINTSCREEN key to capture the desktop.
9. Open the Accessories window.
10. Choose the **Cascade command** from the Window menu. The Cascade command arranges a group of windows so the windows overlap and the title bar of each window is visible.
11. Double-click the Paintbrush icon to start Paintbrush.
12. Click the Maximize button on the Paintbrush window to enlarge the Paintbrush window.
13. Choose the Paste command from the Edit menu to place the picture of the desktop in the window.
14. Choose the Print command from the File menu.

15. Click the Draft option button.
16. Choose the OK button in the Print dialog box to print the desktop.
17. Choose the Exit command from the File menu of the Paintbrush window.
18. Choose the No button to not save current changes and quit Paintbrush.
19. Select the Options menu.
20. If a check mark precedes the Save Settings on Exit command, choose the Save Settings on Exit command.
21. Choose the Exit Windows command from the File menu.
22. Click the OK button.

COMPUTER LABORATORY EXERCISE 4
Backing Up Your Student Diskette

Instructions: Perform the following tasks using a computer to back up your Student Diskette.

Part 1:

1. Start Windows.
2. Double-click the File Manager icon to start the File Manager application.
3. Click the Maximize button on the File Manager window to enlarge the File Manager window.
4. Write-protect the Student Diskette.
5. Choose the Copy Disk command from the Disk menu.
6. Choose the Yes button in the Confirm Copy Disk dialog box.
7. Insert the source diskette (Student Diskette) into drive A.
8. Choose the OK button in the Copy Disk dialog box.
9. When prompted, insert the destination diskette (the formatted diskette created in this project) into drive A.
10. Choose the OK button in the Copy Disk dialog box.
11. Insert and remove the source and destination diskette until the copy process is complete.
12. Click the drive A icon to change the current drive to drive A.
13. Press the PRINTSCREEN key to capture the desktop.
14. Select the Options menu on the File Manager menu bar.
15. If a check mark precedes the Save Settings on Exit command, choose the Save Settings on Exit command.
16. Choose the Exit command from the File menu on the File Manager menu bar to quit File Manager.

Part 2:

1. Double-click the Accessories icon to open the Accessories window.
2. Double-click the Paintbrush icon to start Paintbrush.
3. Click the Maximize button to enlarge the Paintbrush window.
4. Choose the Paste command from the Edit menu to place the picture of the desktop in the window.
5. Choose the Print command from the File menu.
6. Click the Draft option button.
7. Choose the OK button in the Print dialog box to print the picture of the desktop on the printer.
8. Choose the Exit command from the File menu.
9. Choose the No button to not save current changes and quit Paintbrush.
10. Select the Options menu.
11. If a check mark precedes the Save Settings on Exit command, choose the Save Settings on Exit command.
12. Choose the Exit Windows command from the File menu of the Program Manager menu bar.
13. Click the OK button to quit Windows.
14. Remove the diskette from drive A.
15. Remove the write-protection from the Student Diskette.

INDEX

PROGRAMMING

USING MICROSOFT VISUAL BASIC 3.0 FOR WINDOWS

*M*ICROSOFT *V*ISUAL *B*ASIC 3.0 FOR *W*INDOWS

P R O J E C T   O N E

BUILDING AN APPLICATION

▶ Start Visual Basic
▶ Describe the Visual Basic design environment
▶ Change the size and location of a form
▶ Add controls to a form
▶ Describe the function of labels, text boxes and command buttons
▶ Move and resize controls on a form

▶ Set properties of controls
▶ Name a form
▶ Write an event procedure
▶ Save a Visual Basic project
▶ Start a new Visual Basic project
▶ Open an existing Visual Basic project
▶ Use Visual Basic Online Help

▶ WHAT IS VISUAL BASIC?

In *Introduction to Windows* you learned that a user interface allows you to communicate with a computer. Microsoft Windows is called a **graphical user interface (GUI)** because it lets you use both text and graphical images to communicate with the computer. You also learned how to use Windows to run **applications software**, or **applications**, which are computer programs that perform a specific function such as a calendar, word processor, or spreadsheet.

Numerous application software packages are available from computer stores, and several applications are included when you purchase Microsoft Windows. Although many of these Windows applications are created by different companies or individuals, they have a similar *look and feel* to the computer user. They *look* similar because they contain many of the same graphical images, or **objects**. A typical Windows application with common Windows objects is shown in Figure 1-1. Different Windows applications *feel* similar because they respond to the same kinds of user actions, such as clicking or dragging with a mouse.

Visual Basic is itself a Windows application. Its function, however, is to help you build your own special-purpose Windows applications. With Visual Basic, professional-looking applications using the graphical user interface of Windows can be created by persons who have no previous training or experience in computer programming.

VB2

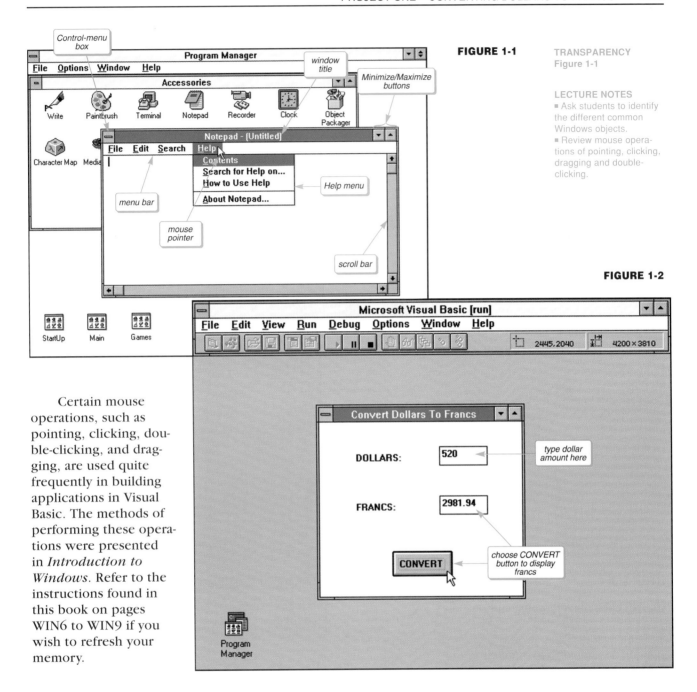

FIGURE 1-1

TRANSPARENCY
Figure 1-1

LECTURE NOTES
■ Ask students to identify
the different common
Windows objects.
■ Review mouse opera-
tions of pointing, clicking,
dragging and double-
clicking.

FIGURE 1-2

Certain mouse operations, such as pointing, clicking, double-clicking, and dragging, are used quite frequently in building applications in Visual Basic. The methods of performing these operations were presented in *Introduction to Windows*. Refer to the instructions found in this book on pages WIN6 to WIN9 if you wish to refresh your memory.

▶ PROJECT ONE – CONVERTING DOLLARS TO FRANCS

To illustrate the major features of Microsoft Visual Basic, this book presents a series of projects using Visual Basic to build Windows applications. Project 1 uses Visual Basic to build the currency conversion application shown in Figure 1-2. In this application, the user enters a number in the box labeled DOLLARS. When the user clicks the CONVERT button, the amount is converted to French francs and appears in the box labeled FRANCS. The Dollars To Francs Converter has some of the common features of Windows applications. It occupies a window that the user can move on the desktop, it can be maximized or minimized, and it has a Control-menu box.

TRANSPARENCY
Figure 1-2

LECTURE NOTES
■ Explain the operation of
the completed currency
conversion application.

▶ STARTING VISUAL BASIC

T o start Visual Basic, Windows must be running. The Program Manager window and the Visual Basic group window must be open. To accomplish these tasks, use the procedures presented in *Introduction to Windows*. Perform the following steps to start Visual Basic.

TO START VISUAL BASIC ▼

STEP 1 ▶

Use the mouse to point to the Microsoft Visual Basic program-item icon in the Visual Basic 3.0 group window (Figure 1-3).

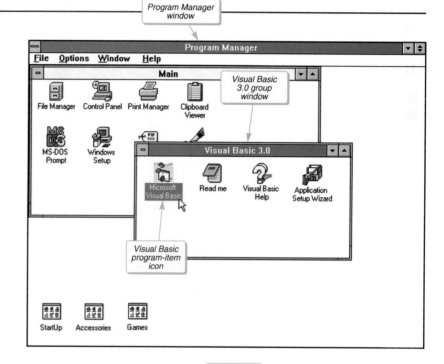

FIGURE 1-3

STEP 2 ▶

Double-click the left mouse button.

Several Visual Basic windows display on the desktop in addition to any other windows that are already open (Figure 1-4).

STEP 3 ▶

Point to an empty area of the Program Manager window (Figure 1-4).

FIGURE 1-4

STEP 4 ▶

Click the left mouse button.

Windows Program Manager becomes the active window. The Visual Basic windows are moved to the background and are no longer visible on the desktop (Figure 1-5).

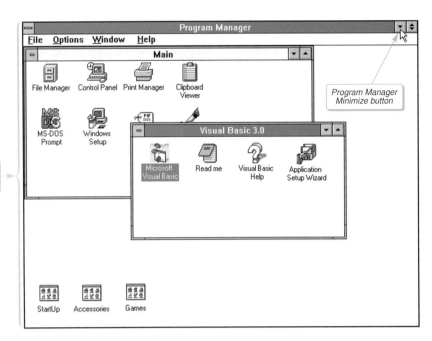

FIGURE 1-5

STEP 5 ▶

Point to the Program Manager minimize button (Figure 1-5).

STEP 6 ▶

Click the left mouse button.

*Program Manager is minimized, and the desktop now displays five windows that make up the **Visual Basic programming environment** (Figure 1-6).*

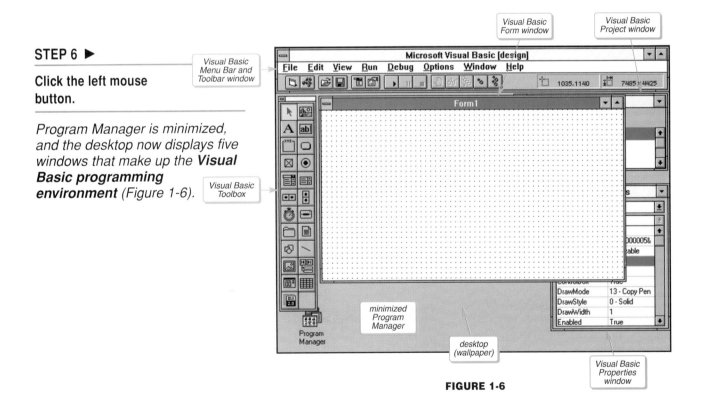

FIGURE 1-6

When you start Visual Basic, several windows are added to the desktop. In the preceding example, you cleared all the windows that are not part of Visual Basic from the desktop by minimizing the Program Manager window. It is possible to work with Visual Basic without clearing the desktop. However, if other windows are already open, the desktop becomes cluttered.

The Active Window

To work in any one of the Visual Basic windows, it must be the active window. Perform the following steps to make the Project window active and then make the Properties window active.

TO MAKE A WINDOW ACTIVE ▼

STEP 1 ▶

Point to any part of the Project window (Figure 1-7).

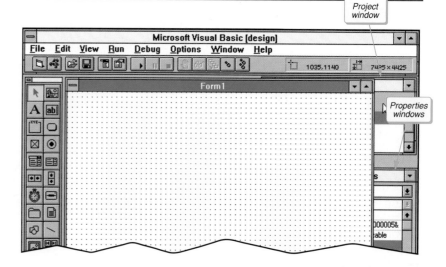

FIGURE 1-7

STEP 2 ▶

Click the left mouse button.

The Project window appears on top of the other windows, and its title bar changes to the active title bar color (Figure 1-8).

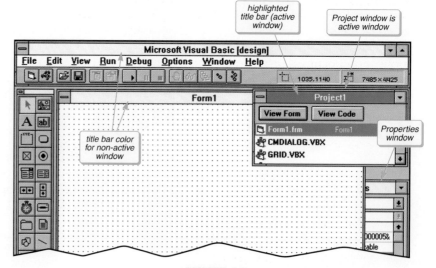

FIGURE 1-8

STEP 3 ▶

Repeat Steps 1 and 2 for the
Properties window.

*The Properties window appears
on top of the other windows
(Figure 1-9). Its title bar changes
to the active title bar color. The
Project window's title bar changes
back to the inactive title bar color.*

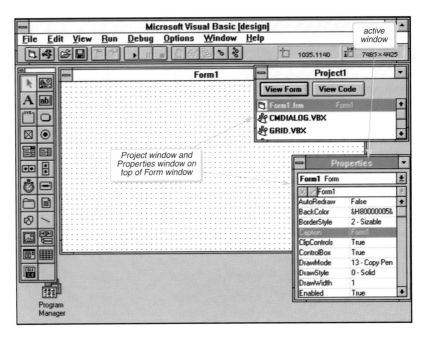

FIGURE 1-9

You can arrange the Visual Basic windows on the desktop in many different ways without affecting Visual Basic's functions. As you become more experienced, you may find a different arrangement that you prefer to work with. For now, use the default sizes and arrangement of the windows as shown in Figure 1-9.

Design Time and Run Time

The time when you build an application in Visual Basic is called **design time**. In contrast, the time when you use an application for its intended purpose is called **run time**. In Visual Basic, the applications you build are called **projects**. A project always begins with a **form**. At run time, a form becomes the window the application occupies on the desktop. Begin building the Dollars To Francs application shown in Figure 1-2 on page VB3 by specifying the size and location where you want the application's window to appear on the desktop during run time.

▶ SETTING THE SIZE AND LOCATION OF FORMS

T he size and location that the application's window will occupy on the desktop during run time is specified by adjusting the size and location of the form during design time. Adjustments to the form's size and location can be made at any time during design time.

Setting the Size of a Form

Perform the following steps to set the size of the Dollars To Francs form.

TO SET THE SIZE OF A FORM ▼

STEP 1 ▶

Point to the form window's title bar (Figure 1-10).

The color of the title bar indicates it is an inactive window.

FIGURE 1-10

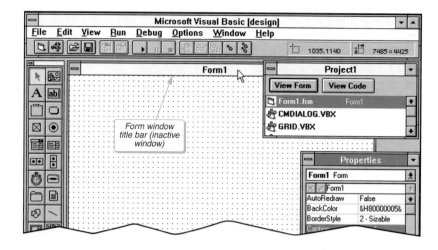

STEP 2 ▶

Click the left mouse button.

The form window becomes the active window (Figure 1-11). This can be seen by the color of the title bar and the form window moving on top of the Project and Properties windows.

FIGURE 1-11

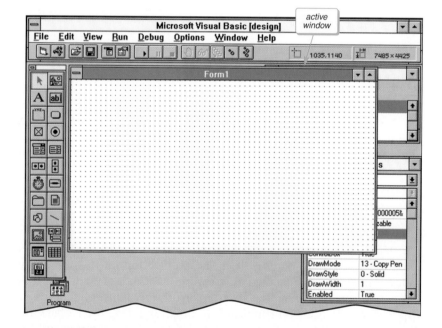

STEP 3 ▶

Point to the form's right border.

The pointer changes to a double arrow (⇔) (Figure 1-12).

FIGURE 1-12

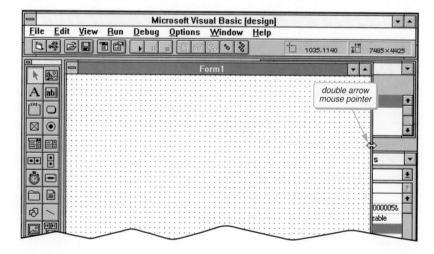

STEP 4 ▶

Drag the form's right border
approximately three inches toward
the left side of the screen.

*The border's new location
appears as a shaded line (Figure
1-13).*

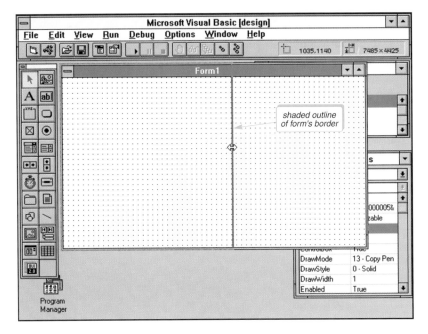

FIGURE 1-13

STEP 5 ▶

Release the left mouse button.

*The form's right border moves to
the location of the shaded line
(Figure 1-14). The Project and
Properties windows again
become visible.*

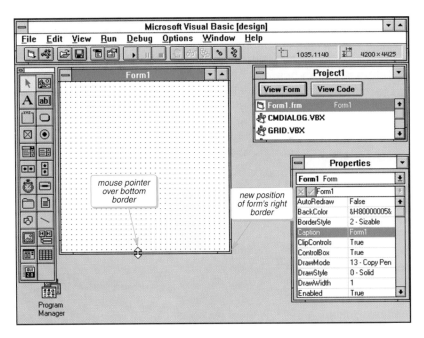

FIGURE 1-14

STEP 6 ▶

Point to the form's bottom border (Figure 1-14). Drag the form's bottom border toward the top of the screen approximately one inch.

The border's new location appears as a shaded line (Figure 1-15).

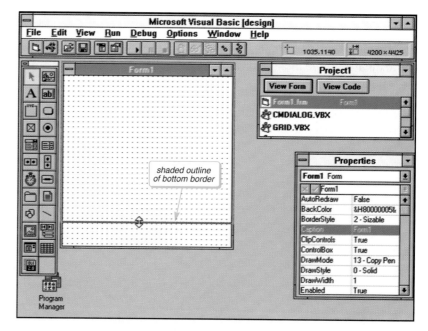

FIGURE 1-15

STEP 7 ▶

Release the left mouse button.

The form's bottom border moves to the location of the shaded line (Figure 1-16). The width and height of the form are shown as two numbers (4200 × 3810) located in the lower right corner of the Menu bar and Toolbar window.

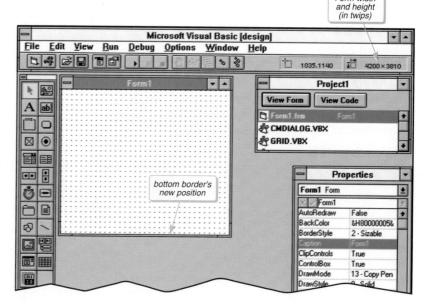

FIGURE 1-16

In the preceding example, the form's width and height were set by dragging the form's right and bottom borders. You can drag any of the form's four borders in either an inward or outward direction to change its size. The form's width and height are measured in units called **twips**. The dimensions of Form1 appear as 4200 × 3810 twips in the lower right corner of the Menu bar and Toolbar window (Figure 1-16). A twip is a printer's measurement equal to 1/1440 inch. However, the width of a twip can vary slightly from one computer monitor to another.

Positioning a Form

Use the following steps to set the location on the desktop for the Dollars To Francs window.

TRANSPARENCIES
Figure 1-17 through
Figure 1-19

TO POSITION A FORM ▼

STEP 1 ▶

Point to the title bar of the form window (Figure 1-17).

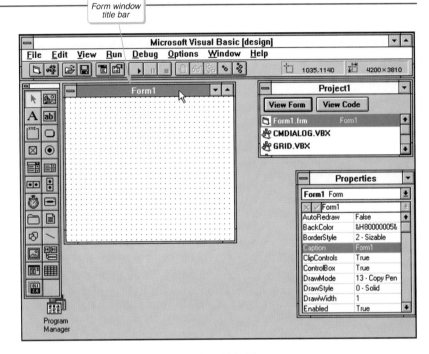

FIGURE 1-17

STEP 2 ▶

Drag the form window down and to the right.

The form window's new location appears as a shaded gray outline on the desktop (Figure 1-18).

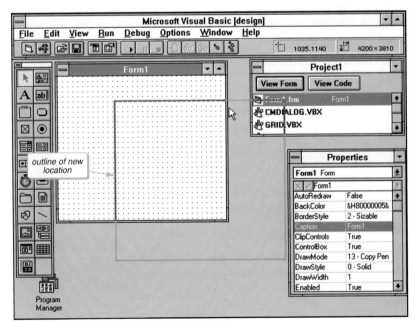

FIGURE 1-18

STEP 3 ▶

When the form is approximately centered on the desktop, release the left mouse button.

The form moves to the location outlined by the shaded lines (Figure 1-19). The location of the form's upper left corner is shown as two numbers (2445, 2040) in the lower right corner of the Menu bar and Toolbar window.

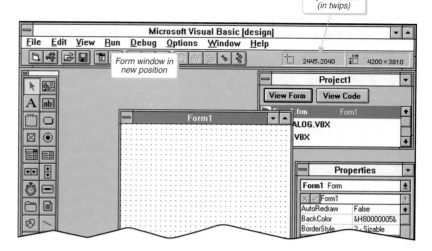

FIGURE 1-19

In the preceding steps, you set the form's location by dragging the form to the desired position. The form's location is given as two numbers. The first number (2445) is the distance in twips between the left side of the desktop and the left border of the form. The second number (2040) is the distance in twips between the top of the desktop and the top border of the form.

The form's location can be changed as often as desired during design time. Sometimes it is useful to temporarily move the form to work more easily in the other Visual Basic windows.

▶ ADDING AND REMOVING CONTROLS

Figure 1-1 on page VB3 shows some of the graphical images, or objects, common to many Windows applications. In Visual Basic, these objects also are called **controls**.

The Dollars To Francs application contains three different types of controls (Figure 1-20). These controls and their functions are:

▶ **Label**   A **label** is used to display text on a form. At run time the person using the application cannot change the text on a label, such as DOLLARS.

▶ **Text box**   A **text box** also is used to display text on a form, but their contents can be changed at run time by the person using the application. It frequently is used as a way for the user to supply information to the application.

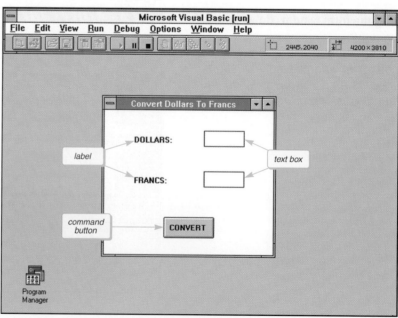

FIGURE 1-20

▸ **Command button** A **command button** is used during run time to initiate actions called **events.**

Adding Controls to a Form

Controls are added to a form by using tools from the group of tools found in the Visual Basic window called the **Toolbox.** Twenty-three tools are in the Toolbox of Visual Basic's standard edition. Additional controls are available in the professional edition of Visual Basic and from third-party vendors. Specific controls and their functions will be discussed as they are used throughout the projects in this book. Figure 1-21 shows the Toolbox containing the three tools that are used to draw controls in Project 1 (label, text box, and command button). The following steps use these tools to add controls to the form.

The names of all tools in the Toolbox are summarized in Figure 1-87 at the bottom of page VB44.

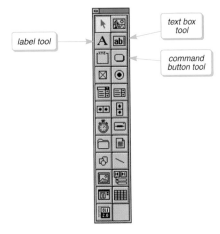

label tool

text box tool

command button tool

FIGURE 1-21

TRANSPARENCIES
Figure 1-20 and
Figure 1-21

LECTURE NOTES
■ Point out the controls
used in this project and
their respective tools in
the Toolbox.
■ Demonstrate moving,
closing and opening the
Toolbox.
■ Refer students to the
Toolbox Reference in
Figure 1-87 on page
VB44 for the names of all
the tools.

VB TIPS
■ The toolbox cannot be
minimized. When closed
it can be opened by
choosing the Toolbox
command from the
Window menu.

TRANSPARENCIES
Figure 1-22 through
Figure 1-26

TO DRAW LABELS ON A FORM ▼

STEP 1 ▶

Point to the label tool (A) in the Toolbox (Figure 1-22).

label tool

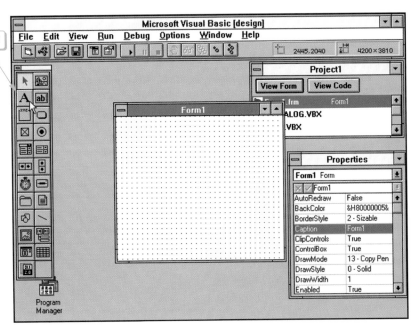

FIGURE 1-22

STEP 2 ▶

Click the left mouse button. Place the cross hair near the upper-left corner of the form by moving the mouse pointer.

The label tool in the Toolbox is highlighted, and the mouse pointer changes to a cross hair (+) when it is over the form (Figure 1-23). The upper-left corner of the label control will be positioned here.

FIGURE 1-23

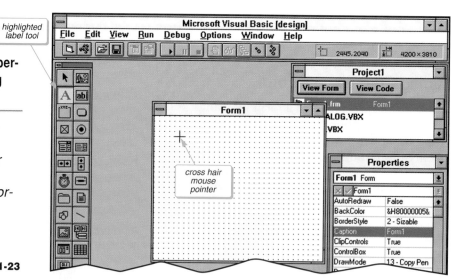

STEP 3 ▶

Drag the cross hair down and to the right.

A gray outline of the label control appears (Figure 1-24).

FIGURE 1-24

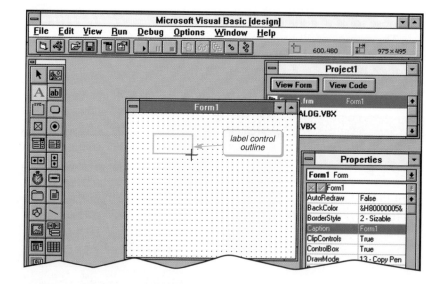

STEP 4 ▶

When the label control outline is the desired size, release the left mouse button.

*The gray outline changes to a solid background. The name of the label control (Label1) appears on the control. Small solid boxes called **sizing handles** appear at each corner and in the middle of each side of the label control (Figure 1-25).*

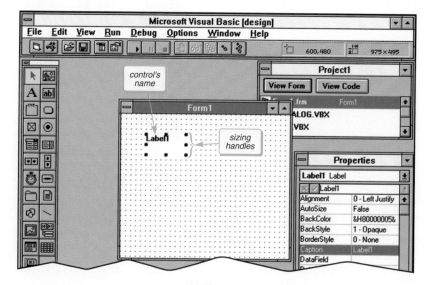

FIGURE 1-25

STEP 5 ▶

Repeat Steps 1 through 4 to draw a second label control on the form as shown in Figure 1-26.

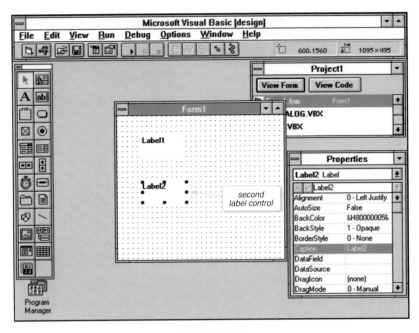

FIGURE 1-26

Two label controls have now been added to the form by drawing them with the label tool selected from the Toolbox. Complete the following steps to add two text box controls to the form.

TO DRAW TEXT BOXES ON A FORM ▼

STEP 1 ▶

Point to the text box tool ( ) in the Toolbox (Figure 1-27).

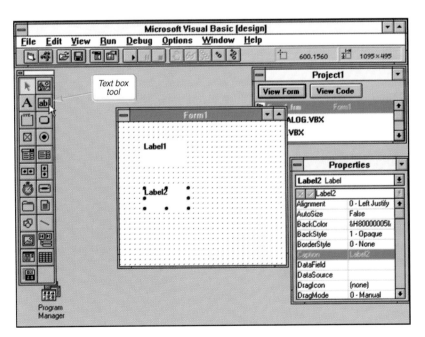

FIGURE 1-27

STEP 2 ▶

Click the left mouse button. Place the cross hair toward the middle-right side of the form.

The text box tool is highlighted in the Toolbox and the mouse pointer changes to a cross hair (Figure 1-28). The upper-left corner of the label control will be positioned here.

FIGURE 1-28

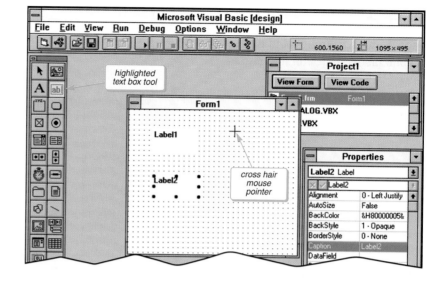

STEP 3 ▶

Drag the pointer down and to the right.

A gray outline of the text box control appears (Figure 1-29).

FIGURE 1-29

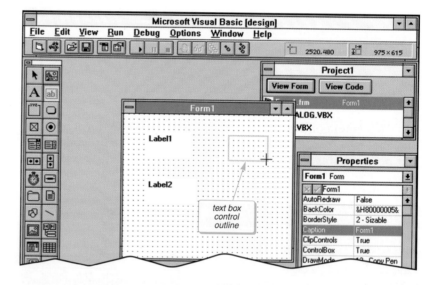

STEP 4 ▶

When the text box control outline is the size you want, release the left mouse button.

The gray outline changes to a solid background. The name of the text box control (Text1) appears on the control. Sizing handles appear at each corner and in the middle of each side of the text box control (Figure 1-30).

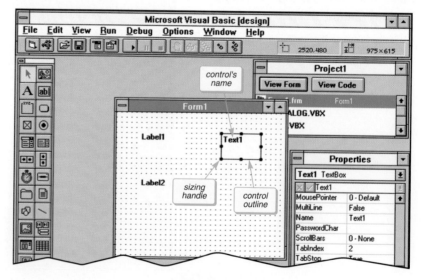

FIGURE 1-30

STEP 5 ▶

Repeat Steps 1 through 4 to place a second text box control on the form as shown in Figure 1-31.

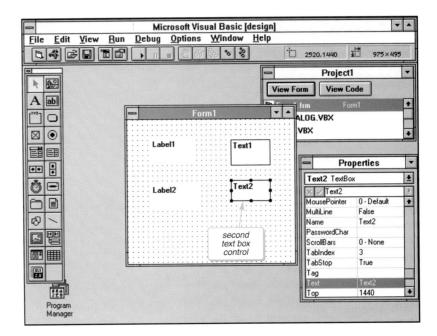

FIGURE 1-31

Two text boxes were added to the form in the same way as the two labels by selecting the tool from the Toolbox and then drawing the control's outline on the form. This method can be used for adding any of the controls in the Toolbox to a form. However, this method is not the only way to add controls to a form.

The following steps use an alternative method to add a command button to the Dollars To Francs form.

TO ADD CONTROLS BY DOUBLE-CLICKING ▼

STEP 1 ▶

Point to the command button tool (▢) in the Toolbox (Figure 1-32).

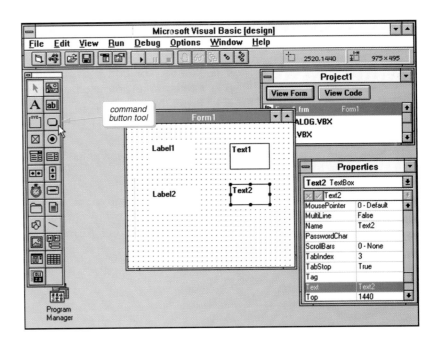

FIGURE 1-32

STEP 2 ►

Double-click the left mouse button.

The command button control appears in the center of the form. The control's name, Command1, appears on the control. Sizing handles appear around the command button control (Figure 1-33).

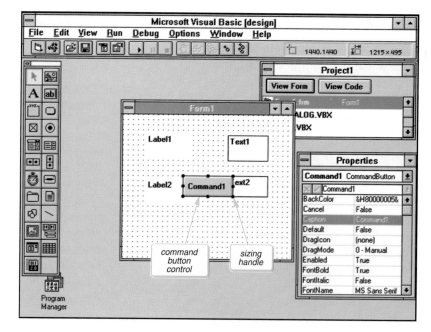

FIGURE 1-33

As you have just seen, double-clicking a tool in the Toolbox adds a default-sized control to the center of the form. If another control already is located in the center of the form, this method will add the new control on top of the previous control.

Removing Controls

If you choose the wrong control from the Toolbox or want to modify the project, controls can be removed from the form at any time during design time. Use the following steps to remove a control.

TO REMOVE A CONTROL

Step 1: Point to the control you want to remove.
Step 2: Click the left mouse button to select the control.
Step 3: Press the DELETE key.

▶ CHANGING THE LOCATION AND SIZE OF CONTROLS

I f you add a control to a form by double-clicking a tool in the Toolbox, you will need to move the control from the center of the form, and you frequently will want to change its size from the default. The location and size of any of the controls on a form can be changed at any time during design time.

Moving a Control on a Form

A control can be moved by dragging it to a new location. Perform the following steps to move the command button control from the center of the Dollars to Francs form.

LECTURE NOTES
■ Point out that dragging
and dropping objects is a
common Windows mouse
operation.

TRANSPARENCIES
Figure 1-34 through
Figure 1-36

TO MOVE A CONTROL ON A FORM ▼

STEP 1 ▶

Point to a location in the interior (not on any of the handles) of the Command1 command button control (Figure 1-34).

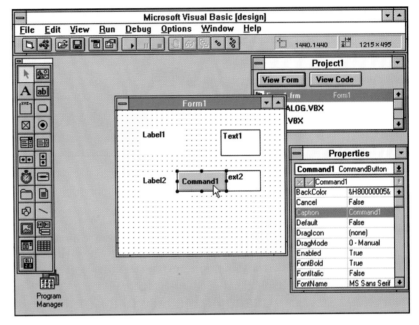

FIGURE 1-34

STEP 2 ▶

Drag the Command1 control toward the bottom of the form.

A gray outline of the command button control appears (Figure 1-35).

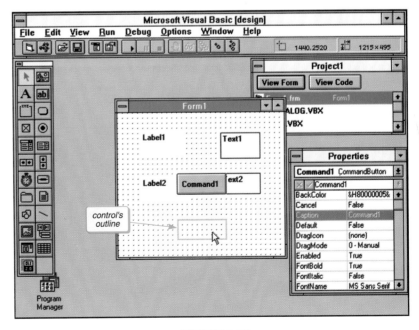

FIGURE 1-35

STEP 3 ▶

Move the pointer until the gray outline is at the desired location on the form, and then release the left mouse button.

The control moves to the location of the outline (Figure 1-36).

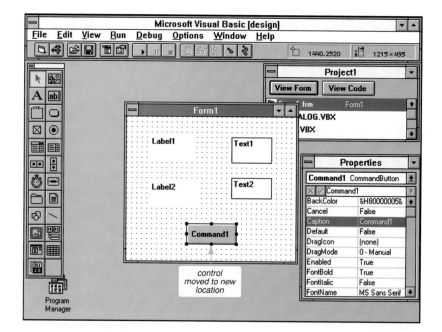

FIGURE 1-36

The location given to a control by dragging it across a form during design time is where the control will appear at the beginning of run time. However, a control doesn't have to remain in that location during run time. Changing a control's location during run time will be covered in a later project.

Changing the Size of a Control

TRANSPARENCIES
Figure 1-37 through
Figure 1-41

Controls can be made larger or smaller by dragging the sizing handles located around the control. Perform the following steps to make the Text1 control smaller.

TO CHANGE A CONTROL'S SIZE ▼

STEP 1 ▶

Select the Text1 text box control by pointing to the Text1 text box control and clicking the left mouse button.

Handles appear around the control (Figure 1-37).

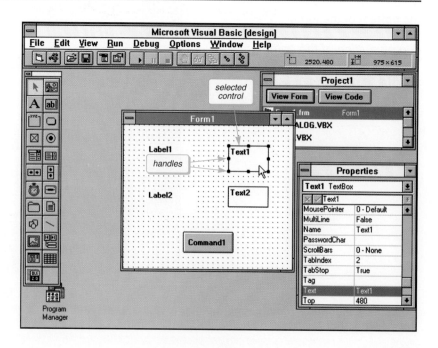

FIGURE 1-37

STEP 2 ▶

Point to the handle located at the center of the bottom border of the control.

The mouse pointer changes to a double arrow (Figure 1-38).

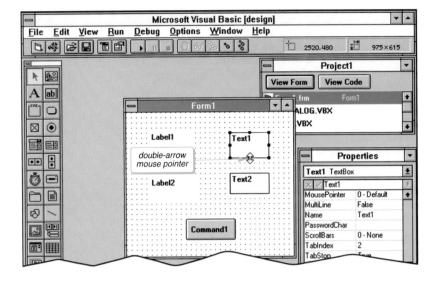

FIGURE 1-38

STEP 3 ▶

Drag the border toward the top of the screen approximately one-quarter of an inch.

The new position of the bottom border appears as a shaded gray line (Figure 1-39). Dragging a handle located in the center of one of the borders of a control moves that one border. Dragging one of the handles located at the corner of a control simultaneously moves the two borders that form the corner.

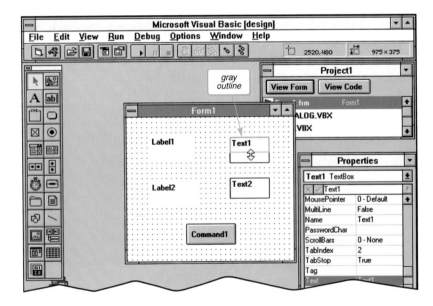

FIGURE 1-39

STEP 4 ▶

Release the left mouse button.

The bottom line of the Text1 text box control moves to the location of the outline (Figure 1-40).

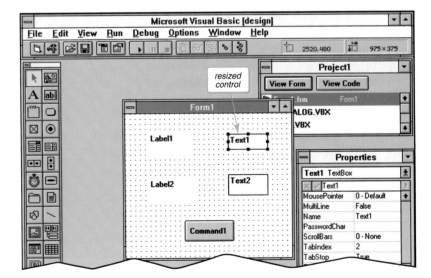

FIGURE 1-40

STEP 5 ▶

Repeat Steps 1 through 4 to resize the Text2 text box control to the size shown in Figure 1-41.

The form window now resembles the one shown in Figure 1-41.

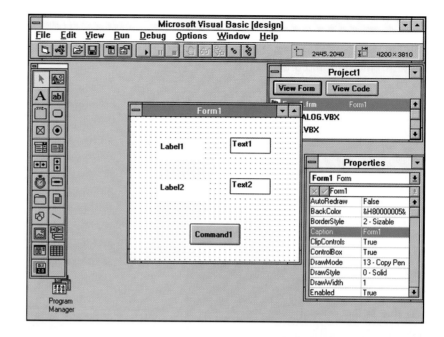

FIGURE 1-41

LECTURE NOTES
■ Point out that it may be necessary to make some adjustments in the controls' sizes and locations in order for the application to appear as shown in Figure 1-41.

TRANSPARENCY
Figure 1-42

Notice how similar the procedures are for setting the location and size of the form and for setting the locations and sizes of the labels, text boxes, and command button on the form. This similarity should not be surprising, though, because a Visual Basic form is a type of control. You will work more with form controls in Project 3.

▶ SETTING PROPERTIES

Now that controls have been added to the form, the next step in Visual Basic application development is to set the controls' **properties**. Properties are characteristics or attributes of a control, such as its color or the text that appears on top of it.

Properties are set at design time by using the Properties window (Figure 1-42). The Properties window consists of three sections:

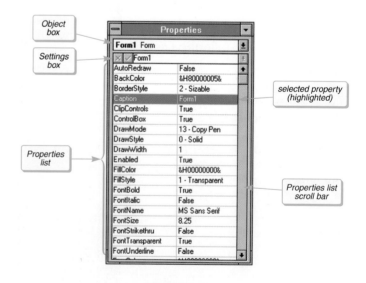

FIGURE 1-42

- ▶ **Object box** The **object box** displays the name of the control whose properties are being set.
- ▶ **Settings box** The **settings box** is where you enter a value for a specific property.
- ▶ **Properties list** The Properties list displays the set of properties belonging to the control named in the object box.

Different controls have different sets of properties. Since some controls' properties lists are very long, the Properties box has a scroll bar to move through the list. It is not necessary to set every property of each control because Visual Basic assigns initial values for each of the properties. Change only the properties that you want to differ from their initial values, called **default values**. The major properties of controls will be discussed as they are used throughout the projects in this book.

The following example sets the **Caption property** of the *Label1* label control. The Caption property of a control contains text that you want to appear on the control.

TO SET THE CAPTION PROPERTY ▼

STEP 1 ▶

Select the Label1 label control by pointing to the control and clicking the left mouse button.

Handles appear around the selected control. The control's name (Label1) appears in the Object box of the Properties window. The currently selected property (Caption) is highlighted in the Properties list, and its current value (Label1) is shown in the Settings box (Figure 1-43).

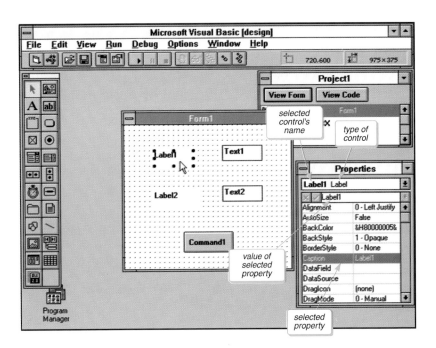

FIGURE 1-43

STEP 2 ▶

Point to the Caption property in the Properties list.

If the property you want to change is not visible in the Properties list (Figure 1-44), use the scroll bar of the Properties window to move the Properties list within the Properties window.

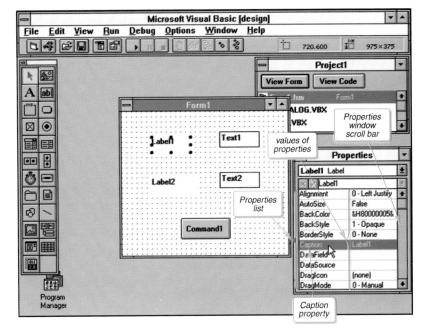

FIGURE 1-44

STEP 3 ▶

Double-click the left mouse button.

The Caption property is highlighted in the Properties list. The current value of the property, Label1, is highlighted in the Settings box (Figure 1-45).

FIGURE 1-45

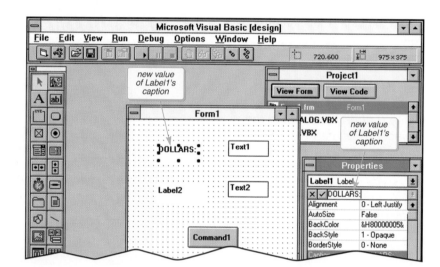

STEP 4 ▶

Type DOLLARS:

When you type the first character, the old value of the caption is replaced by that character. As you continue typing characters, they appear in the Settings box and on the label control on the form (Figure 1-46). If you make a mistake while typing, you can correct it by using the BACKSPACE *key or the* LEFT ARROW *and* DELETE *keys.*

FIGURE 1-46

STEP 5 ▶

Repeat Steps 1 through 4 to change the caption of the second label control from Label2 to FRANCS:

STEP 6 ▶

Repeat Steps 1 through 4 to change the caption of the command button control to CONVERT.

STEP 7 ▶

Select the form control by pointing to an empty area of the form that does not contain any other controls and clicking the left mouse button (Figure 1-47).

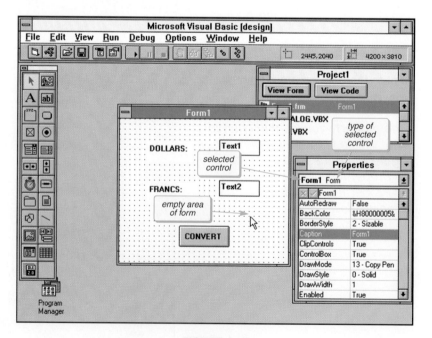

FIGURE 1-47

STEP 8 ▶

Repeat the procedures shown in Steps 2 through 4 to change the form control's caption from Form1 to Convert Dollars To Francs.

The form resembles the one shown in Figure 1-48.

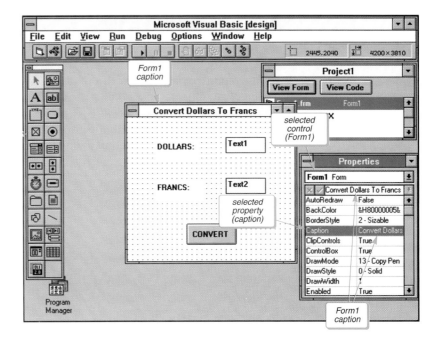

FIGURE 1-48

In the preceding steps, you changed the Caption property of four different types of controls. The caption of a label appears as text in the label control's location. This method is frequently used to place text in different locations on a form. The Caption property of a form appears as text in the title bar of the form.

An alternative method of selecting the control whose properties you want to change is to click the arrow to the right of the Object box (Figure 1-49), and then click the control's name from the drop-down list box that appears. This list expands as you add more controls to a form.

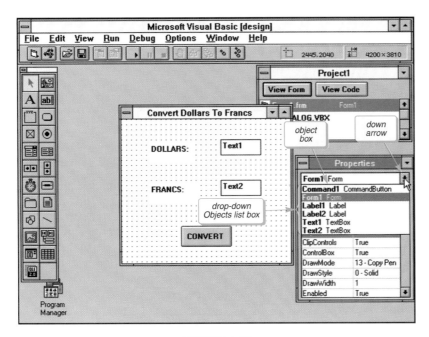

FIGURE 1-49

LECTURE NOTES
■ Demonstrate the use of the BACKSPACE and DELETE keys in the settings box.
■ Demonstrate selecting a control from the drop-down object list.

VB TIPS
■ A third method for selecting a control is listed in the Quick Reference on page VB45.

TRANSPARENCY
Figure 1-49

▶ THE TEXT PROPERTY

T he **Text property** of a text box is similar to the Caption property of a label. That is, whatever value you give to the Text property of a text box control appears in the text box at the beginning of run time. Later in this project you will see how to change the Text property during run time.

The default value of a text box's Text property (the text that appears within its borders) is the name of the control. In the Dollars to Francs application, the two text boxes should be empty when the application begins, so you will set their Text property to be blank, as described in the following steps.

TO SET THE TEXT PROPERTY ▼

STEP 1 ▶

Select the Text1 text box control by pointing to the Text1 text box control and clicking the left mouse button.

The selected control's name appears in the Object box of the Properties window (Figure 1-50).

FIGURE 1-50

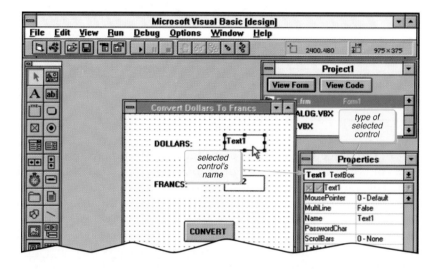

STEP 2 ▶

Point to the Text property in the Properties list.

If the property you want to change is not visible in the Properties list (Figure 1-51), use the scroll bar of the Properties window to move the Properties list within the Properties window.

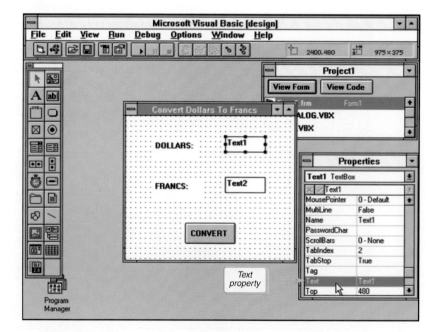

FIGURE 1-51

STEP 3 ▶

Double-click the left mouse button.

The Text property is highlighted in the Properties list, and the current value of the property, Text1, is highlighted in the Settings box (Figure 1-52).

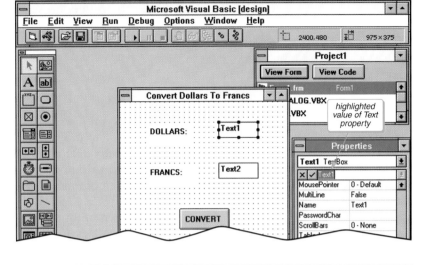

FIGURE 1-52

STEP 4 ▶

Change the contents of the Settings box to be blank by pressing the DELETE key.

The selected text box no longer has any text appearing within its borders (Figure 1-53).

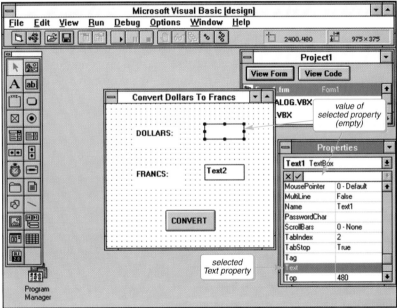

FIGURE 1-53

STEP 5 ▶

Repeat Steps 1 through 4 for the Text2 text box control.

The form appears as shown in Figure 1-54.

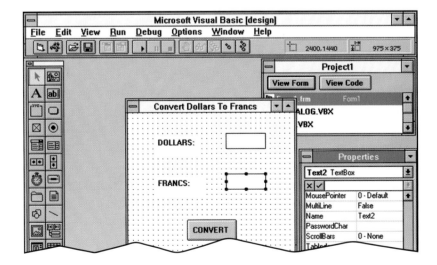

FIGURE 1-54

Notice how similar the procedures are for setting the Text property of the text boxes and for setting the Caption property of the labels. This same basic procedure is used for setting most of the properties of any type of control.

▶ NAMING CONTROLS

LECTURE NOTES
▪ Explain what is meant by a default name of a control.
▪ Explain the difference between a form's name and a form's caption.

VB TIPS
▪ Control names must begin with a letter and can be no longer than 40 characters.

V isual Basic assigns unique **default names** to controls, such as Form1, Label1, Label2, Text1, and Command1. Although Visual Basic initially sets the caption of some controls to be equal to the name of the control, the name of a control and the caption of a control are two different properties. For example, the caption of the command button in your application is CONVERT; its name is Command1.

Each control has its own unique name to distinguish it from a class of similar objects. For example, the Dollars To Francs application has more than one text box. It is very important in the application to distinguish which text box gets what text printed in it. Many times it is useful to give a different name to a control. This renaming often is useful with forms, which are themselves a type of control.

You will see in Project 3 that a single Visual Basic project can have more than one form and that forms created in one project can be can be used in other projects. For these reasons, it is useful to give each form you create a unique name. Forms are named by setting the **Name property** of the *form* control.

TRANSPARENCIES
Figure 1-55 through
Figure 1-59

Perform the following steps to change the Name property of the Form1 control.

TO CHANGE A CONTROL'S NAME ▼

STEP 1 ▶

Point to an empty area of the form that does not contain any other control.

Pointing to an empty area allows you to select the form rather than one of the controls on the form (Figure 1-55).

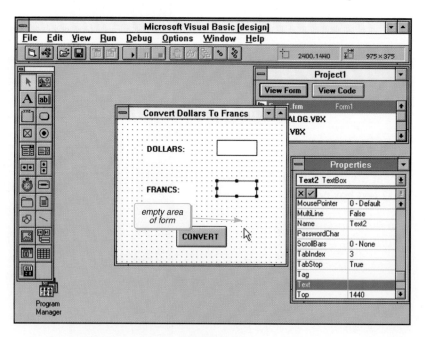

FIGURE 1-55

STEP 2 ▶

Select the Form1 control by clicking the left mouse button.

The form becomes the active window as indicated by the highlighted title bar. The form's name appears in the Object box of the Properties window (Figure 1-56).

FIGURE 1-56

STEP 3 ▶

Point to the down scroll arrow of the Properties box and click the left mouse button several times to bring the Name property into view.

As you click the left mouse button, the Properties list advances within the Properties window (Figure 1-57). An alternative to clicking the down scroll arrow is to drag the scroll box downward.

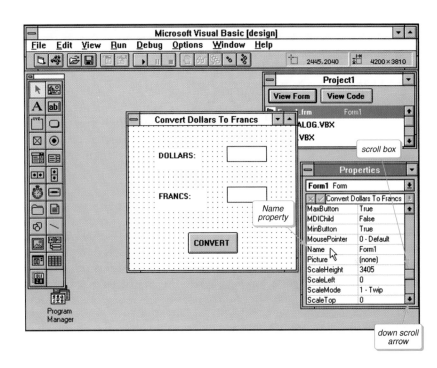

FIGURE 1-57

STEP 4 ▶

Select the Name property by pointing to the Name property in the Properties list and double-clicking the left mouse button.

The Name property is highlighted in the Properties list, and the value of the property, Form1, is highlighted in the Settings box (Figure 1-58).

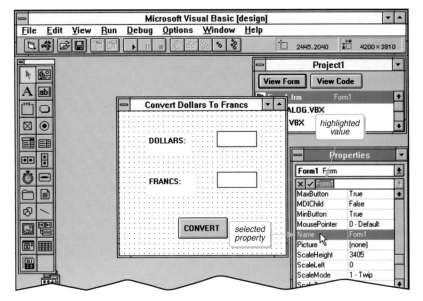

FIGURE 1-58

STEP 5 ▶

Type DLR2FRNC **and press the**
ENTER key.

The value of the form's name in
the Settings box is changed to
DLR2FRNC (Figure 1-59). Note
that the form's caption in the title
bar is unchanged because this
property is different from the
Name property.

FIGURE 1-59

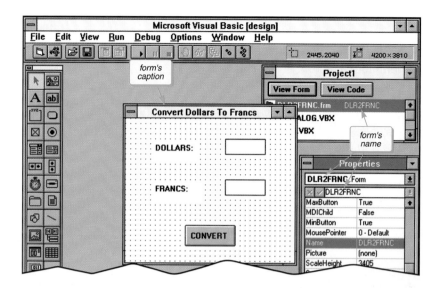

When you save a Visual Basic project, forms are saved as separate files with a
file extension **.frm**. Since filenames cannot be longer than eight characters, the
default filename for the form is the first eight characters of the form's Name property. To make the form's name in Visual Basic the same as its filename, give the
form a name that is no more than eight characters.

▶ EVENT PROCEDURES

LECTURE NOTES
■ Review the three steps
used to build applications
with Visual Basic.
■ Ask the students to
identify some common
events within Windows
applications with which
they are familiar. Ask the
students to give examples
of the actions that occur
in these applications
when the common events
are combined with
specific controls in the
applications.

Development of the Dollars To Francs application began by building the
user interface, which consisted of a form and controls. The properties of
the controls were then set. The remaining step in developing the application is to write the **event procedures** or **events** that will occur within the
application. Events are the actions that occur when the application runs.

Events can be actions by the user, such as clicking or dragging a control.
Events also can be **code statements**, sometimes just called **code**. Code statements
are instructions to the computer written at design time for the computer to execute at run time. Visual Basic has its own **language**, the words and symbols used
to write these instructions. This language is very similar to Beginner's All-Purpose
Symbolic Instruction Code (**BASIC**).

Students who have had previous experience with BASIC language programming will be able to move to much more complex event procedures quite easily.
However, all of the BASIC or BASIC-like code needed for the projects in this book
will be explained at the time it is presented.

In Visual Basic, many predefined events are common to many of the different
types of controls. A control's name is used to associate common events with a specific control on a form. For example, clicking the left mouse button, the **Click**
event, is common to most types of Visual Basic controls. Text boxes are one type,
or *class*, of objects that can be associated with the click event. Each individual text
box on a form is called an *instance* of the class and can be uniquely identified by
its name. When the mouse is clicked with its pointer positioned on a specific
instance of a class, such as the Text1 instance of the text box class, these elements
combine to form a unique event, Text1_Click.

Many times, the things you want to occur in response to events can be expressed as changes in the values of the properties of objects on the form. Although Visual Basic is not truly an Object Oriented Programming language, this type of application development is often referred to as being **event-driven**, and **object-oriented**.

The following steps add the event procedure that converts dollars to francs and displays the result in the Text2 text box when the CONVERT button is clicked during run time.

TRANSPARENCIES
Figure 1-60 through
Figure 1-66

TO WRITE AN EVENT ▼

STEP 1 ►

Point to the Command1 command button control with a caption of CONVERT.

Although you changed the command button's caption to CONVERT (Figure 1-60), its name is still Command1, the name supplied by Visual Basic when you added the control to the form. If you had more than one command button on the form, you might want to change the control's name to cmdConvert or something that more clearly identifies its function.

FIGURE 1-60

STEP 2 ►

Select the command button control by double-clicking the left mouse button.

*The **Code window** opens on the desktop (Figure 1-61). The name of the control you selected appears in the Object box of the Code window. Two lines of code for the Click event procedure display in the Code window.*

FIGURE 1-61

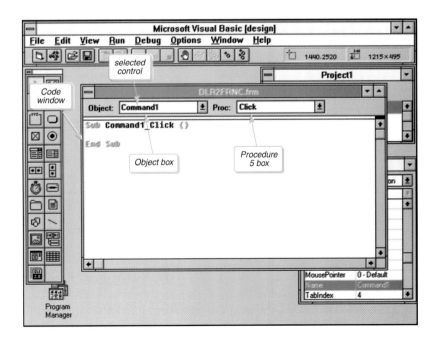

STEP 3 ▶

Point to the arrow to the right of the Procedures box, and then click the left mouse button.

A Procedure list box containing all the event procedures that can be associated with the Command1 control displays (Figure 1-62).

FIGURE 1-62

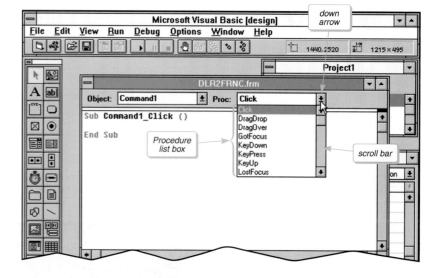

STEP 4 ▶

Point to the Click event procedure in the Procedure list box (Figure 1-63).

FIGURE 1-63

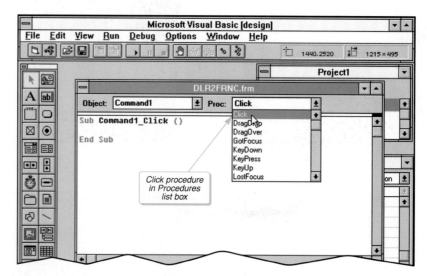

STEP 5 ▶

Click the left mouse button.

The insertion point (|) appears at the beginning of a blank line in between the two code statements (Figure 1-64).

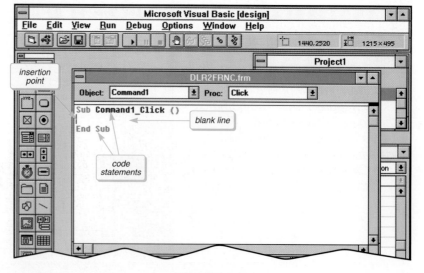

FIGURE 1-64

STEP 6 ▶

Type text2.text = text1.text * 5.7345 **on one line as shown in Figure 1-65.**

The code appears in the second line of the Code window. This code statement changes the value of the text property of the Text2 control to equal the value of the text property of the Text1 control times 5.7345, the exchange rate between dollars and francs. This statement will execute whenever the CONVERT button is clicked during run time.

FIGURE 1-65

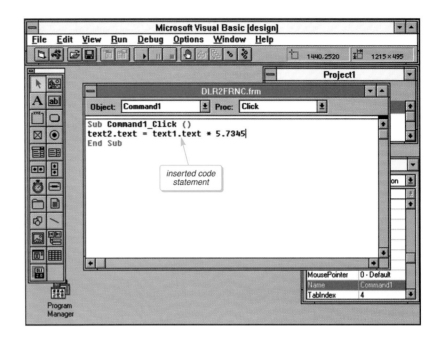

STEP 7 ▶

Close the Code window by pointing at the Code window's Control-menu box and double-clicking the left mouse button (Figure 1-66).

FIGURE 1-66

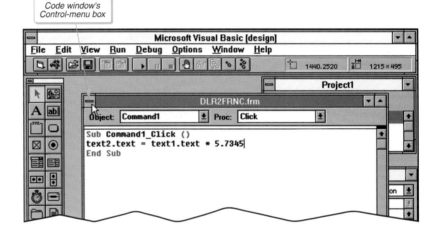

The event procedures in Visual Basic are written in blocks of code called **subroutines**. Each block begins with a statement that includes the subroutine's name and ends with a statement that indicates no further instructions are within that subroutine. These first and last statements are supplied by Visual Basic when you begin a new event subroutine.

The Code window functions as a text editor for writing your code statements. You can add and change text within the window in the same manner presented earlier in the Notepad application in *Introduction to Windows*.

▶ SAVING A PROJECT

T he Dollars To Francs application is now complete. Before starting a new Visual Basic project or exiting Visual Basic, you should save your work. You also should save your project periodically while you are working on it and before you run it for the first time.

LECTURE NOTES
■ Explain that code statements are interpreted when the ENTER key is pressed.
■ Demonstrate typing an incorrect statement in the Code window to show a syntax error dialog box.
■ Demonstrate how to edit code statements within the Code window.

LECTURE NOTES
■ Explain the difference between saving a form to a file and saving a project to a file.
■ Use a text editor to show students the contents of a Visual Basic project (.MAK) file.
■ Explain the difference between a form's name, caption, and filename.

TRANSPARENCIES
Figure 1-67 through Figure 1-71

Visual Basic projects are saved as a set of files. Forms are saved as files with a filename and a .frm extension. Visual Basic creates an additional file to save the project. This file has a filename and a **.mak** extension. You specify the path and filename for these files using the Save File As dialog box and the Save Project As dialog box. The Save File As and Save Project As boxes are the same in many different Windows applications. They are called common dialog boxes. Use both of these dialog boxes in Visual Basic in the same way that you used the *Save As* dialog box to save a file on pages WIN25–WIN27 in *Introduction to Windows*.

The following example illustrates how to save a project to drive A. It is assumed you have a formatted diskette in drive A.

TO SAVE A PROJECT ▼

STEP 1 ▶

Point to the Save Project icon (▣) on the Toolbar, and then click the left mouse button.

The Save File As dialog box opens (Figure 1-67). The default filename in the dialog box is the name you gave to the form previously.

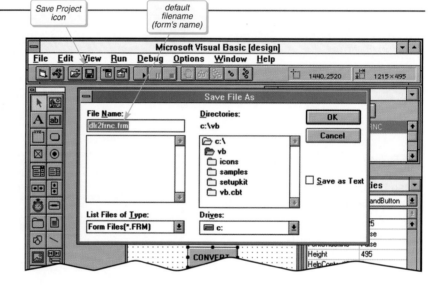

FIGURE 1-67

STEP 2 ▶

Point to the down arrow at the right of the Drives box, and then click the left mouse button.

A drop-down list box of drives appears (Figure 1-68).

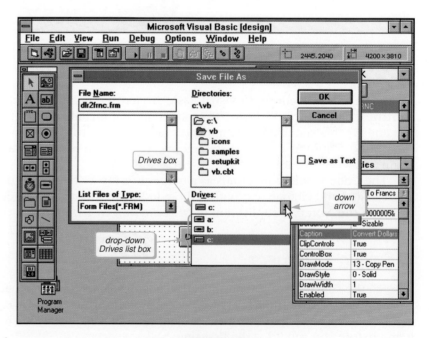

FIGURE 1-68

STEP 3 ►

Point to drive A in the drop-down list box, and then click the left mouse button.

The drop-down list closes, and drive A becomes the selected drive (Figure 1-69).

FIGURE 1-69

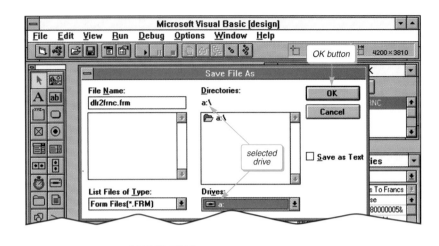

STEP 4 ►

Point to the OK button in the Save File As dialog box, and then click the left mouse button.

The form is saved as the file dlr2frnc.frm, and the Save Project As dialog box appears (Figure 1-70). The default project name, project1.mak, appears in the File Name box.

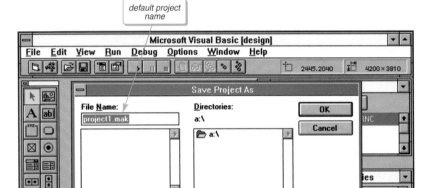

FIGURE 1-70

STEP 5 ►

Type currency

The default name for the project is replaced in the File Name box with the characters you typed (Figure 1-71). If you make an error while typing, you can use the BACKSPACE *key or the* LEFT ARROW *and* DELETE *keys to erase the mistake and then continue typing.*

STEP 6 ►

Point to the OK button in the Save Project As dialog box. Click the left mouse button.

The project is saved as currency.mak and the dialog box closes.

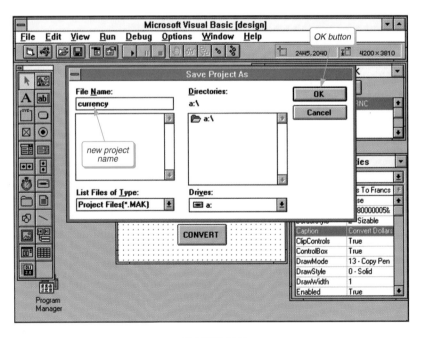

FIGURE 1-71

In the Save File As dialog box you specified the drive used to save the form file, but you did not need to change the drive in the Save Project As dialog box. After you change a drive or directory in any of the common dialog boxes, it remains current in all the dialog boxes until you change it again.

You can resave your work without opening the common dialog box by clicking the Save Project icon on the toolbar. If you want to save your work with a different filename, directory, or drive, you must choose the Save File As command after selecting the File menu from the Menu bar.

▶ STARTING, OPENING, AND RUNNING PROJECTS

 his section shows how to start a new project, open an existing project, and run a project within the Visual Basic environment.

Starting a New Project

When you started Visual Basic, a new project opened automatically. The form had no controls or event procedures, and all properties had their default values. It is not necessary to restart Visual Basic each time you want to build a new application. Before beginning a new application, you should be certain that you have saved any work you don't want to lose. Since you already have saved the Dollars To Francs application, perform the follow steps to begin another project.

TO START A NEW PROJECT ▼

STEP 1 ▶

Point to the File menu in the Menu bar, and click the left mouse button.

The File menu displays (Figure 1-72).

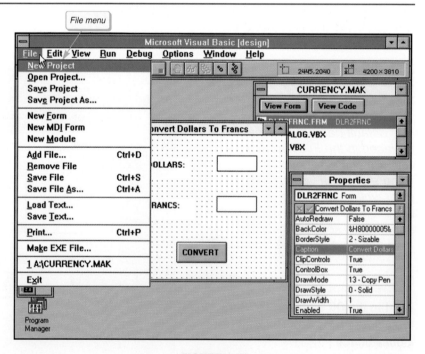

FIGURE 1-72

STEP 2 ▶

Point to the New Project command in the File menu (Figure 1-73).

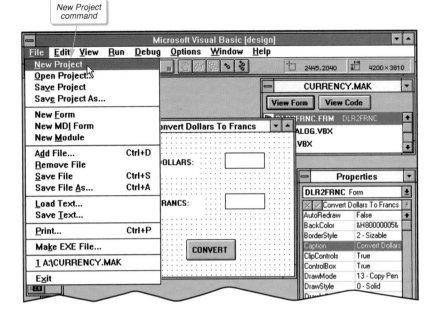

FIGURE 1-73

STEP 3 ▶

Click the left mouse button.

Five Visual Basic windows appear on the desktop with an empty form (Figure 1-74). The new form has the default form name, Form1, and the project has the default project name, Project1.

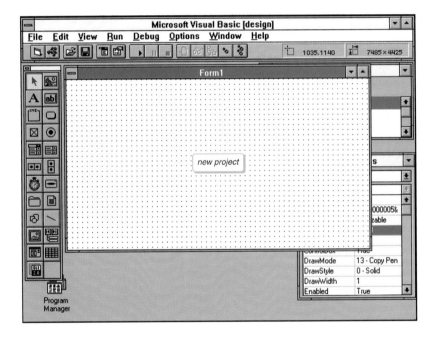

FIGURE 1-74

Each time you start Visual Basic, a new project is opened. In the preceding steps you learned it is not necessary to restart Visual Basic to begin a new project. If you attempt to open a new project before saving the current project, Visual Basic will display a message box asking if you want to save the previous work.

Opening a Project

Once a project has been saved, you can return to that project and make changes. You tell Visual Basic which project you want to use through an Open Project dialog box that is similar to the Save File As dialog box. The example on the following page opens the project completed previously.

TRANSPARENCIES
Figure 1-75 through
Figure 1-77

TO OPEN A PROJECT ▼

STEP 1 ▶

Point to the Open Project icon (▣)
on the Toolbar, and then click the
left mouse button.

*The Open Project dialog box
appears (Figure 1-75). If drive A is
not the selected drive, you can
change it in the same way you
changed the selected drive when
you saved the form file.*

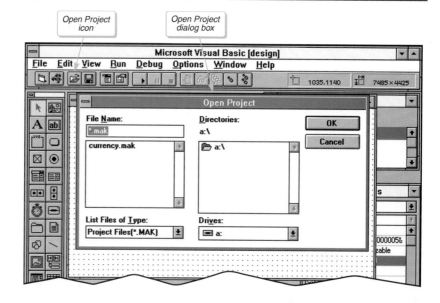

FIGURE 1-75

STEP 2 ▶

Point to the project's name,
currency.mak, in the file list.

*If the project's name is not visible
in the file list, use the scroll bar to
move the list until its name is
visible (Figure 1-76).*

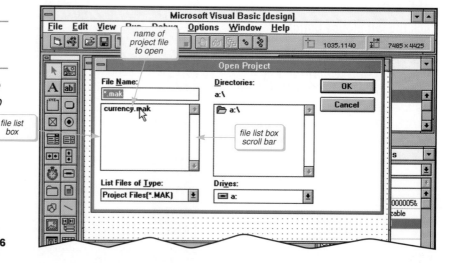

FIGURE 1-76

STEP 3 ▶

Double-click the left mouse button.

*The files are read into memory,
and the Project window listing all
of the files associated with the
project opens on the desktop
(Figure 1-77). The Form window
is reopened by clicking the View
Form button.*

FIGURE 1-77

When you save a project, save the form file first and then save the project file. When you open a project, open only the project file. Any other files associated with that project are opened automatically. All of these files are listed in the Project window.

Running an Application

In the following example, the Dollars To Francs application is run from within the Visual Basic environment. In Project 3, you will learn how to run Visual Basic applications from Windows' Program Manager. In the following example, the application is started by using the Toolbar.

TO RUN AN APPLICATION ▼

STEP 1 ▶

Point to the Run icon (▣) on the toolbar. Click the left mouse button.

The word design in the Visual Basic title bar changes to run. The application's window appears on the desktop, and the cursor moves to the first text box (Figure 1-78).

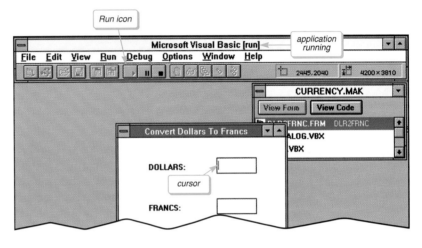

FIGURE 1-78

STEP 2 ▶

Type 520

The number appears in the first text box (Figure 1-79). You can change or edit your entry using the BACKSPACE *key or the* LEFT ARROW *and* DELETE *keys.*

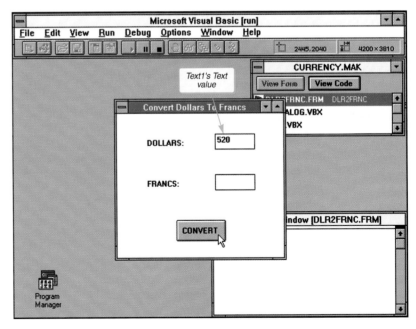

FIGURE 1-79

STEP 3 ▶

Point to the command button with the CONVERT caption. Click the left mouse button.

The number 2981.94 appears in the second text box (Figure 1-80). Thus, $520 = 2981.94 Francs.

STEP 4 ▶

Point to the Stop icon (■) on the toolbar. Click the left mouse button.

The application closes, and the design environment returns to the desktop.

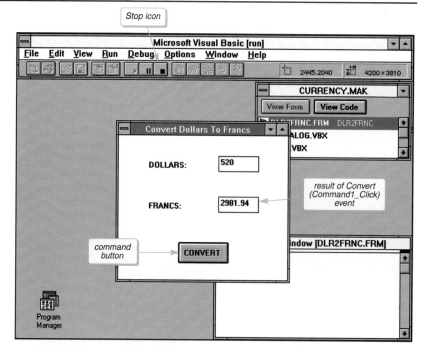

FIGURE 1-80

LECTURE NOTES
■ Point out the many Windows application features automatically added to the application (e.g., Minimize and Maximize buttons, Control menu).

Run your application again, trying different numbers for the Dollars amount. You do not need to restart the application each time you want to do another conversion. Use the mouse to click the first text box, press the DELETE key several times to erase your entry, and type a new number. Click the CONVERT button.

While the application is running, click the application's Minimize button. The application reduces to an icon, just like other Windows applications. Double-click the icon to continue working with the application. You can also close (stop) the application by double-clicking the Control-menu box of the application, like other Windows applications.

LECTURE NOTES
■ Demonstrate minimizing and restoring Visual Basic.

TRANSPARENCY
Figure 1-81

▶ EXITING VISUAL BASIC

J ust like other Windows applications, Visual Basic can be minimized to an icon to allow you to temporarily work with another application such as a spreadsheet or word processor. You then can return by double-clicking the Visual Basic icon.

When you have completed working with Visual Basic, you should exit the Visual Basic program to conserve memory space for other Windows applications. The following step shows how to exit Visual Basic.

TO EXIT VISUAL BASIC ▼

STEP 1 ▶

Point to the Visual Basic Control-menu box. Double-click the left mouse button.

If you made changes to the project since the last time it was saved, Visual Basic displays a dialog box (Figure 1-81). Click the Yes button to resave your project and exit. Click the No button to exit without saving the changes. Click the Cancel button to remove the dialog box.

FIGURE 1-81

An alternative method of exiting Visual Basic is to choose the Exit command from the File menu.

▶ VISUAL BASIC ONLINE HELP FACILITY

The Visual Basic programming system includes an extensive online help facility. You can access the Help facility any time you are working with Visual Basic by selecting the Help menu from the Menu bar (Figure 1-82).

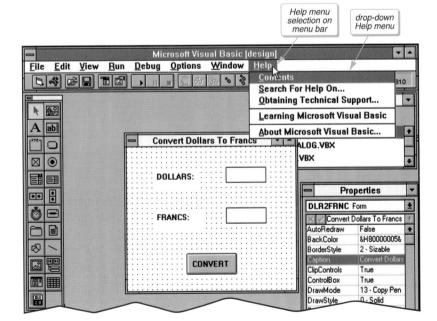

FIGURE 1-82

Help Menu

The Visual Basic Help menu includes a table of contents (Figure 1-83) and a search command for navigating around the Help facility (Figure 1-84). Once you have opened the Help facility, you can get information about how to use it by pressing function key F1.

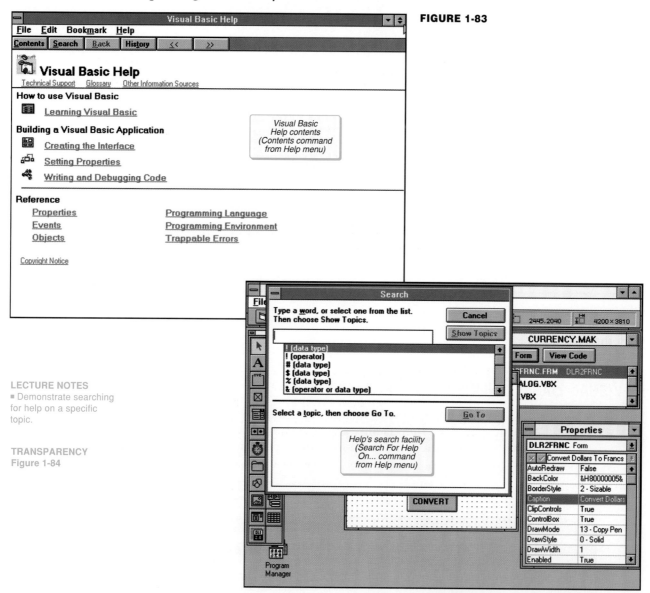

FIGURE 1-83

FIGURE 1-84

Context-Sensitive Help

You can get help on many parts of Visual Basic without using the Help menu. This feature is called **context-sensitive help**. You can get help on any context-sensitive part of Visual Basic by pressing function key F1. For example, to get help about the Menu bar and Toolbar, click the title bar of the Visual Basic Menu bar and Toolbar window, and then press F1. Visual Basic opens the Help facility and displays the section on the Menu bar and Toolbar (Figure 1-85).

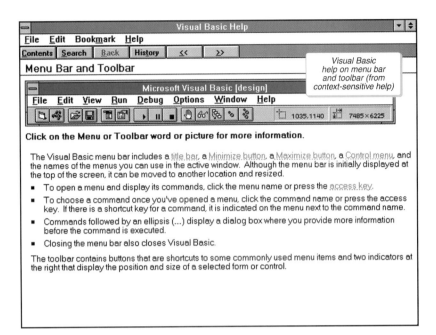

FIGURE 1-85

Double-click the Help window's control-menu box to exit the help facility and return to the design environment.

Visual Basic Tutorial

You can improve your Visual Basic skills by working through the online **tutorial**. The tutorial is accessed by choosing the Learning Microsoft Visual Basic command item in the Help menu. The tutorial contains seven Visual Basic lessons (Figure 1-86). Before starting any of these lessons, you first should complete the lesson on how to use the tutorial by clicking the Instructions button.

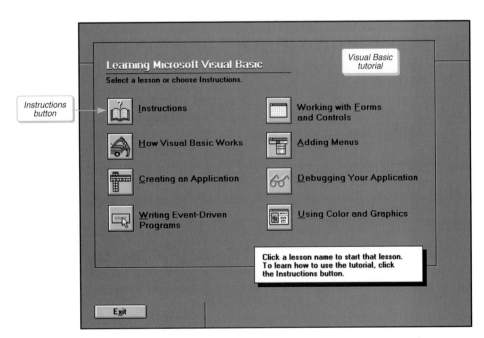

FIGURE 1-86

▶ PROJECT SUMMARY

Project 1 introduced the major elements of Visual Basic by developing a Windows application. The process to build the application consisted of three steps:

- ▶ **Create The User Interface**   Draw the form and controls (objects)
- ▶ **Set Properties**   Set values of properties for the objects added to the form
- ▶ **Write Code**   Create the events and actions that will occur when the application runs

You learned how to start Visual Basic, design a form, and add labels, text boxes, and command buttons to a form. You learned the process for changing the properties of controls by setting caption, text, and name properties. After the graphical user interface of your application was built, you learned how to specify an event procedure. You then learned how to run and save your application and how to start a new project or open an existing project. At the end of Project 1 you learned how to access information about Visual Basic through the Help facility and on-line tutorial.

▶ KEY TERMS

applications (*VB2*)
application software (*VB2*)
BASIC (*VB30*)
caption property (*VB23*)
click event (*VB30*)
code (*VB30*)
code statements (*VB30*)
code window (*VB31*)
command button (*VB13*)
context-sensitive help (*VB42*)
controls (*VB12*)
default names (*VB28*)
default values (*VB23*)
design time (*VB7*)
event (*VB13, VB30*)
event-driven (*VB31*)

event procedures (*VB30*)
form (*VB7*)
.FRM file (*VB30*)
graphical user interface (*VB2*)
GUI (*VB2*)
handles (*VB14*)
Help facility (*VB41*)
label (*VB12*)
language (*VB30*)
.mak file (*VB34*)
Menu bar (*VB5*)
Name property (*VB28*)
Object box (*VB22*)
object-oriented (*VB31*)
objects (*VB2*)
Procedure list box (*VB32*)

project (*VB7*)
properties (*VB22*)
Properties list (*VB22*)
run time (*VB7*)
settings box (*VB22*)
subroutines (*VB33*)
text box (*VB12*)
text property (*VB26*)
toolbar (*VB5*)
Toolbox (*VB13*)
tutorial (*VB43*)
twips (*VB10*)
user interface (*VB2*)
Visual Basic programming
  environment (*VB5*)

▶ TOOLBAR AND TOOLBOX REFERENCE

The Toolbar and Toolbox Reference shown in Figure 1-87 identifies the icons on the toolbar and the tools in the Toolbox.

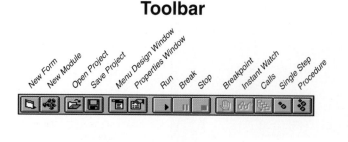

Toolbar

Toolbox

FIGURE 1-87

In Visual Basic you can accomplish a task in a number of ways. The following table provides a quick reference to each of the major tasks presented for the first time in the project with some of the available options. The commands listed in the Menu column can be executed using either the keyboard or mouse.

Task	Mouse	Menu	Keyboard Shortcuts
Activate a Window	Click the window to be activated	From Window menu, choose window title	Press ALT+F6 to toggle between last two active windows
Add a Control to a Form	Double-click control's icon in Toolbox		Press ENTER to add the selected tool in the toolbox
Open a Code Window	Click View Code button in Project window	From View menu, choose Code	Press F7
Open the Help Facility		From Help menu, choose appropriate command	Press F1 for context-sensitive help
Remove a Selected Control from a Form			Press DELETE
Resave a Modified Form with the Same File Name	Click Save Form icon on toolbar	From File menu, choose Save File	
Resave a Modified Project with the Same File Name	Click Save Project icon on toolbar	From File menu, choose Save Project	
Save a Form File with a New File Name		From File menu, choose Save File As	Press CTRL+A (when form window is active)
Save a Project File with a New File Name		From File menu, choose Save Project As	
Select a Control on a Form	Click on Control to be Selected		Press TAB to cycle through control on form (form window must be active window)
Select a Tool in the Toolbox	Click on tool in toolbox		Use arrow keys to move through tools (toolbox must be active window)
Select a Control in the Active Properties Window	Click down arrow next to Object box to open drop-down objects list. Click control's name in objects list.		Press SHIFT+TAB to give object box focus. Press F4 to open list. Use UP and DOWN ARROWS to move through list and press ENTER.
Select a Property in the Active Properties Window	Use scroll bar to move through list and click property's name.		Use UP and DOWN ARROWS to move through list and press ENTER
Start (Run) an Application	Click Run tool in toolbar	From Run menu, choose Start	Press F5
Stop (End) an Application	Click Stop tool in toolbar	From Run menu, choose End	Press CTRL+BREAK

EXERCISE NOTES
■Use Student Assign-
ments 1–6 for classroom
discussion or homework
exercises.

STUDENT ASSIGNMENT 1
True/False

Instructions: Circle T if the statement is true or F if the statement is false.

Ⓣ F   1. Visual Basic is a Windows application.
Ⓣ F   2. Visual Basic is used to build Windows applications.
Ⓣ F   3. A form can be resized by dragging its borders.
T Ⓕ   4. The text in a label control can be changed by the user at run time.
T Ⓕ   5. Controls are added to the form by selecting them from the control list in the Code window.
Ⓣ F   6. The location of a control on a form is changed by dragging the control to the new location.
T Ⓕ   7. The Object box of the Properties window is where you enter a value for a specific property.
T Ⓕ   8. All controls have the same set of properties.
T Ⓕ   9. At design time, you must set the values of all properties of the controls on a form.
Ⓣ F   10. A form is a control.
T Ⓕ   11. A project cannot have the same name as a form used within that project.
T Ⓕ   12. Forms are saved as a file with a filename and .MAK extension.
Ⓣ F   13. Double-clicking a control will open the Code window and show the event code for that control.
T Ⓕ   14. You must exit Visual Basic before you can switch to another Windows application.
Ⓣ F   15. A new project is opened each time you start Visual Basic.
T Ⓕ   16. You can open previously saved projects by using the Save File As dialog box.
T Ⓕ   17. Projects must be saved in the VB30 subdirectory.
T Ⓕ   18. To activate the Help facility, press function key F3.
Ⓣ F   19. To get help about using the Help facility, press function key F1 twice.
T Ⓕ   20. To get help about any topic, you always must use the Help menu.

STUDENT ASSIGNMENT 2
Multiple Choice

Instructions: Circle the correct response.

1. You specify the text you want to appear in a form's title bar by setting the _____ property of the form.
   a. text
   b. title
   ⓒ caption
   d. name
2. The purpose of handles is to _____.
   a. move a form
   b. select controls from the toolbox
   c. grab a drop-down menu list box
   ⓓ resize controls
3. The Code window contains a drop-down list of _____.
   a. properties
   ⓑ controls
   c. code statements
   d. .frm files
4. The _____ property of a command button contains text that will appear on the control.
   a. name
   ⓑ caption
   c. text
   d. label
5. You select a property from the Properties list by _____ the name of the property.
   ⓐ clicking
   b. pointing to
   c. double-clicking
   d. dragging
6. Forms are saved as files that have a filename and _____ extension.
   a. .mak
   ⓑ .frm
   c. .bas
   d. .vbx

7. The Visual Basic window that contains icons representing frequently used menu commands is the
   _____.
   a. Toolbox
   b. Project window
   c. Menu bar and Toolbar window
   d. Menu box
8. The last code statement in an event procedure is _____.
   a. run
   b. end sub
   c. return
   d. run
9. The Visual Basic tutorial is accessed by choosing _____ from the Help menu.
   a. About Microsoft Visual Basic...
   b. Introducing Microsoft Visual Basic
   c. Learning Microsoft Visual Basic
   d. Microsoft Visual Basic Tutorial
10. Context-sensitive help _____.
    a. is not available in Visual Basic
    b. accesses Help without going through the Help menu
    c. can be accessed from the Help menu
    d. provides help on using the Help facility

STUDENT ASSIGNMENT 3
Understanding The Visual Basic Environment

Instructions: In Figure SA1-3, arrows point to the windows that make up the Visual Basic programming environment. Identify these windows in the space provided.

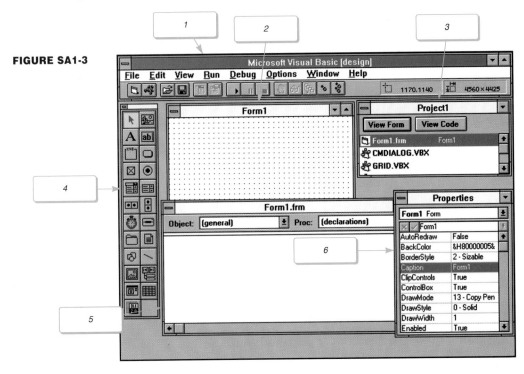

FIGURE SA1-3

1:   Menu bar and Toolbar window
2:   Form window
3:   Project window
4:   Toolbox
5:   Code window
6:   Properties window

STUDENT ASSIGNMENT 4
Understanding the Toolbox and Properties Window

Instructions: In Figure SA1-4, arrows point to some of the tool icons in the Toolbox and to the major components of the Properties window. Identify these in the space provided.

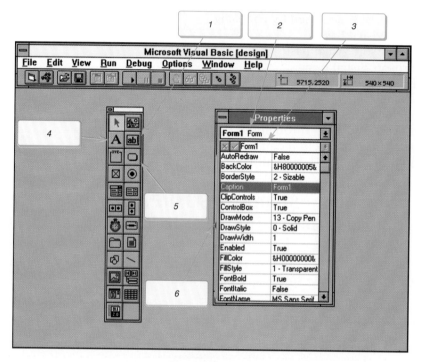

FIGURE SA1-4

1: text box tool
2: object box
3: settings box
4: label tool
5: command button tool
6: properties list

STUDENT ASSIGNMENT 5
Understanding the Menu Bar, Toolbar, and Code Window

Instructions: In Figure SA1-5 on the next page, arrows point to some of the important components of the Menu Bar, Toolbar, and Code window. Identify these components in the space provided.

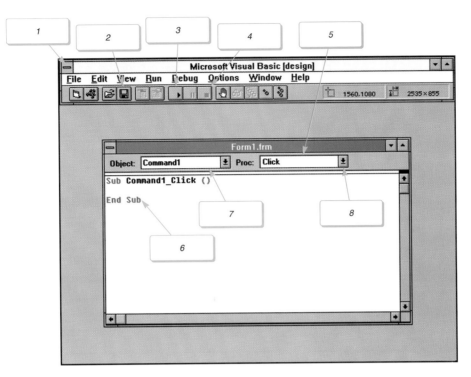

FIGURE SA1-5

1: Control-menu box

2: Save Project icon

3: Run icon

4: Stop icon

5: procedure box

6: ending statement in a subroutine

7: object box

8: down arrow (drop-down procedures list)

STUDENT ASSIGNMENT 6
Understanding Control Names, Properties, and Property Values

Instructions: Three different examples of the Properties window are shown in Figure SA1-6 on the next page. For each of these examples, identify the following:

a. the name of the selected control
b. the type of control
c. the selected property
d. the value of the selected property

STUDENT ASSIGNMENT 6 (continued)

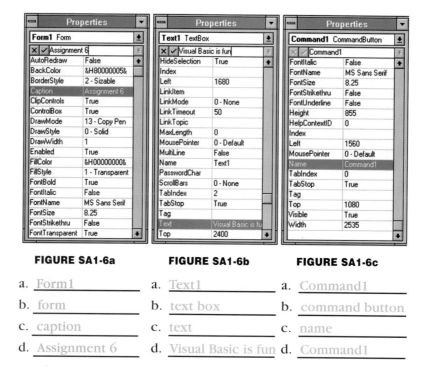

FIGURE SA1-6a   FIGURE SA1-6b   FIGURE SA1-6c

a. Form1   a. Text1   a. Command1

b. form   b. text box   b. command button

c. caption   c. text   c. name

d. Assignment 6   d. Visual Basic is fun   d. Command1

COMPUTER LABORATORY EXERCISES

COMPUTER LABORATORY EXERCISE 1
Using the Help Menu, Context-Sensitive Help, and Visual Basic Tutorial

Instructions: Perform the following tasks using a computer.

1. Start Visual Basic.
2. Minimize Program Manager.
3. Choose the contents command from the Help menu on the menu bar.
4. Click Creating The Interface.
5. Click the word Toolbox in the Creating The Interface Help window.
6. Use the scroll bar to read about Visual Basic's controls.
7. Double-click the Help window's control-menu box.
8. Click the Close button in the Creating The Interface Help window.
9. Click the Caption property in the Properties list of the Properties window.
10. Press function key F1 for context-sensitive help.
11. Read about the Caption property in the Help window.
12. Double click the control-menu box of the Help window.
13. Choose Learning Microsoft Visual Basic from the Help menu on the menu bar.
14. Click How Visual Basic Works, and read through the tutorial.
15. Exit the tutorial.

EXERCISE NOTES
■Exercise 1 introduces students to using the Help menu, context-sensitive help, and the Visual Basic tutorial.

COMPUTER LABORATORY EXERCISE 2
Completing an Animated Application

Instructions: Start Visual Basic. Open the project CLE1-2 from the subdirectory VB3 on the Student Diskette that accompanies this book. Choose the View Form button in the Project window. After you perform the tasks listed below Figure CLE1-2, the completed application should resemble the one shown in Figure CLE1-2.

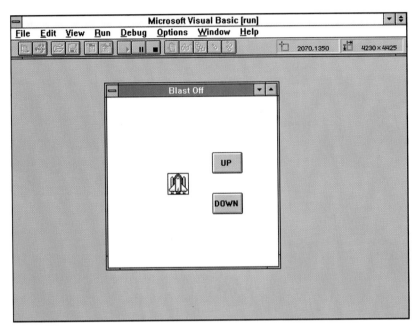

EXERCISE NOTES
■Exercise 2 introduces students to the three-step application development process by adding a control, setting properties, and writing code statements.

FIGURE CLE1-2

1. Add a second command button control below the first.
2. Change the Caption property of Command1 to UP.
3. Change the Caption property of Command2 to DOWN.
4. Add the following code statement to the Command1_Click event:
   ```
   Picture1.Top = Picture1.top - 50
   ```
   (Subtracting the distance between the top of the control and the top of the screen raises the control on the screen.)
5. Add the following code statement to the Command2_Click event:
   ```
   Picture1.Top = Picture1.top + 50
   ```
   (Adding to the distance between the top of the control and the top of the screen lowers the control on the screen.)
6. Save the form as ROCKET.FRM.
7. Save the project as CLE1-2A.MAK.
8. Choose the Start command from the Run menu to start the application.
9. Click the UP control several times and then the DOWN control several times.
10. Double-click the application's control menu box to stop the application.
11. Choose the Exit command from the File menu to exit Visual Basic.
12. Check with your instructor for directions on turning in the exercise.

COMPUTER LABORATORY EXERCISE 3
Working with Controls and Properties

Instructions: Start Visual Basic and minimize Program Manager. Open project CLE1-3 from the sub-directory VB3 on the Student Diskette that accompanies this book. Choose the View Form button in the Project window. After you perform the tasks listed below Figure CLE1-3, your application should look like the one shown in Figure CLE1-3.

EXERCISE NOTES
■Exercise 3 provides students more experience in setting properties of controls.

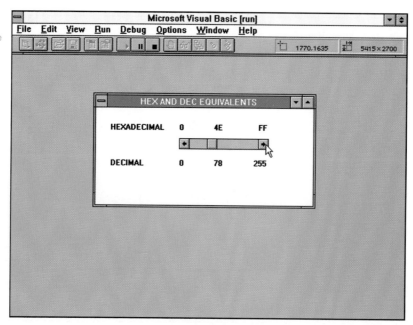

FIGURE CLE1-3

1. Set the properties of the controls as listed in the table on the right:
2. Save the form as HEXDEC.FRM.
3. Save the project as CLE1-3A.MAK.
4. Click the Start tool on the Toolbar to run the application.
5. Click the scroll arrows several times, and then drag the scroll box in both directions.
6. Click the Stop tool on the Toolbar to end the application.
7. Double-click the Control-menu box to exit Visual Basic.
8. Check with your instructor for directions on turning in the exercise.

▸ **WORKING WITH CONTROLS AND PROPERTIES**

CONTROL	PROPERTY	VALUE
Label2	Caption	0
Label4	Caption	FF
Label5	Caption	DECIMAL
Label6	Caption	0
Label7	Caption	[blank]
Label8	Caption	255
Hscroll1	Max	255
Form1	Name	HEXDEC

COMPUTER LABORATORY ASSIGNMENT 1
Building a Metric Conversion Application

Purpose: To gain experience in building an application with three types of controls and a single event.

Problem: Create an application that converts miles to kilometers. The completed application should resemble the one shown in Figure CLA1-1.

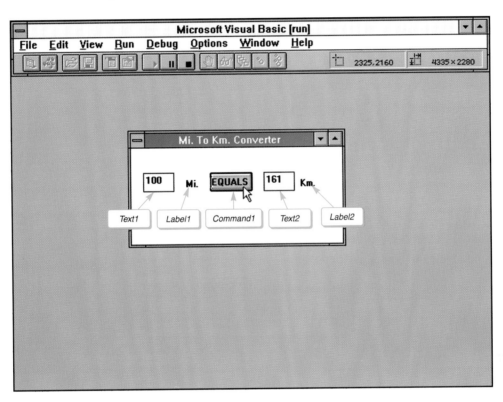

FIGURE CLA1-1

Instructions: Perform the following tasks:

1. Start Visual Basic.
2. Resize and locate the form to resemble the one in Figure CLA1-1.
3. Add two text boxes, two labels, and one command button as shown in Figure CLA1-1.
4. Change label1's caption to Mi:.
5. Change label2's caption to Km:.
6. Change the text boxes' captions to be blank.
7. Change command1's caption to EQUALS.
8. Change the form's name to MItoKM.
9. Change the form's caption to Mi. To Km. Converter.
10. Add the following code to the Command1_Click event:
    ```
    Text2.Text = Text1.Text * 1.61
    ```
11. Save the project as MILEAGE.MAK, and save the form as MITOKM.FRM.
12. Run the application to test it.
13. Exit Visual Basic.
14. Check with your instructor for directions on turning in the assignment.

COMPUTER LABORATORY ASSIGNMENT 2
Maturity Value of an Investment

Purpose: To become familiar with building and saving a Visual Basic application consisting of a form, several controls, and one event.

Problem: Create an application that allows the user to enter the amount of an investment, the annual rate of interest, and the number of years. When the user clicks a control, the application displays the maturity value of the investment based on quarterly compounding. The user interface should resemble the one shown in Figure CLA1-2.

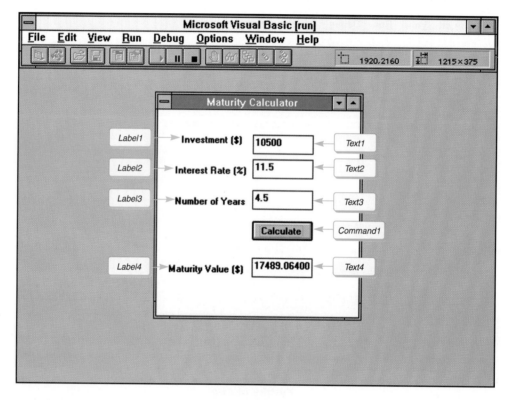

FIGURE CLA1-2

Instructions: Perform the following tasks:

1. Open a new project in Visual Basic.
2. Size and locate the form to resemble the one illustrated in Figure CLA1-2.
3. Add four labels, four text boxes, and one command button to the form.
4. Arrange the controls to resemble Figure CLA1-2.
5. Set the captions of the four labels.
6. Set the value of the Text property of the four text boxes to be blank.
7. Set the form's caption to Maturity Calculator.
8. Save the form as MATURE.FRM.
9. Set the command button's caption.
10. Write the click event for the command1 control. **Hint:** Use text1 for investment, text2 for rate, text3 for years, and text4 for maturity value. Use the following code statement:

```
Text4.text = text1.text * (1 + text2.text/400) ^ (4 * text3.text)
```
11. Save the project as MATURITY.MAK.
12. Check with your instructor for directions on turning in the assignment.

COMPUTER LABORATORY ASSIGNMENT 3
Telephone Directory

Purpose: To become familiar with applications with multiple events and to provide additional practice in building and saving projects.

Problem: You want an application to retrieve the phone numbers of several persons whom you call frequently.

Instructions: Build an application whose user interface is shown in Figure CLA1-3. Whenever you click one of the command buttons, the phone number of the person whose name is on the command button should appear in the text box.

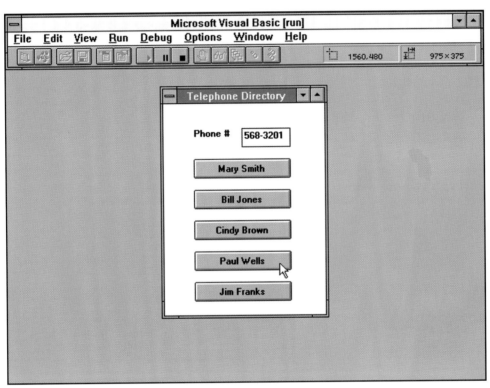

FIGURE CLA1-3

The persons and their phone numbers are as follows:

Mary Smith	549-7637
Bill Jones	863-7740
Cindy Brown	259-0412
Paul Wells	568-3201
Jim Franks	547-2701

Hint: A phone number actually is a set of characters, not numbers. For example, Mary Smith's phone number is not the number 549 minus the number 7,637. In Visual Basic, when you want the value of the text property to be characters rather than a number or numeric expression, it must begin and end with quotation marks. For example,

```
text1.text = "Good Morning"
```
will print the words
```
Good Morning
```
in the text1 text box.

Save the form as TELEPHON.FRM, and save the project as TELEPHON.MAK. Check with your instructor for directions on turning in the assignment.

COMPUTER LABORATORY ASSIGNMENT 4
Currency Exchange

Purpose: To gain additional experience in creating and saving projects, and to gain experience in building applications with increasingly more complex user interfaces.

Problem: You want an application to convert the amount of dollars you input into one of several foreign currencies based on recent exchange rates.

Instructions: Build an application with a user interface that resembles the one shown in Figure CLA1-4.

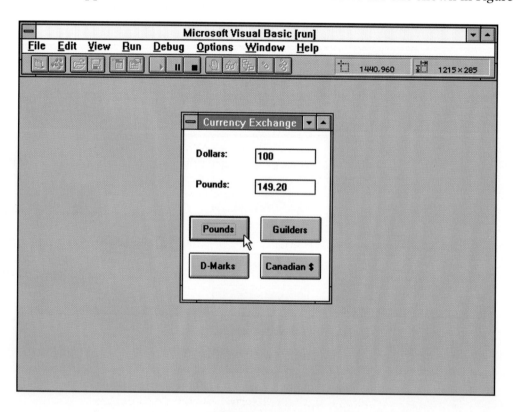

FIGURE CLA1-4

Whenever you click a currency's command button, the dollar amount in the first text box should be converted to the appropriate currency and displayed in the second text box. Note that the label preceding the second text box also should change to reflect the name of the currency. **Hint:** Each event will have two code statements. One will display the converted amount, and the other will change the Caption property of the label control.

Use the following exchange rates. One dollar equals:

1.4920 pounds
.54699 guilders
.61489 marks
.80160 Canadian dollars

Save the form as XCHANGE.FRM, and save the project as XCHANGE.MAK. Check with your instructor for directions on turning in the assignment.

WORKING WITH CONTROLS

OBJECTIVES   You will have mastered the material in this project when you can:

▸ Use a drop-down list box control in an application
▸ Use a shape control in an application
▸ Use a check box control in an application
▸ Use an option button control in an application
▸ Use a frame control in an application
▸ Set the MultiLine, FontSize, and ScrollBars properties of text boxes
▸ Incorporate the ENTER key in applications

▸ Name controls
▸ Copy controls on a form
▸ Copy code between procedures in the Code window
▸ Use code to concatenate text
▸ Use the AddItem method to add items to a list box
▸ Declare a variable with a code statement
▸ Use variables in a code statement
▸ Use the If...Then...Else decision structure

▸ INTRODUCTION

In Project 1, a Windows application that converted an amount of dollars into its corresponding amount of francs was built. The application consisted of one event and three types of controls: labels, text boxes, and command buttons. This project begins building more complex applications with additional controls and multiple events.

▸ PROJECT TWO – MOVIE BOX OFFICE

The application in this project is shown in Figure 2-1 on the next page. This application simulates a ticket vending operation at a movie theater. For each transaction, the name of the movie is selected, whether a matinee discount is available, and the number of tickets to be purchased. When the number of tickets is selected, the total price appears in the Amount Due box. After the money has been accepted, the Enter button is chosen by clicking it, or by pressing the ENTER key on the keyboard. This action adds the name of the movie and number of tickets sold to the transaction list and clears the previous settings.

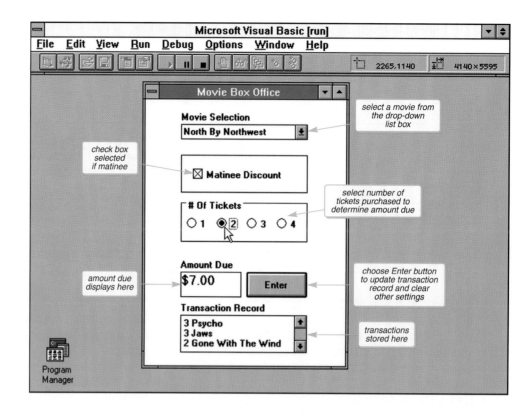

FIGURE 2-1

This project uses the label, text box, and command button controls presented in Project 1. In addition to learning about some additional properties of these controls, you will learn how to use the list box, check box, shape, and frame controls. The controls used in this project are identified in Figure 2-2. This project is built by following the same three-step procedure used in Project 1:

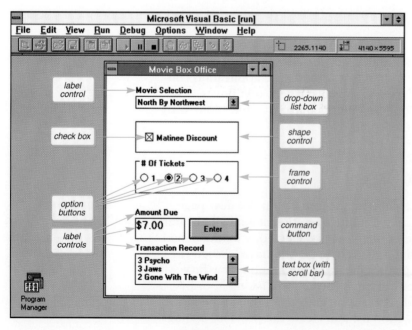

FIGURE 2-2

▶ Create the interface
▶ Set properties
▶ Write code

Begin the project by starting Visual Basic as described on page VB4 in Project 1 or by opening a new project if you are already running Visual Basic. The steps to start Visual Basic are summarized below.

1. Use the mouse to point to the Visual Basic program-item icon in the Visual Basic 3.0 group window.
2. Double-click the left mouse button.
3. Point to an empty area of the Program Manager window and click the left mouse button.
4. Point to the Program Manager minimize button, and click the left mouse button.

▶ THE VISUAL BASIC DESKTOP

I n Project 1, you learned you could change the sizes and positions of the Visual Basic windows on the desktop to whatever arrangement you prefer. Like many other Windows applications, Visual Basic records information about the size and location of the windows when you exit the program. The next time you start Visual Basic, the windows are sized and arranged on the desktop as they were when you last closed the program.

All of the projects in this book begin with the Visual Basic windows in their default sizes and positions. If necessary, you should now arrange the Visual Basic windows on the desktop as shown in Figure 2-3.

VB TIPS
■ Deleting the window size and location statements from the VB.INI file will give the default arrangement shown in Figure 2-3.

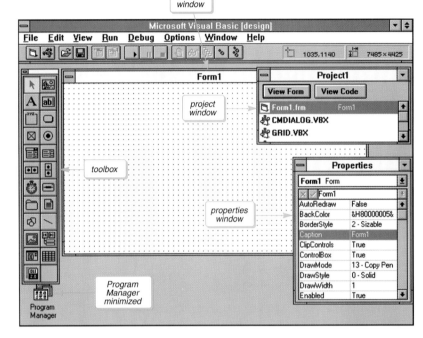

FIGURE 2-3

▶ CREATING THE INTERFACE

B egin building the movie box office project by creating the interface. Creating the interface consists of sizing and locating the form and then adding each of the controls to the form.

Form Size and Position

The following steps use the method presented in Project 1 to set the size and location of the form. Perform the following steps to set the size of the form.

TO SET THE SIZE OF THE FORM ▼

STEP 1 ▶

Click the Form window's title bar.

The Form window becomes the active window (Figure 2-4).

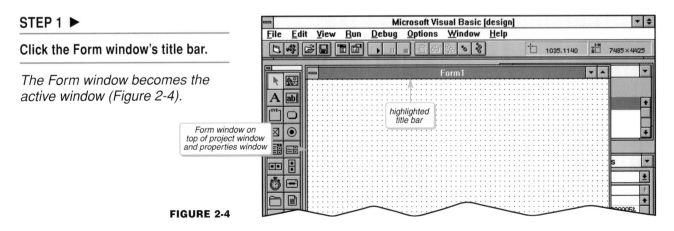

FIGURE 2-4

STEP 2 ▶

Point to the form's left border.

The pointer changes to a horizontal double arrow (⇔) (Figure 2-5). Note the current form's position and size at the right side of the toolbar.

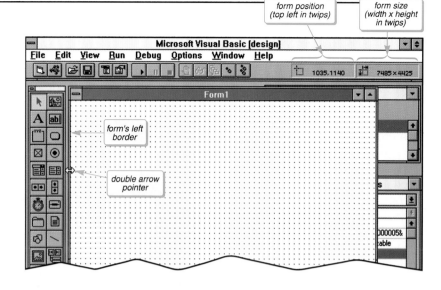

FIGURE 2-5

STEP 3 ▶

Drag the form's left border toward the right side of the screen as shown in Figure 2-6.

As you drag the border, its new position appears as a shaded line.

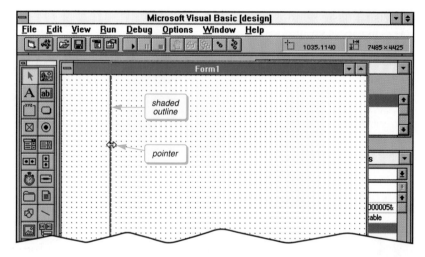

FIGURE 2-6

STEP 4 ▶

Release the left mouse button.

The form's left border moves to the position of the shaded line, and the new width and left position are shown in twips on the right side of the toolbar (Figure 2-7).

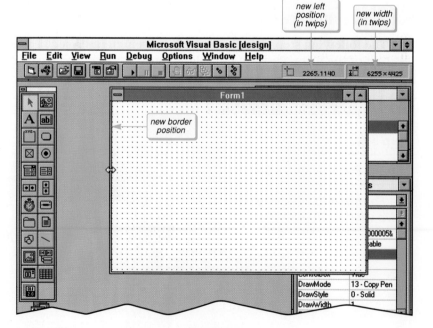

FIGURE 2-7

STEP 5 ▶

Point to the form's right border and drag the border toward the left side of the screen to the position shown in Figure 2-8.

The mouse pointer's shape changes to a horizontal double arrow, and the shaded outline of the right border is moved toward the left side of the screen.

FIGURE 2-8

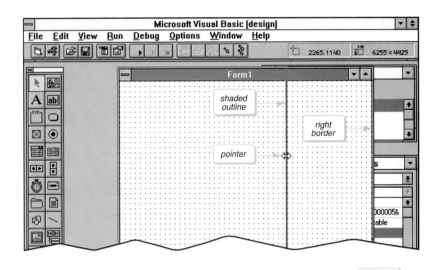

STEP 6 ▶

Release the left mouse button.

The form's right border moves to the position of the shaded line, and the new width appears on the right side of the toolbar (Figure 2-9).

FIGURE 2-9

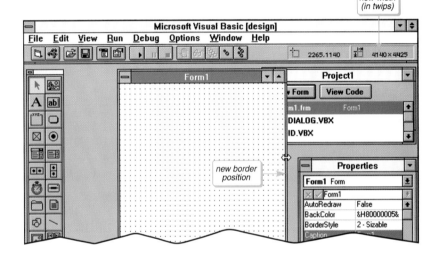

STEP 7 ▶

Point to the form's bottom border and drag the border downward to the position shown in Figure 2-10.

The pointer changes to a vertical double arrow. As you drag the border, the form's new shape appears as shaded lines.

FIGURE 2-10

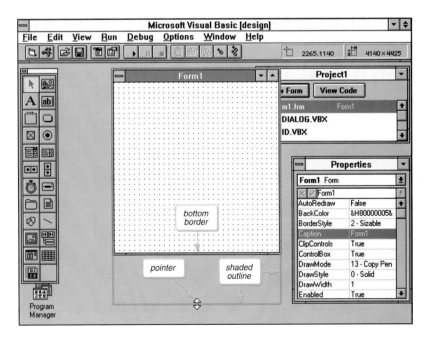

STEP 8 ▶

Release the left mouse button.

The bottom border moves to the position of the shaded line, and the form's new height appears on the right side of the toolbar (Figure 2-11).

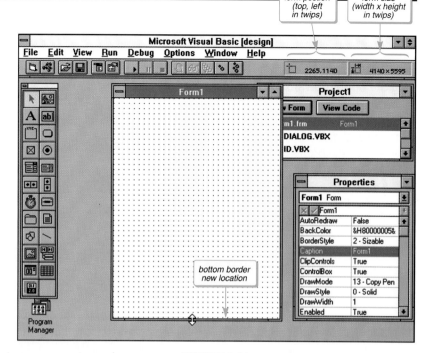

FIGURE 2-11

With the form's size set, the entire form can now be dragged to a position on the desktop where it will appear at run time, as was done in Project 1. However, its current position (Figure 2-11) is satisfactory for the movie box office application.

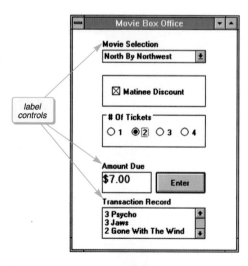

FIGURE 2-12

Adding Labels and Setting the AutoSize Property

The next step is to add the three label controls in the movie box office project shown in Figure 2-12. Recall that unlike a text box, the contents of a label control cannot be directly changed by the user of the application at run time. For example, the words *Movie Selection* can only be changed with code statements at run time since those words are the caption of one of the label controls.

When the **AutoSize** property of a label is set to True, the label's size automatically is adjusted to the size of the label's caption. Although setting properties normally is performed after building the interface, the AutoSize property of three of the labels will be set to make room for the other controls that will be added to the form. The following steps add one label control to the form and set its AutoSize property.

TO ADD AN AUTOSIZE LABEL CONTROL ▼

STEP 1 ►

Double-click the label tool in the Toolbox, and point to the AutoSize property in the Properties list.

A default-size label is added to the center of the form. The Label1 control is the selected control. Its properties appear in the Properties window (Figure 2-13).

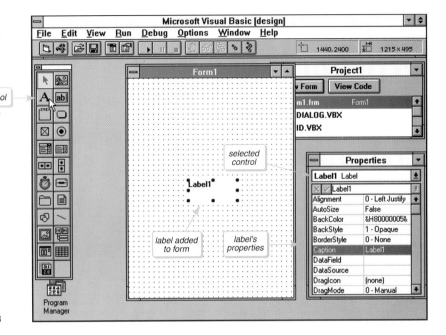

FIGURE 2-13

STEP 2 ►

Double-click the AutoSize property in the Properties list, and point to the Label1 control.

The value of the label's AutoSize property size is changed from False to True in the Properties window, and its size is adjusted on the form (Figure 2-14).

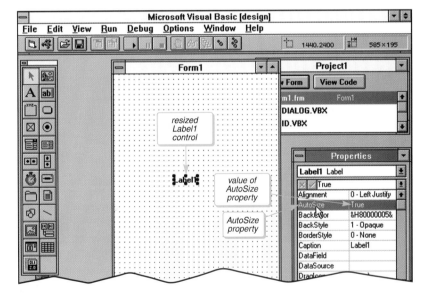

FIGURE 2-14

STEP 3 ►

Drag the Label1 control to the position shown in Figure 2-15.

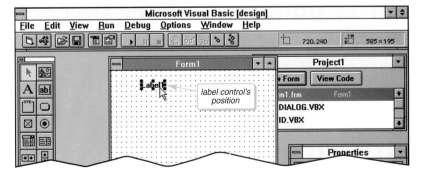

FIGURE 2-15

In Project 1, properties were set by typing their values in the Properties window. When a property has just two values, such as the False/True values of the
AutoSize property, you can switch between those values by double-clicking the
name of the property in the Properties list.

Copying Controls

The two additional label controls identified in Figure 2-12 on page VB62 are similar
to the one that was just added. When you want to add multiple similar controls to
a form, it often is easier to copy the control to the Clipboard and then paste copies
of it from the Clipboard to the form. The following steps add two copies of the
Label1 control to the form.

TO COPY CONTROLS ▼

STEP 1 ▶

**Select the Edit menu from the menu
bar.**

*The Edit menu displays (Figure
2-16).*

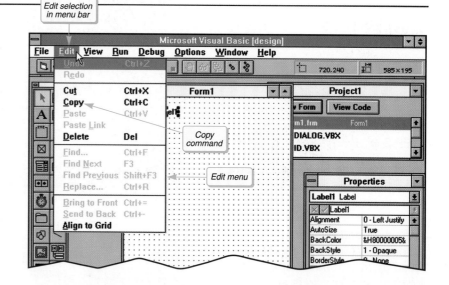

FIGURE 2-16

STEP 2 ▶

**Choose the Copy command from the
Edit menu.**

*The selected control (Label1) is
copied to the Clipboard, and the
Edit menu closes (Figure 2-17).
The selected control changes to
Form1 in the Properties window.*

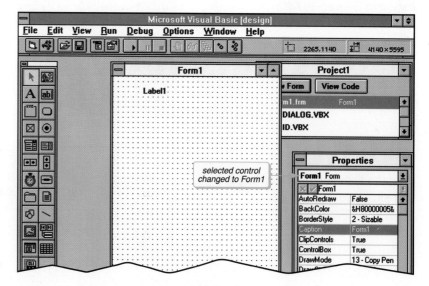

FIGURE 2-17

STEP 3 ▶

Select the Edit menu, and choose the Paste command. Point to No in the dialog box

The dialog box shown in Figure 2-18 displays. The pointer points to No in the dialog box.

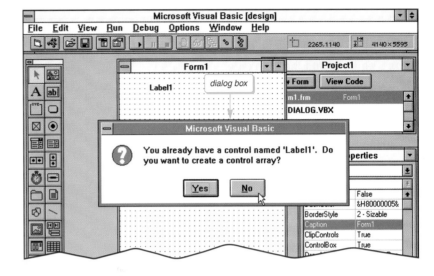

FIGURE 2-18

STEP 4 ▶

Choose No in the dialog box.

The dialog box closes, and a copy of the control is added to the form (Figure 2-19). The control is automatically named Label2 and is the selected control.

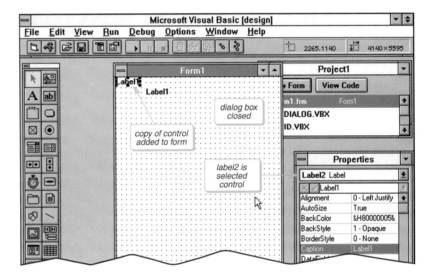

FIGURE 2-19

STEP 5 ▶

Drag the new label control to the position shown in Figure 2-20.

The label's name shown in the Properties window is Label2, but its caption is Label1.

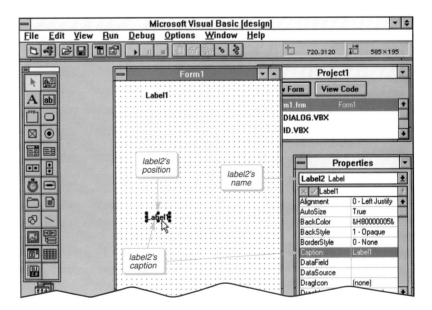

FIGURE 2-20

STEP 6 ▶

Repeat the procedures shown in
Steps 3 and 4 to add the third label,
and drag it to the position shown in
Figure 2-21.

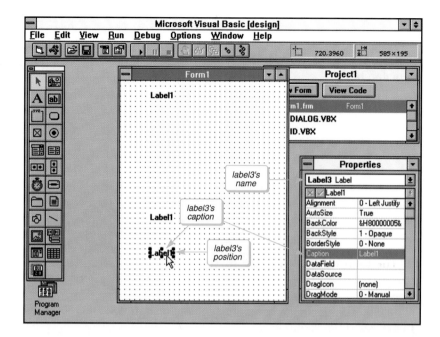

FIGURE 2-21

When you copy a control, the pasted control has a new name but has all of
the other properties of the control you copied. Thus, both additional controls are
AutoSized and have the same caption, Label1. The captions will be changed later
in this project. Once a control is copied to the Clipboard, multiple copies can be
pasted without having to copy the control to the Clipboard each time.

The List Box and Combo Box Controls

List box and **combo box** controls are used in applications to present lists of
choices. In a list box, part or all of the list of choices displays. When the list of
choices is longer than can appear in the list box, a scroll bar automatically is added
to move the list up or down. When an item is selected from the list by clicking it,
the item appears in a highlighted color.

The movie box office application contains a combo
box control with properties set so that the movies
appear in a drop-down list of choices (Figure 2-22).
With a **drop-down list,** the list of choices appears only
when you click the down arrow located next to the list
box. When you select an item from the list by clicking
it, the drop-down list closes, and only the selected item
appears in the list box.

At run time, list box controls always have one way
to select an item from the list. Combo box controls can
have different selection methods and can appear differently, depending on how the properties are set. The
appearance of list box controls and combo box controls
and the method of selecting an item from these controls at run time are summarized in Table 2-1.

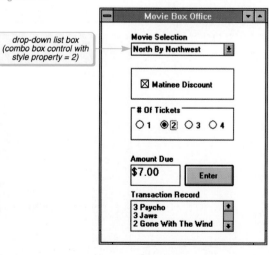

FIGURE 2-22

▸ **TABLE 2-1 LIST BOX AND COMBO BOX CONTROLS**

CONTROL	APPEARANCE OF LIST	SELECTION FROM LIST
List box	List always shows; scrollbar added if list is longer than control's size	Click item from list
Combo box (style 0)	Drop-down list	Click item in list or type item directly in combo box
Combo box (style 1)	List always shows; scrollbar added if list is longer than control's size	Click item in list or type item directly in combo box
Combo box (style 2)	Drop-down list	Click item in list

TRANSPARENCY
Table 2-1

LECTURE NOTES
■ Explain Table 2-1.
■ Explain that a drop-down list box is a combo box and not a list box control.

The following steps add a combo box to the movie box office form. Later, its style is set to 2 (see Table 2-1) to make it a drop-down list box.

TRANSPARENCIES
Figure 2-23 through
Figure 2-26.

TO ADD A COMBO BOX CONTROL ▼

STEP 1 ▶

Double-click the combo box tool ( ) in the Toolbox.

A default-sized combo box is added to the form (Figure 2-23).

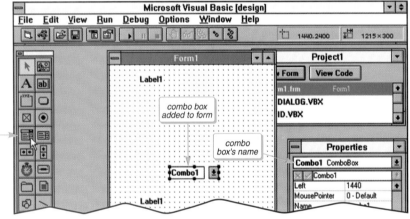

FIGURE 2-23

STEP 2 ▶

Drag the combo box to the position shown in Figure 2-24. Point to the right center sizing handle.

The combo box is moved, and the pointer points to the right center sizing handle.

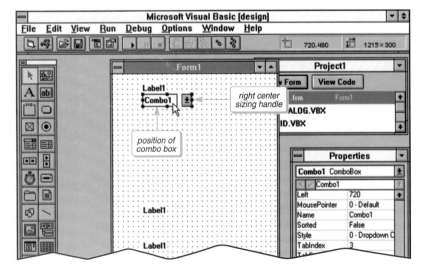

FIGURE 2-24

STEP 3 ▶

Drag the sizing handle on the center right side of the combo box to the position shown in Figure 2-25.

The shaded outline of the control appears on the form.

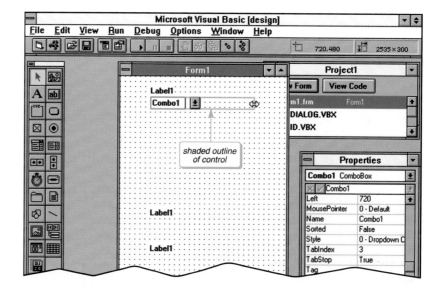

FIGURE 2-25

STEP 4 ▶

Release the left mouse button.

The combo box is resized on the form (Figure 2-26).

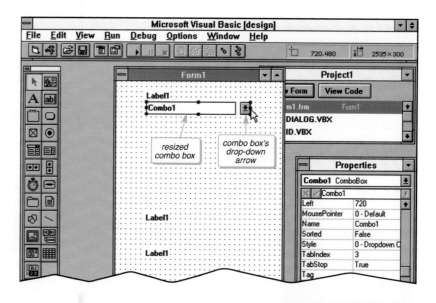

FIGURE 2-26

TRANSPARENCY
Figure 2-27

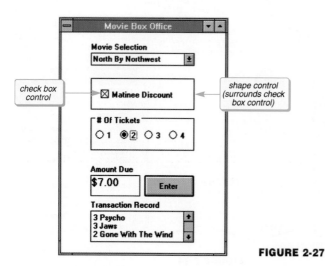

FIGURE 2-27

The names of the movies will be added to the drop-down list box by using code statements later in this project.

The Shape Control

The **shape control** is used to add a rectangle, square, ellipse, or circle to a form. The movie box office application uses a rectangular shape as a border surrounding the matinee discount check box (Figure 2-27). Its only purpose in this application is to enhance the visual balance of the controls on the form.

Perform the following steps to add the shape control to the form.

LECTURE NOTES
■ Explain the functions of shape controls.

TRANSPARENCIES
Figure 2-28 through
Figure 2-30

TO ADD THE SHAPE CONTROL ▼

STEP 1 ▶

Click the shape tool (▣) in the Tool-box, and move the mouse under the lower left corner of the combo box, which is where the top left corner of the shape will appear (Figure 2-28).

The shape tool is highlighted in the Toolbox, and the mouse pointer changes to a cross hair.

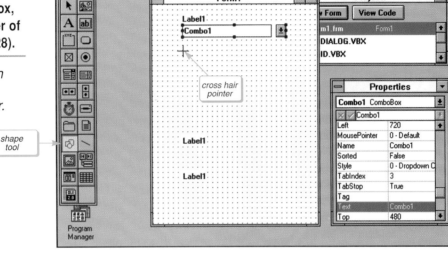

FIGURE 2-28

STEP 2 ▶

Drag the mouse pointer down and to the right as shown in Figure 2-29.

A shaded outline of the control appears on the form.

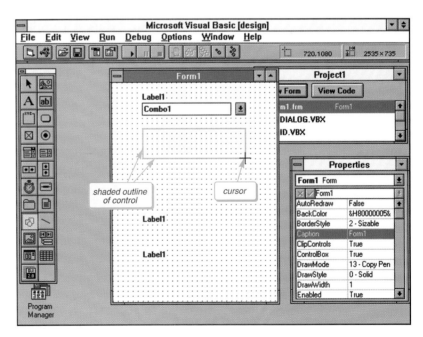

FIGURE 2-29

STEP 3 ►

Release the left mouse button.

The control is sized to fit the area of the shaded outline (Figure 2-30).

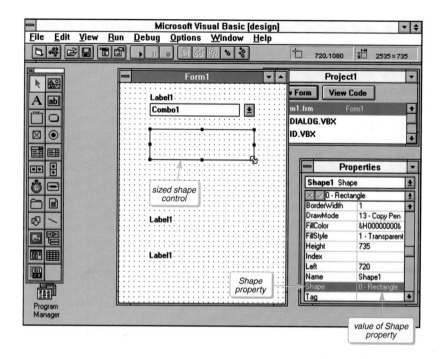

FIGURE 2-30

The different properties of the shape control, such as the Shape property, appear in the Properties list (Figure 2-30). The default shape of a shape control is a rectangle.

LECTURE NOTES
■ Explain the functions of a check box control and its use in the movie box office application.

TRANSPARENCIES
Figures 2-31 and Figure 2-32

The Check Box Control

A **check box** control is used in applications to turn options on or off, such as the matinee discount (Figure 2-27 on page VB68). Clicking an empty check box places an X in the box to indicate the option is selected. Clicking on a selected check box removes the X to indicate the option is not selected.

TO ADD A CHECK BOX CONTROL ▼

STEP 1 ►

Double-click the check box tool (⊠) in the Toolbox.

A default-sized check box is added to the form (Figure 2-31).

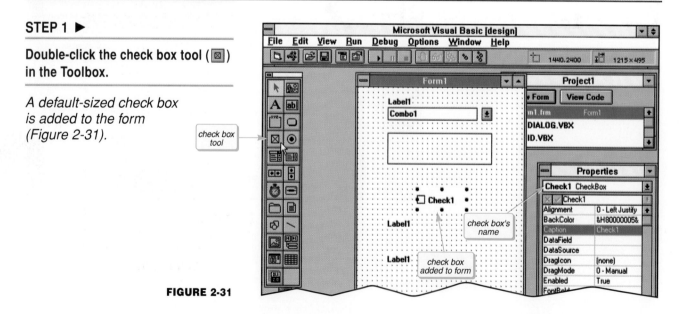

FIGURE 2-31

STEP 2 ▶

Drag the check box to a position inside the shape control. Drag the sizing handle on the right of the control to extend its width, as shown in Figure 2-32.

The check box is positioned inside the shape control, and its width is extended.

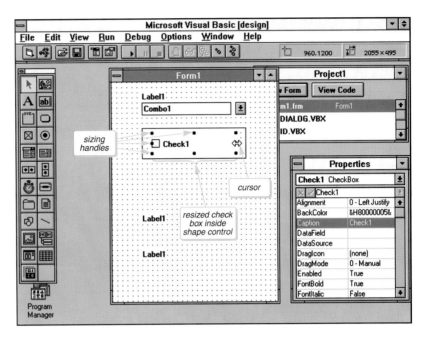

FIGURE 2-32

Check boxes are used to indicate the selection or deselection of individual options. For this reason, any number or combination of check boxes on a form can be checked at the same time. In the movie box office application, the check box is used to switch between the two different prices of the tickets purchased. The two prices will be established later in the code for the application.

The Frame Control

The **frame control** is used as a container for other controls, as shown in Figure 2-33. It has several properties similar to the shape control, but it has some important differences:

▶ A frame can have only a rectangular shape.
▶ A frame can have a caption.
▶ When option buttons are added inside a frame, only one can be selected at a time during run time.

To add the frame control as illustrated in Figure 2-33, perform the steps on the next page.

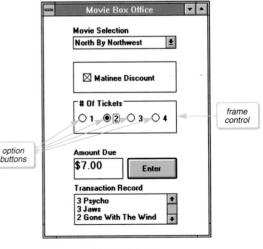

FIGURE 2-33

TO ADD THE FRAME CONTROL ▼

STEP 1 ►

Click the frame tool (▢) in the Tool-box, and move the mouse to the position where the top left corner of the frame will appear (Figure 2-34).

The frame tool is highlighted in the Toolbox, and the mouse pointer changes to a cross hair.

FIGURE 2-34

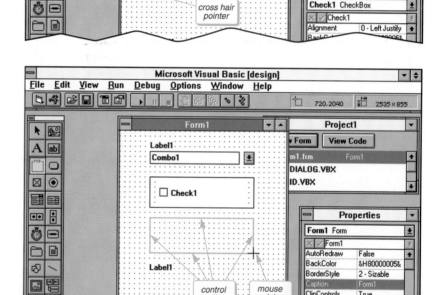

STEP 2 ►

Drag the mouse pointer down and to the right as shown in Figure 2-35.

A gray outline of the control appears on the form.

FIGURE 2-35

STEP 3 ►

Release the left mouse button.

The control is sized to fit the area of the gray outline (Figure 2-36).

FIGURE 2-36

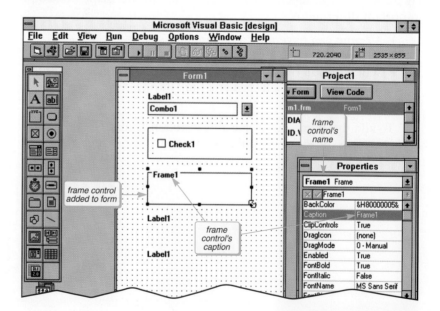

When controls have been added by drawing them inside a frame control, dragging the frame to a new position causes the controls inside to be moved as well.

The Option Button Control

Option buttons present a set of choices, such as the number of tickets bought in a single box office transaction (Figure 2-33 on page VB71). Option buttons are placed in groups that allow you to select only one choice from a group, such as the number of tickets sold. All of the option buttons on a form function as one group unless they are placed inside a frame. Multiple groups of option buttons can be created by adding another frame to the form for each option group.

For an option button to be part of a group, it must be added directly inside the frame. You cannot add an option button to the form and then drag it inside a frame if you want it to be part of the group formed by that frame.

The application in this project offers four choices for the number of tickets sold (1,2,3, or 4). Perform the following steps to create a group of five option buttons within the frame control already added. The reason for the fifth button will be explained later in this project.

LECTURE NOTES
■ Explain the option button control.
■ Describe the use of option buttons in the movie box office application.
■ Explain what is meant by an option button group.

TRANSPARENCIES
Figure 2-37 through
Figure 2-40

TO BUILD AN OPTION BUTTON GROUP ▼

STEP 1 ▶

Click the option button tool ( ) in the Toolbox, and move the mouse to the position where the top left corner of the button will appear (Figure 2-37).

The option button tool is highlighted in the Toolbox, and the mouse pointer changes to a cross hair.

FIGURE 2-37

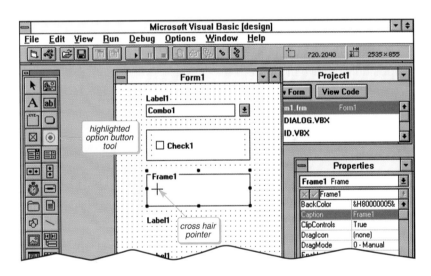

STEP 2 ▶

Drag the mouse pointer down and to the right as shown in Figure 2-38.

A shaded outline of the control appears on the form.

FIGURE 2-38

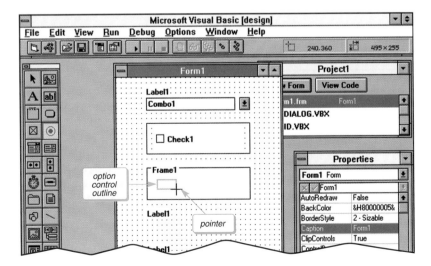

STEP 3 ▶

Release the left mouse button.

The control is sized to fit the area of the gray outline (Figure 2-39). Only the first two letters of the option button's caption, Option1, are visible on the form because of the size of the control.

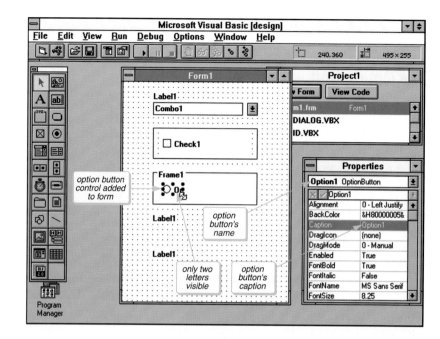

FIGURE 2-39

STEP 4 ▶

Repeat Steps 1 through 3 four times to add four more option buttons in the positions shown in Figure 2-40.

As the option button controls are added, Visual Basic assigns to them the default names Option2 through Option5.

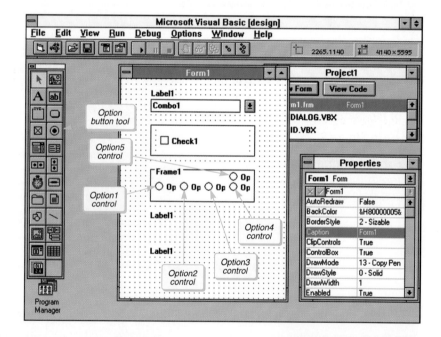

FIGURE 2-40

You may have wondered why Step 4 did not use the cut and paste method or the double-click method to add the last four option buttons. The reason is that both of these methods would have added the option buttons to the form, not to the frame control. To add the option buttons to a frame control, the preceding procedure should be used. The option buttons were added to the form inside the frame control in order to form an option group.

Adding the Remaining Controls

TRANSPARENCY
Figure 2-41

Three controls remain to be added to the form: one additional label, a command button, and a text box as shown in Figure 2-41. You should be familiar with working with these controls from Project 1.

In the movie box office application, a label control with borders around it is used to contain the total cost of the transaction (number of tickets times the ticket price). The command button is used to clear the amount displayed in the label and to add the number of tickets purchased and the name of the movie to a list contained in the Transaction Record text box. Later, some additional properties of these controls will be presented. The following steps add these controls to the movie box office form.

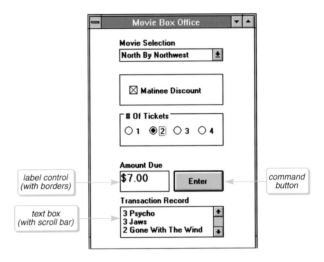

FIGURE 2-41

LECTURE NOTES
■ Point out the remaining controls on the box office form and their functions.

TO ADD A LABEL, COMMAND BUTTON, AND TEXT BOX ▼

STEP 1 ▶

Click the label tool in the Toolbox, and position the cursor under the second label control as shown in Figure 2-42.

The label tool is highlighted in the Toolbox, and the cursor changes to a cross hair.

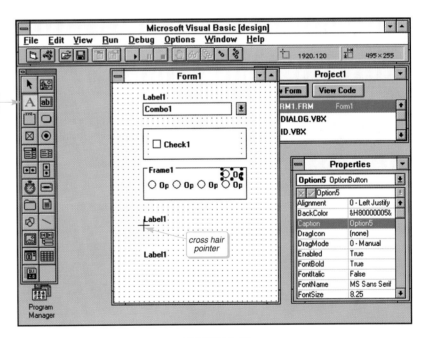

FIGURE 2-42

TRANSPARENCIES
Figure 2-42 through
Figure 2-48

STEP 2 ▶

Drag the cursor down and to the right as shown in Figure 2-43.

As you drag the cursor, a gray outline of the control is drawn.

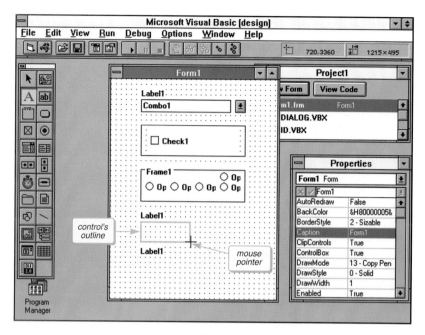

FIGURE 2-43

STEP 3 ▶

Release the left mouse button. Double-click the command button tool in the Toolbox.

When the left mouse button is released, the Label4 control is sized to fit the outline. A default-sized command button is added to the form (Figure 2-44).

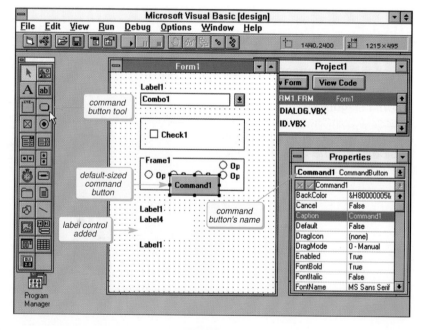

FIGURE 2-44

STEP 4 ►

Drag the command button control's outline down and to the right to the position shown in Figure 2-45.

Dragging the command button control causes an outline of it to move.

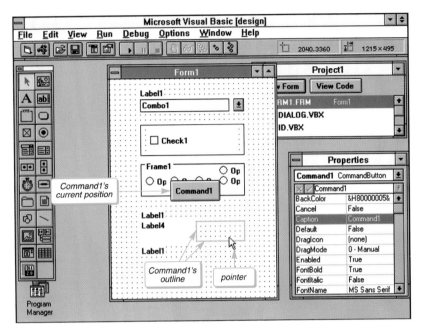

FIGURE 2-45

STEP 5 ►

Release the left mouse button. Double-click the text box tool in the Toolbox.

When the mouse button is released, the Command1 control moves to the position of the outline. A default-sized text box named Text1 is added to the form (Figure 2-46).

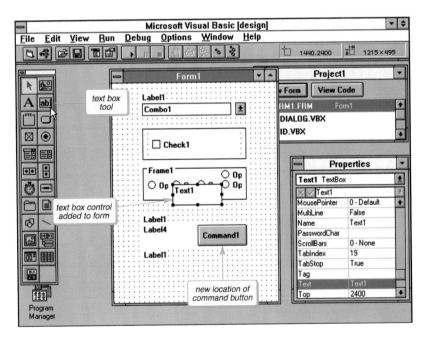

FIGURE 2-46

STEP 6 ▶

Drag the Text1 text box control's outline under the third Label control to the position shown in Figure 2-47.

Dragging the text box control causes an outline of it to move.

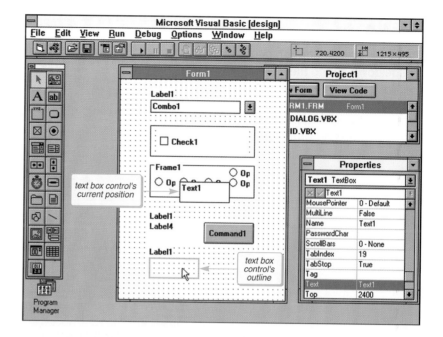

FIGURE 2-47

STEP 7 ▶

Release the left mouse button. Drag the lower right sizing handle of the text box down and to the right, as shown in Figure 2-48 and release the left mouse button.

When the mouse button is released, the Text1 control moves to the position of the outline. When you drag the text box control's handle, a gray outline of the control is drawn.

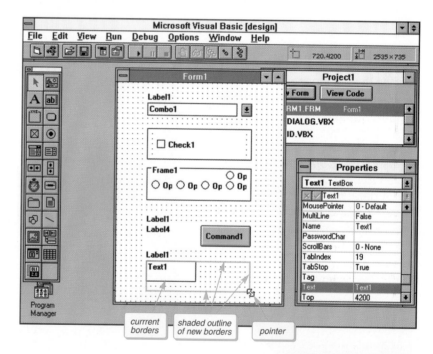

FIGURE 2-48

The text box's borders are moved to the position of the outline when the left mouse button is released. The interface for the movie box office application is now finished. The form should appear as shown in Figure 2-49a. Figure 2-49b shows how the form will appear at run time after the properties of the controls have been set.

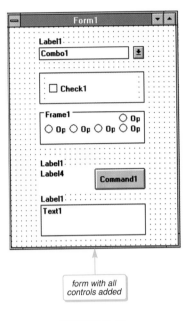

form with all
controls added

FIGURE 2-49a

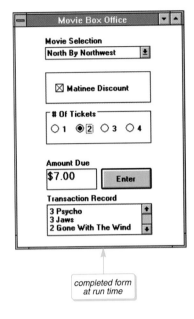

completed form
at run time

FIGURE 2-49b

▶ SETTING PROPERTIES

he following section completes the second phase of application development, setting the properties of the controls.

Naming Controls

When you add controls
to a form, Visual Basic assigns
a name to the control, which
consists of the type of control
and a number, such as Label1.
It often is easier to read and
edit your code if controls
have names that more closely
represent the purpose or
function of the control within
the application. The **name** of
a control is a property of a
control and can be changed
to whatever seems appropriate. Visual Basic has a suggested standard for naming
controls. A control's name
should consist of a three-
letter prefix that designates
the type of control followed
by a unique text description.
Control types and name prefixes are listed in Table 2-2.

▶ TABLE 2-2 CONTROL TYPES AND NAME PREFIXES

CONTROL	PREFIX		CONTROL	PREFIX
form	frm		label	lbl
check box	chk		line	lin
combo box	cbo		list box	lst
command button	cmd		menu	mnu
data	dat		OLE	ole
directory list box	dir		option button	opt
drive list box	drv		picture box	pic
file list box	fil		shape	shp
frame	fra		text box	txt
grid	grd		timer	tmr
horizontal scroll bar	hsb		vertical scroll bar	vsb
image	img			

The following steps assign new names to several of the controls on the movie box office form, following the Visual Basic conventions for naming controls. Table 2-3 lists the current (default) name of each control (shown in Figure 2-49a), its function in the movie box office application, and the new name that will be assigned.

▶ **TABLE 2-3 NAMES AND FUNCTIONS OF MOVIE BOX OFFICE CONTROLS**

CURRENT NAME	CONTROL'S FUNCTION	NEW NAME
Combo1	select name of the move	cboMovie
Check1	selects matinee discount price	chkMatinee
Label4	displays purchase amount	lblAmtdue
Command1	enter transaction in list	cmdEnter
Text1	contains a record of	txtRecord
Form1	the move box office form	frmMovies

TO NAME CONTROLS ▼

STEP 1 ▶

Select the control you want to change (Combo1) by clicking it on the form or by selecting its name from the drop-down Object list in the Properties window.

The name of the selected control and its properties appear in the Properties window (Figure 2-50).

FIGURE 2-50

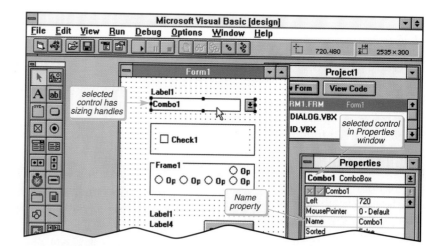

STEP 2 ▶

Double-click the Name property in the Properties window.

The current name of the control (Combo1) appears highlighted in the Settings box (Figure 2-51).

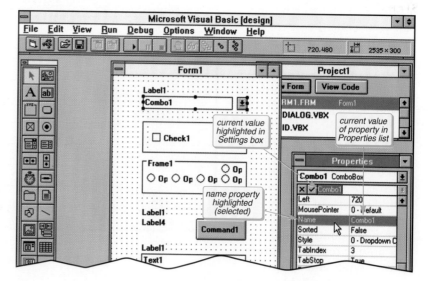

FIGURE 2-51

STEP 3 ▶

Type the new name, `cboMovie` and press the ENTER key.

As you type, the name is replaced in the Settings box. When you press the ENTER key, the value is recorded and appears next to the Name property in the Properties list (Figure 2-52).

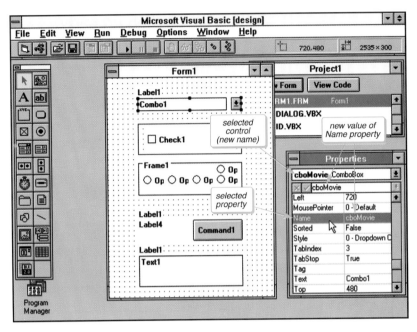

FIGURE 2-52

STEP 4 ▶

Repeat Steps 1 through 3 to name the Check1 control chkMatinee. Repeat Steps 1 through 3 to name the Label4 control lblAmtdue. Repeat Steps 1 through 3 to name the Command1 control cmdEnter. Repeat Steps 1 through 3 to name the Text1 control txtRecord. Repeat Steps 1 through 3 to name the Form1 control frmMovies.

STEP 5 ▶

Click the down arrow next to the Object box in the Properties window.

A drop-down list of objects showing their new names appears (Figure 2-53).

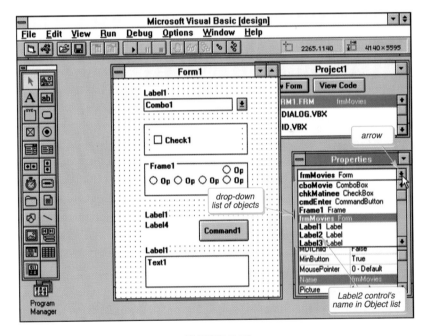

FIGURE 2-53

Changing the control names did not change their appearance on the form because the text that appears on the control is the control's caption, which is separate from the control's name.

VB TIPS
▪ After typing a value for the name property in the settings box, selecting another control or another property eliminates the need to press the ENTER key to record the change in the control's name.

Setting the Caption Property

The following steps add meaningful captions to the controls on the form, as shown in Figure 2-54.

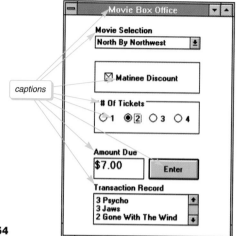

FIGURE 2-54

TO SET THE CAPTION PROPERTY ▼

STEP 1 ▶

Select the Label1 control by clicking its name in the drop-down objects list in the Properties window.

The name of the control and its properties appear in the Properties window (Figure 2-55).

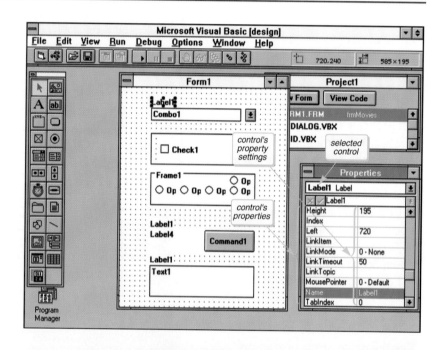

FIGURE 2-55

STEP 2 ▶

Scroll up through the Properties list until the caption property is visible. Double-click the Caption property in the Properties list.

The current value of the control's Caption property appears highlighted in the Settings box (Figure 2-56).

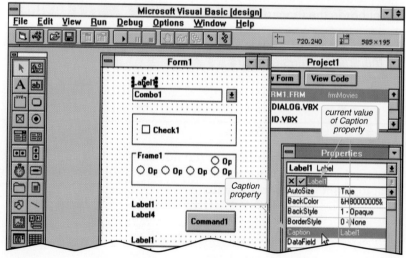

FIGURE 2-56

STEP 3 ▶

Type the new caption, `Movie Selection` and press the ENTER key.

As you type, the caption is replaced in the Settings box. When you press the ENTER key, the value is recorded and appears next to the Caption property in the Properties list (Figure 2-57).

FIGURE 2-57

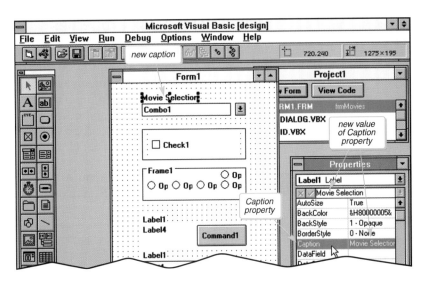

STEP 4 ▶

Repeat Steps 1 through 3 to change the captions of the controls as listed in the new caption column in Table 2-4 below.

The movie box office form (frmMovies) appears as shown in Figure 2-58.

FIGURE 2-58

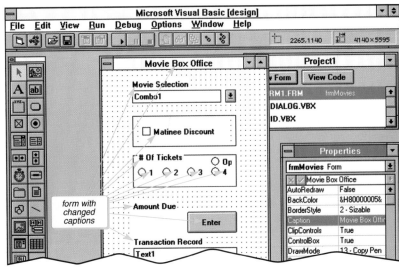

▶ TABLE 2-4 MOVIE BOX OFFICE CONTROL CAPTIONS

CONTROL	CURRENT CAPTION	NEW CAPTION
chkMatinee	Check1	Matinee Discount
Frame1	Frame1	# of Tickets
Option1	Option1	1
Option2	Option1	2
Option3	Option1	3
Option4	Option1	4
Label2	Label1	Amount Due
lblAmtdue	Label4	[blank]
cmdEnter	Command1	Enter
Label3	Label1	Transaction
frmMovies	Form1	Movie Box Office

LECTURE NOTES
■ Review the different
types of combo boxes
(values of the style property) and the difference
between the combo box
control and the list box
control.

TRANSPARENCIES
**Figures 2-59 through
Figure 2-62**

Setting Combo Box Properties

The movie box office application contains a drop-down list box for selecting the name of the movie. A combo box control indicated in Figure 2-59 was added to the form when the other controls were added. Recall from Table 2-1 on page VB67 that a drop-down list is one type of a combo box control. The type of combo box control is set by using the combo box's **style property**. Perform the following steps to make the combo box (cboMovie) a drop-down list box.

TO MAKE A COMBO BOX A DROP-DOWN LIST BOX ▼

STEP 1 ▶

Select the combo box control by clicking on it on the form (its caption is still Combo1 since it was not changed) or by selecting its name, cboMovie, from the drop-down object list in the Properties window.

Sizing handles appear around the control and the control's properties appear in the Properties window (Figure 2-59).

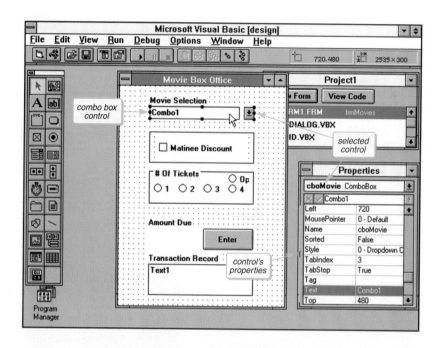

FIGURE 2-59

STEP 2 ▶

Click the style property in the Prop-erties list.

The default value of the Style property, 0-Dropdown Combo, appears in the Settings box (Figure 2-60).

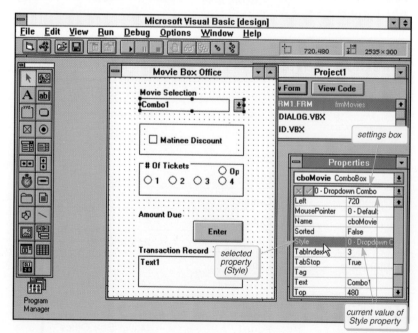

FIGURE 2-60

STEP 3 ▶

Click the down arrow located on the right of the Settings box.

A drop-down list of property values appears (Figure 2-61). Note the down arrow is detached from the combo box in the form window.

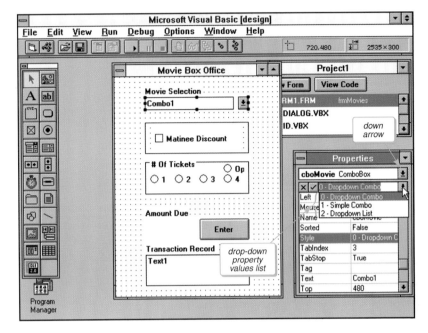

FIGURE 2-61

STEP 4 ▶

Click 2 - Dropdown List in the Property values list.

The selected value of the Style property appears in the Settings box. The drop-down list closes. The control's appearance on the form is changed so the down arrow is now immediately to the right of the control (Figure 2-62).

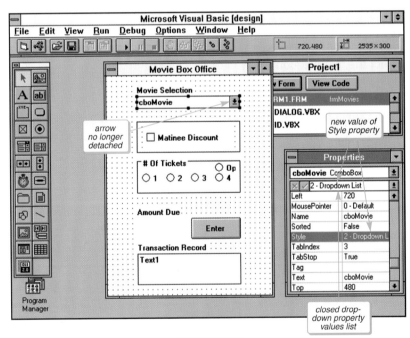

FIGURE 2-62

Although a separate Visual Basic control exists for a simple list box, the drop-down list box is one of three types of combo boxes specified by setting the Style property of the combo box control.

Setting Text Box Properties

The movie box office application contains one text box control. Its appearance in Figure 2-63 is different from the text box controls that were used in Project 1. It contains multiple lines of text (three are visible at a time), and it has a vertical scroll bar to move up and down through the text that extends beyond the borders of the control. The following steps add these features by setting the **MultiLine property** and **ScrollBars property** of the text box control.

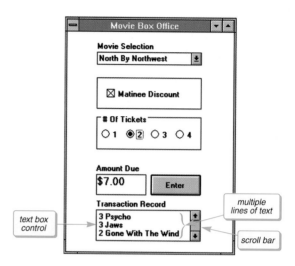

FIGURE 2-63

TO SET THE MULTILINE AND SCROLLBARS PROPERTIES OF TEXT BOXES ▼

STEP 1 ▶

Select the text box control by clicking it on the form or by selecting its name, txtRecord, from the drop-down Object list in the Properties window.

Sizing handles appear around the control, and the control's properties appear in the Properties window (Figure 2-64).

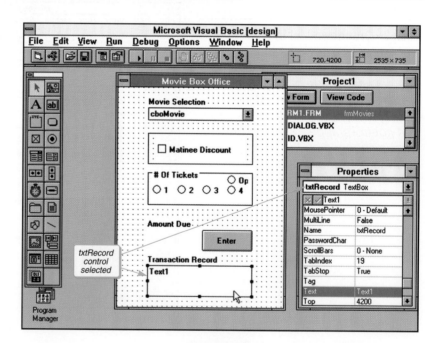

FIGURE 2-64

STEP 2 ▶

Double-click the MultiLine property in the Properties list.

The value of the MultiLine property changes from the default value of False to the new value, True (Figure 2-65).

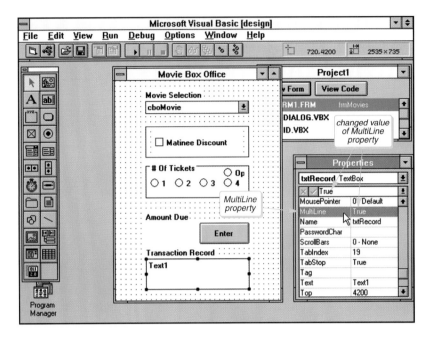

FIGURE 2-65

STEP 3 ▶

Select the ScrollBars property by clicking it in the Properties list. Click the down arrow located on the right of the Settings box.

A drop-down list of ScrollBars property values appears (Figure 2-66).

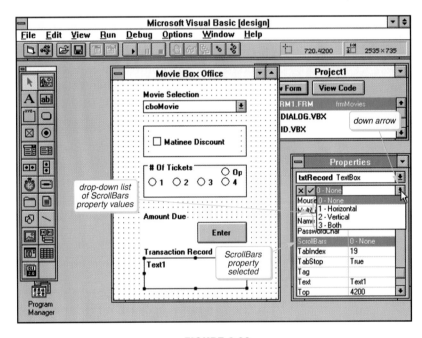

FIGURE 2-66

STEP 4 ▶

Click 2-Vertical in the Property values list.

A vertical scroll bar is added to the control. The selected value of the property appears in the Settings box, and the drop-down list closes (Figure 2-67).

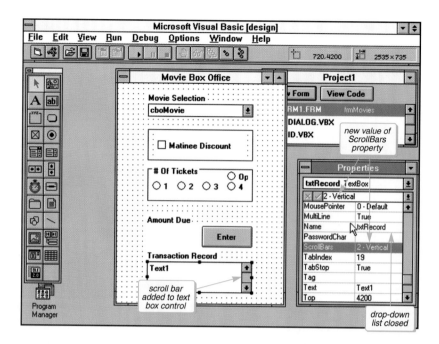

FIGURE 2-67

The drop-down list of property values for the ScrollBars property also has choices for a horizontal scroll bar or both horizontal and vertical scroll bars to be added to text box controls. If the ScrollBars property is not set and the size of the text box control is smaller than the text you want to appear, you are unable to view the text that extends beyond the borders of the text box.

Setting Label Properties

In the movie box office application, a label control (lblAmtdue) is used to display the total purchase price (Figure 2-68). A label control is used rather than a text box so the user of the application cannot change the value displayed during run time. Two features of the label control (lblAmtdue) shown in Figure 2-68 make it different from the other label controls in the movie box office application.

First, you may have thought it was a text box control because it has a border around it. Borders are added to a label control by setting the **Border-Style property**. Second, the size of the characters inside the lblAmtdue control is larger than the size of the characters in the other labels on the movie box office form (Figure 2-68). The size of the characters is set by using the **FontSize property** of the control.

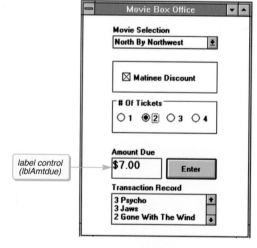

FIGURE 2-68

To set the BorderStyle property and FontSize property of labels, follow the steps on this page and the next page.

TO SET THE BORDERSTYLE PROPERTY AND FONTSIZE PROPERTY OF LABELS ▼

STEP 1 ▶

Select the label control (it appears only as a solid white rectangle on the form) by clicking it or by selecting its name, lblAmtdue, from the drop-down Object list in the Properties window.

Sizing handles appear around the control, and the control's properties appear in the Properties window (Figure 2-69).

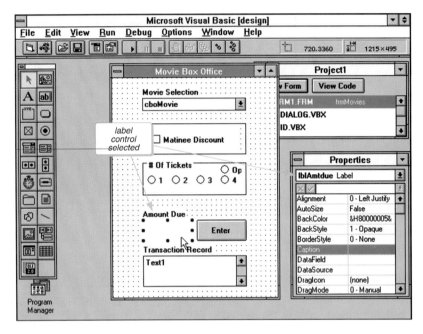

FIGURE 2-69

STEP 2 ▶

Double-click the BorderStyle property in the Properties list.

The value of the BorderStyle property changes from the default value of 0-None to the new value, 1-Fixed Single and a border appears around the control (Figure 2-70).

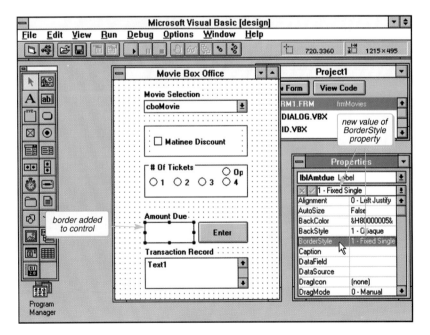

FIGURE 2-70

STEP 3 ▶

Scroll down through the Properties list until the FontSize property is visible. Select the FontSize property by clicking it in the Properties list. Click the down arrow located on the right of the Settings box.

A drop-down list of FontSize property values appears (Figure 2-71).

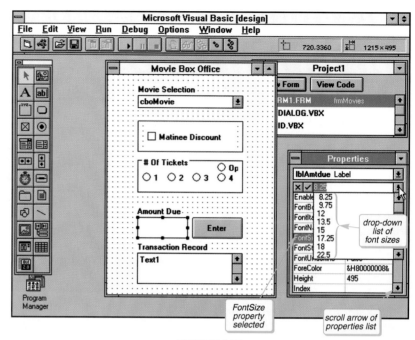

FIGURE 2-71

STEP 4 ▶

Click 12 in the FontSize Properties list.

The selected value of the FontSize property appears in the Settings box, and the drop-down list closes (Figure 2-72). The new value of lblAmtdue's FontSize displays in the Properties list.

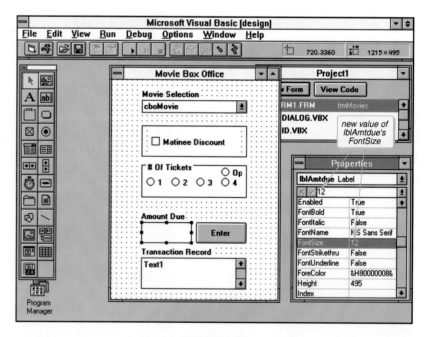

FIGURE 2-72

VB TIPS
■ When a property has a list of possible values (such as FontSize), the value in the list after the current value can be selected by double-clicking the property's name in the Properties window.

All controls that contain text or have caption properties have the FontSize property. In addition, these controls have additional font properties that you may have noticed in the Properties list. You will work with these other font properties in later projects.

The Visible Property

The five option buttons that form the option group within the frame control are shown in Figure 2-73. In the earlier discussion of option buttons, you learned that only one option button in a group can be selected at one time. Selecting a second option button automatically deselects the first option button.

In the movie box office application, you do not want any of the four option buttons representing the number of tickets purchased to be selected when the application starts. When you choose the Enter button on the form, you also want all four of these option buttons to be deselected. The way to accomplish this involves using the fifth option button added earlier.

Later, code will be written so the fifth option button is selected when the Enter button is chosen. Selecting the fifth option button automatically will deselect whichever of the other four had been selected. However, you will make it seem that no button is selected by making the fifth button invisible. The **Visible property** of a control determines whether the control can be seen at run time. Perform the following steps to make the Option5 control invisible.

LECTURE NOTES
■ Explain the visible property of controls.
■ Review what happens when you click an option button that is part of an option group.

TRANSPARENCIES
Figure 2-73 and Figure 2-74

TO SET THE VISIBLE PROPERTY ▼

STEP 1 ►

Select the option button named Option5 by clicking it or by selecting its name from the drop-down Object list in the Properties window.

Sizing handles appear around the control, and the control's properties appear in the Properties window (Figure 2-73).

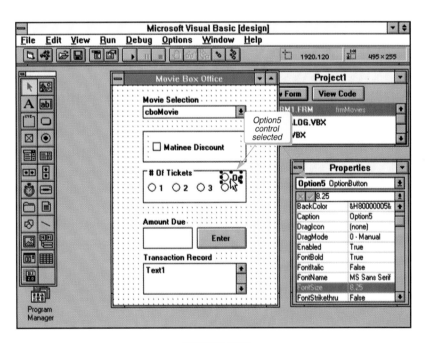

FIGURE 2-73

STEP 2 ▶

Scroll through the properties list, and double-click the Visible property.

The value of the Visible property changes from the default value of True to the new value, False (Figure 2-74).

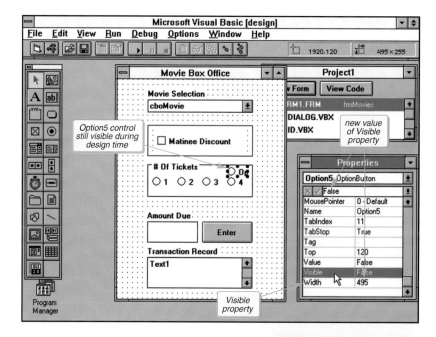

FIGURE 2-74

The Option5 control still is visible on the form during design time. At run time, however, the control will not appear on the form.

The Default Property of Command Buttons

The **Default property** of a command button allows you to press the ENTER key on the keyboard as a substitute for clicking a command button with the mouse during run time. Either action during run time will cause the code statements in the command button's Click event to be executed. Perform the following steps to set this property for the Enter button (cmdEnter) control.

TO SET THE DEFAULT PROPERTY ▼

STEP 1 ▶

Select the Enter button by clicking it or by selecting its name, cmdEnter, from the drop-down Object list in the Properties window.

Sizing handles appear around the control, and the control's properties appear in the Properties window (Figure 2-75).

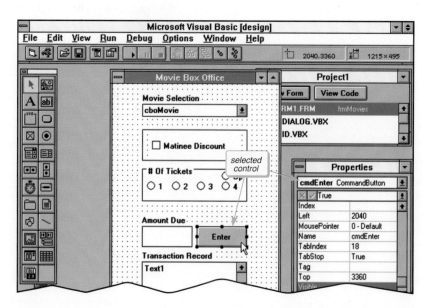

FIGURE 2-75

STEP 2 ▶

Scroll up through the Properties list, and double-click the Default property.

The value of the Default property changes from the value of False to the new value, True (Figure 2-76).

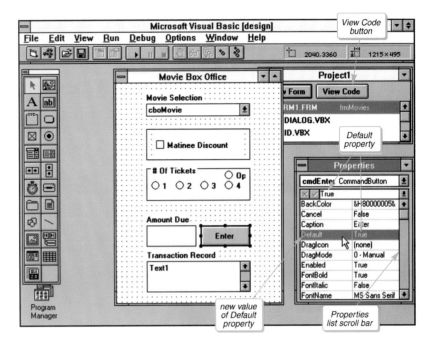

FIGURE 2-76

Only one command button on a form can have its Default property set to true, as has been done with the cmdEnter control in the movie box office application. However, if there were more than one and you changed a second command button's Default property to true, Visual Basic would automatically change the first command button's Default property back to false.

▶ WRITING CODE

LECTURE NOTES
■ Ask students to name the third step in building applications with Visual Basic.
■ Review the general syntax for setting control properties during run time with code statements.

The interface has now been built, and the properties of the controls in the movie box office application have been set. The remaining step is to write the code for the application. Project 1 introduced writing Visual Basic code through the use of statements that change the properties of controls during run time. These statements take the following general form:

```
controlname.property = value
```

The name of the control and the name of the property to be changed are separated with a period, and the value of the property to be set follows an equal sign.

This project requires more complex code statements that incorporate variables and the If...Then...Else statement. This project also shows how to cut and paste (copy) code from one subroutine to another.

Seven events in the movie box office application require event procedures (subroutines). These events and their actions are listed in Table 2-5 on the next page.

▶ **TABLE 2-5 MOVIE BOX OFFICE EVENT SUMMARY**

CONTROL	EVENT	ACTIONS
General	Declarations	Creates a variable that will be used in several of the subroutines
Form	Load	Add the movie names to the drop-down list; places a blank space in the movie name box; clears any text in the transaction list
Option1	Click	Calculates the price of one ticket and displays the amount in the amount due box
Option2	Click	Calculates the price of two tickets and displays the amount in the amount due box
Option3	Click	Calculates the price of three tickets and displays the amount in the amount due box
Option4	Click	Calculates the price of four tickets and displays the amount in the amount due box
cmdEnter	Click	Adds the number of tickets and name of the movie to the transaction list; clears the option buttons, movie name box, and amount due box

The code for the movie box office application will be written one event at a time using the Code window. Before proceeding with the code writing, the form should be saved. In the following steps, the form is saved to a formatted diskette in drive A.

TO SAVE THE FORM

Step 1: Choose the Save File As command from the File menu.
Step 2: Type `Movies` in the File Name box in the Save File As dialog box.
Step 3: Select drive A from the drop-down Drives list box.
Step 4: Choose the OK button.

The form is saved as movies.frm on the diskette in drive A and the Save File As dialog box closes.

The General Declarations Subroutine

Variables are sometimes used in code statements to store the temporary values used by other code statements. Visual Basic variables have a name you create and a data type. The **data type** determines what kind of data the variable can store (numeric or character). You must follow a few rules when choosing names for variables:

▶ the name must begin with a character
▶ the name cannot be more than 40 characters
▶ the name cannot contain punctuation or blank spaces

The easiest way to create a variable is to assign a value to the variable's name in a code statement, such as `rate = 3.5` or `name = "John"`. Variables created in this way can hold either numbers (numeric data) or characters (string data). Character data, called a **string**, is placed within quotation marks. In addition, variables can be assigned the value of another variable or the value of a mathematical expression. Table 2-6 lists several examples of code statements that create a variable and assign a value to it.

▶ **TABLE 2-6 CODE STATEMENTS THAT CREATE VARIABLES**

TRANSPARENCY
Table 2-6

EXAMPLE TYPE	STATEMENT
numeric data	price = 5
numeric data	discount = 1.15
string data	movie = "Jaws"
value of another variable	cost = price
value of an expression	cost = price - discount
value of an expression	amountdue = price * 1.05

LECTURE NOTES
■ Ask students to give
additional examples of
how variables can be
used.

When variables are created simply by using them, they can be used only within the subroutine in which they were created. For code statements in different subroutines to use the value stored in a variable, the variable must be declared. Variables are **declared** in code statements in a special procedure, where both the variable name and data type must be specified. Data types will be discussed in greater detail in Project 5.

The movie box office application uses a variable named *num* that stores the number of tickets to be purchased. The variable is used in more than one event subroutine, and therefore it must be declared. The following steps write a declaration for this variable.

TRANSPARENCIES
Figures 2-77 and Figure
2-78

TO DECLARE A VARIABLE ▼

STEP 1 ▶

Choose the View Code button in the Project window.

The Code window opens (Figure 2-77). The insertion point is located at the top left of the Code window.

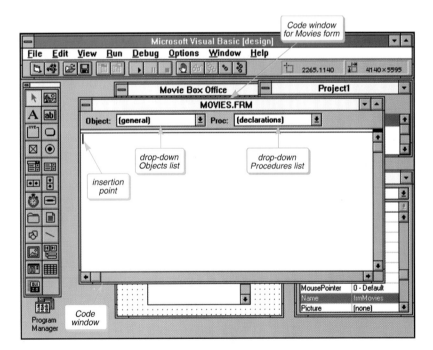

FIGURE 2-77

STEP 2 ▶

Enter the following statement in the Code window:

Dim num as Integer

When you press the ENTER *key, the cursor moves to the beginning of the next line, and some of the typed characters change to upper case or change color (Figure 2-78).*

FIGURE 2-78

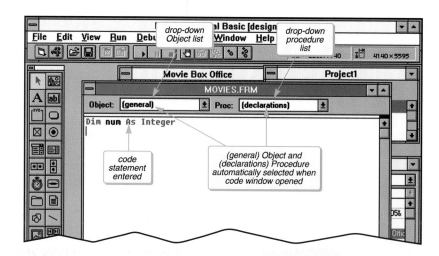

The declaration statement always has the following form:

DIM variablename As datatype

When you press the ENTER key at the end of a code statement, Visual Basic inspects the code for many common errors. If it finds an error, a dialog box opens. Some of the characters' case and color are automatically changed for ease in reading the code.

In Project 1, you learned how to open the Code window and select a control from the object list by double-clicking the control in the Form window. If you are going to write procedures for several controls, it can be awkward to move between the Form window and the Code window just to select different controls in the code window. A more general way to enter, edit, or view a subroutine in the Code window involves these steps (refer to Figure 2-78):

▶ select the control that you wish to assign code to from the drop-down object list
▶ select the desired event from the drop-down procedures list
▶ enter the code statements

When the declaration statement was written, it was not necessary to select an object and a procedure from the drop-down lists in the Code window since the declarations procedure already is selected when the Code window is opened the first time.

The Form_Load Event

The **Form_Load** event causes a subroutine of code statements to be carried out when the form is loaded into the computer's memory at run time. For applications with a single form, such as the movie box office application, this execution occurs when the application starts.

Recall from Table 2-5 on page VB94 that the Form_Load event adds items to the drop-down list of movie names (cboMovie), places a blank line in the movie name box until a movie is selected, and clears any text in the transactions list (txtRecord).

Items such as the list of movie names are added to a list box or combo box by using **ADDITEM** code statements. These statements take the following form:

controlname.ADDITEM "item to be added"

Each item (movie name) added to the list is given a consecutive number (**index**) by Visual Basic that can be used to reference that item in the list. The first item is given an index of 0. When an item is selected during run time, the **ListIndex property** of the control is given the value of that item's index. You can select an item from the list in a code statement by changing the control's ListIndex property.

For the initial movie name displayed in the combo box to be blank, code will be written to add a blank item to the list and to select that blank item by setting the ListIndex property of the movie list box (cboMovie).

One more code statement must be added to cause the transactions list (txtRecord) to be empty. This procedure is done by setting the value of its text property equal to the **null string** (two consecutive quotation marks).

The following steps write the code statements that will occur each time the application starts.

TO WRITE THE FORM_LOAD SUBROUTINE ▼

STEP 1 ▶

Display the drop-down list of controls by clicking the down arrow located next to the Object box in the Code window.

A list of the controls on the Movies form displays (Figure 2-79).

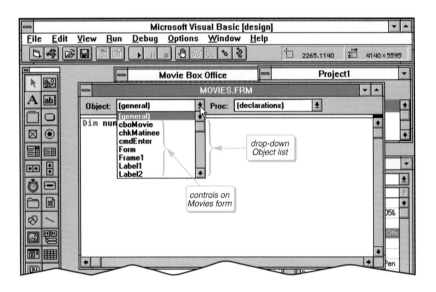

FIGURE 2-79

STEP 2 ▶

Select the form control by clicking the word Form in the Object list.

The Form_Load procedure appears in the Code window. An insertion point appears at the beginning of a blank line located between the first and last statements of the subroutine (Figure 2-80).

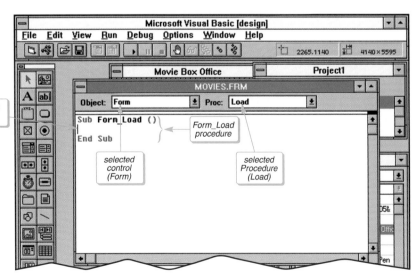

FIGURE 2-80

STEP 3 ▶

Enter the following eight statements in the Code window:

```
cboMovie.Additem " "
cboMovie.Additem "Jaws"
cboMovie.Additem "Gone
With
 The Wind"
cboMovie.Additem "Psycho"
cboMovie.Additem "North
By
 Northwest"
cboMovie.Additem "Exodus"
cboMovie.Listindex = 0
txtRecord.Text = " "
```

The Code window appears as shown in Figure 2-81.

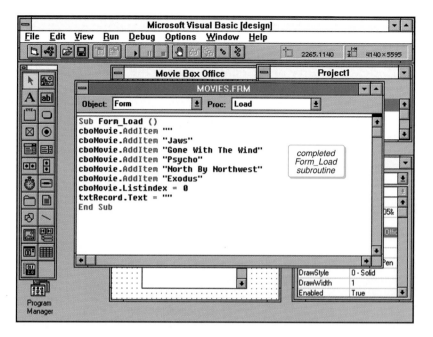

FIGURE 2-81

In the preceding steps you did not have to select the load procedure from the drop-down Procedures list in the Code window since the load procedure is the first one displayed when the form object is chosen from the drop-down Object list.

The Option1_Click Subroutine

LECTURE NOTES
▪ Review the actions that occur when an option button is clicked in the box office application.

TRANSPARENCIES
Table 2-7 and Figure 2-82 and Figure 2-83

LECTURE NOTES
▪ Explain the logic of the If..Then..Else structure.
▪ Define relational operators.
▪ Illustrate the use of the If..Then..Else structure in the box office application.

The next step is to write the code for the four visible option buttons (Option1 through Option4) located inside the frame control labeled # of Tickets (Figure 2-76 on Page VB93). The code for each option button is nearly identical. The following paragraphs describe the code for the Click event of the first option button (Option1_Click subroutine). Later, the code will be copied for the other three option buttons' Click events.

The click subroutine for each option button must do the following:

1. Assign the number of tickets purchased to the num variable.
2. Determine the ticket price.
3. Calculate the amount due as num*price, and display it as dollars and cents in the Amount Due box.

The first code statement must set the variable (num) equal to the number of tickets corresponding to that option button (selecting Opt1 represents 1 ticket). The values assigned to num for the other three option buttons are 2, 3, and 4 respectively. Thus, for the first option button, the following statement sets the variable num equal to 1:

```
num = 1
```

The second code statement will use a single-line If...Then...Else statement to determine the price of the tickets purchased (based on whether the matinee discount is being given). In the movie box office application, the regular price for all movies is $5, and the matinee price for all movies is $3.50.

Single-line **If...Then...Else statements** are used to execute one statement or another conditionally. A partial flowchart and the form of the single-line If...Then...Else statement is shown in Figure 2-82. The condition follows the keyword If. A **condition** is made up of two expressions and a relational operator. Table 2-7 lists the **relational operators** and their meanings.

▸ **TABLE 2-7 RELATIONAL OPERATOR MEANINGS**

RELATIONAL OPERATOR	MEANING
=	is equal to
<	is less than
>	is greater than
<=	is less than or equal to
>=	is greater than or equal
<>	is not equal to

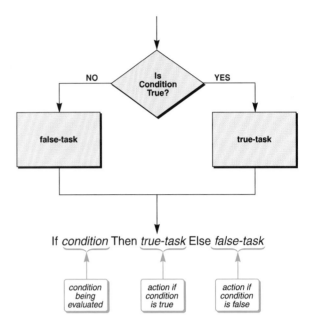

FIGURE 2-82

The statement to be executed when the condition is true follows the keyword Then. The statement to be executed when the condition is false follows the keyword Else. Figure 2-83 shows the logic and single-line If...Then...Else statement to determine the price of the ticket(s) purchased.

Recall that the Value property of a check box control is 1 when the box is checked and 0 when it is not checked. The chkMatinee.Value is equal to 1 or 0 depending on whether the user of the application has selected the option Matinee Discount. If the option Matinee Discount is selected, then the price of a ticket is $3.50, else the price of a ticket is $5.

The amount due is equal to the number of tickets purchased times the price. Thus, the formula num * price determines the amount due. The movie box office application displays amount due as the caption of the lblAmtdue control, using dollars and cents. The following statement determines the amount due and formats the amount due as dollars and cents:

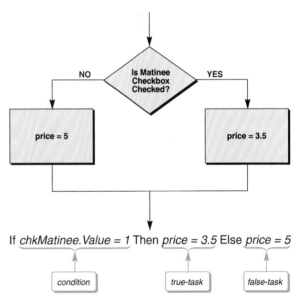

FIGURE 2-83

```
lblAmtdue.Caption = Format$(num * price, "currency")
```

lblAmtdue is the name of the Amount due box. Format$ is a function that takes the first item in parentheses, num * price, and formats it to the second item in the parentheses, "currency". Currency is a **predefined format name**, which means Visual Basic will display the value num * price in a more readable fashion in the Amount Due box. The $ character appended to Format instructs Visual Basic to change the numeric result of num * price to a string before it is assigned as the caption of the label control lblAmtdue.

Table 2-8 summarizes the most often used predefined formats in Visual Basic.

▶ **TABLE 2-8 PREDEFINED FORMATS IN VISUAL BASIC**

FORMAT	DESCRIPTION
General	Displays the number as is.
Currency	Displays number with dollar sign, thousands separator with two digits to the right of the decimal. Negative numbers display enclosed in parentheses.
Fixed	Displays at least one digit to the left and two digits to the right of the decimal separator.
Standard	Displays number with thousands separator. If appropriate, displays two digits to the right of the decimal.
Percent	Displays number multiplied by 100 with percent (%) sign.
Yes/No	Displays No if number is 0; otherwise displays Yes.

Perform the following steps to enter the code for the Option1_Click subroutine.

TO WRITE THE OPTION1_CLICK SUBROUTINE ▼

STEP 1 ▶

Click the arrow located next to the Object box in the Code window.

The drop-down list of Objects opens (Figure 2-84).

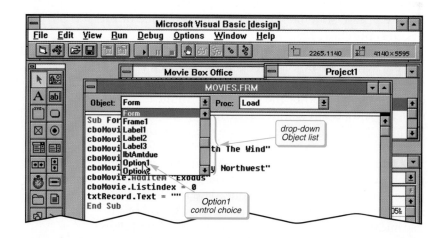

FIGURE 2-84

STEP 2 ▶

Click the Option1 choice in the Object list.

The Option1_Click subroutine appears in the Code window (Figure 2-85).

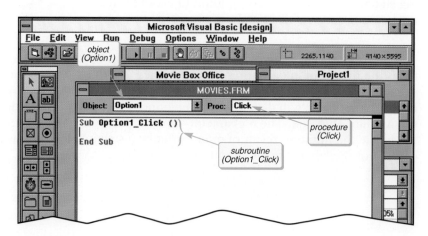

FIGURE 2-85

STEP 3 ▶

Enter the following three statements in the Code window:
```
num = 1
If chkMatinee.Value = 1
  Then price = 3.5
  Else price = 5
lblAmtdue.Caption =
  Format$(num * price,
  "currency")
```

The Code window appears as shown in Figure 2-86.

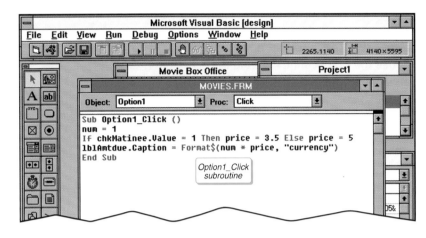

FIGURE 2-86

As mentioned earlier, the subroutines for the other three option button Click events are very similar to this first one. Rather than typing all of the code statements in all of the subroutines, you will copy the code from the first subroutine to the other three and then make the minor changes necessary within the copied subroutines. To copy code between subroutines, perform the following steps.

TRANSPARENCIES
Figure 2-87 through
Figure 2-92

TO COPY CODE BETWEEN SUBROUTINES ▽

STEP 1 ▶

Position the mouse pointer to the left of the first character in the second line of code (Figure 2-87).

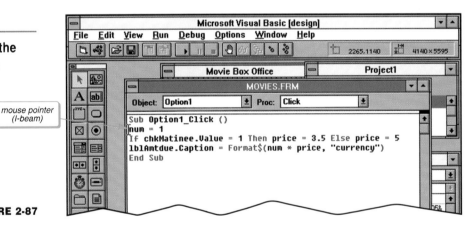

FIGURE 2-87

STEP 2 ▶

Drag the mouse downward through the next to the last line of code.

The code statements are highlighted (Figure 2-88).

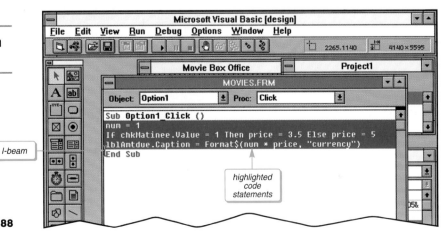

FIGURE 2-88

STEP 3 ▶

Release the left mouse button. Choose the Copy command from the Edit menu (Figure 2-89).

The highlighted text is copied to the Clipboard.

FIGURE 2-89

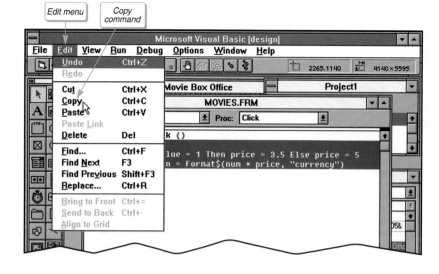

STEP 4 ▶

Select the Option2 control from the drop-down Object list in the Code window.

The Option2_Click subroutine appears with the insertion point at the beginning of the second line (Figure 2-90).

FIGURE 2-90

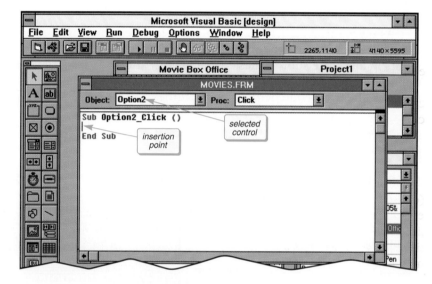

STEP 5 ▶

Choose the Paste command from the Edit menu.

The code is copied from the Clipboard to the procedure in the Code window (Figure 2-91).

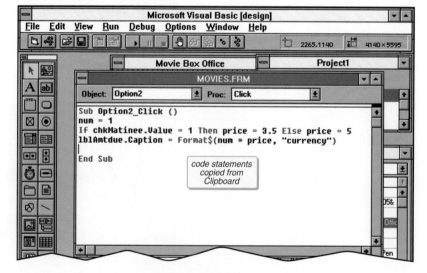

FIGURE 2-91

STEP 6 ▶

Edit the code to change the second line from num = 1 to num = 2

This changes only what is different when 2 tickets are purchased Figure 2-92).

FIGURE 2-92

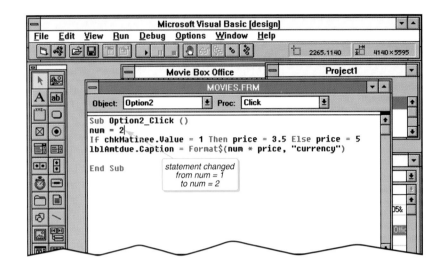

Repeat Steps 4 through 6 to copy the code and edit it for the Option3_Click event and the Option4_Click event.

Once code has been copied to the Clipboard, it is not necessary to recopy it each time. You can continue to paste it as many times as is needed. Each time you copy code to the Clipboard, the previous contents of the Clipboard are erased.

The cmdEnter_Click Subroutine

The cmdEnter_Click event occurs when you click the Enter button (cmdEnter) on the form (Figure 2-93) or press the ENTER key on the keyboard. This event adds the number of tickets and the movie's name to the top of a scrollable list in the transaction record (txtRecord) and clears the movie name, number of tickets, and amount due. To accomplish this task, several functions involving the manipulation of string data are used.

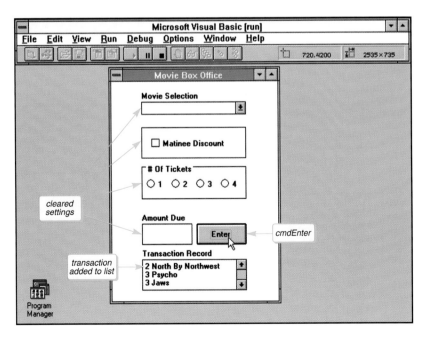

FIGURE 2-93

The value of a text box's text property is a single string (group of characters). To have the transaction record behave the way it does, it is necessary to add special control code characters to the string that cause a new line to be started each time the cmdEnter event occurs. These characters are **chr$(13)** and **chr$(10)**. The characters `chr$(13)` tell Visual Basic to return the cursor to the beginning of the line. The characters `chr$(10)` tell Visual Basic to move the cursor down one line.

Since the record must contain all of the previous sales information, it is necessary to add the new data to the old rather than replace it with the new data. This process of adding strings together is called **concatenation** and is done with the ampersand (&) character. The code statement to accomplish this is as follows:

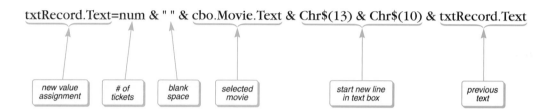

The code statements for the rest of the cmdEnter_Click subroutine are explained as follows:

The list box is returned to an empty state by selecting the blank list item:

    cboMovie.Listindex = 0

The matinee check box is unchecked by setting its Value property:

    chkMatinee.Value = 0

The selected option button is deselected by selecting the Option5 (invisible) option button:

    Option5.Value = True

The amount due is cleared by blanking the caption of the lblAmtdue control:

    lblAmtdue.Caption = " "

Perform the following steps to write the cmdEnter_Click subroutine.

TO WRITE THE CMDENTER_CLICK SUBROUTINE ▼

STEP 1 ▶

Select the cmdEnter control from the drop-down Object list in the Code window.

The cmdEnter_click subroutine appears in the Code window (Figure 2- 94).

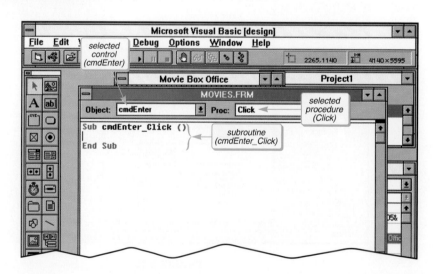

FIGURE 2-94

STEP 2 ▶

Enter the following statement in the Code window:

```
txtRecord.Text = num & "  "
   & cboMovie.Text &
   Chr$(13) & Chr$(10) &
   txtRecord.Text
```

A single code statement must all be placed on a single line in the Code window. As you type the code, the Code window scrolls. Pressing the ENTER key advances the cursor to the beginning of the next line (Figure 2-95).

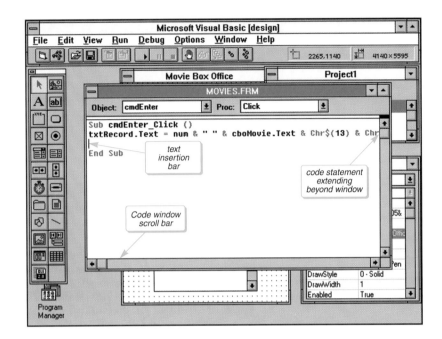

FIGURE 2-95

STEP 3 ▶

Enter the following four statements in the Code window:

```
cboMovie.Listindex = 0
chkMatinee.Value = 0
Option5.Value = True
lblAmtdue.Caption = " "
```

The Code window appears as shown in Figure 2-96.

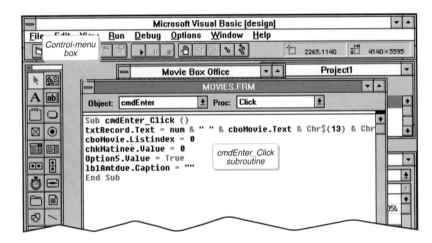

FIGURE 2-96

STEP 4 ▶

Double-click the Code window's Control-menu box.

The Code window closes (Figure 2-97).

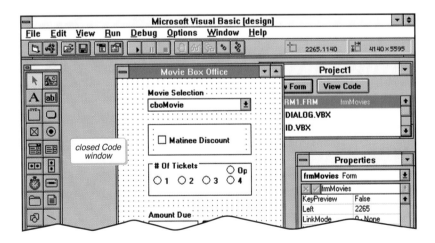

FIGURE 2-97

▶ SAVING AND RUNNING THE APPLICATION

T he movie box office application is now complete. Before running the application, the form and the project should be saved to a formatted diskette in drive A. The form was saved previously, before the subroutines were written. Saving the project will automatically re-save the form with the code included. The following steps save the project as movies.mak and save the amended form as movies.frm.

TO SAVE THE PROJECT

Step 1: Choose the Save Project command from the File menu.
Step 2: Type `Movies` in the File Name box in the Save Project As dialog box.
Step 3: Choose the OK button.

The application is saved to the disk in drive A as two files, one for the form (MOVIES.FRM) and one for the project (MOVIES.MAK).

Perform the following steps to test your movie box office application. After Step 13, your application should appear as shown in Figure 2-98.

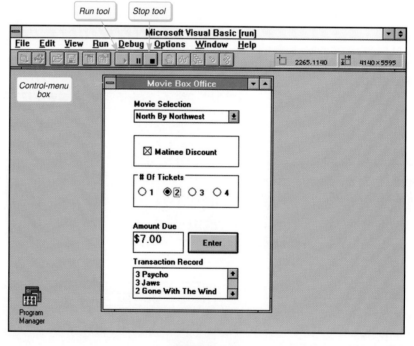

FIGURE 2-98

TO RUN THE APPLICATION

Step 1: Click the Run tool on the toolbar, or choose the Start command from the Run menu.

Step 2: Select *Gone With The Wind* from the Movie Selection list.

Step 3: Choose the *2* tickets option button.

Step 4: Choose the Enter button.

Step 5: Select *Jaws* from the movies list.

Step 6: Choose the *3* tickets option button.

Step 7: Choose the Enter button.

Step 8: Select *Psycho* from the movies list.

Step 9: Choose the *3* tickets option button.

Step 10: Choose the Enter button.

Step 11: Select *North By Northwest* from the movies list.

Step 12: Check the matinee discount box.

Step 13: Choose the *2* tickets option button. The application appears as shown in Figure 2-98.

Step 14: To close (end) the application, click the Stop tool on the toolbar, or double-click the movie box office's Control-menu box.

Step 15: To close Visual Basic, choose Exit from the File menu or double-click the Control-menu box on the menu bar and toolbar window.

▶ PROJECT SUMMARY

Project 2 introduced you to building more complex applications than those built in Project 1. You used additional properties of the controls you learned about in Project 1, as well as several additional controls. You learned more about writing code by writing six event subroutines and a declaration procedure. You learned how to copy controls and to copy code between subroutines. You used variables in code statements and used code statements to concatenate string data.

There is no single, correct interface for a given application, nor is there a single, correct way to write code. In building this application, you may have thought of different ways to design the interface. You may have realized the events and code could have been written in a number of ways. See if you can think of other ways to design the interface and to create the events. Building applications in a graphical environment is an exciting, creative enterprise.

▶ KEY TERMS

ADDITEM *(VB96)*
AutoSize property *(VB62)*
BorderStyle property *(VB88)*
check box *(VB70)*
combo box *(VB66)*
concatenation *(VB104)*
condition *(VB99)*
chr$(10) *(VB104)*
chr$(13) *(VB104)*
data type *(VB94)*
declaration *(VB95)*

default property *(VB92)*
drop-down list box *(VB66)*
FontSize property *(VB88)*
format$ *(VB99)*
Form_Load event *(VB96)*
frame control *(VB71)*
If...Then...Else statement *(VB98)*
index *(VB97)*
list box *(VB66)*
ListIndex property *(VB97)*
MultiLine property *(VB86)*

name property *(VB79)*
null string *(VB97)*
option button *(VB73)*
Predefined format name *(VB99)*
relational operator *(VB99)*
ScrollBars property *(VB86)*
shape control *(VB68)*
string *(VB94)*
style property *(VB84)*
variable *(VB94)*
Visible property *(VB91)*

In Visual Basic you can accomplish a task in a number of ways. The following table provides a quick reference to each of the major tasks presented for the first time in the project with some of the available options. The commands listed in the Menu column can be executed using either the keyboard or mouse.

Task	Mouse	Menu	Keyboard Shortcuts
Copy Code from the Clipboard to a Selected Code Window		From Edit menu, choose Paste	Press CTRL+V
Copy Highlighted Code to the Clipboard		From Edit menu, choose Copy	Press CTRL+C
Copy Selected Control to the Clipboard		From Edit menu, choose Copy	Press CTRL+C
Highlight (Select) Code Statements in the Code Window	Drag mouse across code block to be selected		Press SHIFT+arrow key
Paste a Control from the Clipboard onto a Selected Form		From Edit menu, choose Paste	Press CTRL+V

STUDENT ASSIGNMENTS

EXERCISE NOTES
■ Use Student Assignments 1 through 6 for classroom discussion or homework exercises.

STUDENT ASSIGNMENT 1
True/False

Instructions: Circle T if the statement is true or F if the statement is false.

(T) F 1. Only one command button on a form can have its default property set to True.

T (F) 2. The Copy and Paste commands are found in the Options menu.

T (F) 3. A drop-down list box always has a scroll bar.

T (F) 4. A frame control can have a circular shape.

(T) F 5. When you click an option button during run time, an X appears inside the control.

(T) F 6. When controls have been added inside a frame, you can move all of the controls on the form by dragging just the frame.

T (F) 7. During run time, only one check box can be "checked" at a time.

T (F) 8. Code statements can be used to change the value that a control's property has at design time.

(T) F 9. A common practice in naming controls is to use a three-letter prefix designating to which form the control belongs.

VB108

T̲ F 10. A text box control does not have a Caption property.
T̲ F 11. The Style property is used to determine what type of combo box is displayed.
T F̲ 12. Scroll bars are added automatically to a text box when its text will not fit within its borders.
T F̲ 13. There is no difference between a label control and a text box control whose BorderStyle is fixed single.
T F̲ 14. A label is the only control that has a FontSize property.
T̲ F 15. For a variable to be used in more than one subroutine, it must be declared.
T̲ F 16. The ListIndex property can be set only during run time.
T̲ F 17. Code statements can be cut, copied, and pasted from one subroutine to another.
T F̲ 18. Format$ is a property of all controls that have either Text or Caption properties.
T F̲ 19. When the MultiLine property of a text box is set to True, a scroll bar automatically is added to the text box.
T F̲ 20. Concatenation is a process used to add strings to numbers.

STUDENT ASSIGNMENT 2
Multiple Choice

Instructions: Circle the correct response.

1. If a command button's default property is set to True, pressing the _____ key during run time will have the same effect as clicking the command button.
   a. SPACEBAR
   b. CTRL
   c. ENTER
   d. ALT

2. A shape control cannot appear on a form as a(n) _____.
   a. elipse
   b. circle
   c. square
   d. diamond

3. When a control is copied, the _____ have (has) the same values as those of the control that was copied.
   a. the name property only
   b. all properties
   c. all properties except the name
   d. none of the properties

4. The _____ is not a style of combo box.
   a. drop-down list
   b. simple list
   c. drop-down combo box
   d. simple combo box

5. The _____ can be changed during run time by using the keyboard.
   a. Caption property of labels
   b. Text property of text boxes
   c. both a and b
   d. neither a nor b

STUDENT ASSIGNMENT 2 (continued)

6. The code statement _____ will add the name John to a list that appears in a combo box with the control name of cboNames.
   a. cboNames.ADDITEM = "John"
   b. ADDITEM.cboNames = "John"
   c. ADDITEM."John".cboNames
   d. cboNames.ADDITEM "John"
7. The control code chr$(10) _____.
   a. moves the cursor to the beginning of a new line
   b. signals the end of a line
   c. always must be used with chr$(13)
   d. sets the MultiLine property to True
8. The syntax for a code statement that changes the value of a property of a control is _____.
   a. controlname.property.oldvalue = controlname.property.newvalue
   b. property.controlname.newvalue
   c. controlname.property = newvalue
   d. property.controlname = newvalue
9. The _____ property is used to make a control not visible on a form during run time.
   a. invisible
   b. default
   c. BorderStyle
   d. visible
10. Code statements of the form DIM variablename AS datatype are placed in the _____ subroutine.
    a. form_load
    b. form_declarations
    c. form_general
    d. general_declarations

STUDENT ASSIGNMENT 3
Understanding Visual Basic Tools and Control Name Prefixes

Instructions: Figure SA2-3 shows the Visual Basic Toolbox and lists the prefixes used in naming several controls. In the space provided, match the control name prefix to the tool used to add that control to a form.

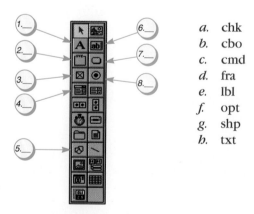

a. chk
b. cbo
c. cmd
d. fra
e. lbl
f. opt
g. shp
h. txt

FIGURE SA2-3

STUDENT ASSIGNMENT 4
Understanding Controls and Properties

Instructions: Figure SA2-4 lists the controls and properties you used in this project. Place an X in the space provided if the control has the property that follows. Hint: A control may have a property that you haven't used yet. If you're unsure, add the control to a form and look at the drop-down Properties list box in the Properties window or use online Help.

PROPERTIES	CONTROLS								
	Form	Check Box	Combo Box	Command Button	Frame	Label	Option Button	Shape	Text Box
AutoSize	[ ]	[ ]	[ ]	[ ]	[ ]	[X]	[ ]	[ ]	[ ]
BorderStyle	[X]	[ ]	[ ]	[ ]	[ ]	[X]	[ ]	[ ]	[X]
Caption	[X]	[X]	[ ]	[X]	[X]	[X]	[X]	[X]	[ ]
Default	[ ]	[ ]	[ ]	[X]	[ ]	[ ]	[ ]	[ ]	[ ]
FontSize	[X]	[X]	[X]	[X]	[X]	[X]	[X]	[ ]	[X]
MultiLine	[ ]	[ ]	[ ]	[ ]	[ ]	[ ]	[ ]	[ ]	[X]
Name	[X]	[X]	[X]	[X]	[X]	[X]	[X]	[X]	[X]
ScrollBars	[ ]	[ ]	[ ]	[ ]	[ ]	[ ]	[ ]	[ ]	[X]
Shape	[ ]	[ ]	[ ]	[ ]	[ ]	[ ]	[ ]	[X]	[ ]
Style	[ ]	[ ]	[X]	[ ]	[ ]	[ ]	[ ]	[ ]	[ ]
Text	[ ]	[ ]	[ ]	[ ]	[ ]	[ ]	[ ]	[ ]	[X]
Visible	[X]	[X]	[X]	[X]	[X]	[X]	[X]	[X]	[X]

FIGURE SA2-4

STUDENT ASSIGNMENT 5
Understanding Code Statements

Instructions: Enter the correct answers.

1. Write a code statement that will display the characters `Hello` in a text box with a control name of txtGreeting.

Statement: txtGreeting.Text = "Hello"

2. Write a code statement that will display the characters `Goodbye` in a label control with a control name of lblGreeting.

Statement: lblGreeting.Caption = "Goodbye"

3. Write a code statement that will create a variable named `Amount`. The variable should have an integer data type and should be able to be used in multiple subroutines.

Statement: Dim Amount As Integer

4. Write a code statement that will add `July` to a list that is displayed in a drop-down list with a control name of cboMonths.

Statement: cboMonths.AddItem "July"

STUDENT ASSIGNMENT 5 (continued)

5. Write a code statement that concatenates the contents of three text boxes (txt1, txt2, txt3) and displays the result in a fourth text box (txt4).

Statement: txt4.Text = txt1.Text & txt2.Text & txt3.Text

6. Write a code statement that displays Hello in a label control (lblGreeting) if a check box (chkOne) is checked and displays Goodbye in the label if the check box is not checked.

Statement:

If chkOne.Checked = True Then lblGreeting.Caption = "Hello" Else lblGreeting.Caption = "Goodbye"

STUDENT ASSIGNMENT 6
Understanding Mathematical and Logical Operators

Instructions: Consider an application with the following controls, property settings and variable assignments.

    txtAmount.text = 45
    rate = .1
    price = 60
    chkDiscount.Value = 1

Fill in the requested value after each of the following code statements.

1. `lblDue.Caption = txtAmount.Text * rate`
   lblDue.Caption: 4.5

2. `If chkDiscount.Value = 0 Then lblDue.Caption = rate * txtAmount.Text`
   lblDue.Caption: value of lblDue.Caption at beginning of run time (unchanged)

3. `If rate <= .5 Then txtAmount.Text = txtAmount.Text - 10`
   txtAmount.Text: 35

4. `price = rate * txtAmount.Text / 5`
   price: .9

5. `lblDue.Borderstyle = 1`
   lblDue.Caption: value of lblDue.Caption at beginning of run time (unchanged)

6. `If chkDiscount.Value = 1 Then price = txtAmount.Text * rate - 5 Else price = txtAmount.Text * rate`
   price: -.5

EXERCISE NOTES
■ Exercise 1 builds an application that uses check boxes to control a demonstration of Font properties.

COMPUTER LABORATORY EXERCISE 1
Changing Properties at Run Time with Check Boxes

Instructions: Start Visual Basic. Open project CLE2-1 from the subdirectory VB3 on the Student Diskette that accompanies this book. Complete the tasks listed below Figure CLE2-1. When you run the application, you can see the effects of different font properties by selecting those properties with check boxes, as shown in Figure CLE2-1.

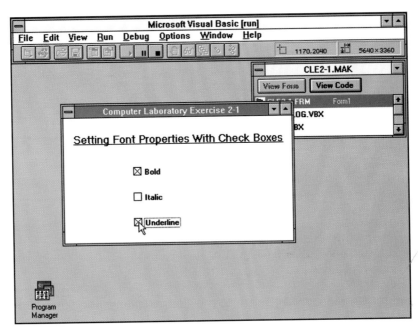

FIGURE CLE2-1

1. Choose the View Form button in the Project window.
2. Choose the View Code button in the Project window.
3. Select the chkBold control from the drop-down Object list in the Code window.
4. Type the following code statement: `lblDisplay.Fontbold = chkBold.Value`
5. Select the chkItalic control from the drop-down Object list in the Code window.
6. Type the following code statement: `lblDisplay.FontItalic = chkItalic.Value`
7. Select the chkUnderline control from the drop-down Object list in the Code window.
8. Type the following code statement: `lblDisplay.FontUnderline = chkUnderline.value`
9. Save the project using the form name CLE2-1A.FRM and the project name CLE2-1A.MAK.
10. Close the Code window by double-clicking its control-menu box.
11. Run the application. Double-click the form's Control-menu box to stop the application.
12. Check with your instructor for directions on turning in the exercise.

EXERCISE NOTES
■ Exercise 2 builds an application that uses an option button group to control a demonstration of mathematical operators.

COMPUTER LABORATORY EXERCISE 2
Mathematical Operators and Option Groups

Instructions: Start Visual Basic. Open project CLE2-2 from the subdirectory VB3 on the Student Diskette that accompanies this book.

Perform the following steps. When you run the completed application, you will enter two numbers and click an option button that designates the operation to perform. The result of the operation then is displayed (Figure CLE2-2).

1. Choose the View Form button in the Project window.
2. Use the Properties window to change the name of the Option1 control to optAdd.
2. Use the Properties window to change the name of the Option2 control to optSubtract.
3. Use the Properties window to change the name of the Option3 control to optMultiply.
4. Use the Properties window to change the name of the Option4 control to optDivide.
5. Use the Properties window to change the name of the Option5 control to optClear.
6. Choose the View Code button in the Project window.

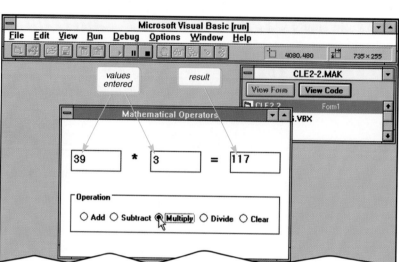

FIGURE CLE2-2

7. Select optAdd from the drop-down Object list in the Code window. Type the following two code statements:
```
lblOperation.Caption = "+"
lblResult.Caption = Val(txtNum1.Text) + Val(txtNum2.Text)
```
8. Select optSubtract from the drop-down Object list in the Code window. Type the following two code statements:
```
lblOperation.Caption = "-"
lblResult.Caption = Val(txtNum1.Text) - Val(txtNum2.Text)
```
9. Select optMultiply from the drop-down Object list in the Code window. Type the following two code statements:
```
lblOperation.Caption = "*"
lblResult.Caption = Val(txtNum1.Text) * Val(txtNum2.Text)
```
10. Select optDivide from the drop-down Object list in the code window. Type the following two code statements:
```
lblOperation.Caption = "/"
lblResult.Caption = Val(txtNum1.Text) / Val(txtNum2.Text)
```
11. Select optClear from the drop-down Object list in the Code window. Type the following four code statements:
```
txtNum1.Text = ""
lblOperation.Caption = ""
txtNum2.Text = ""
lblResult.Caption = ""
```
12. Save the project using the form name CLE2-2A.FRM and the project name CLE2-2A.MAK.
13. Close the Code window. Run the application. Press the TAB key to move between text boxes. Double-click the form's Control-menu box to stop the application.
14. Check with your instructor for directions on turning in the exercise.

COMPUTER LABORATORY EXERCISE 3
Relational Operators and Copying Code

EXERCISE NOTES
■ Exercise 3 builds an application that uses If..Then..Else statements and the Val function to demonstrate relational operators.

Instructions: Start Visual Basic. Open project CLE2-3 from the subdirectory VB3 on the Student Diskette that accompanies this book.

Perform the steps listed below Figure CLE2-3. When you run the completed application, you will enter two numbers and click a command button that designates the relational operation to perform. The result of the operation then is displayed (Figure CLE2-3).

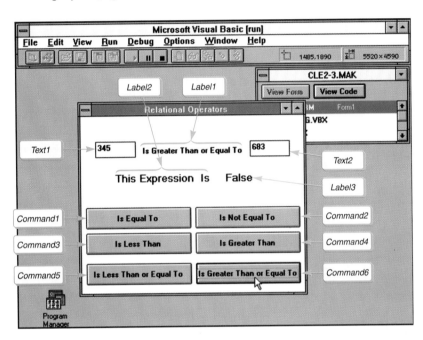

FIGURE CLE2-3

1. Choose the View Form button in the Project window.
2. Choose the View Code button in the Project window.
3. Select the Command1 control from the drop-down Object list in the Code window.
4. Type `Label1.Caption = Command1.Caption` and press the ENTER key.
5. Type `If Val(Text1.Text) = Val(Text2.Text) then Label3.Caption = "True" Else Label3.Caption = "False"`
   Press the ENTER key.
6. Use the mouse to highlight the two code statements, as was done on page VB101.
7. Select Edit from the menu bar. Choose Copy from the Edit menu.
8. Select the Command3 control from the drop-down Object list in the Code window.
9. Select Edit from the menu bar. Choose Paste from the Edit menu. Change `Command1` in the first line to `Command3`. **Change** `If Val(Text1.Text) = Val(Text2.Text)` in the second line to `If Val(Text1.Text)< Val(Text2.Text)`
10. Repeat Steps 8 through 9 for each of the remaining command buttons, changing the name of the command button in the first code statement and the relational operator in the second code statement, so that the relational operators match the captions as shown in Figure CLE2-3. Refer to Table 2-7 on VB99.
11. Save the project using the form name CLE2-3A.FRM and the project name CLE2-3A.MAK.
12. Close the Code window.
13. Run the application. Try different combinations of values and relational operators. Double-click the form's Control-menu box to stop the application.
14. Check with your instructor for directions on turning in the exercise.

EXERCISE NOTES
■ The four Computer Laboratory Assignments increase in
difficulty. Give students directions for turning in the
assignments.

COMPUTER LABORATORY ASSIGNMENT 1
Drop-down Phone List

Purpose: To build an application that allows the addition of items to a drop-down list during run time.

Problem: In Project 2, you added items to a drop-down list using the AddItem method in the Form_Load procedure. In this application you would like to have a drop-down list of phone numbers (Figure CLA2-1), but you also want to be able to add persons to the list during run time. Note: Each time you start the application, the list is empty.

Instructions: Perform the following tasks:

1. Start Visual Basic, or open a new project if Visual Basic already is running.
2. Size and position the form as shown in Figure CLA2-1.

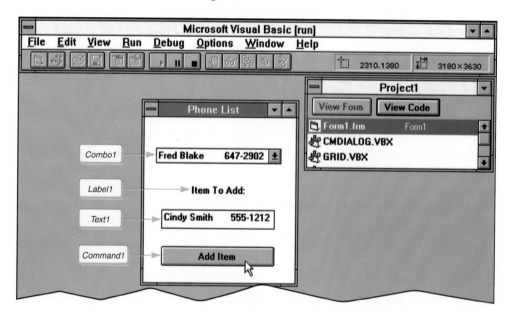

FIGURE CLA2-1

3. Add one text box, one label, one command button, and one combo box as shown in Figure CLA2-1.
4. Set the command buttons's caption to Add Item.
5. Set the label's caption to Item To Add.
6. Set the form's caption equal to Phone List.
7. Set the Text1.Text property equal to blank.
8. Double-click the command button to open the Command1_Click subroutine in the Code window.
9. Type these two statements:
```
Combo1.ADDITEM Text1.Text
Text1.Text = " "
```
10. Select the File menu on the menu bar. Choose Save Project from the File menu.
11. Save the form as CLA2-1.FRM. Save the project as CLA2-1.MAK.
12. Run the application. Add several names and phone numbers to the drop-down list. Double-click the form's Control-menu box to stop the application.
13. Check with your instructor for directions on turning in the assignment.

COMPUTER LABORATORY ASSIGNMENT 2
Shape Control Demonstration

Purpose: To build an application that incorporates multiple option groups.

Problem: You will build the application shown in Figure CLA2-2. The application has two option groups; one group is used to set the Shape property of the Shape control on the form and the other group is used to set the BorderStyle of the shape control.

Instructions: Perform the following tasks:

1. Start Visual Basic, or open a new project if Visual Basic is already running.
2. Size and position the form as shown in Figure CLA2-2.
3. Add the controls shown in Figure CLA2-2.
4. Set the caption properties as shown in the table to the right.
5. Open the Code window by double-clicking the Option1 control. Type `Shape1.Shape = 0`
6. Select the Option2 control from the drop-down Object list in the Code window. Type `Shape1.Shape = 3`
7. Select the Option3 control from the drop-down Object list in the Code window. Type `Shape1.Shape = 2`
8. Select the Option4 control from the drop-down Object list in the Code window. Type `Shape1.Borderstyle = 1`
9. Select the Option5 control from the drop-down Object list in the Code window. Type `Shape1.Borderstyle = 2`
10. Select the Option6 control from the drop-down Object list in the Code window. Type `Shape1.Borderstyle = 3` and double-click the Code window's Control-menu box.
11. Save the form as CLA2-2.FRM. Save the project as CLA2-2.MAK.
12. Run the application. Double-click the form's Control-menu box to stop the application.
13. Check with your instructor for directions on turning in the assignment.

CONTROL	CAPTION
Form1	Shape Properties
Frame1	Shape
Frame2	Borderstyle
Option1	Rectangle
Option2	Circle
Option3	Oval
Option4	Solid
Option5	Dash
Option6	Dot

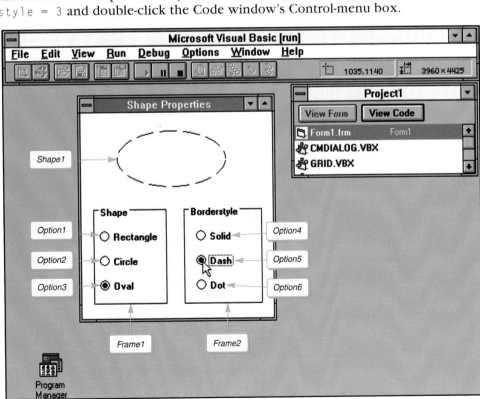

FIGURE CLA2-2

COMPUTER LABORATORY ASSIGNMENT 3
Currency Exchange

Purpose: To build an application that incorporates an option group.

Problem: In Computer Laboratory Assignment 1-4, you built an application that converts an amount of dollars that you enter into one of four foreign currencies. You specified the foreign currency by clicking one of four command buttons. In this assignment you will improve the application by representing the currency choice with an option button group.

Instructions: Build the application with a user interface similar to the one shown in Figure CLA2-3. Name the controls according to Visual Basic conventions. Use a label control rather than text box control for the amount in foreign currency. Use the option button Click event to change the name of the currency on the form and to perform the calculation and display the result.

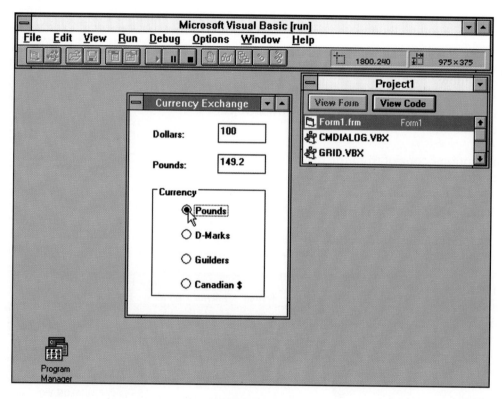

FIGURE CLA2-3

Use the following exchange rates. One dollar equals:

> 1.4920 pounds
> .54699 guilders
> .61489 marks
> .80160 Canadian dollars

Save the form as CLA2-3.FRM. Save the project as CLA2-3.MAK. Check with your instructor for directions on turning in the assignment.

COMPUTER LABORATORY ASSIGNMENT 4
Currency Exchange Revised

Purpose: To build an application that incorporates a drop-down list box and If...Then statements.

Problem: You would like the currency exchange application to be modified so that the foreign currency is selected from a drop-down list.

Instructions: Build an application with a user interface similar to the one shown in Figure CLA2-4. When you click the Convert button, the calculation depends on which item is selected from the drop-down list. Use the exchange rates listed in Assignment 3.

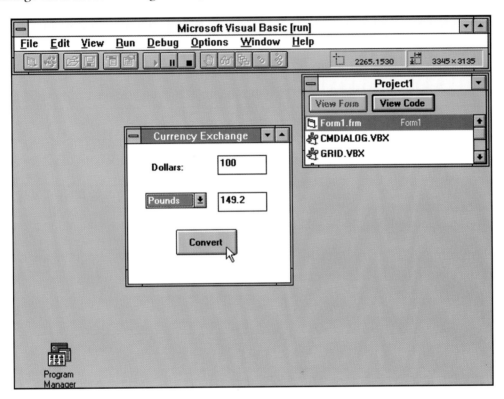

FIGURE CLA2-4

Hint #1: Use the ListIndex property of combo box controls to see which item is currently selected.
Hint #2: You can use a series of If...Then statements without the Else clause. For example:

> If *condition1* Then *action1*
> If *condition2* Then *action2*

Save the form as CLA2-4.FRM. Save the project as CLA2-4.MAK. Check with your instructor for directions on turning in the assignment.

MICROSOFT VISUAL BASIC 3.0 FOR WINDOWS

PROJECT THREE

APPLICATIONS WITH MULTIPLE FORMS AND EXECUTABLE FILES

OBJECTIVES You will have mastered the material in this project when you can:

- ▶ Add forms to a project
- ▶ Work with multiple forms' Code windows
- ▶ Specify a Start Up Form
- ▶ Specify an icon for a form
- ▶ Build an About.. form
- ▶ Add and remove forms from the desktop at run time
- ▶ Center forms on the desktop with code statements
- ▶ Use the MsgBox code statement

- ▶ Use an image control to display an icon
- ▶ Add a scroll bar control to a form and set its properties
- ▶ Add a line control to a form and set its properties
- ▶ Use the built-in financial functions
- ▶ Make and run an executable file
- ▶ Add and remove program items in a program group

▶ INTRODUCTION

LECTURE NOTES
■ Explain what is meant by executable files.
■ Review how applications are launched from program groups within Windows.

VB TIPS
■ Visual Basic .exe files are not completely stand-alone, since they require at a minimum the use of the VBRUN300.DLL file.

To run the applications built in Projects 1 and 2, you must start Visual Basic, open the project for that application, and then run the application from within the Visual Basic environment. Most Windows applications can be started directly from Program Manager and run independently from the software that was used to create them. These applications are called **stand-alone** or **executable** applications. In this project, you will learn how to make your Visual Basic applications executable. You also will learn how to add an icon that represents the application in a program group within Window's Program Manager.

The applications built in Projects 1 and 2 consisted of several controls and one form. In this project, an application with additional controls and multiple forms will be built. Visual Basic's library of built-in financial functions and the use of dialog boxes within applications will also be introduced in this project. Dialog boxes are common in Windows applications and are used during run time to give information about the application to you or to prompt you to supply information to the application.

▶ PROJECT THREE – LOAN PAYMENT CALCULATOR

TRANSPARENCIES
Figure 3-1 through
Figure 3-4

T he application that will be built in this project calculates the amount of the monthly payment on a loan. Since this type of calculation is used frequently for home mortgages and car loans, the program is represented within Program Manager as an icon that consists of a house and car (Figure 3-1). When you double-click the Loan Payment program icon, the Loan Payment Calculator window shown in Figure 3-2 opens on the desktop.

To carry out the calculation, you must supply the amount of the loan, the length of the loan repayment (in years), and the interest rate per year (APR) to the application. The loan amount is entered into a text box from the keyboard (Figure 3-2). The number of years and the APR are entered by using scroll bar controls. As you click the scroll arrows, the value supplied to the loan calculation changes and displays on the form. You can change the value more quickly by dragging the scroll box or by pointing to one of the scroll arrows and holding down the left mouse button.

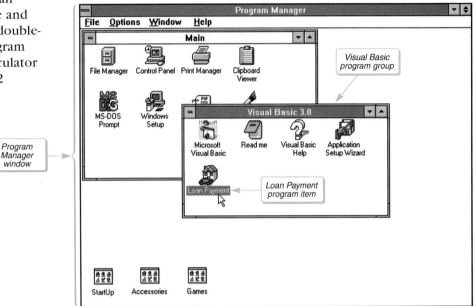

FIGURE 3-1

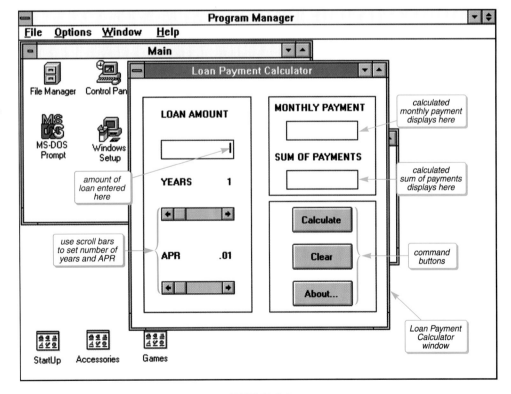

FIGURE 3-2

The Loan Payment window contains three command buttons, labeled Calculate, Clear, and About.. . When you choose the Calculate button or press the ENTER
key, the function is computed, and the monthly payment and the total amount to
be repaid are displayed on the form. If the amount of the loan entered from the
keyboard is not a valid numerical amount, the dialog box shown in Figure 3-3 displays to alert you to this input error. Choosing the OK button closes the dialog box
and clears the text box so a new value can be entered.

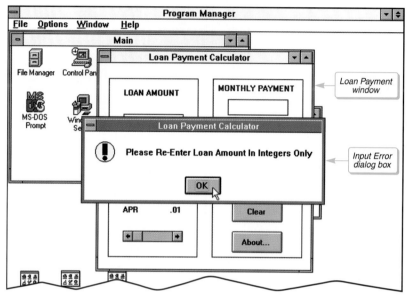

FIGURE 3-3

Choosing the Clear button in the Loan Payment window erases the loan
amount, monthly payment, and sum of payments and returns the scroll bars to
their lowest values. Choosing the About.. button in the Loan Payment window displays the dialog box shown in Figure 3-4. Choosing the OK button in the About..
dialog box closes the dialog box.

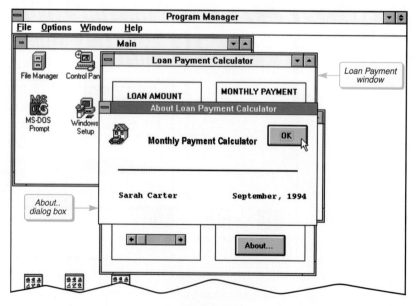

FIGURE 3-4

The Loan Payment window has a control menu (Figure 3-5) that is opened by clicking the Control-menu box. The application can be minimized on the desktop as an icon by choosing Minimize from the control menu or by clicking the window's Minimize button. The window is closed by choosing Close from the control menu or by double-clicking the Control-menu box.

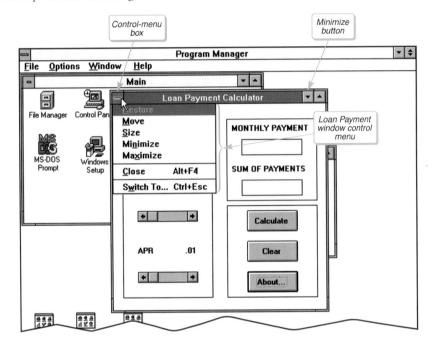

FIGURE 3-5

Starting Visual Basic

Begin this project by starting Visual Basic or by beginning a new project if Visual Basic is already running. If necessary, minimize the Program Manager window and adjust the sizes and locations of the Visual Basic windows to those shown in Figure 3-6. For more information on adjusting the Visual Basic windows, refer to page VB59.

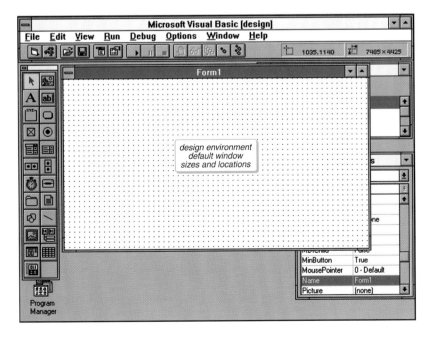

FIGURE 3-6

The application's interface (adding controls and setting properties) will be built one form at a time. After the interface is completed, the code for the application will be written.

▶ **THE ABOUT.. FORM AND ITS CONTROLS**

LECTURE NOTES
■ Show examples of About.. dialog boxes for different Windows applications.

T he About.. dialog box shown in Figure 3-4 on page VB122 is created as a form within the project. The About.. dialog box is common in Windows applications and is used to provide information about the application such as its version number, copyright date, and authors' names. Build the About.. form as follows:

▶ set the size of the form
▶ add the controls
▶ set the properties of the form and its controls
▶ save the form as a file on diskette

Setting the Size of the Form

In Projects 1 and 2, the form's size was set by dragging the form's borders. The values of the form's Height property and Width property changed as the borders were dragged to new locations. In the following example, the size of the About.. form will be changed by directly changing the values of the Height and Width properties in the Properties window.

TRANSPARENCIES
Figure 3-7 through
Figure 3-9

TO SET THE SIZE OF THE FORM USING THE PROPERTIES WINDOW ▼

STEP 1 ▶

Click the Properties window.

The Properties window moves on top of the form window (Figure 3-7).

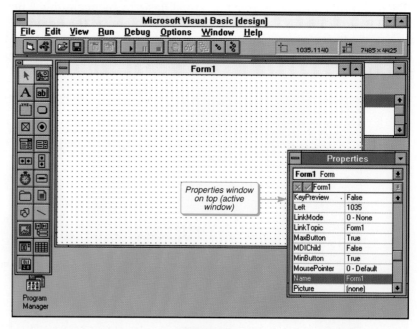

FIGURE 3-7

STEP 2 ▶

Scroll through the Properties list, and then double-click the Height property. Type `3000` and press the ENTER key.

The form's bottom border moves to match the value entered in the Settings box (Figure 3-8).

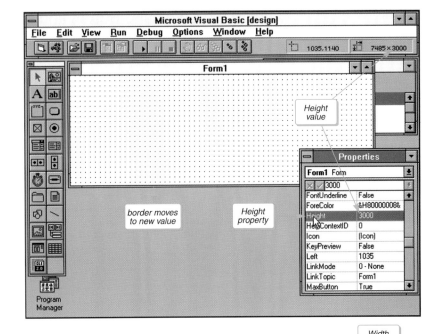

FIGURE 3-8

STEP 3 ▶

Scroll through the Properties list, and then double-click the Width property. Type `5400` and press the ENTER key.

The form's right border moves to match the value entered in the Settings box (Figure 3-9).

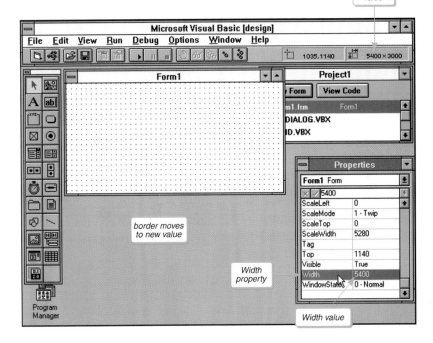

FIGURE 3-9

The form's **Top property** and **Left property** determine the position of the upper left corner of the form on the desktop. Since these properties were not changed, setting values of the form's Height and Width caused only the form's bottom and right borders to move. You can use this method to change a form's size during run time by writing code statements that, when executed, change the values of the form's Height and Width properties.

The form's location can be changed at run time in a similar manner by using code statements that change the values of a form's Top and Left properties. The Loan Calculator application uses this method of locating the form at run time, so it is not necessary to locate the form at this time.

LECTURE NOTES
■ Review the Top, Left, Height and Width properties of forms and other controls.

Adding the Command Button and Label Controls

The About.. form contains three label controls and one command button control, as shown in Figure 3-10. Perform the following steps to add these controls to the form.

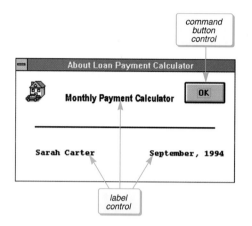

FIGURE 3-10

TO ADD THE COMMAND BUTTON AND LABEL CONTROLS ▼

STEP 1 ▶

Double-click the label tool in the Toolbox. Drag the Label1 control to the position shown in Figure 3-11.

STEP 2

Double-click the label tool in the Toolbox. Drag the Label2 control to the position shown in Figure 3-11.

STEP 3

Double-click the label tool in the Toolbox. Drag the Label3 control to the position shown in Figure 3-11.

STEP 4

Double-click the command button tool in the Toolbox. Drag the Command1 control to the position shown in Figure 3-11.

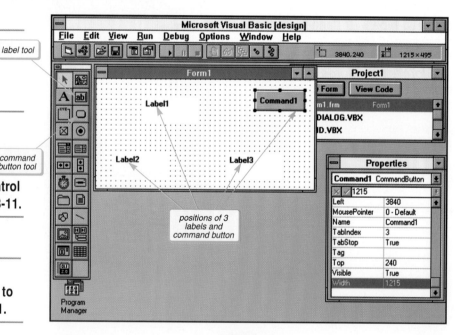

FIGURE 3-11

STEP 5 ▶

Drag the sizing handle on the left side of the Command1 control toward the right border of the form a distance of two grid marks (Figure 3-12). Release the left mouse button to resize the command button.

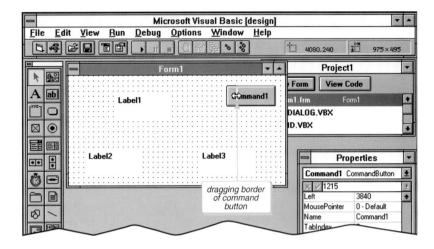

FIGURE 3-12

The Image Control

An image control can be used as a container for graphical images, such as icons or bitmapped graphics files. The image control acts like a command button, so it often is used to create custom buttons like those found in toolbars. An image control is used to add the Loan Payment application's icon to the About.. form (Figure 3-13). Perform the following steps to add an image control to the About.. form.

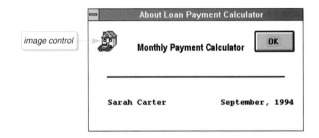

FIGURE 3-13

TO ADD AN IMAGE CONTROL ▼

STEP 1 ▶

Double-click the image tool in the Toolbox.

An image control, Image1, is added to the center of the form (Figure 3-14).

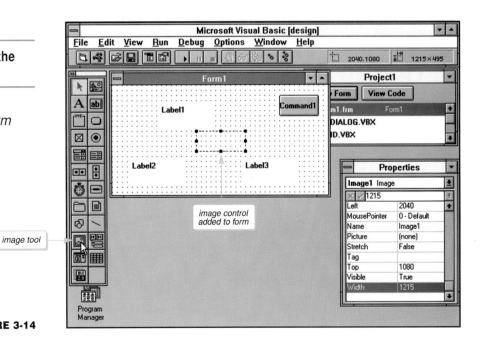

FIGURE 3-14

STEP 2 ▶

Drag the image control to the
location shown in Figure 3-15.

*Do not be concerned that the
image control overlaps the Label1
control. This positioning will be
adjusted later.*

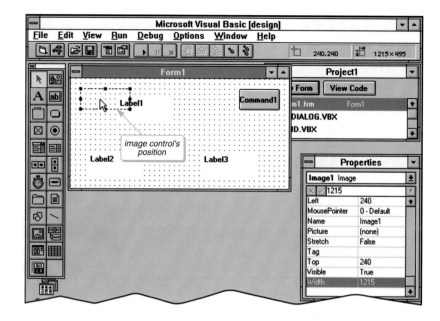

FIGURE 3-15

The Line Control

The **line control** is used to add
straight lines between pairs of points on a
form. The About.. form contains a line
control to visually separate the information on the form into two areas (Figure
3-16). Perform the following steps to add
a line control to the About.. form.

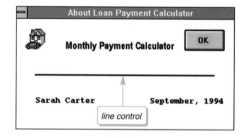

FIGURE 3-16

TO ADD A LINE CONTROL ▼

STEP 1 ▶

Click the line tool in the Toolbox.
Move the mouse pointer to where
you want one end of the line to
appear.

*The mouse pointer changes to a
cross hair (Figure 3-17).*

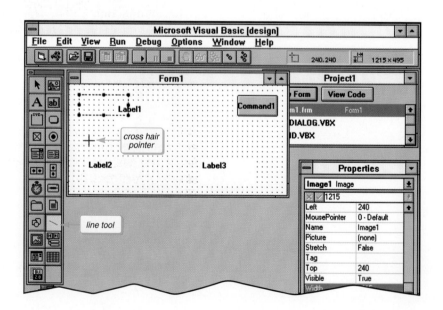

FIGURE 3-17

STEP 2 ▶

Drag the pointer to where you want the other end of the line to appear.

A gray outline of the line appears as you move the pointer (Figure 3-18).

FIGURE 3-18

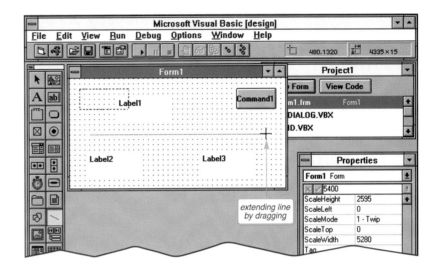

STEP 3 ▶

Release the left mouse button.

A solid line replaces the gray outline (Figure 3-19).

FIGURE 3-19

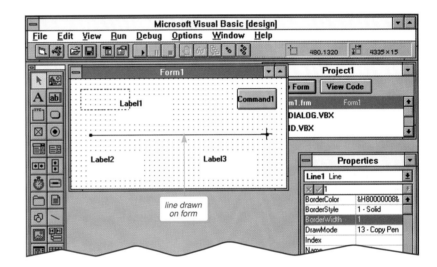

You can lengthen, shorten, or reposition line controls by dragging one end at a time to the new position desired.

▶ SETTING PROPERTIES FOR THE ABOUT.. FORM AND ITS CONTROLS

The next step is to set the properties for the About.. form and its controls. In addition to setting the Name and Caption properties presented in previous projects, the following properties will be set:

- ▶ the WindowState of forms
- ▶ the BorderStyle of forms
- ▶ the font properties of controls
- ▶ the Picture property of image controls
- ▶ the BorderStyle and BorderWidth of line controls

LECTURE NOTES
■ Review the three-step process of building applications.
■ Identify the properties that will be set for the controls on the About.. form.

The WindowState Property of Forms

The **WindowState** is a property of a form that corresponds with the window's size on the desktop during run time. The WindowState property takes one of three values, as listed in Table 3-1.

▶ **TABLE 3-1 WINDOWSTATE VALUES**

VALUE	WINDOW'S SIZE
0-Normal	window open on desktop
1-Minimized	window reduced to an icon
2-Maximized	window enlarged to its maximum size

When the About.. form appears on the desktop at run time, it has a WindowState value of 0-Normal (Figure 3-20). If you look closely, you will see that its WindowState cannot be changed because it does not have a Minimize or a Maximize button in the upper right corner of the window. Also, the usual Minimize and Maximize choices do not appear in the Control menu.

You control the ability to make run-time changes to the WindowState by including or removing minimize and maximize buttons from the form. This control is done by setting the values of the **MinButton property** and the **MaxButton property** of the form to True if you want to include the button or to False to exclude the button. Setting the value to False also removes the corresponding choice from the control menu. Perform the following steps to prevent the About.. form from having its WindowState changed during run time.

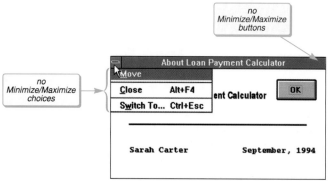

FIGURE 3-20

TO SET THE MINBUTTON AND MAXBUTTON PROPERTIES

Step 1: Select the form object by clicking its name, Form1, in the drop-down Object list in the Properties window.

Step 2: Scroll through the Properties list until the MaxButton property is visible. Double-click the MaxButton property in the Properties list.

Step 3: Double-click the MinButton property in the Properties list.

The new settings of False for each of these properties are shown in the Properties list (Figure 3-21).

When the MinButton or MaxButton properties are set to False, the form still contains Maximize and Minimize buttons at design time (Figure 3-21). However, at run time the buttons will not appear on the form (Figure 3-20).

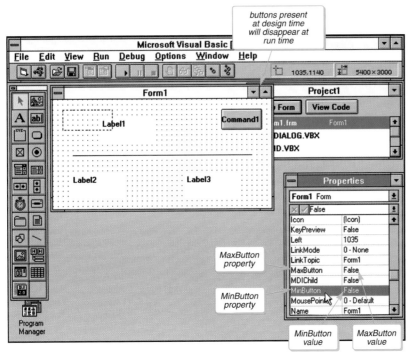

FIGURE 3-21

The BorderStyle Property of Forms

The ability to change the size of a window at run time by dragging its borders is determined by the value of the form's BorderStyle property. The **BorderStyle** property of a form affects the form's appearance and controls. A **sizable form** has borders that can be dragged to new positions. A form's BorderStyle property can take one of four values and affects whether certain controls appear on the form, as listed in Table 3-2.

TRANSPARENCY
Table 3-2

LECTURE NOTES
■ Discuss the different
values of the BorderStyle
property of forms.

▶ **TABLE 3-2 BORDERSTYLE PROPERTY VALUES**

CONTROL	BORDERSTYLE			
	0-None	1-Fixed Single	2-Sizable	3-Fixed Double
Minimize button	no	optional	optional	no
Maximize button	no	optional	optional	no
Control-menu box	no	optional	optional	optional
Title bar	no	optional	optional	optional
Sizable form	no	no	yes	no

The About Loan Payment dialog box is typical of most dialog boxes. Generally, a dialog box's WindowState cannot be changed, and it is not sizable. Perform the following steps to prevent the About.. form from being resized during run time.

VB TIPS
■ When the BorderStyle is
set to either none or
fixed-double, Minimize
and Maximize buttons do
not appear on the form,
regardless of the settings
of the MinButton and
MaxButton properties.

TO SET THE BORDERSTYLE PROPERTY

Step 1: Check to be certain the Form1 form object is selected. If it is not, click its name, Form1, in the drop-down Object list in the Properties window.

Step 2: Scroll through the Properties list until the BorderStyle property is visible. Select the BorderStyle property by clicking its name in the Properties list.

Step 3: Open the drop-down Settings list by clicking the arrow located next to the Settings box.

Step 4: Click the 1-Fixed Single choice in the drop-down Settings list.

The new value appears in the Properties window (Figure 3-22).

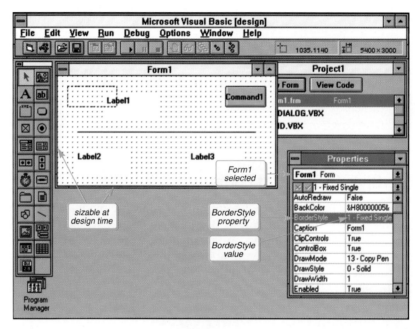

FIGURE 3-22

No matter what value of the BorderStyle is set, the form remains sizable at design time. At run time, however, the form displays with the selected value of the BorderStyle property.

Control Names and Captions

In Project 2, you learned that naming controls makes it easier for you to write code and makes your code easier for other people to understand. Not all of the controls in Project 2 were given names different from their default names. It is important to name forms, especially in projects that contain more than one form. If only one instance of a type of control is on a form, or if a control is not referred to by an event or procedure, it is not as important to have a name other than the default name Visual Basic assigns.

Perform the following steps to name the form and to assign captions to the controls on the About.. form. In order to ensure the entire label captions fit inside the controls, set the labels' AutoSize property to True.

TO SET THE NAME AND CAPTIONS

Step 1: Check to be certain the Form1 form object is selected. If not, click its name in the drop-down Object list in the Properties window. Double-click the Name property in the Properties list.

Step 2: Type `frmLoanabt` and press the ENTER key.

Step 3: Double-click the Caption property in the Properties list.

Step 4: Type `About Loan Payment Calculator` and press the ENTER key.

Step 5: Select the Label1 control by clicking its name in the drop-down Object list in the Properties window. Double-click the AutoSize property in the Properties list.

Step 6: Double-click the Caption property in the Properties list. Type `Monthly Payment Calculator` and press the ENTER key.

Step 7: Select the Label2 control by clicking its name in the drop-down Object list in the Properties window. Double-click the AutoSize property in the Properties list.

Step 8: Double-click the Caption property in the Properties list. Type `Sarah Carter` (or your name) and press the ENTER key.

Step 9: Select the Label3 control by clicking its name in the drop-down Object list in the Properties window. Double-click the AutoSize property in the Properties list.

Step 10: Double-click the Caption property in the Properties list. Type `September, 1994` and press the ENTER key.

Step 11: Select the Command1 control by clicking its name in the drop-down Object list in the Properties window. Double-click the Caption property in the Properties list.

Step 12: Type `OK` and press the ENTER key.

The frmLoanabt form appears as shown in Figure 3-23.

LECTURE NOTES
■ Point out the controls and their captions on the completed About.. form.

VB TIPS
■ Each of the controls in these steps can also be selected by clicking the control in the Form window.

TRANSPARENCY
Figure 3-23

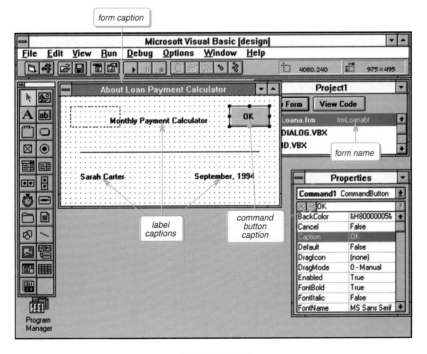

FIGURE 3-23

Font Properties

Project 2 showed how to change the size of text characters on controls by using the FontSize property. The Visual Basic controls containing text have several properties that affect the way text appears. For a detailed description of all the properties, use Visual Basic's online Help to search on the word *font*.

Four major font properties are described in Table 3-3:

▸ **TABLE 3-3 FONT PROPERTIES**

PROPERTY	DESCRIPTION
FontName	the name of the selected font
FontSize	the size (in printer's points)
FontBold	a True value displays the selected font in bold
FontItalic	a True value displays the selected font in italics

As you can see in Figure 3-24, the labels and captions of controls on the frmLoanabt form have different font properties. Perform the following steps to set these font properties.

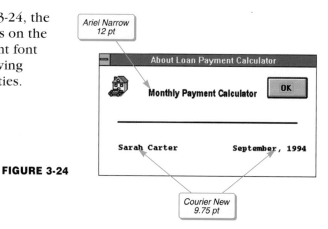

FIGURE 3-24

TO SET THE FONT PROPERTIES

Step 1: Select the Label1 control by clicking its name in the drop-down Object list in the Properties window.

Step 2: Click the FontName property in the Properties list. Open the drop-down list of property settings by clicking the arrow located next to the Settings box. Click the Ariel Narrow choice in the Settings list. Select another font if Ariel Narrow is not in the list.

Step 3: Click the FontSize property in the Properties list. Open the drop-down list of property settings by clicking the arrow located next to the Settings box. Click the 12 choice in the Settings list.

Step 4: Select the Label2 control by clicking its name in the drop-down Object list in the Properties window.

Step 5: Click the FontName property in the Properties list. Open the drop-down list of property settings by clicking the arrow located next to the Settings box. Click the Courier New choice in the Settings list.

Step 6: Click the FontSize property in the Properties list. Open the drop-down list of property settings by clicking the arrow located next to the Settings box. Click the 9.75 choice in the Settings list.

Step 7: Select the Label3 control by clicking its name in the drop-down Object list in the Properties window.

Step 8: Click the FontName property in the Properties list. Open the drop-down list of property settings by clicking the arrow located next to the Settings box. Click the Courier New choice in the Settings list.

Step 9: Click the FontSize property in the Properties list. Open the drop-down list of property settings by clicking the arrow located next to the Settings box. Click the 9.75 choice in the Settings list.

The frmLoanabt form appears as shown in Figure 3-25. The list of available fonts (Step 2) depends on which fonts have been installed in your copy of Windows.

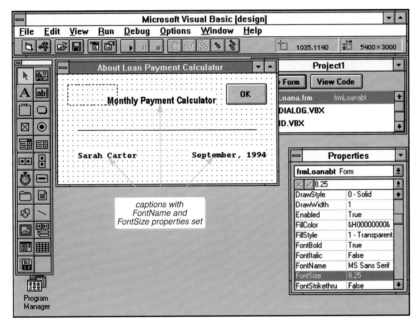

FIGURE 3-25

The FontBold and FontItalic properties can be used alone or in combination. For example, setting the value of both of these properties to True will display the selected font in boldface italics.

The Picture Property of Image Controls

You can add graphics to forms and controls at design time by setting the **Picture property** in the Properties window. The graphic image used on the frmLoanabt form comes from the set of icon files (.ICO) supplied as part of the Visual Basic system. Perform the steps on the next page to add an icon to the Image1 control.

LECTURE NOTES
■ Explain what an .ICO file is.
■ Explain the Picture property of image controls.

TRANSPARENCIES
Figure 3-26 through
Figure 3-29

TO ADD A GRAPHIC TO AN IMAGE CONTROL

STEP 1 ▶

Select the Image1 control by clicking its name in the drop-down Object list in the Properties window. Double-click the Picture property in the Properties list.

The Load Picture dialog box appears (Figure 3-26). The Load Picture dialog box is very similar to other common dialog boxes used in Windows applications.

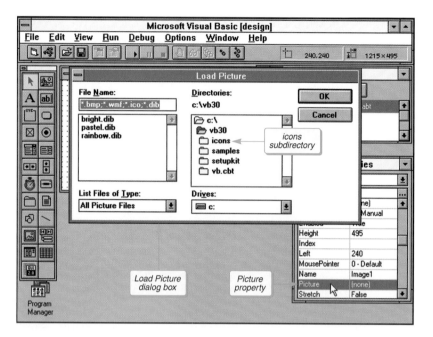

FIGURE 3-26

STEP 2 ▶

Double-click the icons subdirectory in the directory list box.

A list of the subdirectories of the icons subdirectory appears in the directory list box (Figure 3-27).

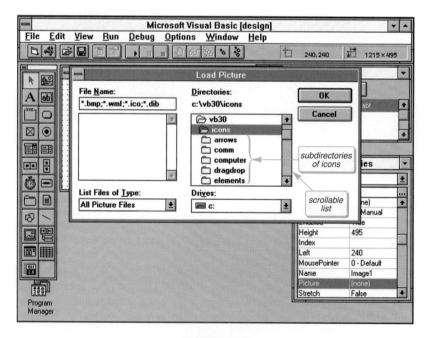

FIGURE 3-27

STEP 3 ▶

Scroll through the directories list, and then double-click the misc subdirectory.

A list of icon files (.ICO) displays in the file list box (Figure 3-28).

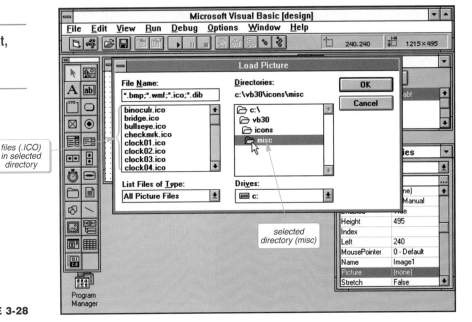

FIGURE 3-28

STEP 4 ▶

Scroll through the file list until the HOUSE.ICO file is visible in the file list box. Select the house icon by double-clicking its file name (HOUSE.ICO) in the file list box.

Visual Basic loads the house icon into the image control located in the upper left of the About.. form (Figure 3-29).

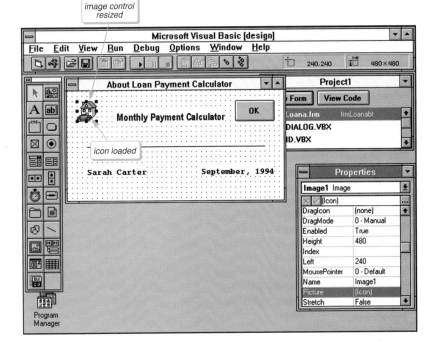

FIGURE 3-29

When Visual Basic loaded the icon, the size of the image control was adjusted automatically to the size of its contents (the house icon). This automatic sizing occurred because the default value of the image control's BorderStyle property is 0-None. If you set the BorderStyle of the image control to 1-Fixed single, Visual Basic does not adjust its size automatically.

VB TIPS
■ Setting the BorderStyle to Fixed and the Stretch property to True will cause the icon to be elongated to fill the size of an image control.

BorderStyle and BorderWidth Properties of Line Controls

The next step is to change the appearance of the horizontal line that runs across the center of the About.. form. The **BorderStyle** property of the line control determines the appearance of the line, such as solid or dashed. The seven possible BorderStyles for the line control are listed in Table 3-4.

▶ **TABLE 3-4 BORDERSTYLE PROPERTIES OF LINE CONTROLS**

SETTING	DESCRIPTION
0	Transparent
1	(Default) Solid — The border is centered on the edge of the shape
2	Dash
3	Dot
4	Dash-Dot
5	Dash-Dot-Dot
6	Inside Solid — The outer edge of the border is the outer edge of the shape

The BorderStyle of the line on the frmLoanabt form is solid, which is the default value (Figure 3-30).

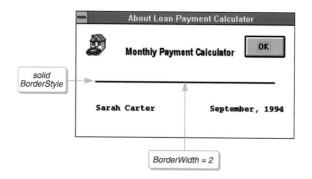

FIGURE 3-30

The **BorderWidth** property is used to set the width of the line. The values of the BorderWidth are integers from 1 to 8192. The line on the frmLoanabt form is wider than the default width of 1 (Figure 3-30). Perform the following steps to change the width of the line control located on the frmLoanabt form.

TO SET THE BORDERWIDTH PROPERTY OF THE LINE CONTROL

Step 1: Select the Line1 control by clicking its name in the drop-down Object list in the Properties window.
Step 2: Double-click the BorderWidth property in the Properties list.
Step 3: Type 2 and press the ENTER key.

The line control appears as shown in Figure 3-31.

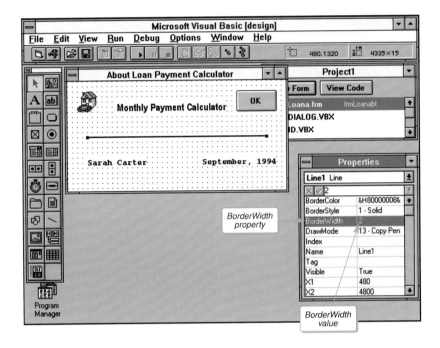

FIGURE 3-31

If the BorderWidth is set to a value greater than 1, the only effective settings of the BorderStyle are 1-Solid and 6-Inside Solid.

▶ SAVING THE FORM

he frmLoanabt form is now complete. Before proceeding with building the second form in the project, save the form. Perform the following steps to save the form to a formatted diskette in drive A.

TRANSPARENCIES
Figure 3-32 through
Figure 3-34

LECTURE NOTES
■ Review the steps to save form files.

TO SAVE A FORM ▼

STEP 1 ▶

Insert a formatted diskette in drive A. Select the File menu on the menu bar. Choose Save File As from the File menu.

The Save File As dialog box appears, and the first eight characters of the form's name appear in the File Name box (Figure 3-32).

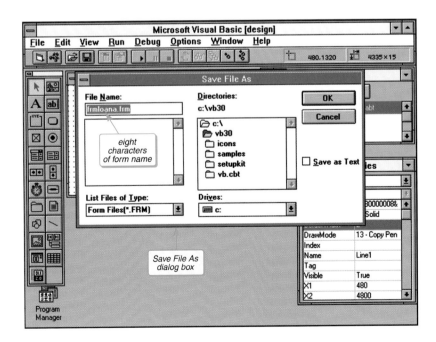

FIGURE 3-32

STEP 2 ▶

Type Loanabt

The file name changes in the File Name box (Figure 3-33).

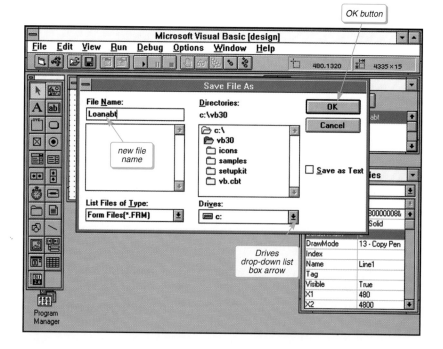

FIGURE 3-33

STEP 3 ▶

Open the Drives drop-down list box by clicking its arrow. Scroll through the list if necessary, and then select drive A from the Drives drop-down list box. Choose the OK button.

The form is saved as a file on the diskette, and the dialog box closes. The form's file name is shown preceding the Visual Basic name of the form in the Project window (Figure 3-34).

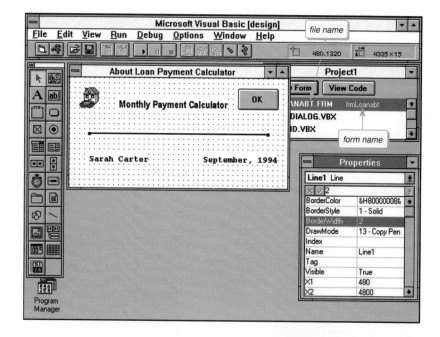

FIGURE 3-34

When the Save File As dialog box opens, only the first eight characters of the name of the form appear in the File Name box. This abbreviation occurs because DOS restricts the file name length to eight characters. Since form files automatically have the .FRM file extension added when you save them, the FRM prefix in the form's name was not included in the file name. You can save a file with any name up to eight characters long, and the file name can be different from Visual Basic's value of the Name property of the form.

▶ THE LOAN PAYMENT FORM AND ITS CONTROLS

The second form to construct in this project is the Loan Payment form shown in Figure 3-35. Since this form is the second one in the project, a new form must be added. The Loan Payment form is built following this sequence of activities:

- ▶ add a new form to the project
- ▶ set the size of the form
- ▶ add the controls
- ▶ set the properties of the form and its controls
- ▶ save the form as a file on a diskette

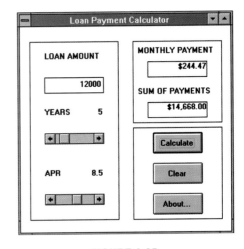

FIGURE 3-35

Adding Additional Forms to the Project

You can have multiple form windows open on the desktop at the same time. However, it reduces confusion if you minimize the windows of forms you are not currently using. Perform the following steps to minimize the About.. form (frmLoanabt) and to add a new form to the project.

TO ADD A NEW FORM

Step 1: Click the About.. form's (frmLoanabt's) minimize button.
Step 2: Click the new form tool on the toolbar.

The About.. form's (frmLoanabt's) window is reduced to an icon on the desktop. A new form with the default name Form2 is added to the project, and its window opens on the desktop (Figure 3-36).

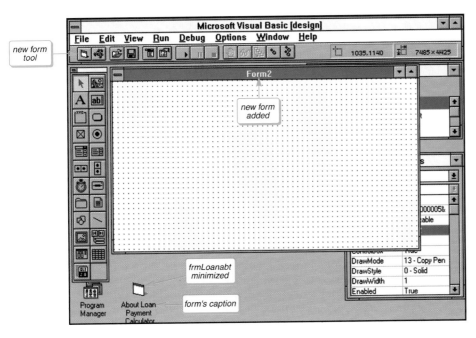

FIGURE 3-36

Setting the Form Size and Position

Perform the following steps to change the size of the Loan Payment form by directly changing the values of the Height and Width properties in the Properties window, as was done with the About.. form.

TO SET THE SIZE OF THE FORM USING THE PROPERTIES WINDOW

Step 1: Make the Properties window the active window by clicking it.
Step 2: Scroll through the Properties list, and then double-click the Height property. Type `5265` and press the ENTER key.
Step 3: Scroll through the Properties list and double-click the Width property. Type `5265` and press the ENTER key.

The form (Form2) appears as shown in Figure 3-37.

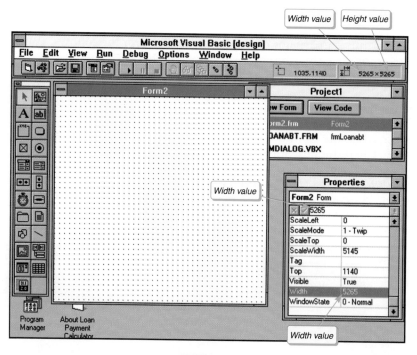

FIGURE 3-37

It is not necessary to locate the second form at this time. The form's location will be changed at run time by using code statements that change the values of the form's Top and Left properties.

Adding Shape Controls

The Loan Payment form has three shape controls, as shown in Figure 3-38. These controls are not functional within the application because no events or code statements are associated with them. However, they do serve an important purpose.

Shape controls are used in the Loan Payment application to visually group related controls on the form. All the controls within the shape on the left of the form are related to the **inputs**, or data needed by the application to carry out its function. The shape on the top, right of the form groups all of the controls related to the results of the application's function, called **outputs**. The shape control located on the bottom, right contains all of the controls used to initiate different actions within the application. Perform the following steps to add three shape controls to the form.

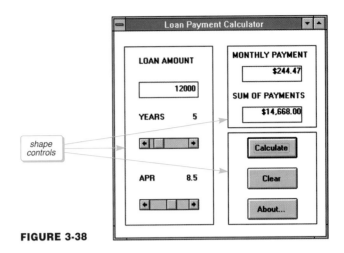

FIGURE 3-38

TO ADD THE SHAPE CONTROLS ▼

STEP 1 ►

Click the shape tool in the Toolbox, and move the mouse to the location where the top left corner of the shape will appear.

The shape tool is highlighted in the Toolbox. The mouse pointer changes to a cross hair (Figure 3-39).

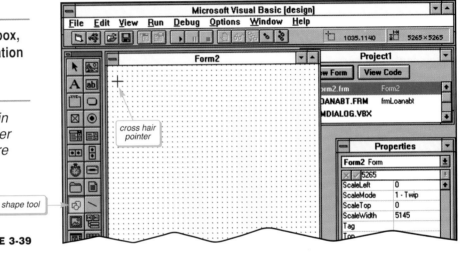

FIGURE 3-39

STEP 2 ►

Drag the mouse pointer down and to the right as shown in Figure 3-40. Release the left mouse button.

As you drag the mouse, a gray outline of the control appears on the form (Figure 3-40). When you release the left mouse button, the shape control is redrawn in the position of the outline.

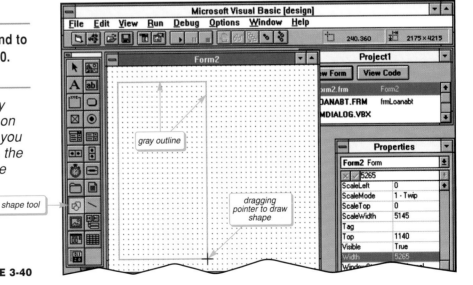

FIGURE 3-40

STEP 3 ▶

Repeat Steps 1 and 2 to draw a
second shape control (Figure 3-41).

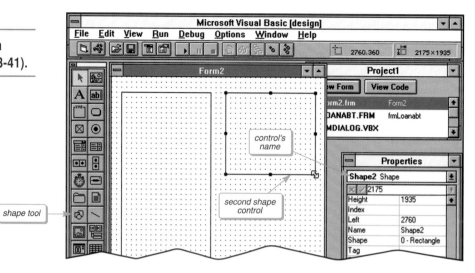

FIGURE 3-41

STEP 4 ▶

Repeat Steps 1 and 2 to draw a third
shape control (Figure 3-42).

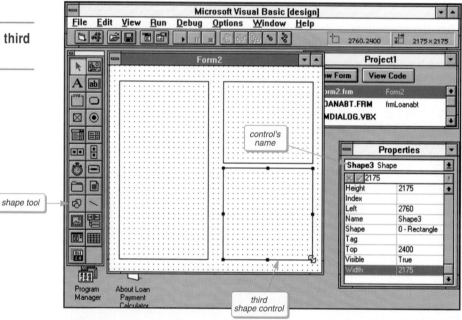

FIGURE 3-42

Adding and Copying Label Controls

The Loan Payment form contains nine labels, as identified in Figure 3-43. The
two labels used to display the outputs of the loan calculation have borders around
them. At run time, their contents (captions) are blank until you click the Calculate
button. The reason for displaying the outputs in this way is that an empty box visually communicates "something goes here." The labels above the boxes communicate what that "something" is.

Project 2 showed how to copy controls using the mouse and the Edit menu. In the following example, controls are copied using the keyboard. Perform the following steps to add the seven borderless labels and then to add the two labels with borders.

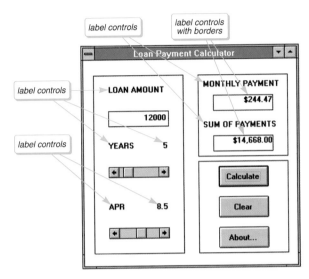

FIGURE 3-43

TRANSPARENCIES
Figure 3-44 through
Figure 3-48

TO ADD THE BORDERLESS LABEL CONTROLS ▼

STEP 1 ▶

Add a default-sized label control to the center of the form by double-clicking the label tool in the Toolbox. Use the mouse to drag the control to the position shown in Figure 3-44.

STEP 2 ▶

Set the label's AutoSize property to True by double-clicking the AutoSize property in the Properties window.

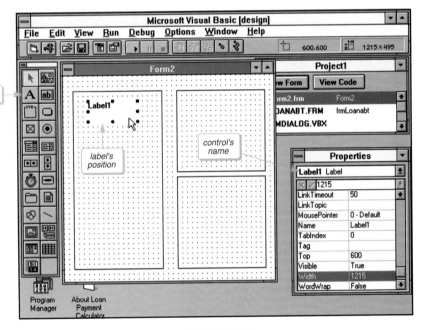

FIGURE 3-44

STEP 3 ▶

Press CTRL+C. Press CTRL+V. In response to the dialog box that appears, type N for No.

An additional label control with its AutoSize property set to True appears on the form. When you copy a control, all of its property settings also are copied. Thus, the second label control has the caption Label1 (Figure 3-45).

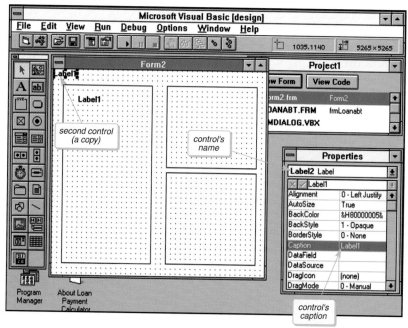

FIGURE 3-45

STEP 4 ▶

Drag the label to the position shown in Figure 3-46.

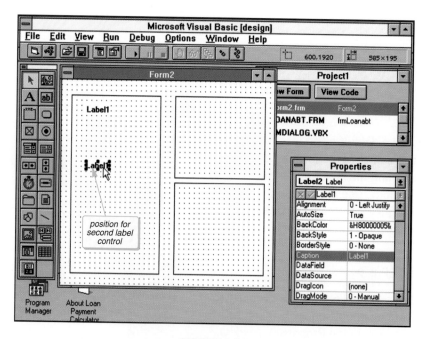

FIGURE 3-46

STEP 5 ▶

Press CTRL+V. In response to the dialog box that appears, type N for No. Drag the control to the position shown in Figure 3-47.

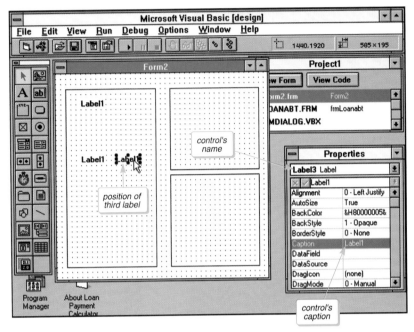

FIGURE 3-47

STEP 6 ▶

Repeat Step 5 four times to add the remaining labels to the positions shown in Figure 3-48. Be careful to locate the labels in the order shown.

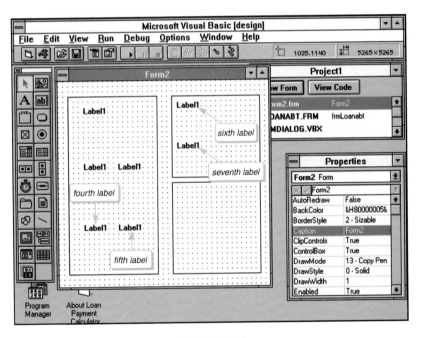

FIGURE 3-48

CTRL+C copies the selected control to the Clipboard. CTRL+V pastes the control from the Clipboard to the form. Seven similar labels have been added to the form. Perform the following steps on the next page to add the remaining two labels used to contain the application's outputs.

LECTURE NOTES
■ Explain why all of the label controls have the characters Label1 on them.

TRANSPARENCIES
Figure 3-49 through Figure 3-53

TO ADD THE REMAINING LABELS ▼

STEP 1 ►

Add a default-sized label control to the center of the form by double-clicking the label tool in the Toolbox. Use the mouse to drag the control to the position shown in Figure 3-49.

STEP 2 ►

Change the label's BorderStyle property from 0-No Border to 1-Fixed Single by double-clicking the BorderStyle property in the Properties window.

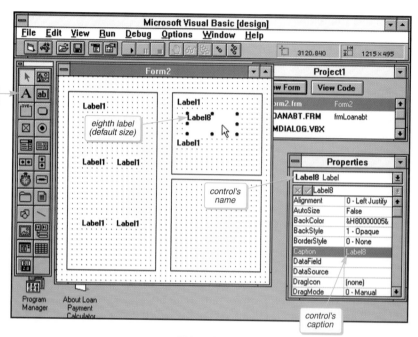

FIGURE 3-49

STEP 3 ►

Drag the control's lower, right sizing handle up and to the right, as shown in Figure 3-50. Release the left mouse button.

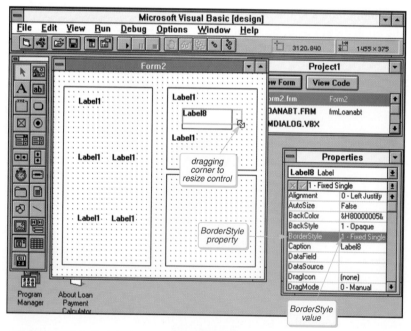

FIGURE 3-50

STEP 4 ▶

Press CTRL+C. Press CTRL+V. In response to the dialog box that appears, type N for No.

An identically sized label control with its BorderStyle property set to 1 appears on the form (Figure 3-51).

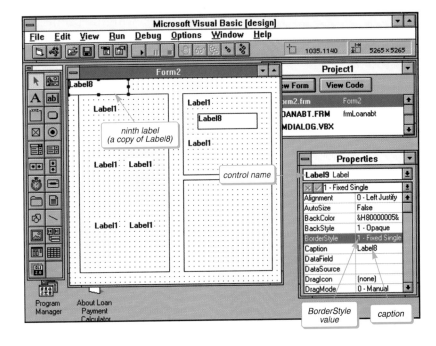

FIGURE 3-51

STEP 5 ▶

Drag the label to the position shown in Figure 3-52.

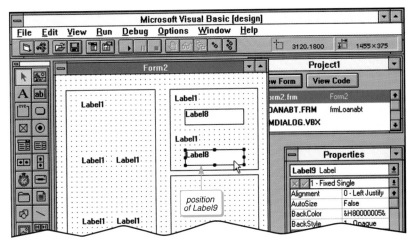

FIGURE 3-52

All of the label controls now have been added to the form. Compare the positions and appearance of the label controls in Figure 3-52 to the completed form shown in Figure 3-53.

Generally, all of the form's controls are added before setting properties. In the preceding example, you set the AutoSize and BorderStyle properties immediately so that you could take advantage of the fact that property values are copied when a control is copied.

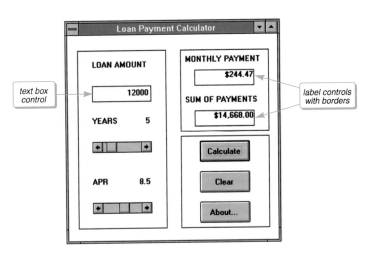

FIGURE 3-53

Copying the labels with the property already set will save you time since you won't have to set each label's AutoSize or BorderStyle property when you set the rest of the properties later. By copying the first output label (Label8), you did not have to draw or resize the second output label (Label9) to match the size of the first.

Adding the Text Box Control

LECTURE NOTES
■ Review why label controls are not used to receive input during run time.

TRANSPARENCIES
Figure 3-54 and Figure 3-55

The Loan Payment form contains one text box control, which is used at run time to accept the loan amount (Figure 3-53). A text box is used for you to enter the loan amount rather than a label since a label's contents can be changed during run time only with a code statement. Perform the following steps to add the text box control to the form.

TO ADD THE TEXT BOX CONTROL ▼

STEP 1 ▶

Add a default-sized text box control to the center of the form by double-clicking the text box tool in the Toolbox. Use the mouse to drag the control to the position shown in Figure 3-54.

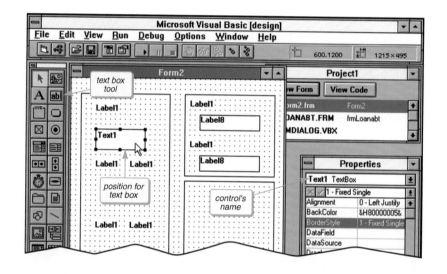

FIGURE 3-54

STEP 2 ▶

Drag the control's lower, right sizing handle up and to the right (Figure 3-55). Release the left mouse button.

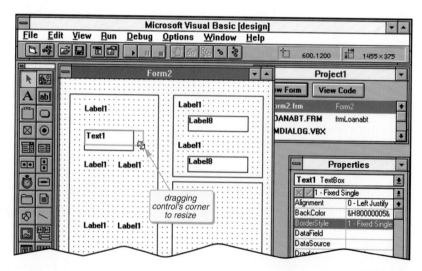

FIGURE 3-55

Adding Scroll Bar Controls

Scroll bars commonly are used to view the contents of a control when the contents cannot fit within the control's borders. An example is the scroll bar on the Properties list in the Properties window. Visual Basic has two different scroll bar controls; the **horizontal scroll bar** and the **vertical scroll bar**. Their names reflect the orientation of the control on the form, not its use. You control its use. For example, you can use a vertical scroll bar to control the horizontal scrolling of a control on a form.

Another use of the scroll bar control is to give a value to an input. One benefit of using a scroll bar for input is that it prevents you from entering an improper value by mistake, such as a letter instead of a number. The two horizontal scroll bar controls shown in Figure 3-56 are used as input controls for the number of years of the loan and for the annual interest rate. Perform the following steps to add the two scroll bar controls.

TRANSPARENCY
Figure 3-56

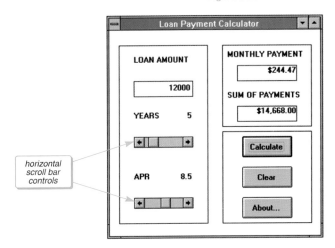

FIGURE 3-56

LECTURE NOTES
■ Ask students to describe the use of scroll bars in applications with which they are familiar.
■ Ask them to identify the scroll bar controls in the loan application.
■ Discuss the two types of scroll bar controls.
■ Discuss the use of scroll bars in the loan application.

TO ADD SCROLL BAR CONTROLS ▼

STEP 1 ►

Double-click the horizontal scroll bar tool in the Toolbox. Extend the scroll bar's width by dragging its sizing handle the distance of one grid mark on the form. Drag the scroll bar to the position shown in Figure 3-57.

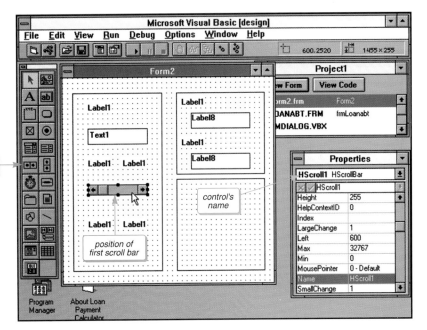

FIGURE 3-57

TRANSPARENCIES
Figure 3-57 and
Figure 3-58

STEP 2 ▶

Double-click the horizontal scroll bar tool in the Toolbox. Extend the new scroll bar's width by dragging its sizing handle the distance of one grid mark on the form. Drag the scroll bar to the position shown in Figure 3-58.

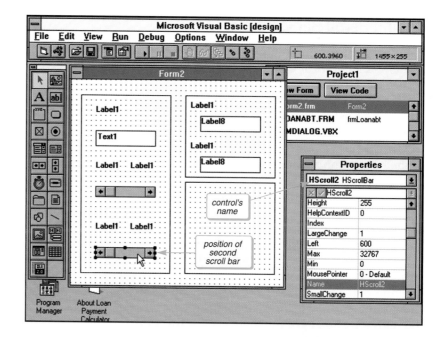

FIGURE 3-58

In the Loan Payment application, the caption of the label located above the right end of the scroll bar is used to display the current value of the input controlled by that scroll bar. When you click a scroll arrow or drag the scroll box, the scroll bar's **Change event** is triggered. A code statement will be written later in this project that will link the caption of the label to the Change event.

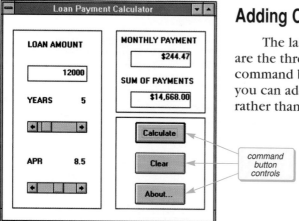

FIGURE 3-59

Adding Command Buttons

The last three controls to be added to the Loan Payment form are the three command buttons identified in Figure 3-59. The command buttons used in this application are the default size, so you can add them to the form by using the double-click method rather than drawing them with the mouse.

TO ADD THE COMMAND BUTTONS

Step 1: Double-click the command button tool in the Toolbox. Drag the Command1 command button inside and to the top, center of the shape control located on the lower right of the form window.

Step 2: Double-click the command button tool in the Toolbox. Drag the Command2 button inside and to the center of the shape control located on the lower right of the form window.

Step 3: Double-click the command button tool in the Toolbox. Drag the Command3 button inside and to the bottom, center of the shape control located on the lower right of the form window.

The command buttons appear as shown in Figure 3-60.

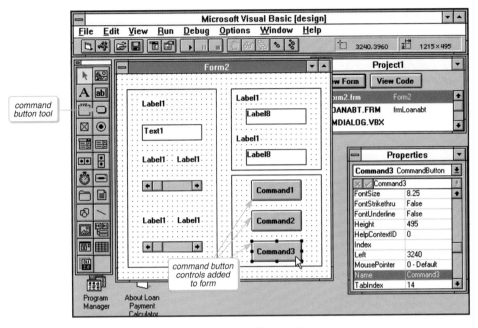

FIGURE 3-60

You now have completed the design of the Loan Payment form. The next step in the development process is to set the properties for the form and its controls.

▶ SETTING PROPERTIES OF THE LOAN PAYMENT FORM AND ITS CONTROLS

I n addition to setting the Caption and Name properties of the controls on the Loan Payment form, you will set the following properties:

▶ the Alignment property of text boxes and labels
▶ the Min and Max properties of scroll bars
▶ the SmallChange and LargeChange properties of scroll bars
▶ the Icon property of forms

Setting the Alignment Property of Text Boxes and Labels

The **Alignment property** specifies where the caption will appear within the borders of a control, regardless of whether the borders are visible. The values of the Alignment property are listed in Table 3-5.

▶ **TABLE 3-5 ALIGNMENT PROPERTY**

VALUE	EXAMPLE
0-Left Justify	loan
1-Right Justify	loan
2-Center	loan

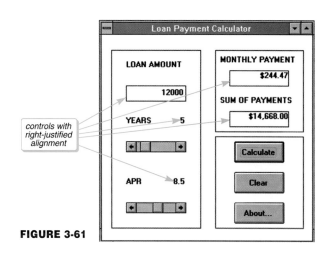

FIGURE 3-61

The default value of the Alignment property is left justified. Since the values appear in the drop-down Properties list in the same order as in Table 3-5, you can change from left justify to right justify by double-clicking the Alignment property in the Properties list rather than opening the Settings list and then selecting 1-Right Justify. The five controls with right-justified alignment are identified in Figure 3-61.

The text box control is among the five right justified controls. To change a text box's alignment, the value of its MultiLine property must be equal to True. Perform the following steps to set the Alignment property.

TO SET THE ALIGNMENT PROPERTY

Step 1: Select the Text1 control by clicking it on the form or by clicking its name in the drop-down Object list in the Properties window. Double-click the Alignment property in the Properties list in the Properties window.

Step 2: Scroll down the Properties list and double-click the MultiLine property in the Properties list.

Step 3: Select the Label3 control by clicking its name in the drop-down Object list in the Properties window. Double-click the Alignment property in the Properties list.

Step 4: Select the Label5 control by clicking its name in the drop-down Object list in the Properties window. Double-click the Alignment property in the Properties list.

Step 5: Select the Label8 control by clicking it on the form or by clicking its name in the drop-down Object list in the Properties window. Double-click the Alignment property in the Properties list.

Step 6: Select the Label9 control by clicking it on the form or by clicking its name in the drop-down Object list in the Properties window. Double-click the Alignment property in the Properties list.

Setting the Caption and Text Properties

Figure 3-62 shows the Loan Payment form as it appears at the current stage of development and as it will appear when completed. The differences between these two figures relate to the Caption property of the form, labels, and command buttons and to the Text property of the one text box control. At run time, the text box should start out empty. This text box is made empty by setting the initial value of its Text property to be blank. Perform the following steps to set the Caption property and Text property.

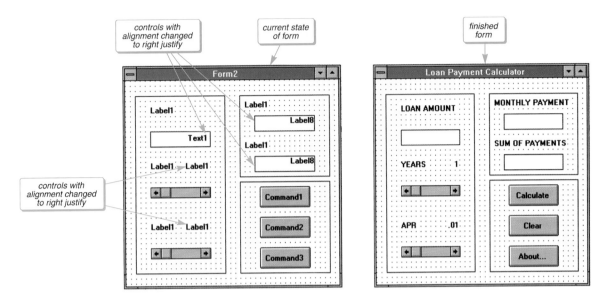

FIGURE 3-62

TO SET THE CONTROLS' CAPTIONS AND TEXT

Step 1: Select the Form2 form control by clicking its name in the drop-down Object list in the Properties window. Double-click the Caption property in the Properties list. Type `Loan Payment Calculator` and press the ENTER key.

Step 2: Select the Label1 control by clicking its name in the drop-down Object list in the Properties window. Double-click the Caption property in the Properties list. Type `LOAN AMOUNT` and press the ENTER key.

Step 3: Select the Text1 control by clicking its name in the drop-down Object list in the Properties window. Double-click the Text property in the Properties list and press the SPACEBAR to clear the text and press the ENTER key.

Step 4: Select the Label2 control by clicking its name in the drop-down Object list in the Properties window. Double-click the Caption property in the Properties list. Type `YEARS` and press the ENTER key.

Step 5: Select the Label3 control by clicking its name in the drop-down Object list in the Properties window. Double-click the Caption property in the Properties list. Type `1` and press the ENTER key.

Step 6: Select the Label4 control by clicking its name in the drop-down Object list in the Properties window. Double-click the Caption property in the Properties list. Type `APR` and press the ENTER key.

Step 7: Select the Label5 control by clicking its name in the drop-down Object list in the Properties window. Double-click the Caption property in the Properties list. Type `.01` and press the ENTER key.

Step 8: Select the Label6 control by clicking its name in the drop-down Object list in the Properties window. Double-click the Caption property in the Properties list. Type `MONTHLY PAYMENT` and press the ENTER key.

Step 9: Select the Label7 control by clicking its name in the drop-down Object list in the Properties window. Double-click the Caption property in the Properties list. Type `SUM OF PAYMENTS` and press the ENTER key.

Step 10: Select the Label8 control by clicking its name in the drop-down Object list in the Properties window. Double-click the Caption property in the Properties list. Press the SPACEBAR on the keyboard. Press the ENTER key.

Step 11: Select the Label9 control by clicking its name in the drop-down Object list in the Properties window. Double-click the Caption property in the Properties list. Press the SPACEBAR. Press the ENTER key.

Step 12: Select the Command1 control by clicking its name in the drop-down Object list in the Properties window. Double-click the Caption property in the Properties list. Type `Calculate` and press the ENTER key.

Step 13: Select the Command2 control by clicking its name in the drop-down Object list in the Properties window. Double-click the Caption property in the Properties list. Type `Clear` and press the ENTER key.

Step 14: Select the Command3 control by clicking its name in the drop-down Object list in the Properties window. Double-click the Caption property in the Properties list. Type `About..` and press the ENTER key.

The Loan Payment form appears as shown in Figure 3-63.

TRANSPARENCY
Figure 3-63

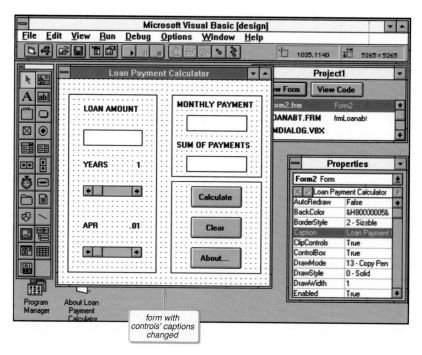

FIGURE 3-63

Naming the Controls

TRANSPARENCIES
Figure 3-64 and
Figure 3-65

LECTURE NOTES
■ Review the reasons for
giving new names to con-
trols and the prefix conven-
tion for naming controls.

In addition to the form control itself, four labels, two scroll bars, three command buttons, and one text box on the Loan Payment Calculator form will be referred to in the events and code statements that will be written later. These controls, with their current (default) names, are shown in Figure 3-64. It would be confusing to write events and code statements using the default names of these controls. Perform the following steps to rename the controls that will be referred to in code statements.

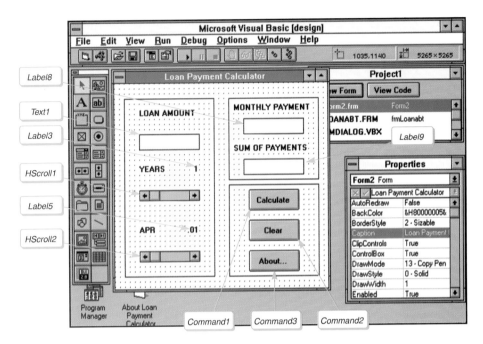

FIGURE 3-64

TO NAME CONTROLS

Step 1: Select the Form2 control by clicking its name in the drop-down Object list in the Properties window. Double-click the Name property in the Properties list. Type the control name `frmLoanpmt` and press the ENTER key.

Step 2: Select the Text1 control by clicking its name in the drop-down Object list in the Properties window. Double-click the Name property in the Properties list. Type the control name `txtAmount` and press the ENTER key.

Step 3: Select the Label3 control by clicking its name in the drop-down Object list in the Properties window. Double-click the Name property in the Properties list. Type the control name `lblYears` and press the ENTER key.

Step 4: Select the HScroll1 control by clicking its name in the drop-down Object list in the Properties window. Double-click the Name property in the Properties list. Type the control name `hsbYears` and press the ENTER key.

Step 5: Select the Label5 control by clicking its name in the drop-down Object list in the Properties window. Double-click the Name property in the Properties list. Type the control name `lblRate` and press the ENTER key.

Step 6: Select the HScroll2 control by clicking its name in the drop-down Object list in the Properties window. Double-click the Name property in the Properties list. Type `hsbRate` and press the ENTER key.

Step 7: Select the Label8 control by clicking its name in the drop-down Object list in the Properties window. Double-click the Name property in the Properties list. Type the control name `lblPayment` and press the ENTER key.

Step 8: Select the Label9 control by clicking its name in the drop-down Object list in the Properties window. Double-click the Name property in the Properties list. Type the control name `lblSumpmts` and press the ENTER key.

Step 9: Select the Command1 control by clicking its name in the drop-down Object list in the Properties window. Double-click the Name property in the Properties list. Type the control name `cmdCalculate` and press the ENTER key.

Step 10: Select the Command2 control by clicking its name in the drop-down Object list in the Properties window. Double-click the Name property in the Properties list. Type the control name `cmdClear` and press the ENTER key.

Step 11: Select the Command3 control by clicking its name in the drop-down Object list in the Properties window. Double-click the Name property in the Properties list. Type the control name `cmdAbout` and press the ENTER key.

The controls are identified by their new names in Figure 3-65.

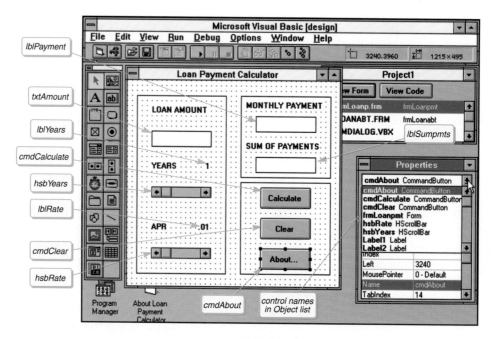

FIGURE 3-65

Setting the Scroll Bar Properties

The **Value property** of a scroll bar is an integer number that changes in relation to the position of the scroll box within the scroll bar. The lowest and highest numbers that the Value property can take are set with the **Min** and **Max** properties of the scroll bar. In a horizontal scroll bar control, these values correspond to the farthest left and farthest right positions of the scroll box.

The amount that the value changes each time you click one of the scroll arrows is set by the **SmallChange property** of the scroll bar. The amount that the value changes by clicking the area between the scroll box and one of the two scroll arrows is set with the **LargeChange property** of the scroll bar. Perform the following steps to set the properties of the scroll bar controls.

TO SET THE SCROLL BAR PROPERTIES

Step 1: Select the Years scroll bar by clicking it on the form or by clicking its name, hsbYears, in the drop-down Object list in the Properties window.

Step 2: Double-click the Max property in the Properties list. Type 30 and press the ENTER key.

Step 3: Double-click the Min property in the Properties list. Type 1 and press the ENTER key.

Step 4: Double-click the LargeChange property in the Properties list. Type 5 and press the ENTER key.

Step 5: Select the APR scroll bar by clicking it on the form or by clicking its name, hsbRate, in the drop-down Object list in the Properties window.

Step 6: Double-click the Max property in the Properties list. Type 1500 and press the ENTER key.

Step 7: Double-click the Min property in the Properties list. Type 1 and press the ENTER key.

Step 8: Double-click the LargeChange property in the Properties list. Type 10 and press the ENTER key.

The new values of these properties are visible by scrolling through the Properties list.

The preceding steps set properties of the scroll bars so that the value of the scroll bar used to set years (hsbYears) will range from 1 to 30 and the value of the scroll bar used to set the APR (hsbRate) will range from 1 to 1500. It was not necessary to set the SmallChange property since its default value is 1. The caption of the label (lblYears), located above the scroll bar, will be the value of the scroll bar hsbYears, representing the number of years to repay the loan (from 1 to 30).

The annual interest rate displayed as the caption of the label (lblAPR), located above the lower scroll bar (hsbRate), will work differently. Percentage rates on loans usually are expressed as a one or two digit number followed by a decimal point and a two digit decimal fraction, such as 12.25 percent or 6.30 percent. Since the value of a scroll bar cannot include a fraction, you will multiply the value of the scroll bar hsbRate by .01 to get the value of the caption of the label (lblAPR), located above the scroll bar. For example, a scroll bar value of 678 will represent an APR of 6.78 percent, and a scroll bar value of 1250 will represent an APR of 12.50 percent. Multiplying a scroll bar value by a decimal is a common way to make scroll bars able to represent numbers with fractional parts. You set the range of the APR scroll bar (hsbRate) values from 1 to 1500 so that it can be used as described above to represent .01 to 15.00 percent.

The Icon Property of Forms

When a window is minimized, it appears on the desktop as a small graphical image called an icon. You can specify the graphical image used to represent the form by setting the form's **Icon property.** In the example on the next page, an icon for the Loanpmt form will be selected.

TO SELECT AN ICON ▼

STEP 1 ►

Select the Loanpmt form by clicking an empty area of the form. Scroll through the Properties list until the Icon property is visible (Figure 3-66).

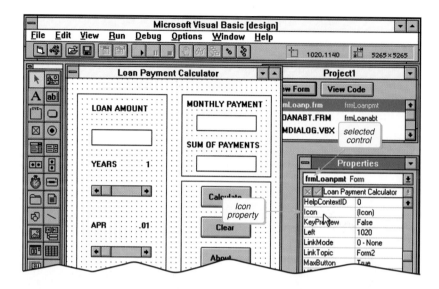

FIGURE 3-66

STEP 2 ►

Double-click the Icon property in the Properties list.

The Load Icon dialog box appears (Figure 3-67). The Load Icon dialog box is similar to other common dialog boxes such as the Save File As dialog box. The current drive and directory are those that were last selected when you added the icon to the image control in Figure 3-28 on page VB137.

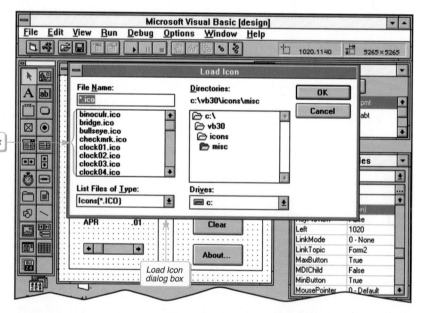

FIGURE 3-67

STEP 3 ►

Scroll through the file list box until the HOUSE.ICO file is visible. Select the house icon by double-clicking its file name (HOUSE.ICO) in the files list box (Figure 3-68).

The Load Icon dialog box closes.

FIGURE 3-68

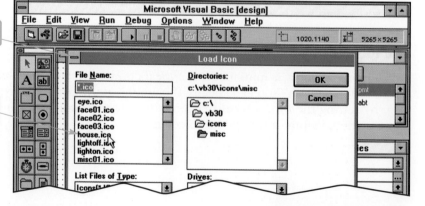

In the preceding example, an icon was selected from the set of icon files provided with the Visual Basic system. You are not limited to using this set of icons in your applications. Visual Basic also includes a sample application called Icon-Works, which you can use to view, edit, or create icons. See your instructor for additional information on using IconWorks.

▶ SAVING THE FORM

The frmLoanpmt form is now complete. Before proceeding, you should save the form to a formatted diskette in drive A.

TO SAVE THE FORM

Step 1: Select the File menu on the menu bar. Choose Save File As from the File menu.

Step 2: Type `Loanpmt` and with the Drives box set to drive A choose the OK button.

Step 3: Minimize the frmLoanpmt window by clicking the form window's minimize arrow.

The frmLoanpmt's file name appears in the Project window, followed by its name (Figure 3-69).

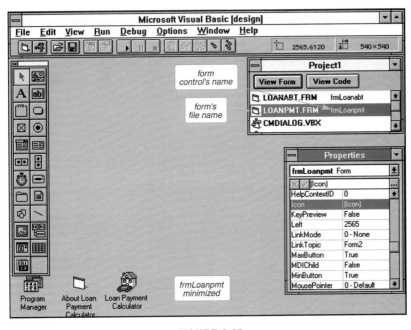

FIGURE 3-69

▶ WRITING CODE

Event procedures (subroutines) must be written for seven events in the Loan Payment Application. These events and their actions are listed in Table 3-6 on the next page.

▸ **TABLE 3-6 LOAN PAYMENT APPLICATION EVENT PROCEDURES**

FORM	CONTROL	EVENT	ACTIONS
frmLoanpmt	Form	Load	Position the form in the center of the desktop
frmLoanpmt	hsbYears	Change	Update the caption of lblYears
frmLoanpmt	hsbRate	Change	Update the caption lblRate
frmLoanpmt	cmdCalculate	Click	Perform the monthly payment and sum of payments calculations, and display results in lblPayment and lblSumpmts
frmLoanpmt	cmdClear	Click	Clear the contents of txtAmount, lblPayment, and lblSumpmts; reset hsbYears and hsbRate to lowest values
frmLoanpmt	cmdAbout	Click	Add About.. dialog box to desktop
frmLoanabt	Command1	Click	Remove About.. dialog box from desktop

The code for the Loan Payment application will be written one event at a time using the Visual Basic Code window in the same manner as in Projects 1 and 2. However, in a project that has more than one form, each form has its own Code window. Before writing the subroutines, a Start Up Form for the project will be specified.

The Start Up Form

At run time, the **Start Up form** is the first form in a project loaded into the computer's memory and added to the desktop. By default, the Start Up Form is the first form you create in a project. The Loan Payment application begins by displaying the frmLoanpmt form on the desktop. Since frmLoanpmt was not the first form created, it must be specified as the Start Up Form.

TO SPECIFY A START UP FORM ▼

STEP 1 ▶

Select the Options menu from the menu bar (Figure 3-70).

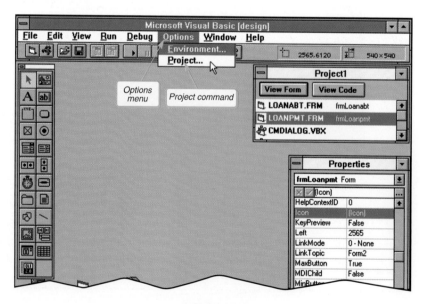

FIGURE 3-70

STEP 2 ▶

Choose Project... from the Options menu.

The Project Options dialog box appears (Figure 3-71).

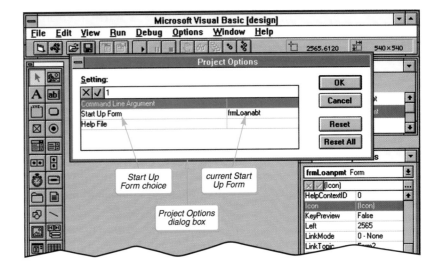

FIGURE 3-71

STEP 3 ▶

Double-click Start Up Form

The Project Options dialog box resembles the Properties window. Start Up Form is selected, and a drop-down list of possible values is displayed (Figure 3-72).

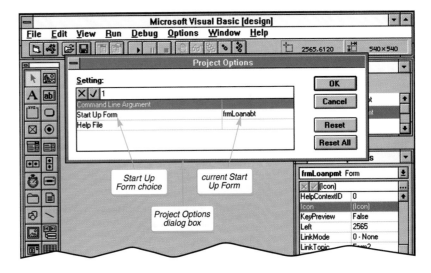

FIGURE 3-72

STEP 4 ▶

Select frmLoanpmt by clicking its name in the list.

frmLoanpmt is now the Start Up Form (Figure 3-73).

STEP 5 ▶

Choose the OK button to close the dialog box.

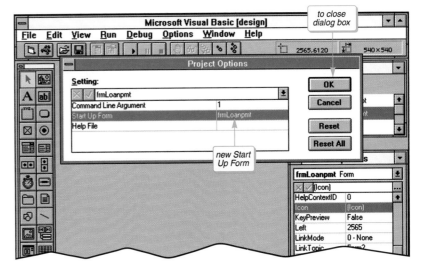

FIGURE 3-73

In Projects 1 and 2, a Start Up Form was not specified explicitly because when a project consists of just one form (as those projects did), the form is automatically set as the Start Up Form.

The frmLoanpmt Form_Load Subroutine

In Project 2, the Form_Load event was presented and used to add items to a drop-down list. Project 3 uses the Form_Load event to set the location of the form on the desktop by specifying its Top and Right properties. Recall that control properties are set at run time by using a code statement consisting of the control's name, a period, the name of the property you want to change (with no blank spaces) followed by an equal sign, and the new value of the property, such as

```
Label1.Caption = "John" or chkMatinee.Value = True
```

LECTURE NOTES
■ Review the syntax for setting properties with code statements.
■ Explain the code statements that center a form on the desktop.

A simple procedure exists for placing any form in the center of the desktop, regardless of its dimensions. The total height and width of the desktop (in twips) are kept by Visual Basic as the values of Screen.Height and Screen.Width, respectively. A form is centered top to bottom by placing its top at a position that is half the difference between the total height of the desktop and the height of the form. A form is centered left to right on the desktop in a similar way by placing its left border at a position that is half the difference between the total width of the desktop and the width of the form. Perform the following steps to open the frm-Loanpmt Code window and to write the Form_Load event subroutine.

TO WRITE THE FORM_LOAD SUBROUTINE

Step 1: Be certain the frmLoanpmt form is selected. If not, click its name, frmLoanpmt, in the Project window. Click the View Code button.

Step 2: Select the Form object from the drop-down Object list in the Code window.

Step 3: Enter the following statements in the Code window:
```
frmLoanpmt.Top = (Screen.Height - frmLoanpmt.Height) / 2
frmLoanpmt.Left = (Screen.Width - frmLoanpmt.Width) / 2
```

TRANSPARENCY
Figure 3-74

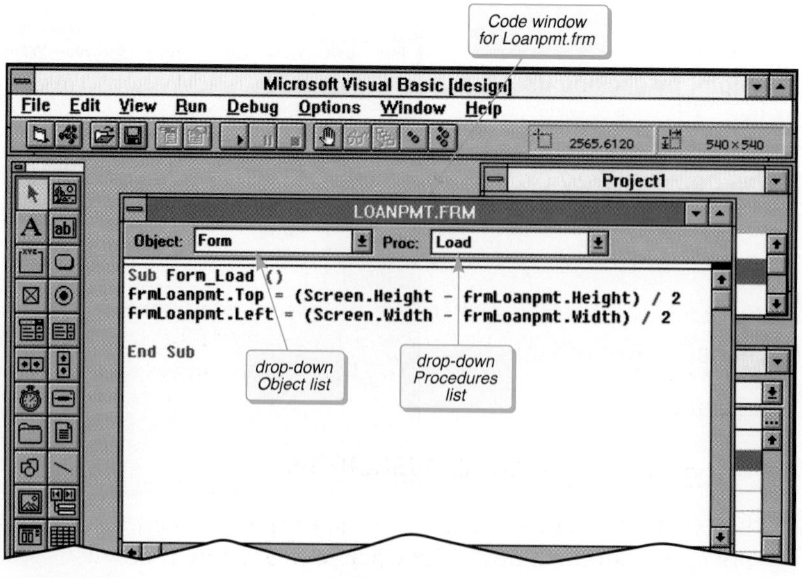

The code appears as shown in Figure 3-74.

FIGURE 3-74

The frmLoanpmt hsbYears_Change Subroutine

A scroll bar control's **Change event** is triggered any time the control's scroll box is moved by clicking a scroll arrow, dragging the scroll box, or clicking the space between the scroll box and scroll arrow. Each of these three movements also changes the Value property of the scroll bar.

In the Loan Application, a movement of the scroll box must be linked to a new number displayed in the caption located above the scroll bar. Perform the following steps to establish this link by setting the Caption property of the label used to display the years (lblYears) to equal the Value property of the scroll bar located beneath it on the form (hsbYears).

TO WRITE THE HSBYEARS_CHANGE SUBROUTINE

Step 1: Select the hsbYears control from the drop-down Object list in the frm-Loanpmt Code window. The Change procedure is already selected.

Step 2: Enter the following statement in the Code window:

```
lblYears.Caption = hsbYears.Value
```

The Code window appears as shown in Figure 3-75.

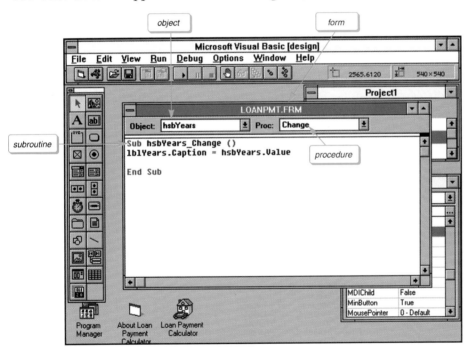

FIGURE 3-75

The frmLoanpmt hsbRate_Change Event

This event is very similar to the Change event for hsbYears. The only difference is the interest rate displayed as the caption of lblApr must be converted from the value of hsbRate by multiplying it by .01. Perform the following steps to write the hsbRate_Change subroutine.

TO WRITE THE HSBRATE_CHANGE SUBROUTINE

Step 1: Select the hsbRate control from the drop-down Object list in the frm-Loanpmt Code window. The Change procedure is already selected.

Step 2: Enter the following statement in the Code window:
```
lblRate.Caption = hsbRate.Value * .01
```

The Code window appears as shown in Figure 3-76.

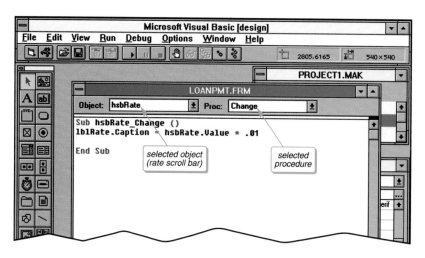

FIGURE 3-76

The frmLoanpmt cmdCalculate_Click Subroutine

The cmdCalculate_Click subroutine is used to perform the loan calculation and to display the results. The actual computation is performed by one of Visual Basic's financial functions, the Pmt function. For a complete list and descriptions of all the Visual Basic financial functions, use online Help to search on the words *financial functions*. The **Pmt function** returns the payment for a loan based on periodic, constant payments and a constant interest rate. The function is used in a code statement in the following manner:

Pmt(*rate, nper, pv, fv, due*)

The entries within parentheses are called **arguments**. Arguments within the Pmt function are described in table 3-7.

▶ **TABLE 3-7 PMT FUNCTION ARGUMENTS**

ARGUMENT	DESCRIPTION
rate	Interest rate per period. For example, if you get a car loan at an annual percentage rate of 9 percent and make monthly payments, the rate per period is 0.09/12 or 0.0075.
nper	Total number of payment periods in the loan. For example, if you make monthly payments on a five-year car loan, your loan has a total of 5 * 12 (or 60) payment periods.
pv	Present value that a series of payments to be paid in the future is worth now (to the lender). For example, if you borrow $10,000 to buy a car its pv is -10,000.
fv	Future value or cash balance you want after you've made the final payment. The future value of a loan is $0.
due	Number indicating when payments are due. Use 0 if payments are due at the end of the payment period, and use 1 if payments are due at the beginning of the period. In the Loan application you will use 1 to indicate payments are due on the first day of the month.

In the cmdCalculate_Click subroutine, the inputs of the loan application are substituted for the arguments of the Pmt function described in Table 3-7. Remember that the value of hsbRate runs from 1 to 1500 and that the decimal interest rate is .0001 times that value. The Pmt function arguments and values assigned in this project are listed in Table 3-8.

▸ **TABLE 3-8 ARGUMENTS IN LOAN PAYMENT APPLICATION**

ARGUMENT	VALUE
rate	.0001 * hsbRate.Value / 12
nper	hsbYears.Value * 12
pv	-1 * txtAmount.Text
fv	0
due	1

When you use the Pmt function, all of the arguments must be numbers (or variables whose value is a number). What if you typed `Hello` as the amount of the loan in the txtAmount text box at run time and then chose the Calculate button? The function would be unable to calculate a value, and the program would end abruptly. It is possible for you to make an error when typing the loan amount, so you want some way to trap this error and to correct it without the program ending abruptly.

Since the Text property of a text box can be either numbers (numeric) or text (string), you need to write some additional code that checks to see if the contents are numeric. This checking is done with the Visual Basic **IsNumeric** function. The function is used within code statements as follows:

IsNumeric(txtAmount.text)

The function will return a True value if the contents are a number and a False value if the contents are not a valid number. The logical flow of actions within the cmdCalculate_Click subroutine is shown in Figure 3-77.

TRANSPARENCIES
Figure 3-77 and
Figure 3-78

LECTURE NOTES
■ Explain the IsNumeric function.
■ Review the conditions and actions that occur when the Calculate button is clicked in the loan payment application.
■ Review the If..Then statement.
■ Explain the If..Then block.
■ Explain the use of the If...Then block in the cmdCalculate_Click event.

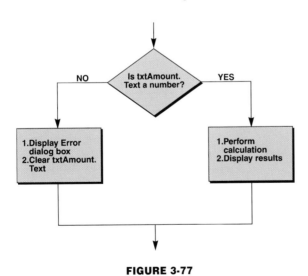

FIGURE 3-77

In Project 2, this type of logical structure was represented in code by using an If...Then statement. This project uses an extension to the If...Then statement called an **If...Then block**. The If...Then block evaluates a condition like the If...Then statement. However, the block allows you to have multiple code statements executed, as illustrated in Figure 3-78.

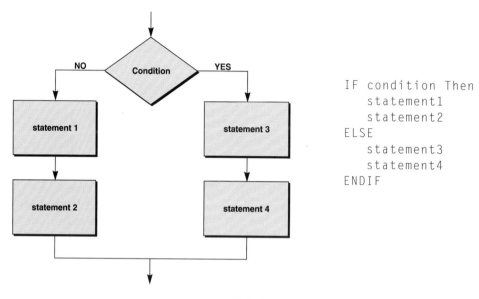

```
IF condition Then
      statement1
      statement2
ELSE
      statement3
      statement4
ENDIF
```

FIGURE 3-78

If the value is not a number, you want to first display a dialog box that alerts you to the error, and then erase the contents of txtAmount. Creating customized forms is one way that you can add dialog boxes to your applications (as you did with the About.. dialog box). Another way is to use the Visual Basic **MsgBox** statement to display message dialog boxes.

The dialog box shown in Figure 3-79 is used to alert you when an error has been made in entering a value for the loan amount. The dialog box is created with a MsgBox statement in the application's code. The generalized form of the MsgBox code statement consists of three parts: Msgbox *text,type,title,* which are described in Table 3-9.

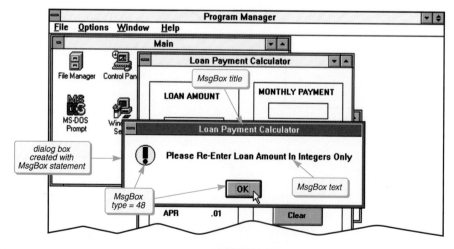

FIGURE 3-79

▸ **TABLE 3-9 MESSAGE BOX CODE STATEMENT ARGUMENTS**

ARGUMENT	DESCRIPTION
text	The text that appears in the body of the message box. It is enclosed in quotes.
type	A number that represents the type of button displayed, the icon displayed, and whether or not the dialog box is modal.
title	The text that appears in the title bar of the dialog box. It is enclosed in quotes.

For a detailed description of how to use different values of *type* for various combinations of buttons, icons, and modality, use the Visual Basic online Help facility to search for help on the MsgBox topic.

After these actions are completed, you want to place the cursor back in the txtAmount control for a new loan amount to be entered. You could select the textAmount control during run time by clicking it, which would place the cursor in the text box. However, you can cause this event to occur through code using the **SetFocus** statement. The syntax of the statement is:

controlname.Setfocus

The single argument *controlname* is the name of the control that you want to select.

The code statements that make up the cmdCalculate_Click subroutine are shown in Figure 3-80.

TRANSPARENCIES
Figure 3-80 and
Figure 3-81

LECTURE NOTES
■ Review the function of each code statement in the subroutine.
■ Emphasize that an individual code statement must be entered on only one line in the Code window. Review resizing and scrolling the code window to view or edit the code statement.

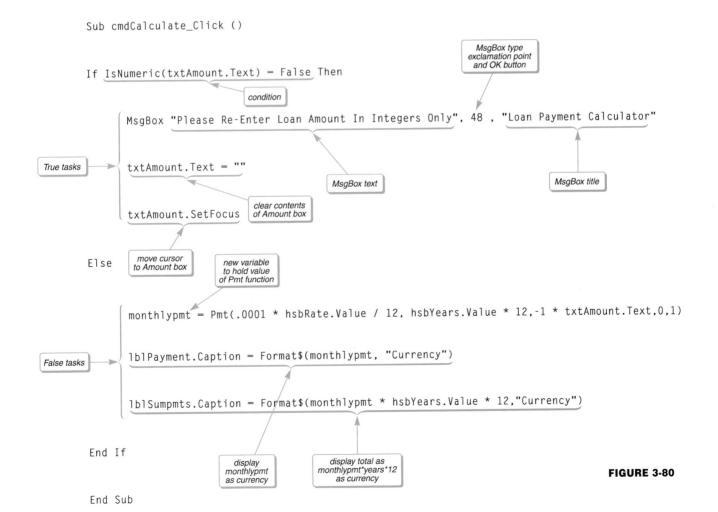

FIGURE 3-80

Perform the following steps to write the cmdCalculate_Click subroutine.

TO WRITE THE CMDCALCULATE_CLICK SUBROUTINE

Step 1: Select cmdCalculate from the drop-down Object list in the Code window.
Step 2: Enter the following statements in the Code window:

```
If IsNumeric(txtAmount.Text) = False Then
   Msgbox "Please Re-Enter Loan Amount In Integers Only", 48,"Loan Payment Calculator"
   txtAmount.Text = ""
   txtAmount.SetFocus
Else
   monthlypmt = Pmt(.0001 * hsbRate.Value / 12, hsbYears.Value * 12,-1 *
txtAmount.Text,0,1)
   lblPayment.Caption = Format$(monthlypmt,"Currency")
   lblSumpmt.Caption = Format$(monthlypmt * hsbYears.Value *12, "Currency")
End If
```

The Code window should appear as shown in Figure 3-81.

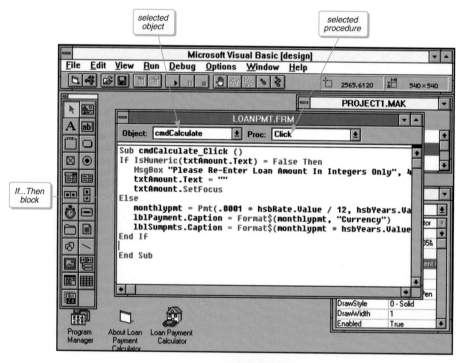

FIGURE 3-81

Line 6 in Step 2 (above) creates a variable named monthlypmt to hold the value returned by the Pmt function. This step makes the statement in Step 7 easier to read, where that value (monthlypmt), formatted as currency, is assigned to the Caption property of the lblPayment control. In Line 8, the sum of payments is calculated as the monthly payment times the number of years times 12 months in a year, and it also is formatted as currency.

The frmLoanpmt cmdClear_Click Subroutine

During run time, you choose the Clear button (cmdClear) to remove any currently displayed inputs or outputs from the form. These include the loan amount (txtAmount.Text), length of loan period (lblYears.Caption), APR (lblRate.Caption), monthly payment (lblPayment.Caption), and sum of payments (lblSumpmts.Caption). You also want the scroll bars (hsbYears and hsbRate) to return to their farthest left positions. Each of these actions will be accomplished by a statement that changes the value of the appropriate property of each control.

You do not need to directly change the number of years (the caption of lblYears) or the APR (the caption of lblRate). A code statement that changes the Value property of the scroll bar controls activates their Change event, which sets the captions of those labels.

After these actions are completed, you want the cursor to move back to the Loan Amount box (txtAmount control) for a new amount to be entered. This procedure will be accomplished using the SetFocus method described on page VB169. Perform the following steps to write the subroutine.

LECTURE NOTES
■ Review the actions that occur when the Clear button is clicked.
■ Review the use of the null string, "".

TRANSPARENCY
Figure 3-82

TO WRITE THE CMDCLEAR SUBROUTINE

Step 1:   Select cmdClear from the drop-down Object list in the Code window.

Step 2:   Enter the following statements in the Code window:

```
txtAmount.Text = " "
hsbYears.Value = 1
hsbRate.Value = 1
lblPayment.Caption = " "
lblSumpmts.Caption = " "
txtAmount.SetFocus
```

The Code window appears as shown in Figure 3-82.

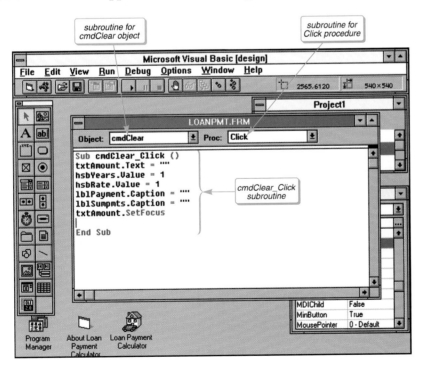

FIGURE 3-82

The frmLoanpmt cmdAbout_Click Event

TRANSPARENCIES
Table 3-10 and
Figure 3-83

LECTURE NOTES
■ Ask students to give
examples of modal and
modeless windows in
applications with which
they are familiar.
■ Explain the Form.Show
statement and its parts.

This event is triggered at run time when you click the About..command button. This event is used to display the frmLoanabt form. In Windows applications, a dialog box usually appears on top of all other open windows on the desktop, and you cannot work with any other window until the dialog box is closed. A form or window with these characteristics is called a **modal** form. Forms without these properties are called **modeless**.

You make forms visible on the desktop and control their modality at run time with the **Form.Show** code statement. The statement has these parts: *form*.SHOW *style*, as described in Table 3-10.

▸ **TABLE 3-10 ARGUMENTS OF SHOW STATEMENT**

ARGUMENT	DESCRIPTION
form	Name of form to display
style	Integer value that determines if the form is modal or modeless. If style is 0, the form is modeless; if style is 1, then form is modal; if a value for style is not included, the form is modeless

In addition to being modal, you want the About.. dialog box to appear in the center of the desktop. This project uses the method presented earlier to center the About.. dialog box when it appears during run time. Perform the following steps to write the cmdAbout_Click subroutine.

TO WRITE THE CMDABOUT_CLICK SUBROUTINE

Step 1: Select the cmdAbout control from the drop-down Object list in the frmLoanpmt Code window.

Step 2: Enter the following statements in the Code window:

```
frmLoanabt.Top = (Screen.Height - frmLoanabt.Height) / 2
frmLoanabt.Left = (Screen.width - frmLoanabt.Width) / 2
frmLoanabt.Show 1
```

The code appears as shown in Figure 3-83.

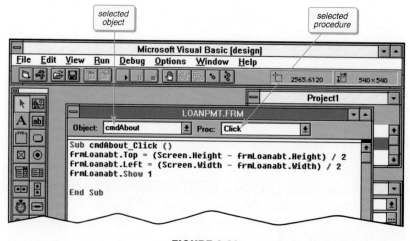

FIGURE 3-83

The frmLoanAbt Command1_Click Subroutine

This event is triggered when you click the command button labeled OK. The action of this event removes the About.. dialog box from the desktop. You remove forms from the desktop during run time by using the **Form.Hide** code statement. Perform the following steps to minimize the frmLoanpmt Code window, to open the frmLoanabt Code window, and to write the subroutine.

TO WRITE THE COMMAND1_CLICK SUBROUTINE

Step 1: Click the minimize button on the frmLoanpmt Code window.

Step 2: Select the frmLoanabt form by clicking its name in the Project Window. Choose the View Code button.

Step 3: Select the Command1 control from the drop-down Object list in the Code window.

Step 4: Enter the following statement in the Code window:
```
frmLoanabt.Hide
```

The Code window appears as shown in Figure 3-84.

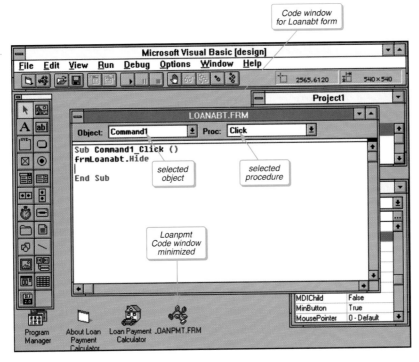

FIGURE 3-84

▶ SAVING THE PROJECT

The Loan Payment project is complete. When you save a form, the subroutines that you wrote for that form are saved as part of the .FRM file. The forms were saved earlier, but it was before the code had been written. Before making a project executable, you should save the project as a .MAK file. Perform the following steps to save the project and to resave the form files to a formatted diskette in drive A.

TO SAVE THE PROJECT

Step 1:   Choose Save Project from the File menu, or click the Save Project tool on the toolbar.
Step 2:   Type `Loan` in the File Name box.
Step 3:   With the Drives box set to drive A, choose the OK button.

The forms are automatically resaved, and the project is saved as LOAN.MAK.

▶ Making Executable Files

I n order to run an application without Visual Basic, you must convert the application into an executable file. The executable file will have the name that you give to the application and an .EXE extension. Perform the following steps to make an executable file for the Loan Payment application.

TO MAKE EXECUTABLE FILES ▼

STEP 1 ▶

Minimize the Loanabt code window. Select File from the Visual Basic menu bar.

The File menu opens (Figure 3-85).

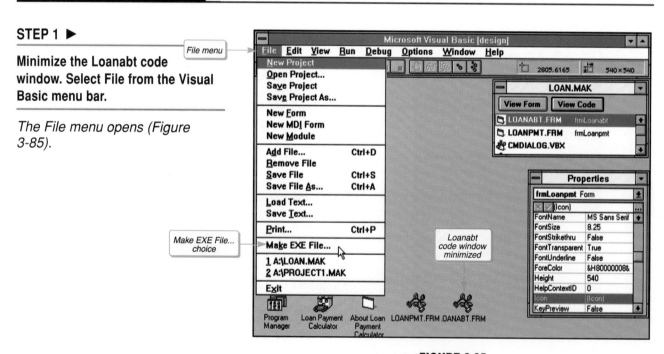

FIGURE 3-85

STEP 2 ▶

Choose Make EXE File.

The Make Exe File dialog box appears (Figure 3-86). The default name of the .EXE file is the name you gave to the .MAK file. The default icon that will be used when the program is minimized is the one that you attached to the main form. You can use the drop-down list boxes to select an icon from a different form or from an .ICO file.

STEP 3 ▶

Type Loancalc **and with drive A selected in the Drives box, choose the OK button.**

The .EXE file is created and written to the drive you specified. The Make EXE File dialog box closes, and Visual Basic returns to the design environment.

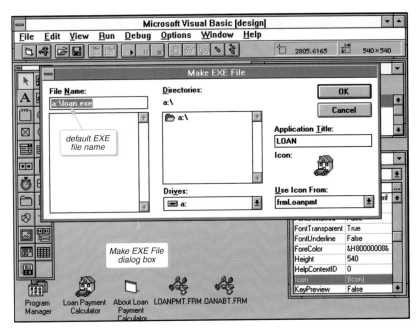

FIGURE 3-86

The Loan Payment application has been compiled and written to a file named LOAN.EXE on the disk in drive A. The application can now be run independently from the Visual Basic design environment. Close the Visual Basic program by double-clicking the Control-menu box. Respond Yes if prompted to save changes to LOAN.MAK.

▶ ADDING AND DELETING PROGRAM ITEMS

I n *Using Microsoft Windows* at the beginning of this book, you learned how to open program group windows and to start application programs within Windows' Program Manager. It is very easy to add, delete, and rearrange the program items within Program Manager.

Adding a Program Item

The following steps add a new program item, the Loan Payment program, to a program group. This example adds the loan program to the Visual Basic program group, but you could use the same steps to add it to any of the other program groups. It is also possible to create a new program group for your application.

TO ADD A PROGRAM ITEM ▼

STEP 1 ▶

Restore the Program Manager window by double-clicking the Program Manager icon. If the program group window where you want to place the item is not open (Visual Basic group), double-click the Visual Basic program group icon to open the window and to make it active.

STEP 2 ▶

Select the File menu from the Program Manager menu bar.

The File menu opens (Figure 3-87).

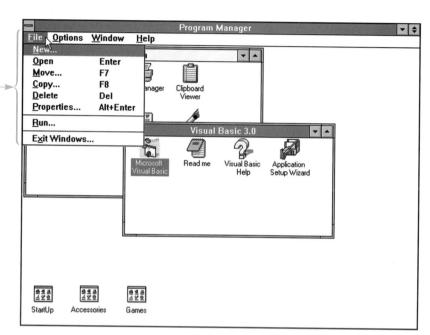

FIGURE 3-87

STEP 3 ▶

Choose New from the File menu.

The New Program Object dialog box appears (Figure 3-88).

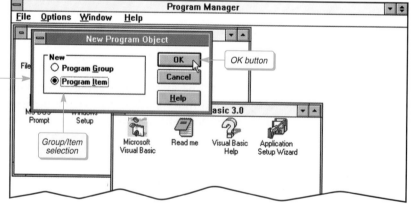

FIGURE 3-88

STEP 4 ▶

Choose the OK button to indicate you want to add a program item.

The Program Item Properties dialog box opens (Figure 3-89).

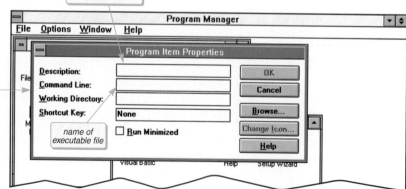

FIGURE 3-89

STEP 5 ▶

Type Loan Payment

The characters appear in the Description box (Figure 3-90). This title will appear below the icon.

STEP 6 ▶

Click the Command Line box. Type a:loancalc.exe

This area is where you enter the drive, directory, and file name of the item you are adding. Normally, you would copy the .EXE file to your hard disk. Right now this program will launch only when the current diskette is in drive A.

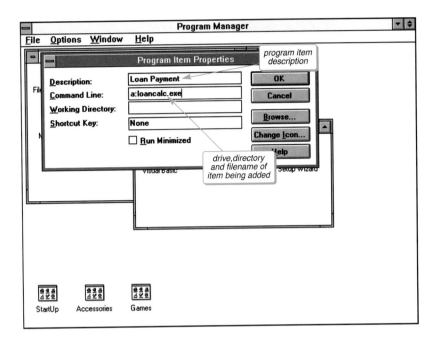

FIGURE 3-90

STEP 7 ▶

Choose the OK Button.

Windows adds the program item icon to the program group (Figure 3-91).

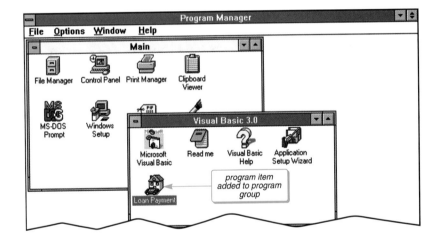

FIGURE 3-91

If you decide later to place the program item within another program group, you can do so by dragging and dropping the program item icon into the new program group window where you want it to appear. For more information on adding and managing program items, refer to the online Program Manager Help facility.

▶ RUNNING AND REMOVING THE APPLICATION

he Loan Payment application now can be opened and closed in the same way that you run other Windows applications. Perform the steps on the next page to test your application.

LECTURE NOTES
■ Explain how to move program items from one program group to another.
■ Review how programs are started by double-clicking their program items.
■ Demonstrate or discuss the operation of the completed executable loan payment calculator.

TRANSPARENCIES
Figure 3-92 through Figure 3-95

TO RUN THE APPLICATION ▼

STEP 1 ▶

Double-click the Loan Payment icon as shown in Figure 3-91 on page VB177 to launch the Loan Payment Calculator. Type `Hello` in the Loan Amount box. Choose the Calculate button.

The input error dialog appears (Figure 3-92).

FIGURE 3-92

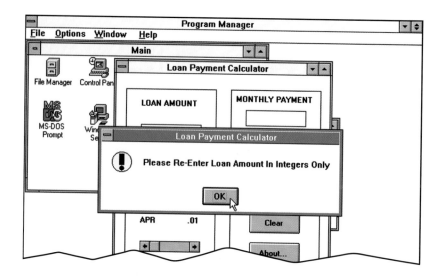

STEP 2 ▶

Choose the OK button on the input error dialog box. Choose the About.. button in the Loan Payment Calculator window.

The About.. dialog box opens (Figure 3-93).

FIGURE 3-93

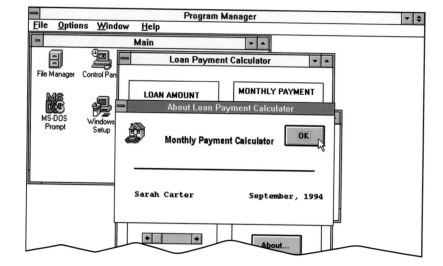

STEP 3 ▶

Choose the OK button. Type `18000` in the Loan Amount box. Use the Years scroll bar to set the number of years to 5. Use the APR scroll bar to set the rate to 8.9. Choose the Calculate button.

The application computes and displays as currency the monthly payment ($370.03) and the sum of the payments ($22,201.98) (Figure 3-94).

FIGURE 3-94

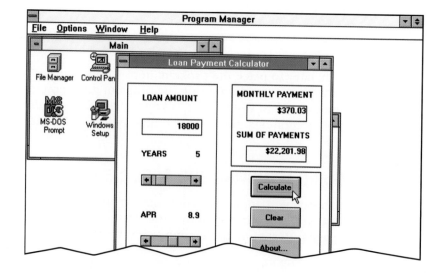

STEP 4 ▶

Choose the Clear button.

The inputs and outputs are cleared (Figure 3-95).

STEP 5 ▶

Try several different sets of input values. Minimize the window on the desktop. Restore the window. Try some more calculations.

STEP 6 ▶

Double-click the Loan window's Control-menu box.

The application closes.

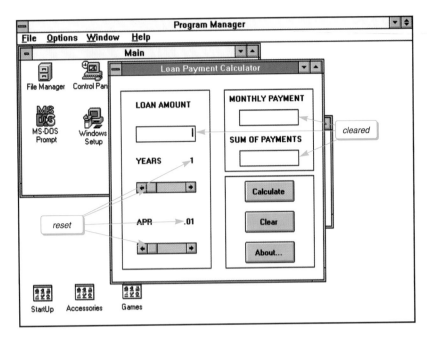

FIGURE 3-95

After the Loan Payment application is closed, perform the following steps to remove the program item from the Visual Basic 3.0 program group window.

TO REMOVE A PROGRAM ITEM ▼

STEP 1 ▶

If the item is not already selected, click the item icon to select it.

The program icon is highlighted in the active color (Figure 3-96).

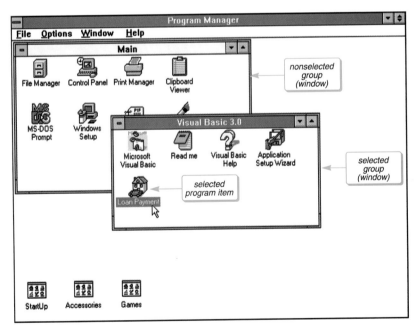

FIGURE 3-96

STEP 2 ▶

Press and release the DELETE key.

*The Delete dialog box appears
(Figure 3-97).*

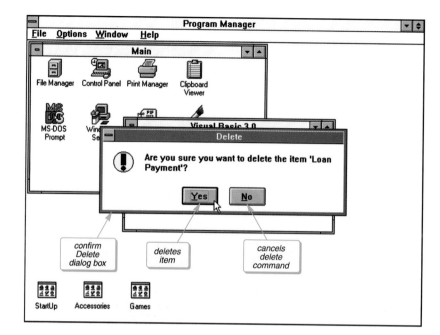

FIGURE 3-97

STEP 3 ▶

Choose the Yes button.

*The Delete dialog box closes, and
the program icon is removed from
the program group (Figure 3-98).*

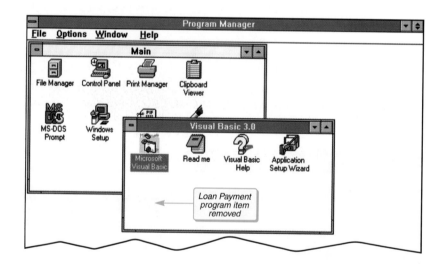

FIGURE 3-98

Although you removed the Loan Payment item from Program Manager, these
steps did not do anything to the LOANPMT.EXE file, the LOANPMT.MAK file, or
either of the two form files that you saved to the disk in drive A.

▶ PROJECT SUMMARY

Project 3 extended the basics of building an application that were presented in Projects 1 and 2. You built
an application by designing the interface and then writing code. The application in this project consisted
of multiple forms and dialog boxes. You learned more about the form control's properties, WindowState,
and modality. You also learned how to add an icon to a form.

Several new properties of familiar controls were presented. You also learned about image, line, and
scroll bar controls. After building the Loan Payment application, you compiled it into an executable file.

At the end of the project, you learned how to add and remove program items from program groups.

▶ KEY TERMS

About.. dialog box *(VB122)*
Alignment property *(VB153)*
argument *(VB166)*
AutoSize property *(VB132)*
dialog box *(VB120)*
BorderStyle property *(VB131)*
Change event *(VB152)*
executable *(VB120)*
font *(VB134)*
FontBold property *(VB134)*
FontItalic property *(VB134)*
FontName property *(VB134)*

FontSize property *(VB134)*
Icon property *(VB159)*
inputs *(VB143)*
image control *(VB127)*
LargeChange property *(VB158)*
line control *(VB128)*
Max property *(VB158)*
MaxButton property *(VB130)*
Min property *(VB158)*
MinButton property *(VB130)*
modal *(VB172)*
modeless *(VB172)*

MsgBox statement *(VB168)*
outputs *(VB143)*
Pmt function *(VB166)*
scroll bar control *(VB151)*
shape control *(VB142)*
SetFocus method *(VB169)*
sizable form *(VB131)*
SmallChange property *(VB158)*
stand-alone *(VB120)*
Value property *(VB158)*
WindowState *(VB130)*

QUICK REFERENCE

In Visual Basic you can accomplish a task in a number of ways. The following table provides a quick reference to each of the major tasks presented for the first time in the project with some of the available options. The commands listed in the Menu column can be executed using either the keyboard or mouse.

Task	Mouse	Menu	Keyboard Shortcuts
Add an Additional Form to a Project	Click the New Form icon on the toolbar	From File menu, choose New Form	
Copy a Selected Control to the Clipboard		From Edit menu, choose Copy	Press CTRL+C
Delete a Selected Program Item from a Program Item Group	From Program Manager File menu, choose Delete		Press DELETE
Open the Project Options Dialog Box	From Options menu, choose Project		
Open the Make EXE File Dialog Box	From File menu, choose Make EXE File...		
Paste a Control from the Clipboard onto a Selected Form		From Edit menu, choose Paste	Press CTRL+V

EXERCISE NOTES
■ Use Student Assignments 1 through 6 for classroom discussion or homework exercises.

STUDENT ASSIGNMENT 1
True/False

Instructions: Circle T if the statement is true or F if the statement is false.

T (F) 1. Dialog boxes rarely are used in Windows applications.
T (F) 2. A form's width can be changed only by dragging its borders.
(T) F 3. Top and Left properties determine the position of the upper left corner of the form on the desktop.
(T) F 4. A shape control can be displayed as a circle.
T (F) 5. Label controls cannot have borders.
T (F) 6. The AutoSize property has three values.
T (F) 7. A label control's borders can be resized at run time by dragging them.
T (F) 8. The default value of the Alignment property is Centered.
(T) F 9. Clicking a scroll arrow changes the value of the scroll bar by an amount equal to the value of the SmallChange property.
(T) F 10. Dragging the scroll box of a scroll bar control causes the scroll bar's Change event to occur.
T (F) 11. The WindowState property of a form determines whether the form has a title bar.
T (F) 12. All windows must have minimum and maximum buttons.
(T) F 13. When a form's BorderStyle is set to None, the form does not have a title bar.
(T) F 14. A minimized window appears as an icon.
T (F) 15. A form's Icon property has values of True or False.
(T) F 16. IconWorks is a program for creating and editing .ICO files.
T (F) 17. A modal dialog box does not have a Control-menu box.
T (F) 18. A font cannot be displayed as both bold and italics at the same time.
(T) F 19. An image control can be used as a container for graphical images.
T (F) 20. The Load Icon dialog box is opened by clicking the icon tool in the toolbar.

STUDENT ASSIGNMENT 2
Multiple Choice

Instructions: Circle the correct response.

1. The _____ property of the line control determines its appearance (solid, dotted, etc).
   a. BorderWidth
   b. LineStyle
   (c.) BorderStyle
   d. FrameStyle
2. The _____ form is the first form loaded into the computer's memory and displayed on the desktop.
   a. default
   b. Form1
   (c.) start up
   d. .FRM
3. Each _____ in an application has its own Code window.
   a. event
   b. control
   (c.) form
   d. procedure

4. Stand-alone application files have a _____ extension.
   a. .FRM
   b. .MAK
   c. .VBX
   d. .EXE ⟵ (circled)
5. Executable files are added to Windows Program Manager as _____.
   a. program groups
   b. group icons
   c. program items ⟵ (circled)
   d. program icons
6. _____ is a property of scroll bar controls.
   a. scroll box
   b. scroll arrow
   c. LargeChange ⟵ (circled)
   d. ScrollChange
7. A shape control can be displayed as a(n) _____.
   a. oval ⟵ (circled)
   b. triangle
   c. both a and b
   d. neither a nor b
8. A scroll bar's Change event occurs when a user _____.
   a. clicks a scroll arrow
   b. drags the scroll box
   c. both a and b ⟵ (circled)
   d. neither a nor b
9. _____ is a Visual Basic financial function.
   a. Ipv
   b. Npr
   c. Pmt ⟵ (circled)
   d. none of these
10. The default value of a label control's BorderStyle property is_____.
    a. 0-none ⟵ (circled)
    b. True
    c. False
    d. fixed-single

STUDENT ASSIGNMENT 3
Understanding the Procedure for Copying Controls

Instructions: Fill in the step numbers below to correctly order the process of making two copies of a control and locating them on a form.

Step __4 or 7__ :   Type N for No.

Step __3 or 6__ :   Press CTRL+V.

Step __6 or 3__ :   Press CTRL+V.

Step __5 or 8__ :   Drag the copy of the control to its location.

Step ____1____ :   Click the control to be copied.

Step __7 or 4__ :   Type N for No.

Step __8 or 5__ :   Drag the copy of the control to its location.

Step ____2____ :   Press CTRL+C.

STUDENT ASSIGNMENT 4
Understanding Controls and Properties

Instructions: The following table lists several controls and several properties. Place an "x" in the space provided if the control has that property.

PROPERTY	CONTROLS				
	Label	Form	Text Box	Image	Scroll Bar
AutoSize	[X]	[ ]	[ ]	[ ]	[ ]
BorderStyle	[X]	[X]	[X]	[X]	[ ]
LargeChange	[ ]	[ ]	[ ]	[ ]	[X]
Alignment	[X]	[ ]	[X]	[ ]	[ ]
MaxButton	[ ]	[X]	[ ]	[ ]	[ ]
Max	[ ]	[ ]	[ ]	[ ]	[X]
MinButton	[ ]	[X]	[ ]	[ ]	[ ]
Min	[ ]	[ ]	[ ]	[ ]	[X]
SmallChange	[ ]	[ ]	[ ]	[ ]	[X]
Caption	[X]	[X]	[ ]	[X]	[ ]
Text	[ ]	[ ]	[X]	[ ]	[ ]
Name	[X]	[X]	[X]	[X]	[X]
Value	[ ]	[ ]	[ ]	[ ]	[X]
Icon	[ ]	[X]	[ ]	[ ]	[ ]

STUDENT ASSIGNMENT 5
Understanding Code Statements

Instructions: Enter the correct answers.

1. Write a code statement that will center a form named Form1 vertically on the desktop.

Statement: Form1.Top = (Screen.Height – Form1.Height) / 2

2. Write a code statement that will center a form named Form2 horizontally on the desktop.

Statement: Form1.Left = (Screen.Width – Form.Height) / 2

3. Write a code statement that will display a message box titled *My Application*. The message box should display an exclamation point icon and an OK button. The text should read *Important Message*.

Statement: MsgBox"Important Message",48,"My Application"

4. Write a code statement that will cause a form named Form3 to appear on the desktop in a modal state.

Statement: Form3.Show 1

5. Write a code statement that will cause a form named Form4 to be removed from the desktop.

Statement: Form4.Hide

6. Write a code statement that will cause a form named Form5 to be minimized on the desktop.

Statement: Form5.Windowstate = 1

STUDENT ASSIGNMENT 6
Understanding Commands in Menus

Instructions: Write the appropriate command name to accomplish each task and the menu in which each command is located.

TASK	COMMAND NAME	MENU NAME
Add a new form to a project	[NewForm]	[File]
Begin execution of an application	[Start]	[Run]
Open the dialog box used to specify the Start Up Form	[Project]	[Options]
Copy a control or code statements to the Clipboard	[Copy]	[Edit]
Stop execution of an application	[End]	[Run]
Save a form to a file	[SaveFile]	[File]
Copy a control or code statements from the Clipboard	[Paste]	[Edit]
Make an executable file for the application	[MakeEXEFile]	[File]
Close Visual Basic	[Exit]	[File]

C O M P U T E R   L A B O R A T O R Y   E X E R C I S E S

COMPUTER LABORATORY EXERCISE 1
Using Scroll Bar Controls

EXERCISE NOTES
■ Exercise 1 provides students with experience in using scroll bar and image controls.

Instructions: Start Visual Basic. Open the project CLE3-1 from the subdirectory VB3 on the Student Diskette that accompanies this book. Complete the following tasks.

1. Choose the View Form button in the Project window.
2. Add a vertical scroll bar to the form, as shown in Figure CLE3-1 on the next page.
3. Add a horizontal scroll bar to the form, as shown in Figure CLE3-1.

COMPUTER LABORATORY EXERCISE 1 (continued)

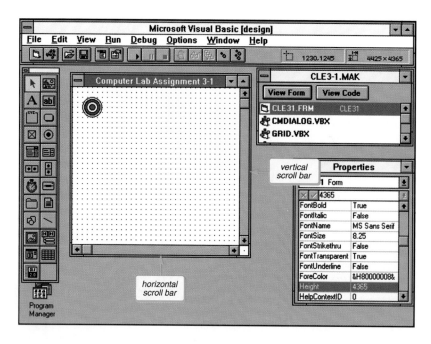

FIGURE CLE3-1

4. Set the following ScrollBars property values:

PROPERTY	CONTROL	
	HSCROLL	VSCROLL1
Min	480	
Max	3600	
Largechange	200	
Smallchange	50	
Value	480	

5. Choose the View Code button in the Project window.
6. Choose the HScroll1 control from the drop-down Object list in the Code window.
8. Type the following code statement: `Image1.Width = HScroll1.Value`
9. Choose the VScroll1 control from the drop-down Object list in the Code window.
10. Type the following code statement: `Image1.Height = VScroll1.Value`
11. Save the form using the file name CLE3-1A.FRM, and save the project using the file name CLE3-1A.MAK.
12. Run the application. Stretch the image's size by clicking the scroll arrows, dragging the scroll boxes, and clicking the spaces between the scroll boxes and the scroll arrows. Double-click the form's Control-menu box to stop the application.
13. Check with your instructor for directions on turning in the exercise.

COMPUTER LABORATORY EXERCISE 2
The BorderStyle of Forms

Instructions: Start Visual Basic. Open the project CLE3-2 from the subdirectory VB3 on the Student Diskette that accompanies this book. Perform the following steps:

1. Select Form1 in the Project window, and then click the View Form button.
2. Select Form2 in the Project window, and then click the View Form button.
3. Select Form3 in the Project window, and then click the View Form button.
4. Select Form4 in the Project window, and then click the View Form button.
5. Add one label control to each of the forms, and set the labels' AutoSize property to True and set their captions as shown in Figure CLE3-2.

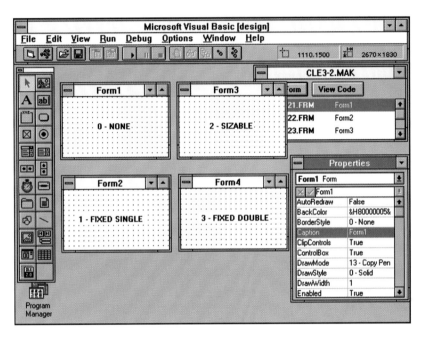

FIGURE CLE3-2

6. Set the BorderStyles as shown on the right, for the forms in the Properties window:
7. Double-click an empty area of Form1 to open Form1's Code window.
8. Type the following code statements in the Form1_Load subroutine:

```
Form1.Show
Form2.Show
Form3.Show
Form4.Show
```

FORM	BORDERSTYLE
Form1	0-None
Form2	1-Fixed Single
Form3	2-Sizable
Form4	3-Fixed Double

9. Save the forms using the file names CLE3-21A.FRM, CLE3-22A.FRM, CLE3-23A.FRM, and CLE3-24A.FRM. Save the project with the file name CLE3-2A.MAK.
10. Run the application. Try many different actions on each form, such as minimizing the form or dragging its borders.
11. To end the application, click the Stop icon on the toolbar.
12. Check with your instructor for directions on turning in the exercise.

EXERCISE NOTES
■ Exercise 3 gives students experience in using the Alignment property and making executable applications.

COMPUTER LABORATORY EXERCISE 3
The Alignment Property and .EXE Files

Instructions: Start Visual Basic. Open the project CLE3-3 from the subdirectory VB3 on the Student Diskette that accompanies this book. Perform the following steps.

1. Choose the View Form button in the Project window.
2. Draw three option buttons within the frame labeled Alignment, and then set their Caption properties as shown in Figure CLE3-3.

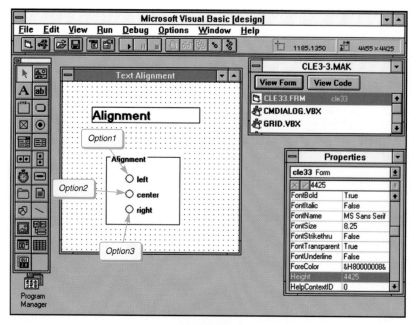

FIGURE CLE3-3

3. Use the Code window to write the following code statements for the Click event for each of the option buttons:

SUBROUTINE	CODE STATEMENT
Option1_Click	
Option2_Click	
Option3_Click	

4. Save the form as CLE3-3A.FRM, and then save the project as CLE3-3A.MAK.
5. Select the File menu.
6. Choose Make .EXE File.
7. Type `Align` in the File Name box.
8. Choose the OK button.
9. Close the Visual Basic program by double-clicking the Control-menu box.
10. Select the File menu in the Program Manager window.
11. Choose Run...
12. Type `a:\vb3\align.exe` in the Command Line box.
13. Choose the OK button in the Run dialog box.
14. Click the different option buttons. Minimize the window. Restore the window.
15. End the Alignment application by double-clicking its Control-menu box.
16. Check with your instructor for directions on turning in the exercise.

COMPUTER LABORATORY ASSIGNMENT 1
Tailor's Calculations

EXERCISE NOTES
■ The four Computer Laboratory Assignments increase in difficulty. Assignments 2 and 4 are suitable for either individual or small group projects.

Purpose: To build an application that performs mathematical computations and uses the IsNumeric function and If...Then block.

Problem: A tailor would like to have an application that calculates the average neck size, hat size, and shoe size for male customers, given the customer's weight and waistline. The interface should resemble the one shown in Figure CLA3-1. Text boxes should be used for the inputs, and labels should be used for the outputs. The calculations are as follows:

Neck size = 3 * (Weight / Waistline)
Hat Size = (3 * Weight) / (2.125 * Waistline)
Shoe size = 50 * (Waistline / Weight)

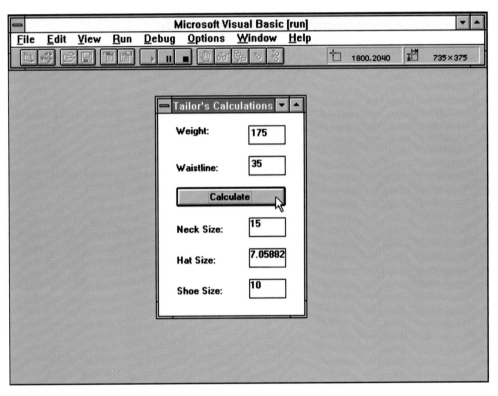

FIGURE CLA3-1

Instructions: Perform the following tasks:

1. Start Visual Basic, or open a new project if Visual Basic is already running.
2. Size and locate the form, as shown in Figure CLA3-1.
3. Add two text boxes, eight labels, and one command button, as shown in Figure CLA3-1.
4. Set the appropriate captions for the form, labels, and command button.
5. Set the text boxes' text values to be blank.
6. Set the BorderStyle of the three labels used for displaying the outputs so that the labels have borders.

COMPUTER LABORATORY ASSIGNMENT 1 (continued)

7. Write the code for the command button_click event. A partial structure for the code is shown below:

```
If IsNumeric(Text1.Text) = False OR IsNumeric(Text2.Text) = False Then
```
    (add statements here to clear the text boxes)

```
Else
```
    (add statements here to perform the calculations and to display the results in the appropriate labels)

```
EndIf
```

8. Save the form as CLA3-1.FRM. Save the project as CLA3-1.MAK.
9. Run the application to test it.
10. Check with your instructor for directions on turning in the assignment.

COMPUTER LABORATORY ASSIGNMENT 2
Future Value Calculation

Purpose: To build an application that uses Visual Basic's library of financial functions and the Format$ function.

Problem: Build an application with an interface similar to the one shown in Figure CLA3-2. The application uses the future value (FV) function to compute the future value of a series of payments when the interest is compounded on a quarterly basis.

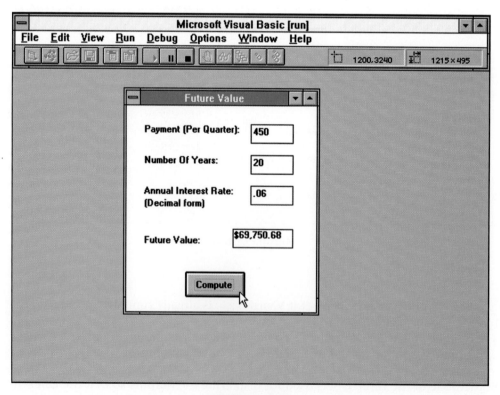

FIGURE CLA3-2

Instructions: Perform the following tasks:

1. Start Visual Basic, or open a new project if Visual Basic is already running.
2. Size and position the form, as shown in Figure CLA3-2.
3. Add the controls shown in Figure CLA3-2.
4. Choose Search For Help On from the Help menu.
5. Type `Financial Functions`
   Choose the Show Topics button. Choose the Go To button. Click FV.
6. Scroll through the Help file to see the correct syntax for the FV function. Close the Help window.
7. Write the code for the command button Click event. Use the Format$ function for the output displayed as the future value. Note: Quarterly compounding means the number of periods is 4 times the number of years, and the rate per period is the annual rate divided by 4.
8. Save the form as CLA3-2.FRM. Save the project as CLA3-2.MAK.
9. Run the application. Double-click the form's Control-menu box to stop the application.
10. Check with your instructor for directions on turning in the assignment.

COMPUTER LABORATORY ASSIGNMENT 3
An About.. Dialog Box

Purpose: To build an application that incorporates a second form.

Problem: Add an About.. dialog box similar to the one developed in Project 3 to either Computer Laboratory Assignment 3-1 or Computer Laboratory Assignment 3-2. (Check with your instructor.) You will need to add a command button to the original form and to use the Form.Show and Form.Hide code statements to open and close the About.. dialog box.

Instructions: Follow the steps listed below to add an About.. dialog box as a second form to a previously completed application.

1. Start Visual Basic if it is not currently running.
2. Open the project that you will modify.
3. Add a command button with the caption About.. to the application's form.
4. Choose the New Form command from the File menu.
5. Design the new form to resemble the About.. form created in Project 3 (Figure 3-4 on page VB122).
6. Write the appropriate Form.Show code statement for the About.. button click event.
7. Write the appropriate code statement for the About.. form's OK button Click event.
8. Resave the main form as CLA3-31.FRM. Save the About.. form as CLA3-32.FRM. Save the project as CLA3-3.MAK.
9. Check with your instructor for directions on turning in the assignment.

COMPUTER LABORATORY ASSIGNMENT 4
Ideal Age of a Spouse

Purpose: To build an application that incorporates an If...Then statement, IsNumeric function, mathematical calculations, and message box.

Problem: Plato said that the ideal age of a man's wife is one-half the man's age, plus seven years. If this is true, then the ideal age of a woman's husband is two times the woman's age, minus fourteen years. Create an application that will calculate the ideal age of a person's spouse, using Plato's formula.

Instructions: Use your creativity to build an application that calculates the ideal spouse's age as described above. The application must include some method for the user to indicate his or her gender, since the choice of formulas for the spouse's age depends on this fact. Include an IsNumeric function to test the value of age entered by the user. If the input is not numeric, the application should display a message box similar to the one in Project 3 (page VB122) and then clear the input for the user to start over. Include a command button that "clears" the application so that additional calculations can be completed without having to restart the application.

Save the form as CLA3-4.FRM. Save the project as CLA3-4.MAK. Check with your instructor for directions on turning in the assignment.

USING COLOR, MENUS, THE DATA CONTROL AND COMMON DIALOG CONTROL

OBJECTIVES   You will have mastered the material in this project when you can:

▶ Build applications that contain menus and submenus
▶ Add access keys, separator bars, and check marks to menus
▶ Build applications that use the data control
▶ Bind data-aware controls to a data control

▶ Add color to applications
▶ Build applications that use common dialog controls
▶ Create control arrays
▶ Write code to select records in a database
▶ Use the For...Next statement in subroutines

▶ INTRODUCTION

O ne of the most powerful features of Visual Basic Version 3.0 is the ability to create sophisticated database applications with minimal programming. A **database** is a collection of related facts organized in a systematic manner. A telephone book is an example of a database that contains the names, addresses, and phone numbers of persons and businesses in a community. Many database management products, such as Microsoft Access, are available for personal computers and they allow you to store, maintain, and retrieve data quickly and efficiently.

Visual Basic can be used to build applications that display, edit, and update information from databases created by the following database management products: Microsoft Access, Btrieve, dBase, FoxPro, and Paradox. Project 4 provides an introductory exposure to accessing a database by building an application that displays information from a World Geography database created with Microsoft Access. The World Geography database is included on the Student Diskette that accompanies this text. This project describes only how to display information in a database. You should be aware that Visual Basic can be used to create applications that also query, add, change, or delete information in a database.

LECTURE NOTES
▪ Explain what a database is, and what database management software does.
▪ Ask students to describe databases or database management products.

CAUTION
▪ Before beginning this project, certain data access features must be installed. These features are installed as part of the normal VB setup process, unless they were purposely bypassed. Be sure the data tool is present in the Toolbox and the share.exe file is in memory (usually in the autoexec.bat file). If these are not present, you must reinstall Visual Basic, using a normal setup, in order to complete the database access application in this project.

VB193

Many of the application-building activities in Projects 1 through 3 involved choosing commands from drop-down menus selected from the Visual Basic menu bar. This structure of menus and commands is common in many types of Windows applications. These previous projects also required using common dialog boxes, such as the Open and Save As dialog boxes, in building the applications. The application built in this project includes a menu bar and drop-down menus, as well as a common dialog box, the Color dialog box.

▶ PROJECT FOUR – GEOGRAPHY DATABASE VIEWER

The application that will be built in this project is shown as it appears on the desktop during run time in Figure 4-1. This application accesses an existing database of information about different countries and displays that information one country at a time. The name of the database is World.

Each characteristic or attribute of a country, such as its name or capital city, is represented in a database by a **field**. In addition to fields that contain text and numbers, the World database has a field that contains a graphical image of each country's flag. Information about a specific country (the values for that country contained in a group of fields) is represented in a database by a single **record**. A group of records within a database that have the same fields is called a **table**. Although databases can contain more than one table, the World database contains only one table, named Countries.

The information contained in the Countries table of the World database is shown in Table 4-1, where each column represents a field, and each row represents a record.

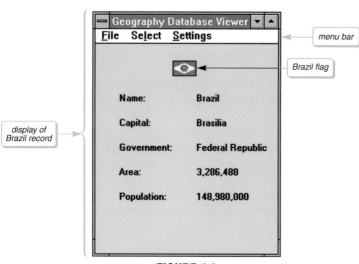

menu bar

Brazil flag

display of Brazil record

FIGURE 4-1

▶ TABLE 4-1 COUNTRIES TABLE OF THE WORLD DATABASE

NAME	CAPITAL	GOVERNMENT	AREA	POPULATION	FLAG
USA	Washington DC	Federal Republic	3,679,245	250,150,000	Image
Italy	Rome	Republic	116,324	57,625,000	Image
France	Paris	Republic	211,208	52,210,000	Image
Denmar	Copenhagen	Const. Monarchy	2,045	650,000	Image
Turkey	Ankara	Republic	300,948	54,075,000	Image
Mexico	Mexico City	Federal Republic	756,066	85,090,000	Image
Brazil	Brasilia	Federal Republic	3,286,488	148,980,000	Image
Japan	Tokyo	Monarchy	145,870	123,350,000	Image
Ireland	Dublin	Republic	169,235	17,745,000	Image

Unlike the applications built in previous projects, the Geography Database Viewer application does not have any controls, such as command buttons, option buttons, or check boxes, for you to initiate events or to choose options during run time (Figure 4-1). The reason for this omission is that all run-time interaction with the application occurs by using drop-down menus.

You can view the information in Table 4-1 during run time by moving forward or backward one record (country) at a time or by moving directly to the first record or to the last record. These actions are initiated by choosing the Next, Previous, First, and Last commands in the Select menu (Figure 4-2). Choosing Color from the Settings menu (Figure 4-3) opens the Color common dialog box (Figure 4-4). The Color dialog box is used in this application to set the background color of the form and its controls during run time.

Choosing View from the Settings menu opens a submenu (Figure 4-3) that allows you to choose whether the Name and/or Flag of the country appear(s) in the window. This on/off state is indicated by a check mark being added or removed in front of the command in the menu.

The application can be minimized at run time by choosing Minimize from the Control menu or by clicking its Minimize button. The application is closed by choosing Close from the Control menu, by double-clicking its Control-menu box, or by choosing the Exit command from the application's File menu (Figure 4-5 on the next page).

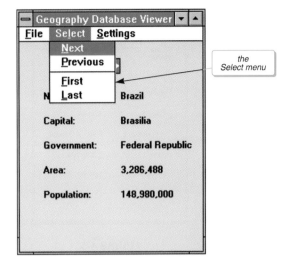

FIGURE 4-2

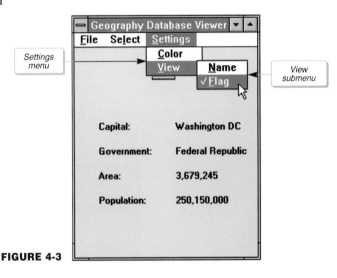

FIGURE 4-3

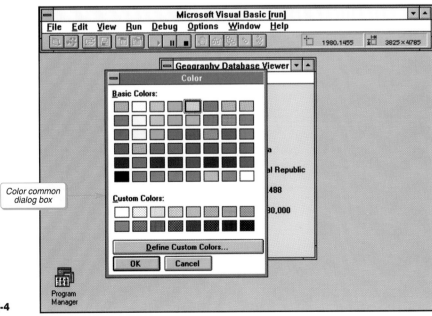

FIGURE 4-4

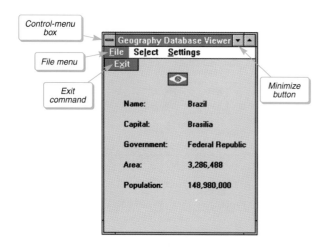

FIGURE 4-5

The Geography Database Viewer application is created in this project by following the same three-step approach used in previous projects:

▶ create the interface
▶ set properties
▶ write code

Getting Started

The database file that is used in this project is contained in the VB3 subdirectory of the Student Diskette that accompanies this book. The file is named WORLD.MDB. Before building the Geography Database Viewer, this file should be copied to another diskette that will be used later to save the completed application.

If you have any questions about how or where to copy this file, you should see your instructor prior to building the application.

Starting Visual Basic

Begin this project by starting Visual Basic or by beginning a new project if Visual Basic is already running. If necessary, minimize the Program Manager window and adjust the sizes and locations of the Visual Basic windows to those shown in Figure 4-6. For more information on adjusting the Visual Basic windows, refer to page VB59.

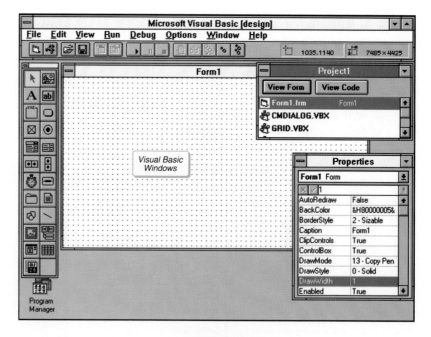

FIGURE 4-6

▶ CREATING THE INTERFACE

I n this step, the size and location of the form will be determined, and the controls will be added to the form. The Viewer form contains one image control, ten label controls, one data control and one common dialog control. These controls are shown as they appear on the completed form during design time in Figure 4-7. In addition to the two new controls — the data control and common dialog control — control arrays will be presented for the first time. The menu will be created by using Visual Basic's Menu Design window.

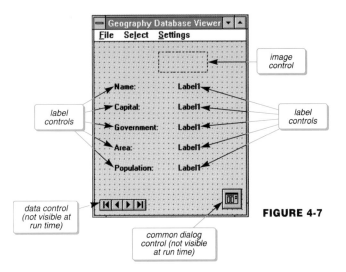

FIGURE 4-7

Setting the Location and Size of the Form

At run time, the form is centered on the desktop. This placement will be accomplished later in the project, through code statements, as was done in Project 3. In the steps that follow, the form's size will be set by setting the form's Height and Width properties.

TO SIZE THE FORM

Step 1: Select the form control by clicking it or by selecting its name, Form1, from the drop-down Object list in the Properties window.

Step 2: Double-click the Height property in the Properties list in the Properties window.

Step 3: Type 4500 and press the ENTER key.

Step 4: Double-click the Width property in the Properties list in the Properties window.

Step 5: Type 3825 and press the ENTER key.

Step 6: Drag the form to the center of the desktop to make it easier to use during design time.

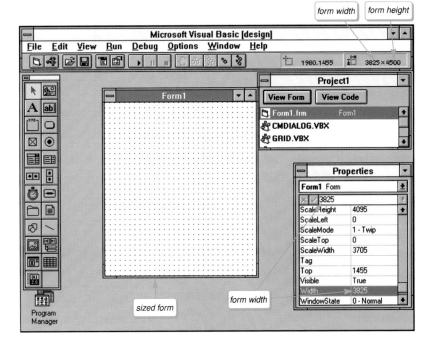

FIGURE 4-8

The form appears as shown in Figure 4-8.

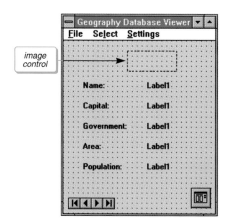

FIGURE 4-9

Adding the Image Control

An image control is used in the Geography Database Viewer application to contain graphical images of the flags of the different countries (Figure 4-9). Perform the following steps to add the image control.

TO ADD THE IMAGE CONTROL

Step 1: Double-click the image tool (🖼) in the Toolbox.

Step 2: Drag the control, Image1, to the location shown in Figure 4-10.

It is not necessary to change the size of the image control because it will be sized automatically each time a flag graphic is loaded.

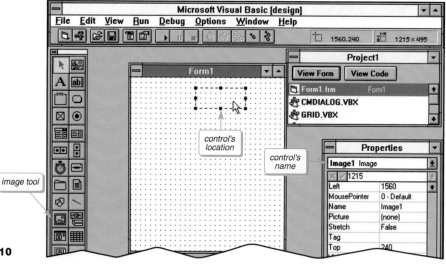

FIGURE 4-10

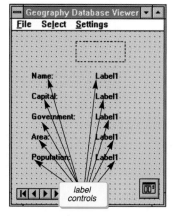

FIGURE 4-11

Adding the Label Control Array

Ten label controls are used in the Geography Database Viewer application (Figure 4-11). The five labels on the left are used to indicate the names of the fields in the database. The five labels on the right are used to display the field values for the current record. The ten labels are added to the form as a control array.

A **control array** is made up of a group of controls of the same type (for example, all labels) that share a common control name and a common set of event procedures. For example, clicking any label in the array triggers the same Click event subroutine.

Each control in an array has a unique index number assigned by Visual Basic when the array is created. The value of the index begins at zero for the first control and increases by one for each new control. All items in a control array must have the same Name property setting. All other property settings apply only to the individual control. For example, Label1(0) can have a caption and other property settings different from Label1(1).

Arrays make it easier to change a property of a group of controls to a common value during run time. For example, suppose you wanted to change the FontSize of all ten labels to 12 at run time. As separate controls, this change would require ten similar, but separate, code statements. As an array, the FontSize can be changed much more easily through a simple code structure that will be presented later.

The ten labels have their AutoSize property set to True and have the same BackColor property. Since the controls will be added to the form with the copy method, these two properties will be set for the first control during the interface building step, rather than during the setting properties step. This procedure will eliminate having to set the two properties individually for each of the ten labels later.

The **BackColor property** sets the background color of an object. The Back-Color property will be set by using the Visual Basic Color Palette. The following steps add one label and set its AutoSize and BackColor properties. The control is then copied nine times to a control array.

TRANSPARENCY
Figure 4-11

LECTURE NOTES
■ Identify the two groups of label controls in the Viewer application and explain their functions.
■ Explain the concept of a control array.
■ Describe the BackColor property of controls.
■ Explain why the Auto-Size and BackColor properties are set before copying the label control.

TRANSPARENCIES
Figure 4-12 through
Figure 4-22

TO ADD THE LABEL ARRAY ▼

STEP 1 ▶

Double-click the Label tool ( ) in the Toolbox.

A default-sized label, Label1, is added to the form (Figure 4-12).

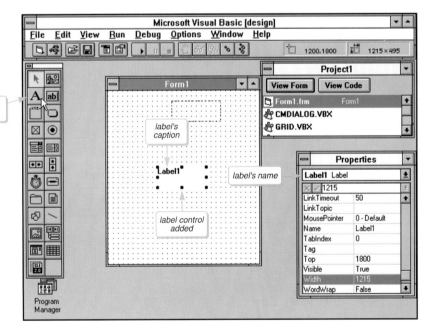

FIGURE 4-12

STEP 2 ▶

Double-click the AutoSize property in the Properties list in the Properties window.

The value of the AutoSize property changes to True (Figure 4-13).

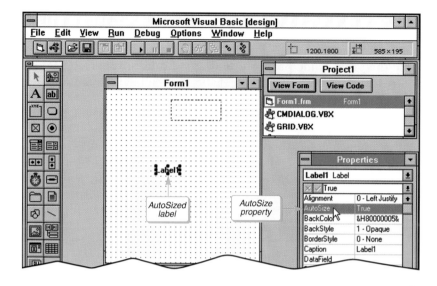

FIGURE 4-13

STEP 3 ▶

Double-click the BackColor property in the Properties list in the Properties window.

The Color Palette opens (Figure 4-14).

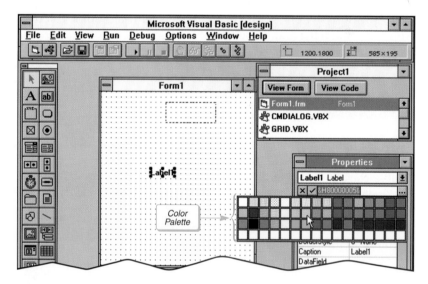

FIGURE 4-14

STEP 4 ▶

Click the light blue color pointed out in the Color Palette shown in Figure 4-14.

The background color of the Label1 control changes to the selected color, and the Color Palette closes (Figure 4-15).

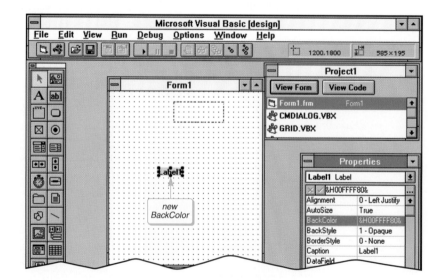

FIGURE 4-15

STEP 5 ▶

Drag the label control to the location shown in Figure 4-16.

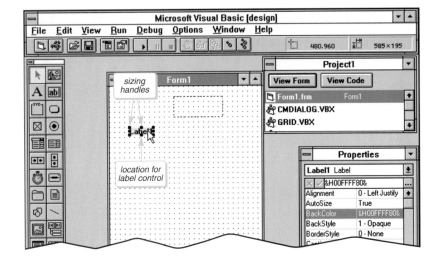

FIGURE 4-16

STEP 6 ▶

Click the Label1 control on the form. Press CTRL+C.

The control is copied to the Clipboard, and its sizing handles disappear (Figure 4-17).

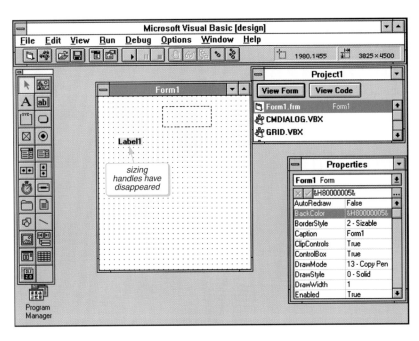

FIGURE 4-17

STEP 7 ▶

Press CTRL+V.

The Control Array dialog box opens (Figure 4-18).

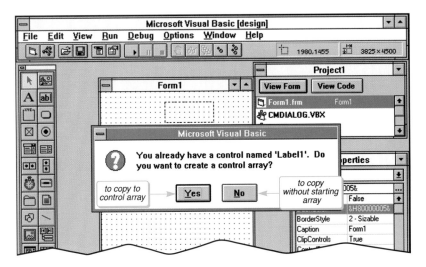

FIGURE 4-18

STEP 8 ▶

Choose Yes from the dialog box.

The name of the first label changes to Label1(0). A second label control, Label1(1), is added to the upper left corner of the form (Figure 4-19). The dialog box closes.

FIGURE 4-19

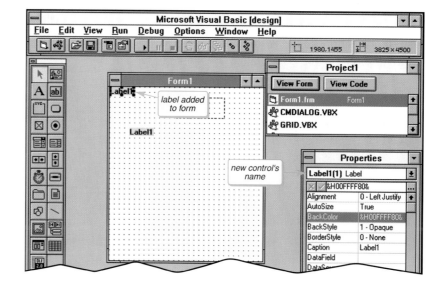

STEP 9 ▶

Drag the second label control, Label1(1), to the location shown in Figure 4-20.

The property values of the second label control (including the Caption property) are identical to the property values of the control that was copied (Label1(0)).

FIGURE 4-20

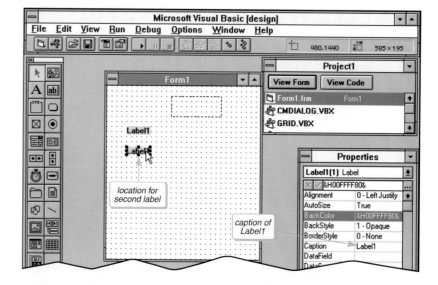

STEP 10 ▶

Press CTRL+V.

A third label control is added to the form (Figure 4-21).

FIGURE 4-21

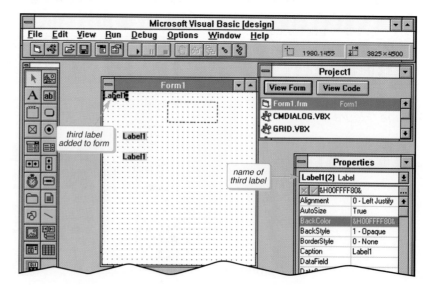

STEP 11 ▶

Repeat Steps 9 and 10 seven times. Drag the labels to the locations shown in Figure 4-22.

Be careful to locate the controls in the order shown in Figure 4-22. They can be confused easily at this point because they have the same caption, Label1.

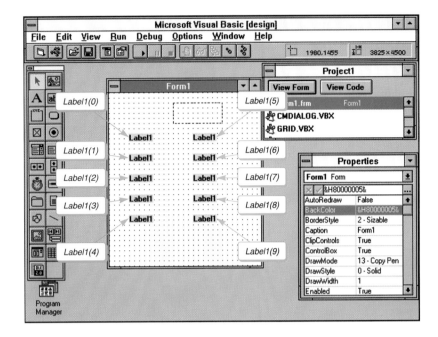

FIGURE 4-22

When controls were copied in previous projects, the Create Array dialog box appeared each time a copy of a control was placed on the form. This is because you responded No to the dialog box each time you were asked if you wanted to start a new control array. Once you responded Yes to the Create Array dialog box in the previous steps, it never appeared again because all subsequent copies were added to the array. If you had wanted to add an additional Label control to the form but not as part of the array, you would have had to use a method other than copying, such as double-clicking the label tool.

Adding the Data Control

A **data control** is used in Visual Basic applications to provide the necessary links to a database file. The data control is added to a form in the same manner as other controls. A form can contain more than one data control, and generally one data control exists for each database table accessed by the application. The data control has four arrow buttons used during run time to move between records in a database, as shown in Figure 4-23. Perform the steps on the next page to add a data control and to locate it on the form.

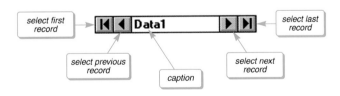

FIGURE 4-23

TO ADD A DATA CONTROL ▼

STEP 1 ▶

Double-click the data tool (▦) in the Toolbox.

A default-sized data control, Data1, is added to the form (Figure 4-24).

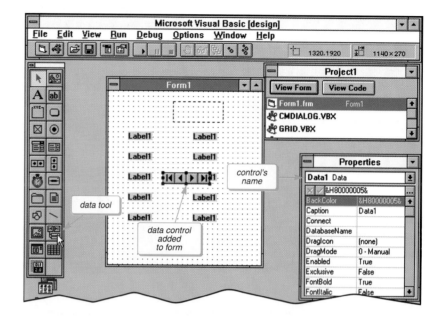

FIGURE 4-24

STEP 2 ▶

Drag the Data1 control to the location shown in Figure 4-25.

The location is not important because the control is not visible at run time in this application.

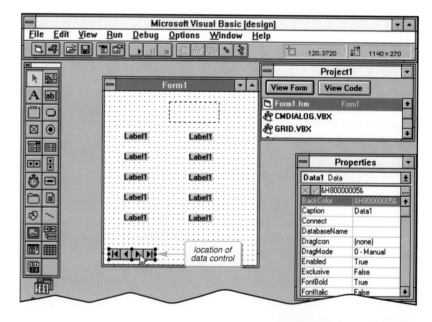

FIGURE 4-25

LECTURE NOTES
■ Explain why the data control is not visible in the Viewer application.
■ Explain why the data control is still necessary.

The Geography Database Viewer application contains a data control to link to the World database. The data control is not visible at run time, however, because record selection is controlled through the Select menu. Later, code will be written that causes the Select menu commands to trigger the data control events that make different records in the database the current record. Even though the Select menu commands initiate the record selection actions in this application, a data control still must be added to make the link between the application and the database.

Adding the Common Dialog Control

A **common dialog control** is used in applications to display one of five common dialog boxes at run time: Open, Save As, Print, Color, and Font. The common dialog control itself never is visible at run time. When you Choose OK from an open dialog box during run time, the settings specified in the dialog box are recorded as properties of the common dialog control. You write code that then transfers those properties to the appropriate controls.

For example, when you select a color in the Color common dialog box and choose OK, the selected color becomes the value of the common dialog control's Color property. You then can set (through a code statement) the BackColor property of another control to equal the value of the common dialog control's Color property. The actions from the user's perspective are that 1) a color was selected in the dialog box, 2) the OK button was chosen, and 3) a control's color then changed to the selected color.

The Geography Database Viewer application uses the common dialog control to display the Color common dialog box for you to set the color of the form and its controls during run time. Perform the following steps to add a common dialog control to the form.

LECTURE NOTES
■ Describe the different dialog boxes the common dialog control can display.
■ Explain the use of the common dialog control in the Database Viewer application.

TRANSPARENCIES
Figure 4-26 and Figure 4-27

TO ADD A COMMON DIALOG CONTROL ▼

STEP 1 ►

Double-click the common dialog tool (▦) in the Toolbox.

A common dialog control, CMDialog1, is added to the form (Figure 4-26).

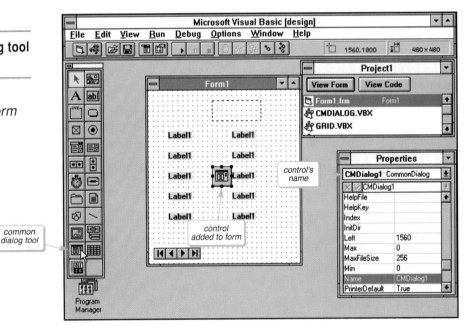

FIGURE 4-26

STEP 2 ▶

Drag the common dialog control to the location shown in Figure 4-27.

The location is not important because the common dialog control is not visible at run time.

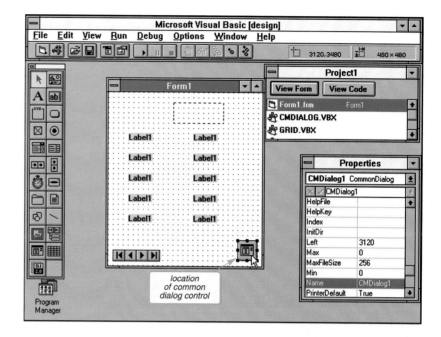

location of common dialog control

FIGURE 4-27

TRANSPARENCIES
Figure 4-28 and
Figure 4-29

LECTURE NOTES
■ Demonstrate or discuss
the menu structure in the
Viewer application.
■ Describe the function of
menu access keys.
■ Describe the use of sep-
arator bars in menus.

A common dialog box is opened at run time by a code statement. A statement to open the Color dialog box when Color is chosen from the Settings menu during run time will be added to the project later.

Creating the Menus

The Geography Database Viewer contains three menus in the menu bar: File, Select, and Settings (Figure 4-28). These menus are selected during run time either by clicking their names in the menu bar or by pressing ALT and an access key.

menu names

access key indicated in menu name

menu bar

Access keys allow you to open a menu at run time by pressing the ALT key and a letter. Access key assignments are common in Windows applications and appear as an underlined letter in the menu control's caption. For example, the letter F is the access key for the File menu (Figure 4-28). Access keys also are used in menu choices. However, when a menu is open, you press only the access key of a command (not the ALT key) to choose that command. In the following steps, the three menus in the Geography Database Viewer are created one at a time.

FIGURE 4-28

Creating the File Menu

LECTURE NOTES
■ Discuss the components
and functions of the Menu
Design Window.

The File menu in the Visual Basic menu bar follows a standard layout for this type of menu in Windows applications. Although the Visual Basic application can be closed by double-clicking its Control-menu box, File menus always include an Exit command as an alternate way to close the application. The File menu in the Geography Database Viewer contains only the Exit command, as shown in Figure 4-29.

Each command you add to a menu is an additional control within the application, and it has a name and a Click event. Menus are created during design time with Visual Basic's **Menu Design Window**. The Menu Design Window is shown with its major components identified in Figure 4-30. Perform the following steps to create the File menu for the Geography Database Viewer.

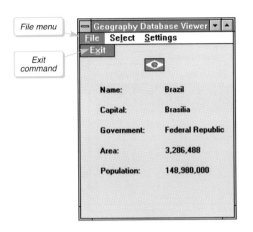

FIGURE 4-29

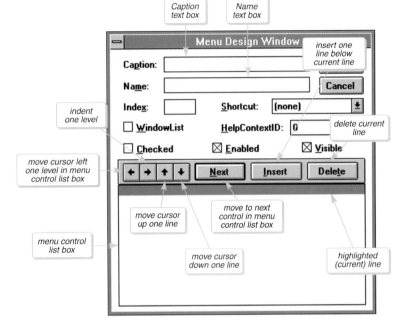

FIGURE 4-30

TO CREATE THE FILE MENU ▼

STEP 1 ▶

Click the Menu Design Window tool (📖) on the toolbar, or choose Menu Design from the Window menu.

The Menu Design Window opens on the desktop (Figure 4-31).

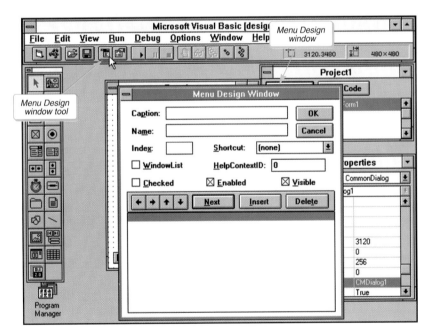

FIGURE 4-31

STEP 2 ▶

Type &File **in the Caption text box.**

The caption that will appear on the menu bar appears in the Caption text box and in the menu control list box (Figure 4-32). The ampersand (&) is placed before the letter in the caption to be used as the access key. At run time, the ampersand is not visible, and the access key letter is underlined.

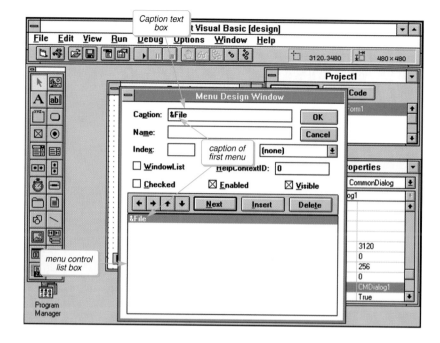

FIGURE 4-32

STEP 3 ▶

Press the TAB key or click the Name text box to move the cursor to that box. Type mnuFile **and point to the Next button.**

The name of the menu control, mnuFile, appears in the Name text box (Figure 4-33).

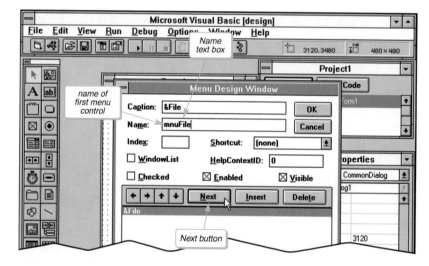

FIGURE 4-33

STEP 4 ▶

Choose Next in the Menu Design Window.

The highlighted line in the menu control list box advances to the next line, and the menu control properties boxes are blank (Figure 4-34).

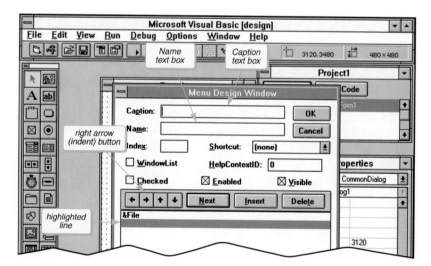

FIGURE 4-34

STEP 5 ►

Click the right arrow (▶) button in the menu control list box. Select the Caption text box by clicking it. Type `E&xit` in the Caption text box.

*A new menu control with the run time caption E*x*it is added. The caption is preceded by a series of hyphens in the menu control list box (Figure 4-35). Clicking the right arrow button indents the control's caption and adds the hyphens in the menu control list box. This step is how you indicate Exit is a command within the File menu.*

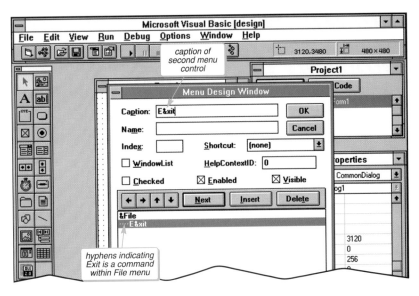

FIGURE 4-35

STEP 6 ►

Type `mnuExit` in the Name text box. Choose Next. Click the left arrow button in the menu control list box.

Clicking the left arrow button moves the cursor flush left in the menu control list box to indicate the next item will be a new menu (Figure 4-36).

FIGURE 4-36

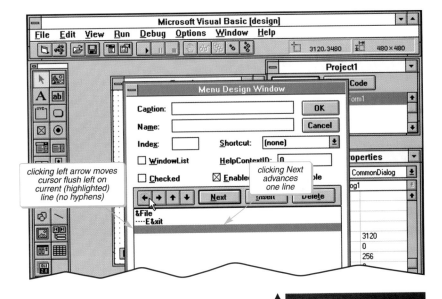

Creating the Select Menu

The Select menu is shown in Figure 4-37. The four commands in the menu correspond to the options to move between the records in the database during run time. The Select menu also includes a separator bar. A **separator bar** is a horizontal line used to visually group related commands in a menu. Separator bars are added to the menu at design time by typing a hyphen (–) in the Caption text box in the Menu Design Window. Perform the steps on the next page to create the Select menu.

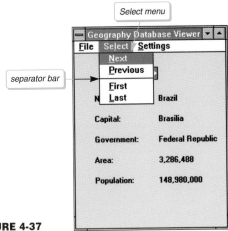

FIGURE 4-37

TO CREATE THE SELECT MENU ▼

STEP 1 ▶

Type `Se&lect` in the **Caption text box.** Type `mnuSelect` in the **Name text box. Choose Next.**

The Menu Design Window appears as shown in Figure 4-38. The letter l was chosen for the access key rather than the letter S because S will be used for the Settings menu access key. An access key cannot be used for more than one menu control in one level of a menu. Different menus can use the same access keys for different menu controls.

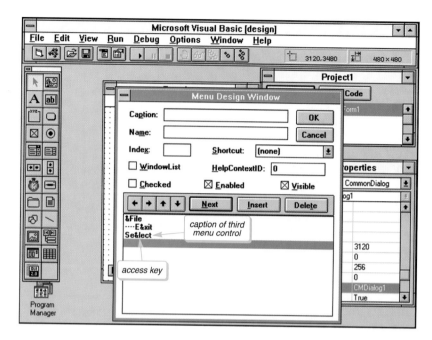

FIGURE 4-38

STEP 2 ▶

Click the right arrow button to indicate a command within the Select menu. Type `&Next` in the **Caption text box. Type** `mnuNext` in **the Name text box. Choose Next.** Type `&Previous` in the **Caption text box. Type** `mnuPrev` in the **Name text box. Choose Next.**

The Menu Design Window appears as shown in Figure 4-39.

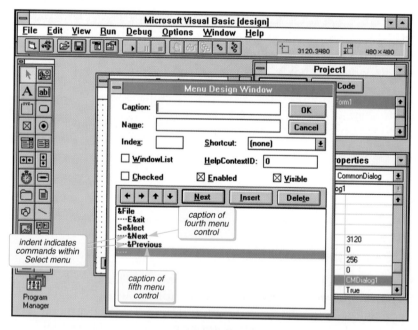

FIGURE 4-39

STEP 3 ▶

Add the separator bar to the Select menu by typing a hyphen (–) in the Caption text box. Type `Separator` in the Name text box. Choose Next. Type `&First` in the Caption text box. Type `mnuFirst` in the Name text box. Choose Next. Type `&Last` in the Caption text box. Type `mnuLast` in the Name text box.

The Menu Design Window appears as shown in Figure 4-40. Each separator bar in a menu must be given a unique name even though it doesn't have a function at run time.

FIGURE 4-40

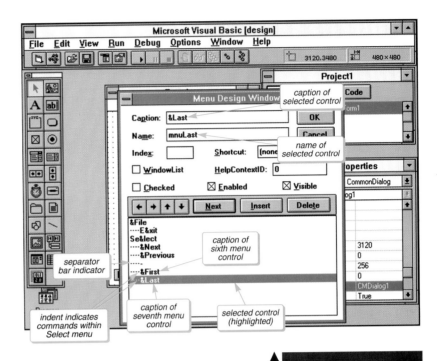

Creating the Settings Menu

The Settings menu is shown in Figure 4-41. The Settings menu contains one command, Color, and a submenu, View. A **submenu** branches off another menu to present an additional set of commands in a separate grouping. Each menu created in Visual Basic can have up to four levels of submenus. Menu choices that display submenus have an arrowhead symbol (▶) at their right edge (Figure 4-41).

The View submenu (Figure 4-42) is used in this application to set whether the country's name and/or flag appear(s) during run time. During run time, the status of the on/off choice is indicated by the presence or absence of a check mark, similar to the check box control. The steps on the next page create the Settings menu.

TRANSPARENCIES
Figure 4-41 and
Figure 4-42

LECTURE NOTES
▪ Explain the function of submenus in applications.
▪ Ask students to describe submenus in applications they are familiar with.
▪ Explain the submenu structure in the Database Viewer application.

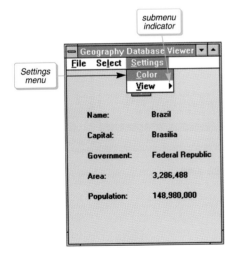

FIGURE 4-41

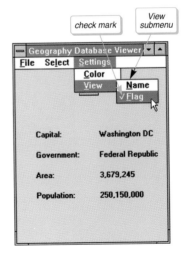

FIGURE 4-42

TRANSPARENCIES
Figure 4-43 through
Figure 4-47

TO CREATE THE SETTINGS MENU ▼

STEP 1 ▶

Choose Next. Click the left arrow button to move the cursor flush left in the menu control list box. Type &Settings in the Caption text box. Type mnuSet in the Name text box. Choose Next. Click the right arrow.

The menu control named mnuSet is added. Its caption, &Settings, appears in the menu control list box. The cursor is advanced to the next line and is indented once to indicate the next control added will be a command within the Settings menu (Figure 4-43).

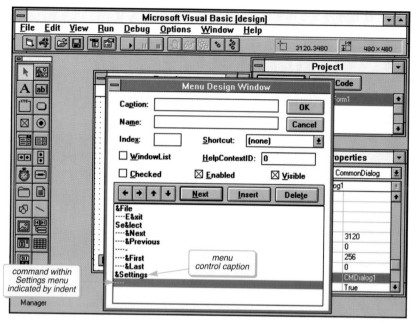

FIGURE 4-43

STEP 2 ▶

Type &Color in the Caption text box. Type mnuColor in the Name text box. Choose Next. Type &View in the Caption text box. Type mnuView in the Name text box.

The Menu Design Window appears as shown in Figure 4-44.

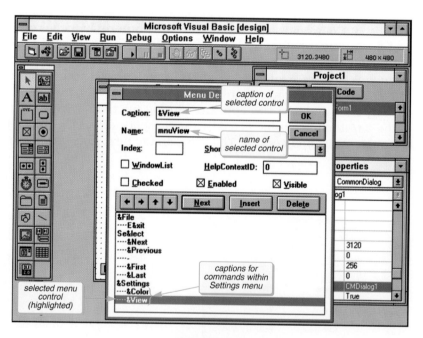

FIGURE 4-44

STEP 3 ▶

Choose Next. Indicate the next control to be added is a submenu item by clicking the right arrow button. Type &Name in the Caption text box. Type mnuNameshow in the Name text box. Click the check box labeled Checked in the Menu Design Window.

The Menu Design Window appears as shown in Figure 4-45. Checking the Checked box indicates the current menu control, mnuNameshow, will have a check mark added to or removed from its caption, Name, during run time each time the command is chosen.

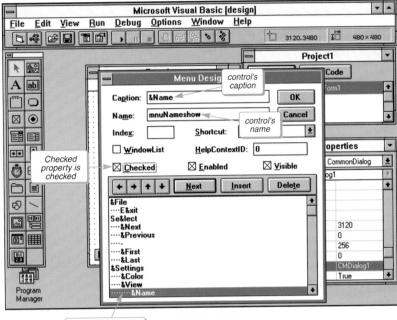

FIGURE 4-45

STEP 4 ▶

Choose Next. Type &Flag in the Caption text box. Type mnuFlagshow in the Name text box. Click the check box labeled Checked in the Menu Design Window.

The Menu Design Window appears as shown in Figure 4-46.

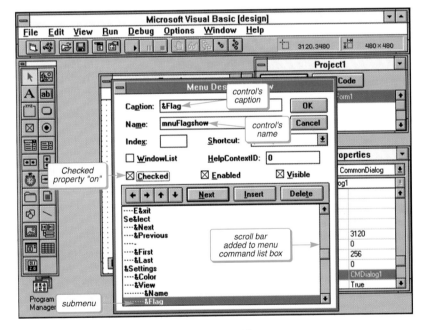

FIGURE 4-46

STEP 5 ▶

Choose the OK button in the Menu Design Window.

The Menu Design Window closes, and the menus appear on the form (Figure 4-47).

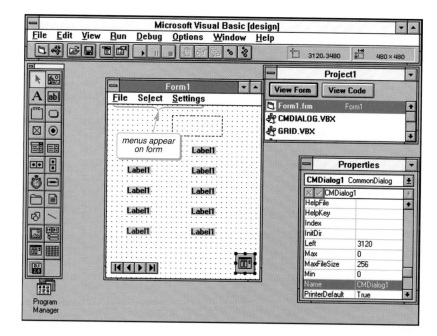

FIGURE 4-47

The menus for the Geography Database Viewer are complete. During design time, menus can be opened in the form window by clicking the menu title. Click the menu title for each of the three menus you just created.

The interface for the Geography Database Viewer is now complete. The second step of application development is to set the properties of the form and other controls.

▶ SETTING PROPERTIES

In this section, control properties are set in the following groups of steps:

▶ the properties of the form
▶ the properties of the five labels used to display the names of the fields of the database
▶ the properties of the data control
▶ the properties of the five label controls and one image control used to contain information from the database (the data-aware controls)

Setting Properties of the Form

In the following steps, the name of the form is set. No other control names need to be set because all the labels in the array must have the same name and each of the remaining types of controls appears only once. The form is given a caption to appear in its title bar. Additionally, the form's BackColor is set to match the BackColor of the label controls, and an icon is specified to represent the form when it is minimized. The following steps set these properties for the form control.

TO SET THE FORM'S PROPERTIES ▼

STEP 1 ▶

Select the form by clicking an area that does not contain any other controls. Double-click the Name property in the Properties list. Type `frmGeoView` and press the ENTER key.

The form's new name appears in both the Project window and the Properties window (Figure 4-48).

FIGURE 4-48

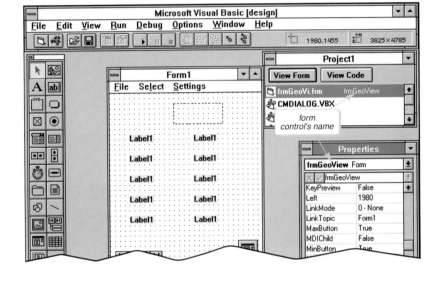

STEP 2 ▶

Double-click the Caption property in the Properties window. Type `Geography Database Viewer` and press the ENTER key.

The form's caption appears in the form's title bar (Figure 4-49).

FIGURE 4-49

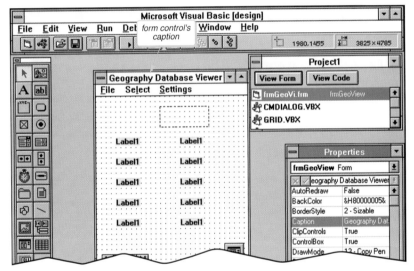

STEP 3 ▶

Double-click the BackColor property in the Properties window. Point to the light blue color identified in Figure 4-50.

The Color Palette opens (Figure 4-50).

FIGURE 4-50

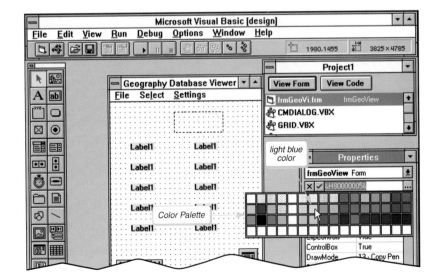

STEP 4 ▶

Click the left mouse button.

The background color of the form control changes to the selected color, and the Color Palette closes (Figure 4-51).

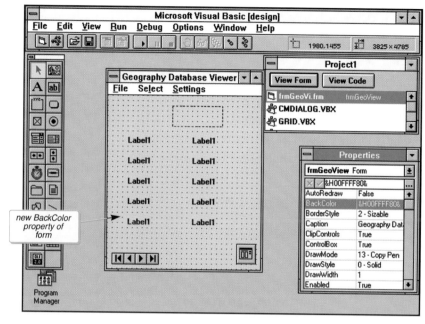

FIGURE 4-51

STEP 5 ▶

Double-click the Icon property in the Properties list.

The Load Icon dialog box opens (Figure 4-52).

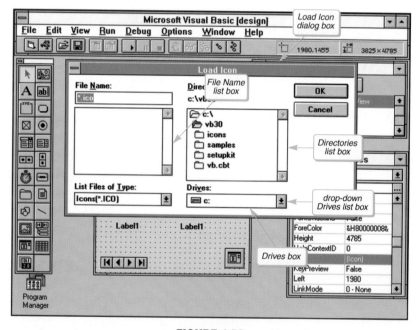

FIGURE 4-52

STEP 6 ►

Double-click icons in the Directories list box. Double-click elements in the Directories list box. Double-click earth.ico in the File Name list box (Figure 4-53).

Visual Basic loads the icon and closes the Load Icon dialog box.

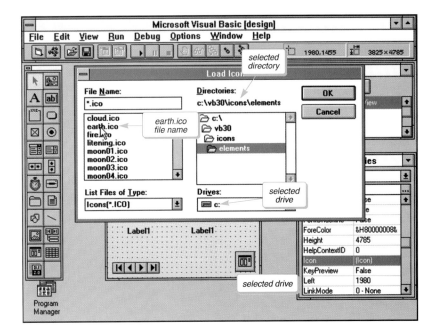

FIGURE 4-53

All of the necessary property settings for the form are complete. View the form's icon by minimizing the form. The icon loaded into the Icon property of a form appears when the form is minimized during design time as well as run time. Restore the form by double-clicking its icon.

Setting Caption Properties

The captions of the first five labels (Label1(0) through Label1(4)) are used to show the names of the fields in the database. The captions of the remaining five labels are used as containers for the values of the corresponding fields in the current record. Perform the following steps to add the field names to the form as captions of the label controls.

TO SET CAPTION PROPERTIES

Step 1: Select Label1(0) by clicking its name in the drop-down Object list in the Properties window. Double-click the Caption property in the Properties list. Type `Name:` and press the ENTER key.

Step 2: Select Label1(1) by clicking its name in the drop-down Object list in the Properties window. Double-click the Caption property in the Properties list. Type `Capital:` and press the ENTER key.

Step 3: Select Label1(2) by clicking its name in the drop-down Object list in the Properties window. Double-click the Caption property in the Properties list. Type `Government:` and press the ENTER key.

Step 4: Select Label1(3) by clicking its name in the drop-down Object list in the Properties window. Double-click the Caption property in the Properties list. Type `Area:` and press the ENTER key.

Step 5: Select Label1(4) by clicking its name in the drop-down Object list in the Properties window. Double-click the Caption property in the Properties list. Type `Population:` and press the ENTER key.

The form appears as shown in Figure 4-54.

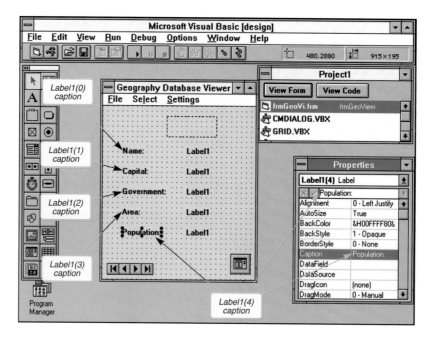

FIGURE 4-54

Setting the Properties of the Data Control

In the following steps, the DatabaseName and RecordSource properties of the data control named Data1 are set. The **DatabaseName property** is used to supply the file name of the database to which the data control is linked. The **Record-Source property** is used to specify the table name in the database to which the data control is linked. The **Connect property** is used to specify the type of database (Microsoft Access, FoxPro, dBASE, etc.). When the database to be accessed is a Microsoft Access database (as in this application), it is not necessary to set the Connect property. The data control's Visible property is set to False so that it will not appear at run time in the Geography Database Viewer. Perform the following steps to set the properties of the Data1 control.

TO SET THE DATA CONTROL'S PROPERTIES ▼

STEP 1 ▶

Select the data control by clicking it or by clicking its name, Data1, in the drop-down Object list in the Properties window. Double-click the DatabaseName property in the Properties list.

The DatabaseName dialog box appears (Figure 4-55).

FIGURE 4-55

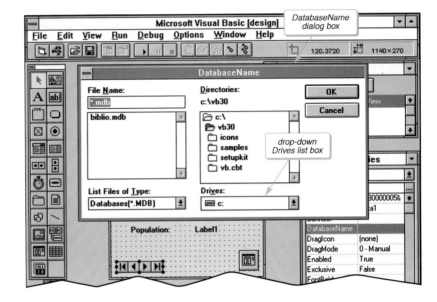

STEP 2 ▶

Make sure the diskette that you copied the WORLD.MDB file to earlier is in drive A. Click drive A in the drop-down Drives list box.

The database file name appears in the File Name list box (Figure 4-56).

FIGURE 4-56

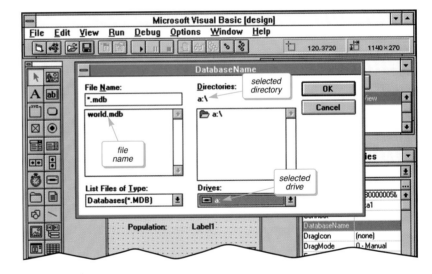

STEP 3 ▶

Double-click the WORLD.MDB file in the File Name list box.

The file's name appears in the Properties list (Figure 4-57).

FIGURE 4-57

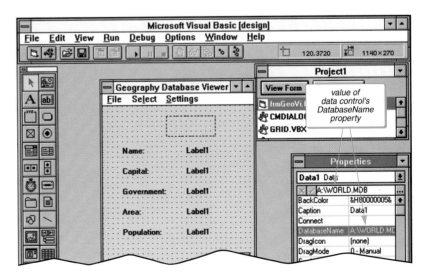

STEP 4 ▶

Scroll through the Properties list until the RecordSource property is visible. Click the RecordSource property. Click the arrow located to the right of the Settings box.

A drop-down list of property settings opens (Figure 4-58). The name of the one table of the World database, Countries, appears in the drop-down Settings list.

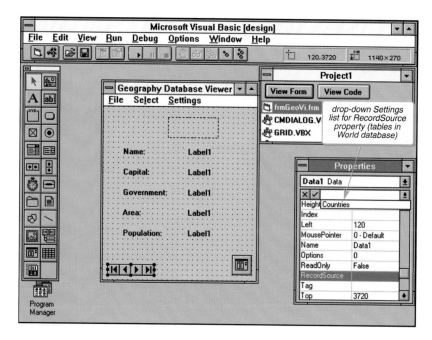

FIGURE 4-58

STEP 5 ▶

Click Countries in the drop-down Settings list.

The drop-down list closes, and the Property setting appears in the Settings box (Figure 4-59).

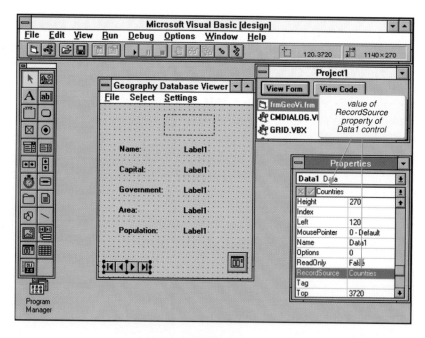

FIGURE 4-59

STEP 6 ▶

Double-click the Visible property in the Properties list.

The value of Data1's Visible property changes to False (Figure 4-60).

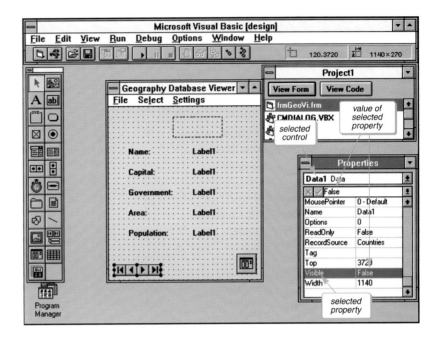

FIGURE 4-60

In Step 4, the drop-down Settings list contained only the name of the Countries table. If the World database contained more than one table, the drop-down Settings list for the RecordSource property would contain all the available tables.

Setting Properties of the Data-Aware Controls

The controls within Visual Basic that can be linked to information in a database are said to be **data-aware**. The data-aware controls are check boxes, images, labels, picture boxes, and text boxes. To use these controls to access a database, the controls must be **bound** to a data control on the form. In a multiform application, the bound control and the data control to which it is bound must be on the same form.

Data-aware controls are bound to a data control by setting their DataSource and DataField properties. The **DataSource property** of a control specifies the name of the data control to which it is bound. The **DataField property** of a bound control specifies the name of a field in the database to which the control is linked. Perform the following steps on the next page to bind the five label controls and one image control in the Geography Database Viewer application used to display information from the Countries table of the World database.

TO BIND THE DATA-AWARE CONTROLS ▼

STEP 1 ▶

Select the Label1(5) control by clicking its name in the drop-down Object list in the Properties window. Click the DataSource property in the Properties list. Click the arrow next to the Settings box.

The drop-down Settings list for the DataSource property lists all the data controls on the form (Figure 4-61).

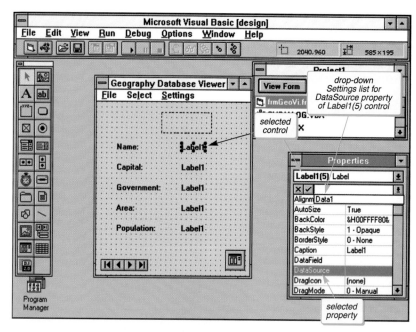

FIGURE 4-61

STEP 2 ▶

Select the Data1 control by clicking its name in the drop-down Settings box. Click the DataField property in the Properties list. Click the arrow next to the Settings box.

The drop-down Settings list for the DataField property lists all the fields in the Countries table of the World database (Figure 4-62).

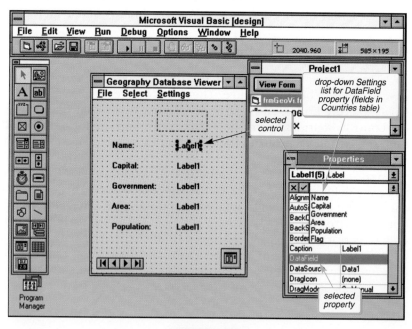

FIGURE 4-62

STEP 3 ▶

Select the Name field by clicking it in the Settings list.

The list closes, and the property value appears in the Settings box (Figure 4-63).

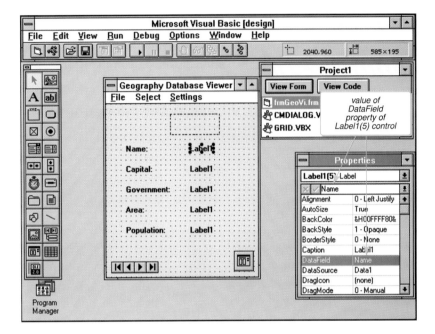

FIGURE 4-63

STEP 4 ▶

Repeat Steps 1 through 3 five times to accomplish the following: Bind the Label1(6) control to the Data1 control, and then set the DataField property equal to Capital. Bind the Label1(7) control to the Data1 control, and then set the DataField property equal to Government. Bind the Label1(8) control to the Data1 control, and then set the DataField property equal to Area. Bind the Label1(9) control to the Data1 control, and then set the DataField property equal to Population. Bind the Image1 control to the Data1 control, and then set the DataField property equal to Flag.

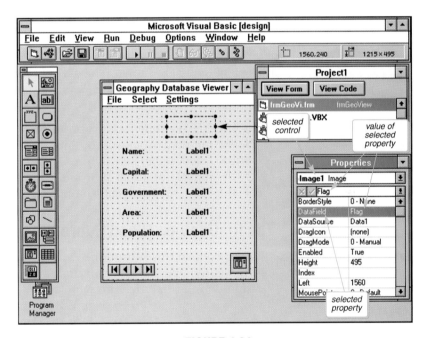

FIGURE 4-64

The form appears as shown in Figure 4-64.

It is not necessary to change the Caption property of the bound labels to blank because their captions will be given the field values of the first record in the table as soon as the application starts.

The property-setting stage of application development is complete. The third and last stage is to write the code for the application.

▶ WRITING CODE

ode must be written for nine events in the Geography Database Viewer application. The control, procedure, and a description of the action are listed in Table 4-2.

▸ TABLE 4-2 DATABASE VIEWER EVENT PROCEDURES

CONTROL	PROCEDURE	ACTIONS
frmGeoView	Load	Center the form on the desktop
mnuExit	Click	Closes the application
mnuNext	Click	Makes the next record in the database the current record
mnuPrev	Click	Makes the previous record in the database the current record
mnuFirst	Click	Makes the first record in the database the current record
mnuLast	Click	Makes the last record in the database the current record
mnuColor	Click	Opens the Color dialog box; when the dialog box closes, changes the color of the form and controls
mnuFlagshow	Click	Makes the image control containing country's flag visible/not visible
mnuNameshow	Click	Makes the label control containing country's name visible/not visible

The code statements (subroutines) for the four menu controls that make up the Select menu are similar. The subroutines for the two menu controls that make up the View submenu also are similar. The code-writing activities for the Geography Database Viewer are grouped as follows:

▸ the frmGeoView_Load subroutine
▸ the mnuExit_Click subroutine
▸ the Select menu subroutines (mnuNext, mnuPrev, mnuFirst, mnuLast)
▸ the mnuColor_Click subroutine
▸ the View submenu subroutines (mnuFlagshow, mnuNameshow)

The frmGeoView_Load Subroutine

The code in this subroutine causes the GeoView form to be centered on the desktop at the beginning of run time. However, you can drag the form to another location during run time. The same code statements used to center the form in Project 3 are used. Refer to page VB164 for a review of this method. The following steps write the Load procedure for the frmGeoView control.

TO WRITE THE FRMGEOVIEW_LOAD SUBROUTINE

Step 1: Minimize the form window. Open the Code window by choosing the View Code button in the Project window.

Step 2: Select the Form control from the drop-down Object list in the Code window.

Step 3: Enter the following two statements in the Code window:
```
frmGeoView.Top = (Screen.Height - frmGeoView.Height) / 2
frmGeoView.Left = (Screen.Width - frmGeoView.Width) / 2
```

The Code window appears as shown in Figure 4-65.

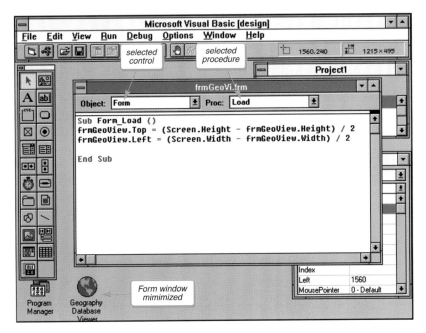

FIGURE 4-65

The mnuExit_Click Subroutine

When you trigger this event during run time by choosing Exit from the File menu, the Geography Database Viewer application closes. This procedure is accomplished in code by using the **End statement**. While the End statement never is required to terminate program execution, it is generally accepted as good programming practice because it closes any files that the application opened, removes forms from the computer's memory, and clears the value of all variables. Perform the following steps to write the mnuExit_Click subroutine.

LECTURE NOTES
■ Review the function of the mnuExit_Click subroutine.
■ Explain the code statement in the subroutine.

TO WRITE THE MNUEXIT_CLICK SUBROUTINE

Step 1: Select the mnuExit control from the drop-down Object list in the Code window.

Step 2: Enter the following statement in the Code window:

```
End
```

TRANSPARENCY
Figure 4-66

The Code window appears as shown in Figure 4-66.

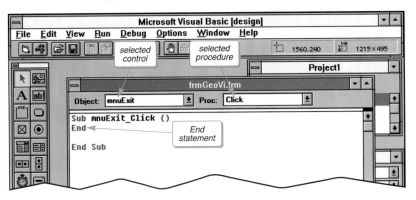

FIGURE 4-66

In the preceding steps, it was not necessary to select the Click event from the drop-down Procedures list in the Code window because menu controls have only the Click procedure.

The Select Menu Subroutines

One event is associated with each of the four commands in the Select menu: mnuNext_Click, mnuPrev_Click, mnuFirst_Click, and mnuLast_Click. When you trigger the mnuNext_Click event during run time by choosing Next from the Select menu, the next record (the one after the current record in the table) becomes the current record, and its information displays in the window. A similar record selection action occurs for each of the other three commands.

As discussed earlier, these actions are the same as if the data control were visible on the form and you clicked on the appropriate arrow button for the next, previous, first, or last record to become the current record. These actions are accomplished in code with the **MoveNext**, **MovePrevious**, **MoveFirst** and **MoveLast** methods. The code statement has the form:

```
DataControlName.Recordset.MoveNext
```

When the current record is the last record in the table and the Next arrow button on a data control is clicked, the last record remains the current record, so nothing happens. However, when the MoveNext method is used, a blank record becomes the current record and the end of file, or **EOF**, **property** of the recordset changes from False to True. A similar set of events occurs with the MovePrevious method and the beginning of file, **BOF**, **property**.

The subroutine for the Next command includes an If...Then statement to check if the application has gone past the last record by seeing if the value of EOF is true. If it has, the routine issues a command to make the first record current. The code to do this procedure is as follows:

```
Data1.Recordset.MoveNext
If Data1.Recordset.EOF = True Then Data1.Recordset.MoveFirst
```

If the MoveNext command causes the current record to move past the last record, then the first record in the table becomes the current record. That is, when the information displayed on the form is from the last country in the table and you choose Next from the Select menu, the information changes to that of the first country in the table. In this way the Geography Database Viewer "loops" through the records.

A similar code structure is used in the mnuPrev_Click subroutine. The following steps write the subroutines for the four commands in the Select menu of the application.

TO WRITE THE SELECT MENU SUBROUTINES ▼

STEP 1 ►

Select the mnuNext control from the drop-down Object list in the Code window. Enter the following two statements in the Code window:

```
Data1.Recordset.MoveNext
If Data1.Recordset.EOF =
  True
  Then Data1.Recordset.
  MoveFirst
```

The Code window appears as shown in Figure 4-67.

FIGURE 4-67

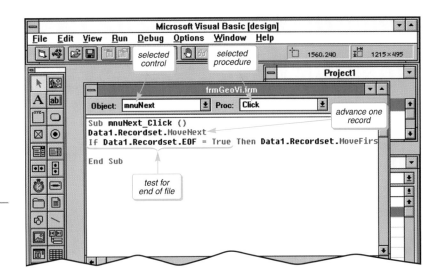

STEP 2 ►

Select the mnuPrev control from the drop-down Object list in the Code window. Enter the following two statements in the Code window:

```
Data1.Recordset.MovePrevious
If Data1.Recordset.BOF =
  True
  Then Data1.Recordset.
  MoveLast
```

The Code window appears as shown in Figure 4-68.

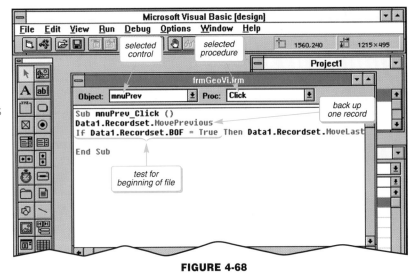

FIGURE 4-68

STEP 3 ►

Select the mnuFirst control from the drop-down Object list in the Code window. Enter the following statement in the Code window:

```
Data1.Recordset.MoveFirst
```

The Code window appears as shown in Figure 4-69.

FIGURE 4-69

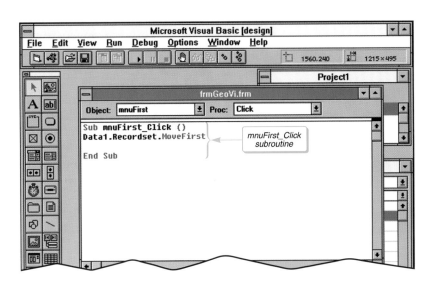

STEP 4 ▶

Select the mnuLast control from the drop-down Object list in the Code window. Enter the following statement in the Code window:
`Data1.Recordset.MoveLast`

The Code window appears as shown in Figure 4-70.

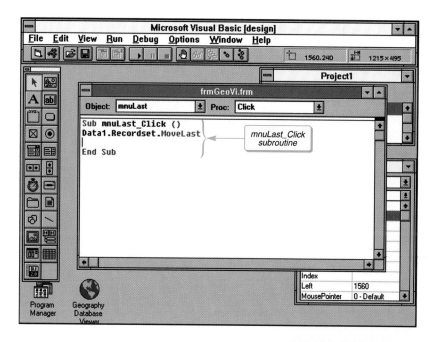

FIGURE 4-70

The mnuColor_Click Subroutine

This subroutine performs two actions when you choose the Color command from the Settings menu during run time. First, it opens the Color common dialog box. Second, after you select a color in the dialog box and choose the OK button, the subroutine changes the BackColor property of the form and the ten labels.

As discussed previously, the common dialog control can be used to open any of five common dialog boxes. You specify which type of dialog box to open by setting the common dialog control's **Flags property** and **Action property** in two code statements. The statements to open a Color dialog box are

```
controlname.Flags = &H1&
controlname.Action = 3
```

where *controlname* is the value of the Name property of the common dialog control.

When you close the Color dialog box, the selected color becomes the value of the common dialog control's **Color property**. The second action in this subroutine is to set the BackColor property of the form and labels to equal the Color property of the common dialog control. For the form control the statement is

```
frmGeoView.BackColor = CMDialog1.Color
```

This type of property assignment has been used many times in previous projects. A similar code statement could be added for each of the ten labels on the form to change their BackColor. However, a simpler way to accomplish this change is by using a code structure called a For...Next statement.

A **For...Next statement**, also called a For...Next loop, repeats a group of code statements a specified number of times. Its syntax is

```
For counter = start To end
   [statements]
Next
```

The parts of the statement are described in Table 4-3.

TRANSPARENCY
Table 4-3

LECTURE NOTES
■ Explain the For..Next
statement and its use in
this subroutine.
■ Explain the code
statements in the
mnuColor_Click
subroutine.

▶ **TABLE 4-3 PARTS OF A FOR...NEXT STATEMENT**

PART	DESCRIPTION
For	Begins a For...Next loop control structure; must appear before any other part of the structure
counter	Numeric variable used as the loop counter
start	Initial value of counter
to	Separates start and end values
end	Final value for counter
[statements]	Code statements between For and Next executed the specified number of times
Next	Ends a For...Next loop; causes 1 to be added to counter

A flowchart representation of the For...Next loop is shown to the right

In the mnuColor_Click subroutine, the *start* and *end* values of the counter are set to the values of the index of the first and last labels in the label array (0 and 9). The counter increases by one each time it performs the statements. However, the statements themselves use the counter's value for the index value of the label whose color is being changed as follows:

```
For index = 0 To 9
    Label1(index).BackColor = CMDialog.Color
Next
```

The following steps write the subroutine.

TO WRITE THE MNUCOLOR_CLICK SUBROUTINE

Step 1: Select the mnuColor control from the drop-down Object list in the Code window.

Step 2: Enter the following six statements in the Code window:

```
CMDialog1.Flags = &H1&
CMDialog1.Action = 3
frmGeoView.BackColor = CMDialog1.Color
For index = 0 To 9
 Label1(index).BackColor =
CMDialog1.Color
Next
```

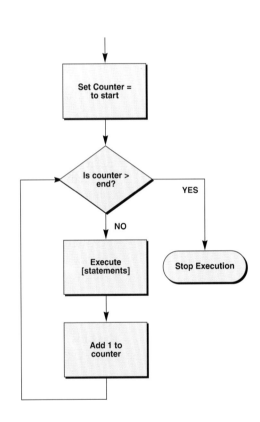

The Code window appears as shown in Figure 4-71 on the next page.

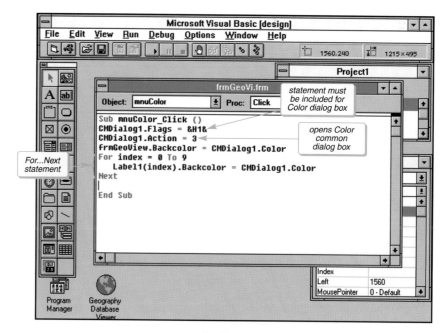

FIGURE 4-71

Writing the Subroutines for the View Submenu

Two similar subroutines correspond to the two commands in the View submenu in the Geography Database Viewer: mnuFlagshow_Click and mnuNameshow_Click. When the application starts, these commands are preceded in the menu by check marks, indicating that the Flag and Name fields are visible on the form. Choosing one of the commands removes the check mark preceding that command and changes the Visible property of the appropriate control on the form to False. When the command is chosen again, the check mark returns, and the control is visible. The two menu controls were set to receive check marks by checking the Checked box in the Menu Design Window when the menu was created. Checks are added or removed during run time by setting the menu control's **Checked property** to True or False with code statements.

The subroutines must evaluate whether the check mark is present and then take one of two courses of action based on that evaluation. The code structure for accomplishing this evaluation is the For...Next block used in Project 3. The form of the block for the mnuFlagshow_Click is:

```
If mnuFlagshow.Checked = True Then
    mnuFlagshow.Checked = False
    Image1.Visible = False
Else
    mnuFlagshow.Checked = True
    Image1.Visible = True
End If
```

The code structure for the mnuNameshow_Click event is similar, but the Visible property for both the label that names the field as well as the label that contains the value of the Name field of the current record must be set. Perform the following steps to write these subroutines.

TO WRITE THE MNUFLAGSHOW_CLICK SUBROUTINE

Step 1: Select the mnuFlagshow control from the drop-down Object list in the Code window.

Step 2: Enter the following statements in the Code window:

```
If mnuFlagshow.Checked = True Then
    mnuFlagshow.Checked = False
    Image1.Visible = False
Else
    mnuFlagshow.Checked = True
    Image1.Visible = True
End If
```

TRANSPARENCIES
Figure 4-72 and
Figure 4-73

The Code window appears as shown in Figure 4-72.

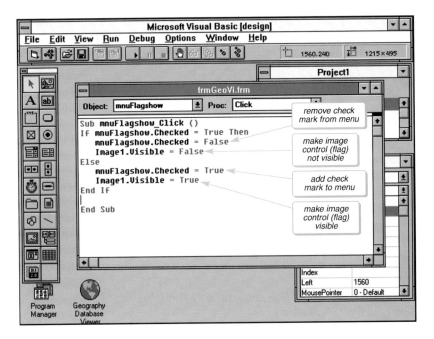

FIGURE 4-72

TO WRITE THE MNUNAMESHOW_CLICK SUBROUTINE

Step 1: Select the mnuNameshow control from the Object list in the Code window.

Step 2: Enter the following statements in the Code window:

```
If mnuNameshow.Checked = True Then
    mnuNameshow.Checked = False
    Label1(0).Visible = False
    Label1(5).Visible = False
Else
    mnuNameshow.Checked = True
    Label1(0).Visible = True
    Label1(5).Visible = True
End If
```

The Code window appears as shown in Figure 4-73 on the next page.

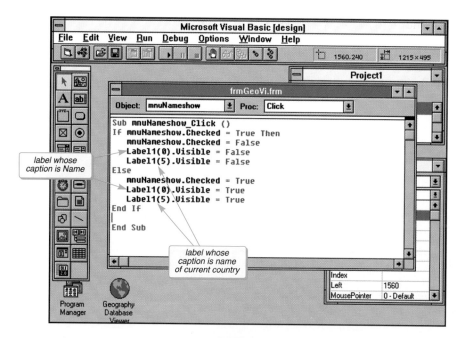

FIGURE 4-73

▶ SAVING THE PROJECT

LECTURE NOTES
■ Ask students why they should save their work periodically and why they should always save a project before running it.
■ Introduce students to what is meant by debugging.
■ Review the steps to save forms and projects.

CAUTION
The form and project file should be saved to the same diskette that the WORLD.MDB file was copied to earlier.

T he Geography Database Viewer project is complete. Before running an application, it always should be saved. Possibly the application contains errors. Depending on the severity of the error, it is possible (although generally not very likely) that the computer will "lock up" when the application runs. If so, all execution stops, and you have no control from the keyboard or mouse. The only recourse in this event is to reboot the computer. If the project has not been saved, all work on the project is lost. If the project has been saved, you can restart Visual Basic, open the project, and begin the process of detecting and correcting errors.

In the following steps, the project is saved to the diskette in drive A that contains the database file, WORLD.MDB. The following steps save the form file and the project file.

TO SAVE THE PROJECT

Step 1: Click the Save Project tool (▢) in the toolbar.
Step 2: Type `Geoview` in File Name text box in the Save File As dialog box.
Step 3: Select drive A from the drop-down Drives list box in the Save File As dialog box.
Step 4: Choose the OK button in the Save File As dialog box.
Step 5: Type `Geoview` in the File Name box in the Save Project As dialog box.
Step 6: Choose the OK button in the Save Project As dialog box.

The form file is saved on the diskette in drive A as GEOVIEW.FRM. The project file is saved on the diskette in drive A as GEOVIEW.MAK.

Even though Save Project was chosen in the preceding Step 1, the Save File As dialog box opened, and then the Save Project As dialog box opened. Visual Basic automatically opened these dialog boxes because neither the form nor the project had been saved previously. With the project saved, it can now be run without risk of losing the work that has been completed.

▶ RUNNING THE APPLICATION

When the Geography Database Viewer application starts, it looks for the World database file (WORLD.MDB) on the diskette in drive A because *A:\WORLD.MDB* is the value assigned to the DatabaseName property of the data control in the application. A diskette containing the WORLD.MDB file must be in drive A before running the application. For this reason, the two project files were saved to the diskette, which already contained the WORLD.MDB file.

An alternative to this procedure is to copy the WORLD.MDB file to a directory on the hard disk. However, if this copying is done, the DatabaseName property must be changed to the new drive and directory where the database file is located. Perform the following steps to run the application.

LECTURE NOTES
■ Demonstrate the operation of the completed application.

TRANSPARENCIES
Figure 4-74 through Figure 4-76

TO RUN THE APPLICATION ▼

STEP 1 ▶

Double-click the Code window's Control-menu box. Click the Run icon (▣) in the toolbar, or choose Start from the Run menu.

The application takes a few seconds to load. The first record is read, and the application appears as shown in Figure 4-74.

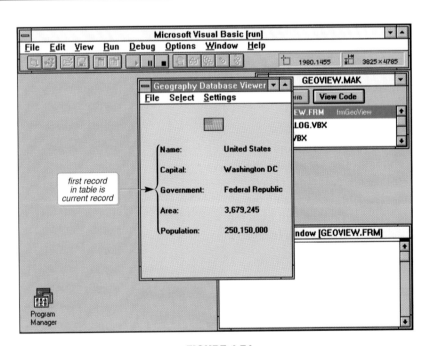

FIGURE 4-74

STEP 2 ▶

Choose Last from the Select menu.

The last country in the table appears in the window (Figure 4-75).

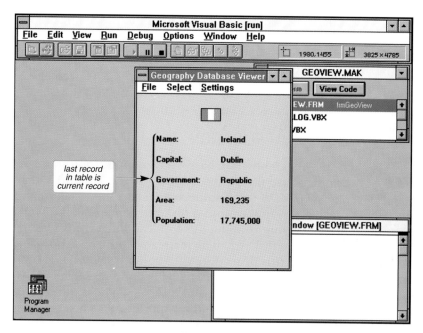

FIGURE 4-75

STEP 3 ▶

Choose Next from the Select menu.

The record selection "loops" back to the first record (Figure 4-76).

STEP 4 ▶

Try all of the different options and features such as changing the color, turning off the display of the flag, and minimizing the application. Choose Exit from the application's File menu to close the application.

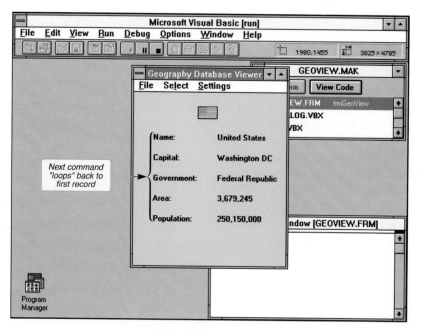

FIGURE 4-76

▶ PROJECT SUMMARY

Project 4 extended the basics of building applications presented in the first three projects. An application was built by creating the interface, setting properties and writing code. The data control was introduced to link the application to a database. The use of color within applications was introduced. Menus were created for the application using the Menu Design Window. The application included the use of a control array and the For...Next statement. The common dialog control was incorporated to improve the sophistication of user interaction with the application during run time.

▶ KEY TERMS

Action property *(VB228)*
access key *(VB206)*
BackColor property *(VB199)*
BOF property *(VB226)*
bound *(VB221)*
Checked property *(VB230)*
Color property *(VB228)*
common dialog control *(VB205)*
Connect property *(VB218)*
control array *(VB198)*
database *(VB193)*

DatabaseName property *(VB218)*
DataField property *(VB221)*
DataSource property *(VB221)*
data-aware *(VB221)*
data control *(VB203)*
End statement *(VB225)*
EOF property *(VB226)*
field *(VB194)*
Flags property *(VB228)*
For...Next statement *(VB228)*
Menu Design Window *(VB207)*

MoveFirst *(VB226)*
MoveLast *(VB226)*
MoveNext *(VB226)*
MovePrevious *(VB226)*
record *(VB194)*
RecordSource property *(VB218)*
separator bar *(VB209)*
submenu *(VB211)*
table *(VB194)*

QUICK REFERENCE

In Visual Basic you can accomplish a task in a number of ways. The following table provides a quick reference to each of the major tasks presented for the first time in the project with some of the available options. The commands listed in the Menu column can be executed using either the keyboard or mouse.

Task	Mouse	Menu	Keyboard Shortcuts
Display the Menu Design Window	Click Menu Design icon on toolbar	From Window menu, choose Menu Design	Press CTRL+M
Open the Code Window for a Selected Object (Form Window Active)	Double-click object on form		Press F7
Open the Color Palette for the Active Control (Design Time)	Double-click ForeColor or BackColor property in Properties window	From Window menu, choose Color Palette	

EXERCISE NOTES
■ Use Student Assign-
ments 1 through 6 for
classroom discussion or
homework exercises.

STUDENT ASSIGNMENT 1
True/False

Instructions: Circle T if the statement is true or F if the statement is false.

(T) F   1. A database may contain more than one table.

T (F)   2. In a database, characteristics or attributes of an object are called tables.

T (F)   3. A control array can contain different types of controls.

T (F)   4. The index value of the first control in an array is 1.

T (F)   5. Controls are copied from the Clipboard by pressing CTRL+Z.

(T) F   6. It is not necessary to press the ALT key when using an access key for a command within a menu.

T (F)   7. The value of the Display property of a common dialog control determines which type of common dialog box is opened.

(T) F   8. Common dialog controls never are visible during run time.

T (F)   9. Separator bars can have Click event subroutines.

T (F) 10. The RecordSource property is used to specify the name of the database file to which the data control is linked.

(T) F   11. Check box controls are data-aware.

T (F) 12. The variable incremented in a For...Next statement is called an index.

(T) F   13. Submenus may contain additional submenus.

T (F) 14. Data controls never are visible during run time.

(T) F   15. All of the controls in an array must have the same name.

(T) F   16. Clicking any control that is part of an array will trigger the same Click event subroutine.

T (F) 17. Code statements used to center a form on the desktop must be part of the Form_Load subroutine.

T (F) 18. Submenus are indicated by a check mark located on the right of the caption.

T (F) 19. File menus in Windows applications seldom contain an Exit command.

T (F) 20. Control arrays are created by clicking the Array icon in the toolbar.

STUDENT ASSIGNMENT 2
Multiple Choice

Instructions: Circle the correct response.

1. The _____ control is not data-aware.
    a. image
    b. text box
    (c.) common dialog
    d. label

2. The common dialog control can be used to display _____ common dialog boxes.
    a. Font
    b. Open
    c. Save As
    (d.) all of the above

3. _____ is a property of data controls.
   (a.) DatabaseName
   b. DataSource
   c. DataField
   d. all of the above

4. _____ is a property of bound controls.
   a. RecordSource
   (b.) DataSource
   c. Connect
   d. all of the above

5. Access keys are set by preceding the designated letter in the menu control's caption with _____.
   a. %
   b. $
   (c.) &
   d. @

6. _____ is not a command button in the Menu Design Window.
   a. Next
   b. OK
   (c.) Previous
   d. Delete

7. The menu control list box contains menu controls' _____.
   a. names
   b. values of the Checked property
   (c.) captions
   d. all of the above

8. The type of common dialog box displayed is determined by the value of the _____ property of the common dialog control.
   a. Flags
   (b.) Action
   c. Show
   d. none of the above

9. The _____ property is used to bind a data-aware control to a data control.
   (a.) DataSource
   b. DatabaseName
   c. RecordSource
   d. Connect

10. The Menu Design Window can be opened by _____.
    a. choosing Menu Design from the Option menu
    b. clicking the Menu Design tool in the Toolbox.
    (c.) both a and b
    d. neither a nor b

STUDENT ASSIGNMENT 3
Understanding the Menu Design Window

Instructions: In Figure SA4-3, arrows point to some of the major components in the Menu Design Window. Identify these in the space provided.

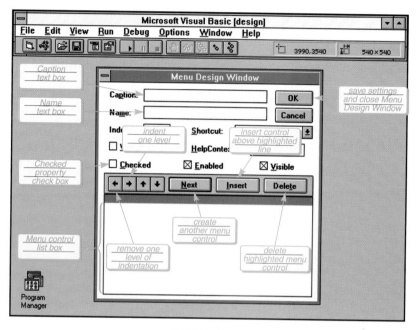

FIGURE SA4-3

STUDENT ASSIGNMENT 4
Understanding Controls and Properties

Instructions: The following table lists several controls and several properties. Place an "x" in the space provided if the control has that property.

PROPERTIES	DATA CONTROL	COMMON DIALOG CONTROL	FORM CONTROL	MENU CONTROL
Color	[ ]	[X]	[ ]	[ ]
Checked	[ ]	[ ]	[ ]	[X]
BackColor	[X]	[ ]	[X]	[ ]
RecordSource	[X]	[ ]	[ ]	[ ]
Connect	[X]	[ ]	[ ]	[ ]
Action	[ ]	[X]	[ ]	[ ]
Visible	[X]	[ ]	[X]	[ ]
MinButton	[ ]	[ ]	[ ]	[ ]
Caption	[X]	[ ]	[X]	[X]
Name	[X]	[X]	[X]	[X]

STUDENT ASSIGNMENT 5
Understanding Menus

Instructions: The Menu Design Window for an application is shown in Figure SA4-5. On a separate sheet of paper draw a picture of the menu bar and the menus for this application. Include submenus, access key markings, separator bars, and check marks.

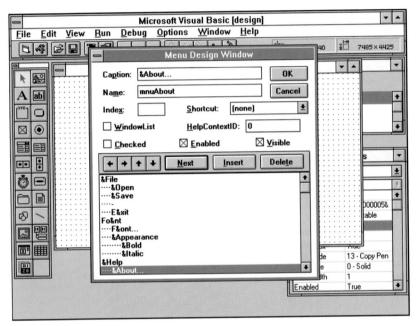

FIGURE SA4-5

STUDENT ASSIGNMENT 6
Understanding the Visual Basic Toolbar and Toolbox

Instructions: In Figure SA4-6, arrows point to some of the tools on the toolbar and in the Toolbox. Identify these in the space provided.

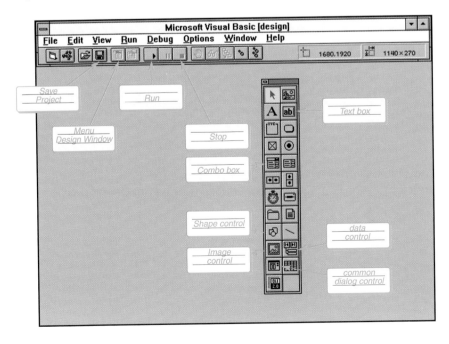

FIGURE SA4-6

EXERCISE NOTES
■ Exercise 1 provides
students with experience
using the common dialog
control to control Font
properties during run time.

COMPUTER LABORATORY EXERCISE 1
Using Common Dialog Control

Instructions: Start Visual Basic. Open the project CLE4-1 from the subdirectory VB3 on the Student Diskette that accompanies this book. Complete the following tasks.

1. Choose the View Form button in the Project window. The form appears as shown in Figure CLE4-1.

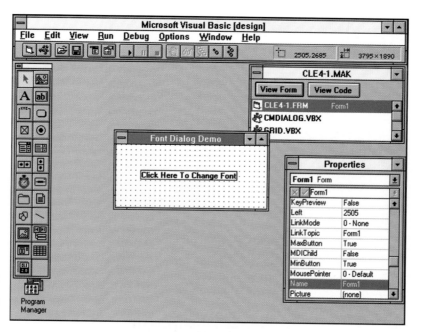

FIGURE CLE4-1

EXERCISE NOTES
■ Explain to students that
the last 4 code state-
ments in instruction 5 are
used to resize the form
and reposition it in the
center of the desktop
when the FontSize is
changed.

2. Add a common dialog control to the form by double-clicking the common dialog tool in the Toolbox.
3. Choose the View Code button in the Project window.
4. Select the Label1 control from the drop-down Object list in the Code window.
5. Write the Label1_Click subroutine as follows:

```
CMDialog1.Flags = &H1&
CMDialog1.Action = 4
Label1.Fontname = CMDialog1.Fontname
Label1.Fontsize = CMDialog1.Fontsize
Form1.Width = Label1.Width + 1200
Form1.Height = Label1.Height + 1635
Form1.Left = (Screen.Width - Form1.Width)/2
Form1.Top = (Screen.Height - Form1.Height)/2
```

6. Describe the action of each of the code statements in Step 5 on a separate piece of paper.
7. Save the form as CLE4-1A.FRM, and save the project as CLE4-1A.MAK. Close the Code window.
8. Run the application. Select different values for FontName and FontSize in the Font dialog box, and choose OK.

9. Select Bold in the Font dialog box. What happens (or doesn't happen) when you choose OK? Why?
10. To end the application, click the Stop icon on the toolbar, or double-click the form's Control-menu box.
11. Check with your instructor for directions on turning in the exercise.

EXERCISE NOTES
■ Exercise 2 provides students with experience using control arrays and using the common dialog control to set Color properties during run time.

COMPUTER LABORATORY EXERCISE 2
The Color Dialog Box and Control Arrays

Instructions: Start Visual Basic. Open the project CLE4-2 from the subdirectory VB3 on the Student Diskette that accompanies this book.

Perform the following steps.

1. Choose the View Form button. The form contains an array of 24 label controls arranged in a checkerboard pattern, as shown in Figure CLE4-2.

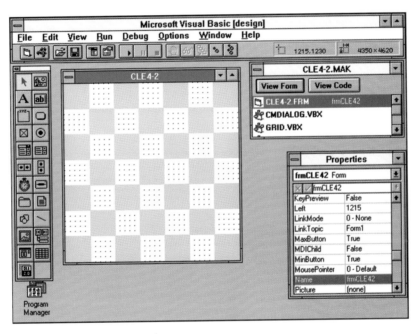

FIGURE CLE4-2

2. Add a common dialog control to the form by double-clicking the common dialog tool in the toolbox.
3. Choose the View Code button in the Project window.
4. Select the Form control from the drop-down Object list in the Code window.
5. Select the Click event from the drop-down Procedures list in the Properties window.
6. Write the Form_Click subroutine as follows:

```
CMDialog1.Flags = &H1&
CMDialog1.Action = 3
frmCLE42.BackColor = CMDialog1.Color
```

7. Select the Label1 control array from the drop-down Object list in the Code window.

COMPUTER LABORATORY EXERCISE 2 (continued)

8. Write the Label1_Click subroutine as follows:

```
CMDialog1.Flags = &H1&
CMDialog1.Action = 3
For Index = 0 to 24
    Label1(Index).BackColor = CMDialog1.Color
Next
```

9. Save the form as CLE4-2A.FRM, and save the project as CLE4-2A.MAK. Close the Code window.
10. Run the application. Click any of the boxes on the form. Change its color. Click any other box on the form. Change its color.
11. To end the application, click the Stop icon on the toolbar, or double-click the form's Control-menu box.
12. Check with your instructor for directions on turning in the exercise.

EXERCISE NOTES
■ Exercise 3 provides students with experience creating and using menus in applications.

COMPUTER LABORATORY EXERCISE 3
Creating Menus

Instructions: Start Visual Basic. Open the project CLE4-3 from the subdirectory VB3 on the Student Diskette that accompanies this book. In this exercise you will create a menu for the Alignment demo built in Computer Laboratory Exercise 3-3 on page VB187. The completed application will appear as shown in Figure CLE4-3.

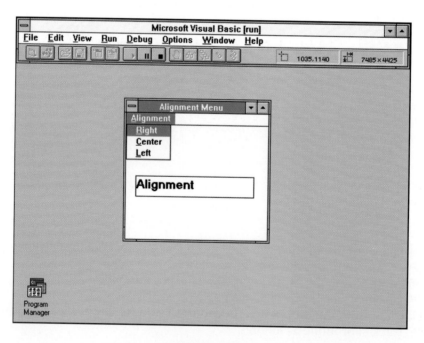

FIGURE CLE4-3

Perform the following steps.

1. Choose the View Form button in the Project window.
2. Open the Menu Design Window.
3. Add a menu control with the caption &Alignment and the name mnuAlign.
4. Choose Next. Click the right arrow to indent once. Add a menu control with the caption &Right and the name mnuRight.

5. Choose Next. Add a menu control with the caption &Center and the name mnuCenter.
6. Choose Next. Add a menu control with the caption &Left and the name mnuLeft.
7. Choose the OK button in the Menu Design window. Choose the View Code button in the Project window.
8. Select the mnuRight control from the drop-down Object list in the Code window. Write the following mnuRight_Click subroutine statement: `Label1.Alignment = 1`
9. Select the mnuCenter control from the drop-down Object list in the Code window. Write the following mnuCenter_Click subroutine statement: `Label1.Alignment = 2`
10. Select the mnuLeft control from the drop-down Object list in the Code window. Write the following mnuLeft_Click subroutine statement: `Label1.Alignment = 0`
11. Save the form as CLE4-3A.FRM, and save the project as CLE4-3A.MAK.
12. Close the Code window. Run the application. Make menu selections by clicking as well as by using the menu access keys.
13. Close the Alignment application by double-clicking its Control-menu box or by clicking the Stop icon on the toolbar.
14. Check with your instructor for directions on turning in the exercise.

COMPUTER LABORATORY ASSIGNMENTS

COMPUTER LABORATORY ASSIGNMENT 1
Tailor's Calculations Revisited

EXERCISE NOTES
■ The four Computer Laboratory Assignments increase in difficulty. Assignment 3 and Assignment 4 are suitable for either individual or small group assignments.

Purpose: To build an application that uses a menu to trigger subroutines that contain mathematical computations.

Problem: A tailor would like to have an application that calculates the average neck size, hat size, and shoe size for male customers, given the customer's weight and waistline. The interface should resemble the one shown in Figure CLA4-1a. Text boxes should be used for the inputs, and a label should be used for the output. The calculations are as shown on the next page.

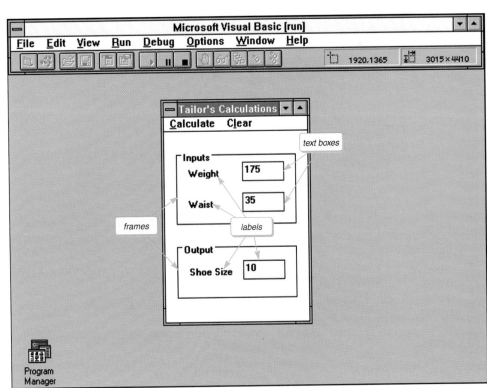

FIGURE CLA4-1a

COMPUTER LABORATORY ASSIGNMENT 1 (continued)

Neck size = 3 * (Weight / Waistline)
Hat Size = (3 * Weight) / (2.125 * Waistline)
Shoe size = 50 * (Waistline / Weight)

Instructions: Perform the following tasks.

1. Start Visual Basic, or open a new project if Visual Basic is already running.
2. Size and locate the form, as shown in Figure CLA4-1a on page VB243.
3. Add two frames, two text boxes, and four labels, as shown in Figure CLA4-1a.
4. Set the appropriate captions for the form and labels.
5. Set the text boxes' text values to be blank.
6. Set the BorderStyle of the label used for displaying the outputs so that it is visible.
7. Create a menu, as shown in Figure CLA4-1b.

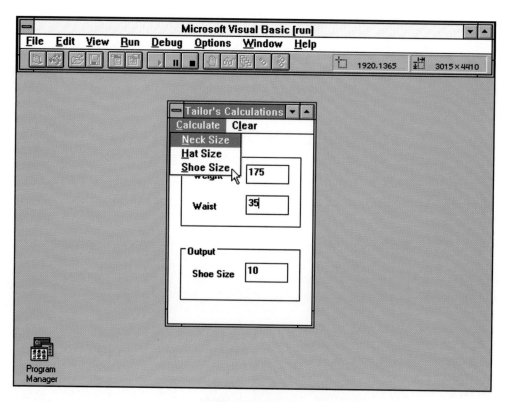

FIGURE CLA4-1b

8. Write the code for the Click event for each of the three commands in the Calculate menu. Each sub-routine should perform the appropriate calculation, change the caption of the output label, and display the result.
9. Clicking the Clear choice in the menu bar should clear the data on the form and return the cursor to the first input box. (Hint: Use the SetFocus method.)
10. Save the form as CLA4-1.FRM. Save the project as CLA4-1.MAK.
11. Run the application to test it.
12. Check with your instructor for directions on turning in the assignment.

COMPUTER LABORATORY ASSIGNMENT 2
Shape Control Demonstration Revisited

Purpose: To build an application that incorporates menus and submenus.

Problem: You will build the application shown in Figure CLA2-2. The application has one menu used to access the two submenus. One submenu is used to set the Shape property of the shape control on the form, and the other submenu is used to set the BorderStyle property of the shape control.

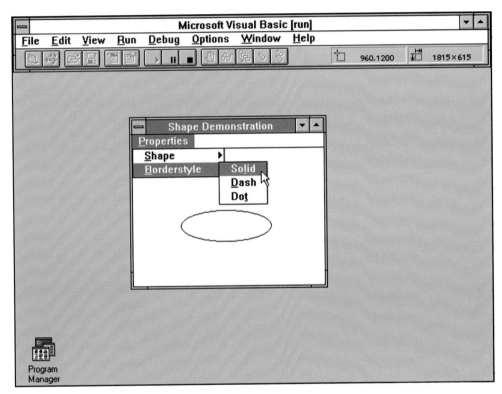

FIGURE CLA4-2

Instructions: Perform the following tasks.

1. Start Visual Basic, or open a new project if Visual Basic is already running.
2. Size and position the form, as shown in Figure CLA4-2.
3. Add a shape control, as shown in Figure CLA4-2.
4. Set the form's Caption property.
5. Open the Menu Design Window. Create the menu. Include access keys. An outline of the menu is as follows:

Properties
    Shape
        Rectangle
        Square
        Oval
        Circle
    BorderStyle
        Solid
        Dash
        Dot

COMPUTER LABORATORY ASSIGNMENT 2 (continued)

6. Write the Click subroutines for each of the menu commands. The subroutines should change the appropriate property of the shape control to the value listed in the menu control's caption.
7. Save the form as CLA4-2.FRM. Save the project as CLA4-2.MAK.
8. Run the application. Double-click the form's Control-menu box to stop the application.
9. Check with your instructor for directions on turning in the assignment.

COMPUTER LABORATORY ASSIGNMENT 3
Creating Menus that Include Check Marks

Purpose: To build an application that contains menus with check marks.

Instructions: Build a menu-driven interface for the application described in Computer Laboratory Assignment 4-2. Include three menus in the application's menu bar: File, Shape, and Borderstyle. The File menu should contain one command — Exit. Include access keys. The commands in the Shape and Borderstyle menus should include check marks to indicate the currently selected property value. Note: You will have to include If...Then blocks in the menu command subroutines that add the check mark to the caption of the command chosen and remove the check mark from the previously chosen command. Save the form as CLA4-3.FRM. Save the project as CLA4-3.MAK. Run the application. Choose Exit from the application's File menu to close the application. Check with your instructor for directions on turning in the assignment.

COMPUTER LABORATORY ASSIGNMENT 4
Accessing a Database

Purpose: To build an application that accesses a database and displays information from that database.

Instructions: The Visual Basic programming system includes a sample database of information about books, authors, and publishers, named BIBLIO.MDB. The database contains several tables. One of the tables, named Publishers, includes the name, address, city, and phone number of several publishing companies. Create an application that will access the Publishers table of the BIBLIO.MDB database and display the information one record at a time. The data control should be used during run time for record selection. The BIBLIO.MDB file is located in the VB3 subdirectory. Save the form as CLA4-4.FRM. Save the project as CLA4-4.MAK. Check with your instructor for directions on turning in the assignment.

MICROSOFT VISUAL BASIC 3.0 FOR WINDOWS
PROJECT FIVE

BUILDING APPLICATIONS WITH DRAG-AND-DROP FUNCTIONALITY

OBJECTIVES You will have mastered the material in this project when you can:

- Add drag-and-drop functionality to applications
- Add and remove custom controls
- Write code that calls other subroutines
- Copy code using keyboard commands
- Understand Visual Basic data types
- Include comments in subroutines
- Write subroutines with nested code structures

- Use the Select Case structure in applications
- Use the Do...Loop structure in applications
- Use the InputBox and UCase$ functions in applications
- Print an application's form and subroutines
- Distribute your applications to other users

▶ INTRODUCTION

You interact with many Windows applications by dragging and dropping objects. A good example is Windows' Solitaire game (page WIN43 in the Microsoft Windows section of this book). The application built in this project incorporates the activities necessary to add drag-and-drop functionality to your applications.

You previously have worked with form files (.FRM), project files (.MAK), and executable (.EXE) files. This project extends the concepts of managing Visual Basic project files by discussing other files used by Visual Basic. Additional information about documenting applications and distributing applications is presented.

Project 4 introduced control arrays. In this project, subroutines are written for common events shared by the controls in an array. In addition, a code method is used that allows one event procedure to initiate another event procedure. Several additional code structures are introduced in this project: nested If...Then blocks, Select Case blocks, and Do...Loop statements.

▶ PROJECT FIVE – TRAFFIC SIGN TUTORIAL

The application built in this project is shown in Figure 5-1 as it appears on the desktop during run time. The application is a tutorial that teaches you the meanings of several traffic signs. At run time, you are presented with several traffic signs and several containers having labels. You are instructed to drag and drop the signs into the correct containers. If you attempt to drop a sign into an incorrect container, the sign snaps back to its original location.

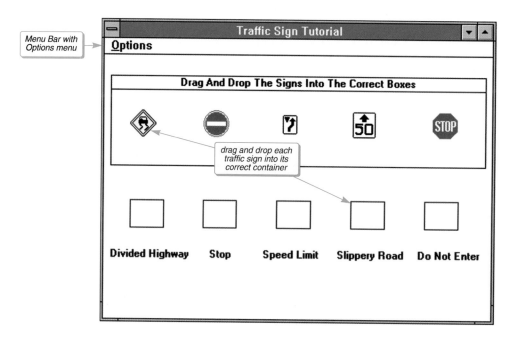

FIGURE 5-1

Three commands are available in the application by using the Options menu (Figure 5-2). The menu and commands include access keys, such as the Q is Quiz. Choosing the Clear command returns all the signs to their original locations. Choosing the Show command places all the signs in their correct containers. Choosing the Quiz command presents a series of three questions about the shapes of the signs.

The Traffic Sign Tutorial application is created by following the same three-step approach used in previous projects:

- ▶ create the interface
- ▶ set properties
- ▶ write code

FIGURE 5-2

Starting Visual Basic and Removing Custom Controls

Begin this project by starting Visual Basic, or by beginning a new project if Visual Basic is already running. If necessary, minimize the Program Manager window and adjust the sizes and locations of the Visual Basic windows to those shown in Figure 5-3. For more information on adjusting the Visual Basic windows, refer to page VB59.

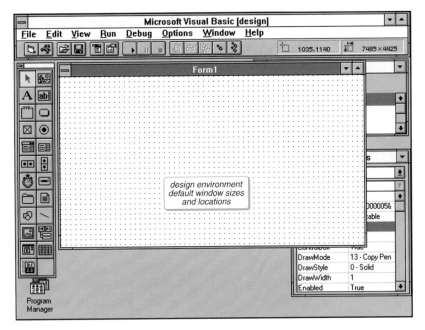

FIGURE 5-3

Custom controls can be added to applications in addition to the standard set of controls available within Visual Basic. Custom controls are stored in files with a **.VBX** file extension. The file contains the information Visual Basic needs to add the control to a project. Custom controls are added to the Toolbox by choosing the Add File command from the Visual Basic File menu (Figure 5-4) or by including the files in the AUTOLOAD.MAK file. When you open a new project, Visual Basic automatically adds the files listed in the **AUTOLOAD.MAK** file.

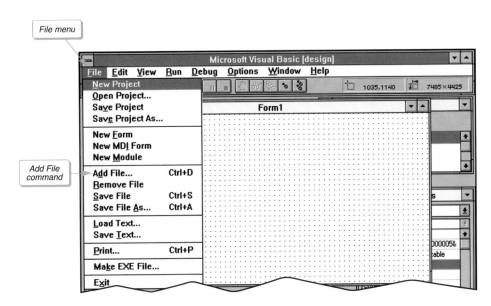

FIGURE 5-4

Many custom controls are available from third-party software vendors. Visual Basic has three custom controls that automatically are added to projects. (They are included in the AUTOLOAD.MAK file.) These controls can be recognized by their .VBX extension in the Project window (Figure 5-5). It is a good practice to include only those custom controls actually used in a project. The reasons for this practice are discussed in the section on distributing applications presented later in this project. Since the three custom controls are not used in this project, they are removed in the following steps.

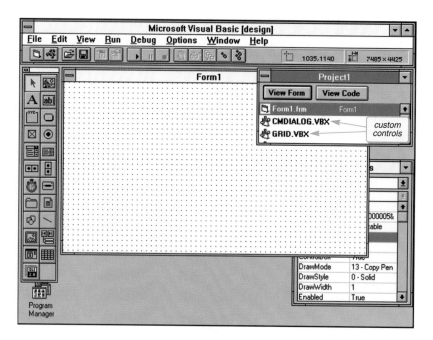

FIGURE 5-5

TO REMOVE CUSTOM CONTROLS ▼

STEP 1 ▶

Select the CMDIALOG.VBX file by
clicking its name in the Project1
window.

*The file name is highlighted, and
the View Form and View Code
buttons are disabled (Figure 5-6).*

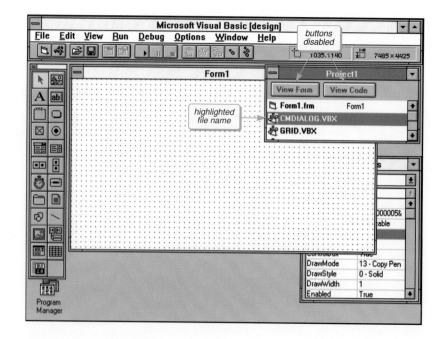

FIGURE 5-6

STEP 2 ▶

Select the File menu from the Menu Bar, and then choose the Remove File command.

The file is removed from the project. It is no longer listed in the Project1 window, and its icon is removed from the Toolbox (Figure 5-7).

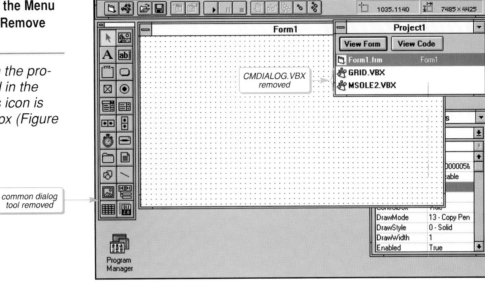

FIGURE 5-7

STEP 3 ▶

Repeat Steps 1 and 2 to remove the GRID.VBX file and the MSOLE2.VBX file.

The file names are removed from the Project window and the controls' icons are removed from the Toolbox (Figure 5-8).

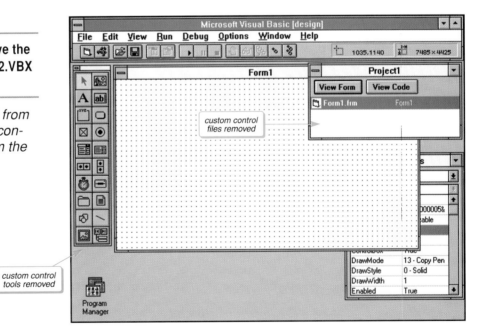

FIGURE 5-8

An alternative to removing custom controls from every project in which they are not used is to remove them from the AUTOLOAD.MAK file and then add them to projects only when they are needed. Consult with your instructor before editing the AUTOLOAD.MAK file.

▶ CREATING THE INTERFACE

I n this step, the size and location of the form is determined, and the controls are added to the form. The Traffic Sign Tutorial form contains one shape control, one individual image control, one individual label control, two arrays of image controls, and one array of label controls, as identified in Figure 5-9. After these controls are added to the form, the menu is created using Visual Basic's Menu Design window.

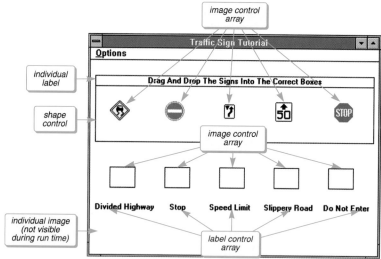

FIGURE 5-9

Setting the Location and Size of the Form

At run time, the form is centered on the desktop. This positioning will be accomplished later in the project through code statements, as was done in Project 4. In the steps that follow, the form is sized by setting the form's Height and Width properties.

TO SIZE THE FORM

Step 1: Select the form control by clicking it.
Step 2: Click the Properties window. Double-click the Height property in the Properties list.
Step 3: Type 4995 and press the ENTER key.
Step 4: Double-click the Width property in the Properties list in the Properties window.
Step 5: Type 7080 and press the ENTER key.

The form's width and height values appear as shown in Figure 5-10.

FIGURE 5-10

Adding the Individual Label, Shape, and Image Controls

TRANSPARENCY
Figure 5-11

The individual label, shape, and image controls are identified in Figure 5-11. The label control is used to contain the run-time instructions for the application. The shape control is used to visually group the traffic signs that are to be dragged and dropped. The individual image control is left blank and is not visible at run time. Its purpose is explained later in this project.

TO ADD THE INDIVIDUAL CONTROLS

Step 1: Add a label control to the form by double-clicking the label tool in the Toolbox. Adjust the label's size to that shown in Figure 5-12, and then drag it to the location shown.

Step 2: Add a shape control to the form by double-clicking the shape tool in the Toolbox. Adjust the shape control's size to that shown in Figure 5-12, and then drag it to the location shown.

Step 3: Add an image control to the form by double-clicking the image tool in the Toolbox. Drag it to the location shown in Figure 5-12.

The form appears as shown in Figure 5-12.

FIGURE 5-11

LECTURE NOTES
■ Point out the controls that are not part of control arrays (the individual controls) in the Traffic Sign Tutorial.
■ Emphasize that the image control in the lower left corner of the form is not visible at run time.

TRANSPARENCY
Figure 5-12

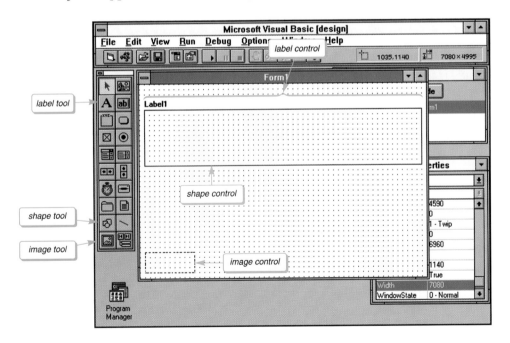

FIGURE 5-12

Adding the imgSign Array

Run-time dragging and dropping of a control does not automatically change its location. When the left mouse button is released to drop the control, the control retains its original position. Any relocation must be specifically programmed with code statements to occur when the left mouse button is released. Many times the control does not actually relocate. The control only appears to relocate by changing the properties of it and other controls, such as the Visible property.

LECTURE NOTES
■ Explain how controls can appear to move at run time by changing their Visible property.
■ Review the concept of a control array that was introduced in Project 4.

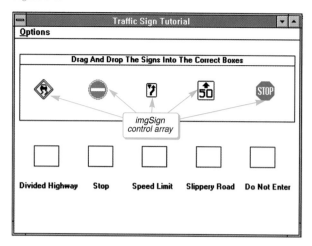

FIGURE 5-13

In Visual Basic, the control being dragged is called the **source control**. The control over which the source control is located during the dragging operation is called the **target control**.

In the Traffic Sign Tutorial, a sign appears to move into a container by changing the Picture property of the container from being blank to being equal to the Picture property of the image being dropped. Much of the apparent movement in the Traffic Sign Tutorial is the result of changing the values of the Picture and Visible properties of image controls on the form.

The first set of image controls in this application contains the graphical images of the five signs (Figure 5-13). These controls are grouped in an array to simplify the code writing later. The control array is given the name imgSign.

The ability to drag a control during run time is determined by the value of the control's **DragMode** property. When the DragMode property is set to Automatic, the dragging operation is initiated during run time by positioning the mouse pointer on the control and pressing the left mouse button. The DragMode property can be set through code statements or in the Properties window. In this application, the DragMode property is set to Automatic for the first image control in the array so that the property will be copied to all image controls in the array. The following steps add the imgSign control array.

TO ADD THE IMGSIGN ARRAY ▼

STEP 1 ▶

Double-click the image tool (▣) in the Toolbox.

A default-sized image control, Image2, is added to the form (Figure 5-14).

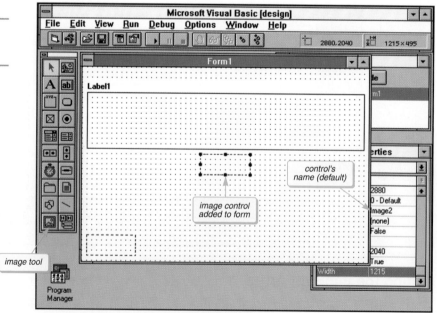

FIGURE 5-14

STEP 2 ▶

Drag the image control to the location shown in Figure 5-15.

Its size will be adjusted later.

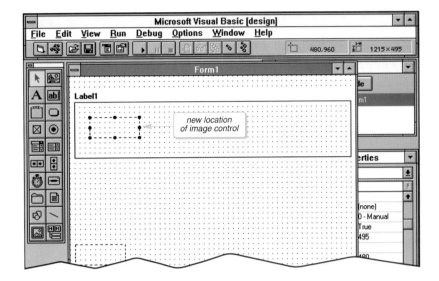

FIGURE 5-15

STEP 3 ▶

Click the Properties window. Double-click the Name property in the Properties list. Type `imgSign` and press the ENTER key. Double-click the DragMode property in the Properties list.

The control's new name (imgSign) appears in the Object box, and the value of the DragMode property changes to 1-Automatic (Figure 5-16).

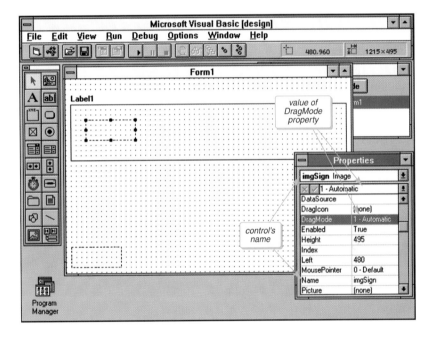

FIGURE 5-16

STEP 4 ▶

Click the imgSign control on the form. Press CTRL+C to copy the control to the Clipboard. Press CTRL+V to paste the contents of the Clipboard to the form. Choose Yes from the dialog box to begin a control array.

The name of the first image changes to imgSign(0). A second image control, imgSign(1), is added to the upper left corner of the form (Figure 5-17).

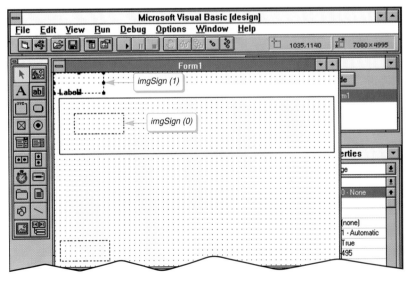

FIGURE 5-17

STEP 5 ▶

Drag the second image control, imgSign(1), from the upper left corner of the form to the location shown in Figure 5-18. Press CTRL+V to paste the Clipboard contents to the form.

A third label control, imgSign(2), is added to the form (Figure 5-18).

FIGURE 5-18

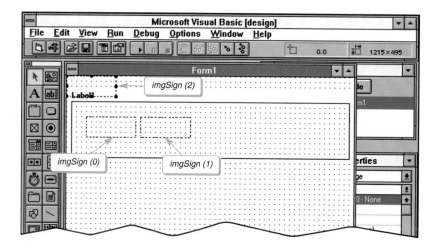

STEP 6 ▶

Drag the third image control in the array to the location shown in Figure 5-19. Press CTRL+V. Drag the fourth image control, imgSign(3), to the position shown in Figure 5-19. Press CTRL+V to paste the Clipboard contents to the form. Drag the fifth image control, imgSign(4), to the position shown in Figure 5-19.

Locating the controls in the order shown in Figure 5-19 is important. They easily can be confused because they all have the same appearance on the form.

FIGURE 5-19

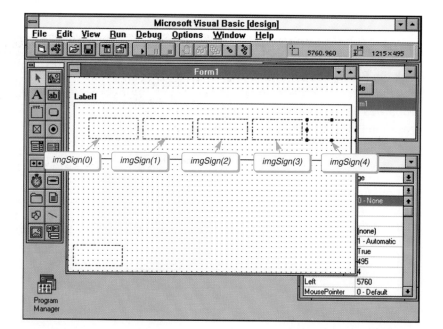

Adding the imgContainer Control Array

The second set of image controls is indicated in Figure 5-20. These controls also are grouped as an array and act as the containers into which the signs will be dropped. These controls have their Border-Style set to Fixed Single to display as empty boxes. Perform the following steps to create this array, imgContainer, and to locate the controls on the form.

TRANSPARENCY
Figure 5-20

FIGURE 5-20

TO ADD THE IMGCONTAINER ARRAY

Step 1: Double-click the image tool (🖾) in the Toolbox.

Step 2: Double-click the Name property in the Properties list in the Properties window. Type `imgContainer` and press the ENTER key. Double-click the BorderStyle property in the Properties list to change the value to 1-Fixed Single. Drag the image control to the location shown in Figure 5-21.

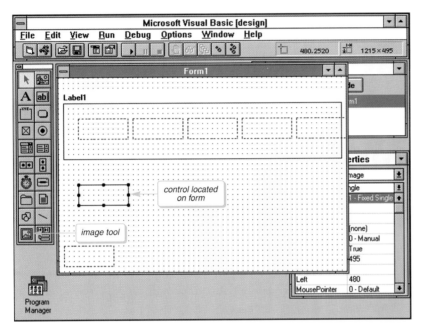

FIGURE 5-21

Step 3: Click the imgContainer control on the form. Press CTRL+C to copy the control to the Clipboard. Press CTRL+V to paste the Clipboard's contents to the form. Choose Yes from the dialog box to start a control array.

Step 4: Drag the second image control, imgContainer(1), to the location shown in Figure 5-22.

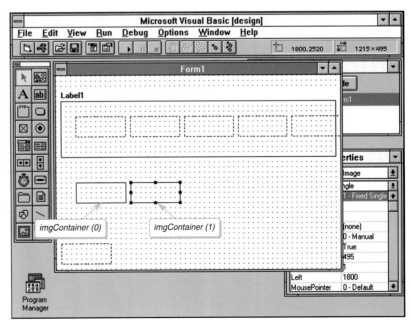

FIGURE 5-22

Step 5: Press CTRL+V to paste the Clipboard's contents to the form. Drag the third image control to the location shown in Figure 5-23.

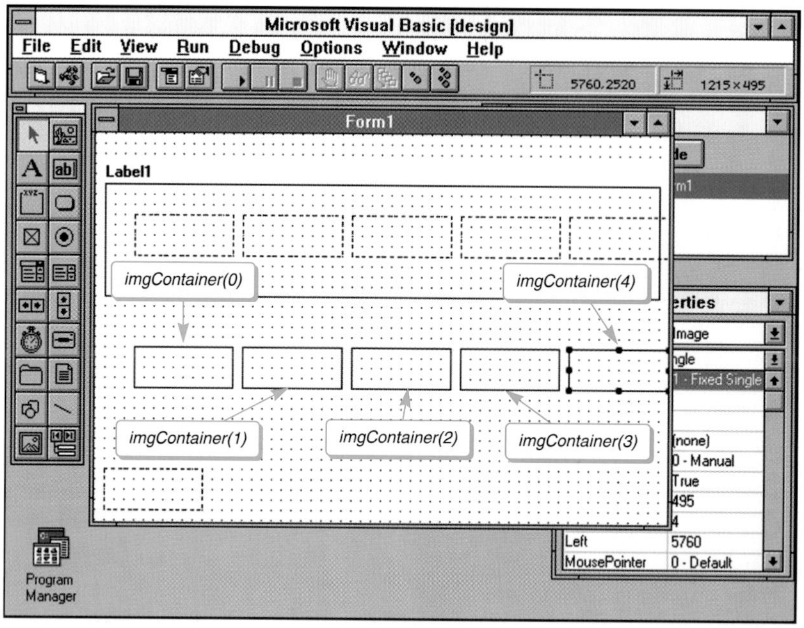

FIGURE 5-23

Step 6: Repeat Step 5 two times, dragging the controls to the locations shown in Figure 5-23.

Locating the controls in the order shown in Figure 5-23 is important. They easily can be confused because they all have the same appearance on the form.

Adding the Label Control Array

TRANSPARENCY
Figure 5-24

LECTURE NOTES
■ Point out and explain the function of the label control array.

The label control array is indicated in Figure 5-24. These controls are used for the names of the containers. The labels in the array have their AutoSize property set to True. The following steps create this array using the default name Label2 and locate the controls on the form.

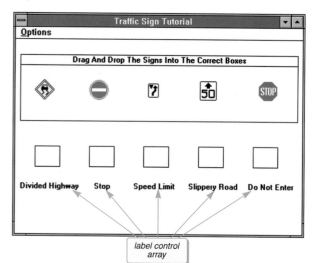

FIGURE 5-24

TO ADD THE LABEL2 ARRAY

Step 1: Double-click the label tool (A) in the Toolbox.

Step 2: Double-click the AutoSize property in the Properties list to change the value to True. Drag the label control to the location shown in Figure 5-25.

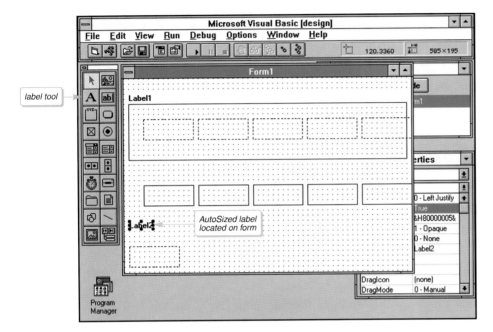

FIGURE 5-25

Step 3: Click the Label2 control on the form. Press CTRL+C to copy the control to the Clipboard. Press CTRL+V to paste the Clipboard's contents to the form. Choose Yes from the dialog box.

Step 4: Drag the second label control, Label2(1), to the location shown in Figure 5-26.

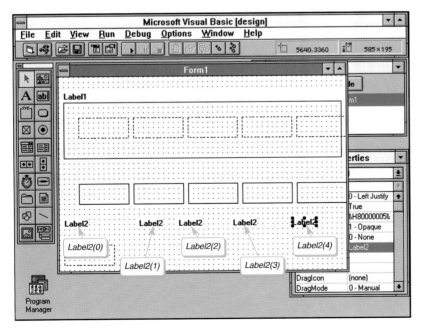

FIGURE 5-26

Step 5: Press CTRL+V to paste the Clipboard's contents to the form. Drag the third label control to the location shown in Figure 5-26.

Step 6: Repeat Step 5 two times, dragging the label controls to the locations shown in Figure 5-26 on page VB259.

Locating the controls in the order shown in Figure 5-26 is important. They easily can be confused because they all have the same caption, Label2.

Adjusting the Size and Location of Controls

LECTURE NOTES
■ Explain why the sizes of only the container images need to be adjusted.

The size of the image controls in the imgSign array will be set automatically when the traffic sign icons are loaded. However, the size of the imgContainer controls must be set manually. The following steps adjust the size and location of controls on the form.

TO SIZE THE IMGCONTAINER CONTROLS

Step 1: Click the first control in the imgContainer array.

Step 2: Drag its right border to the left the distance of 5 gridmarks on the form.

Step 3: Repeat Step 2 for each of the remaining 4 controls in the imgContainer array.

Step 4: Make any additional adjustments so the form appears as shown in Figure 5-27.

The location of the labels in the Label2 array is not critical at this time. Their location can be adjusted more easily after they have been given captions.

TRANSPARENCY
Figure 5-27

VB TIPS
■ When a graphic is loaded into an image control whose BorderStyle is none, the image control size is automatically adjusted to the size of the graphic.

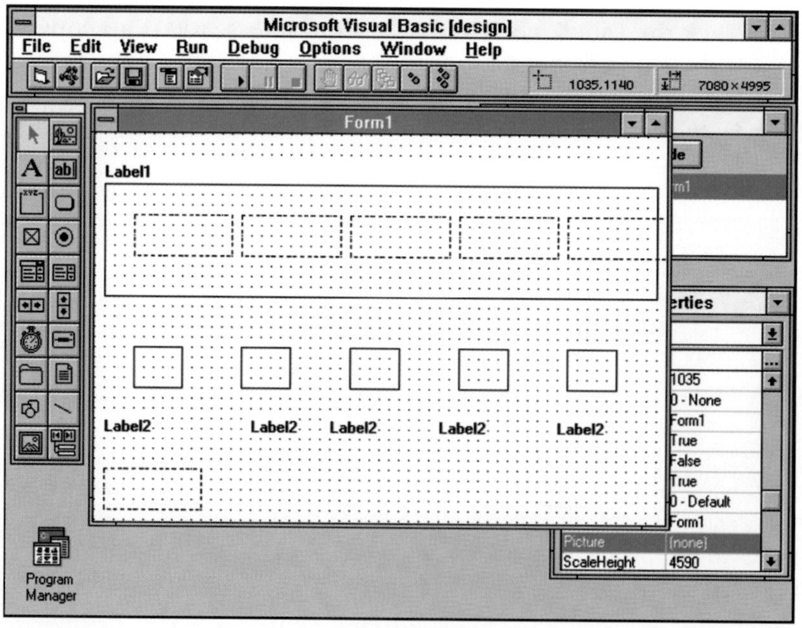

FIGURE 5-27

Creating the Menu

The Options menu in the Traffic Sign Tutorial contains three commands, as shown in Figure 5-28. Access keys are designated for the menu selection and command choices. The following steps create the menu using the Menu Design Window.

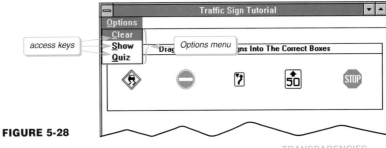

FIGURE 5-28

TO CREATE THE MENU ▼

STEP 1 ►

Click the Menu Design Window icon (🔳) in the toolbar, or choose Menu Design from the Window menu.

The Menu Design Window opens on the desktop (Figure 5-29).

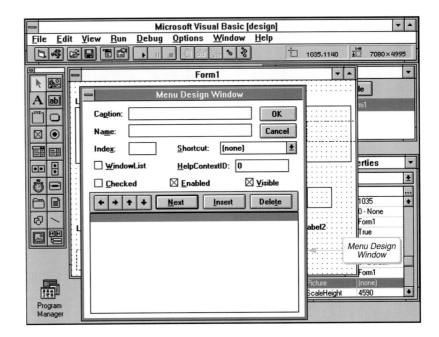

FIGURE 5-29

STEP 2 ►

Type &Options in the Caption box. Press the TAB key. Type mnuOptions in the Name box. Choose Next.

The mnuOptions control is added to the menu. Its caption appears in the menu control list box. The cursor advances to the next line in the menu control list box (Figure 5-30).

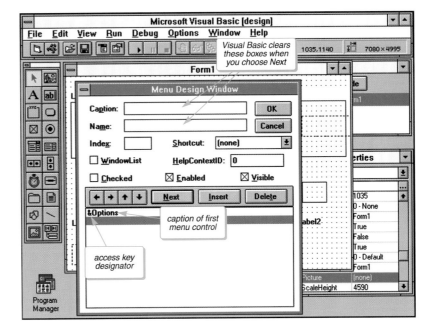

FIGURE 5-30

STEP 3 ▶

Click the right arrow (▣) button in the menu control list box. Type &Clear in the Caption box. Press the TAB key. Type mnuClear in the Name box. Choose Next.

The Menu Design Window appears as shown in Figure 5-31.

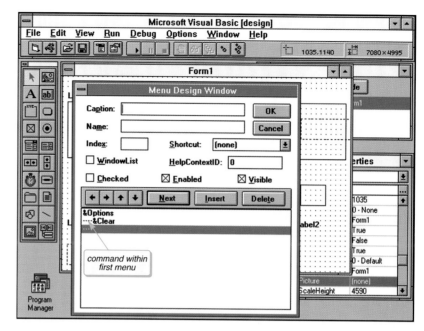

FIGURE 5-31

STEP 4 ▶

Type &Show in the Caption box. Press the TAB key. Type mnuShow in the Name box. Choose Next.

The Menu Design Window appears as shown in Figure 5-32.

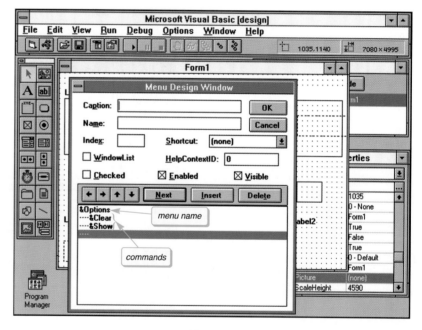

FIGURE 5-32

STEP 5 ▶

Type &Quiz **in the Caption box. Press the TAB key. Type** mnuQuiz **in the Name box. Choose the OK button.**

The Menu Design Window closes, and the menu is added to the form (Figure 5-33).

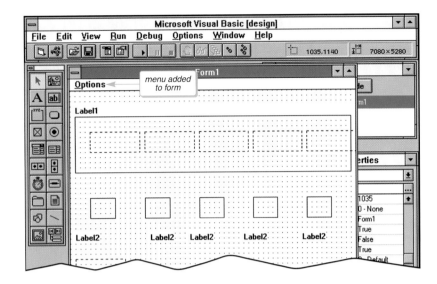

FIGURE 5-33

STEP 6 ▶

Click the menu title, Options, to view the menu structure.

Menus can be viewed during design time, as shown in Figure 5-34. Click anywhere on the form, or press the ESC key to close the menu.

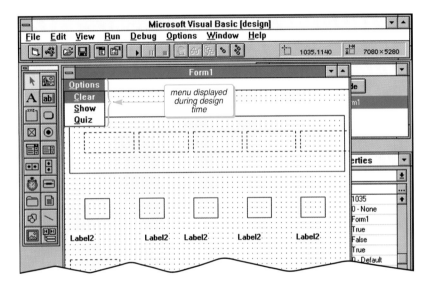

FIGURE 5-34

The interface for the Traffic Sign Tutorial is now complete. The next step of application development is to set the properties of the form and other controls.

▶ SETTING PROPERTIES

n this section, control properties are set in the following groups of steps:

▶ the properties of the form
▶ the properties of the five label controls used to display the names of the containers
▶ the properties of the controls in the imgSign array
▶ the properties of the individual image and label controls

Setting Properties of the Form

In the following steps, the name of the form is set, it is given a caption to appear in its title bar and an icon is specified to represent it when it is minimized. The following steps set these properties for the form control.

TO SET THE FORM'S PROPERTIES ▼

STEP 1 ▶

Make the Properties window visible by clicking it. Select the Form1 control from the drop-down Object list. Double-click the Name property in the Properties list. Type `frmTraffic` **and press the ENTER key. Click the Project window to make it visible.**

The form's new name appears in both the Project window and the Properties window. The form is given a default file name even though it has not yet been saved (Figure 5-35).

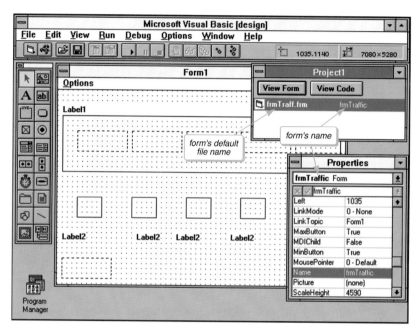

FIGURE 5-35

STEP 2 ▶

Double-click the Caption property in the Properties window. Type `Traffic Sign Tutorial` **and press the ENTER key. Double-click the Icon property in the Properties list.**

The Load Icon dialog box opens (Figure 5-36).

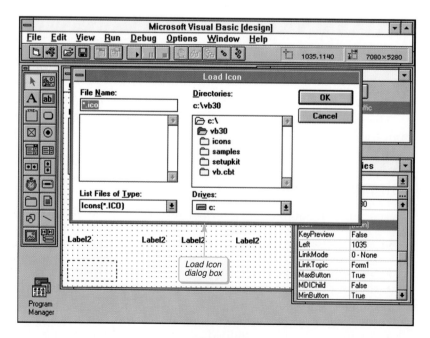

FIGURE 5-36

STEP 3 ▶

Double-click *icons* in the Directories list box. Double-click *traffic* in the Directories list box. Double-click the *trffc09.ico* (stoplight) icon in the File Name list box (Figure 5-37).

The icon is loaded, and the Load Icon dialog box closes. When the Form window is minimized, it appears as a stoplight icon (Figure 5-42 on page VB272).

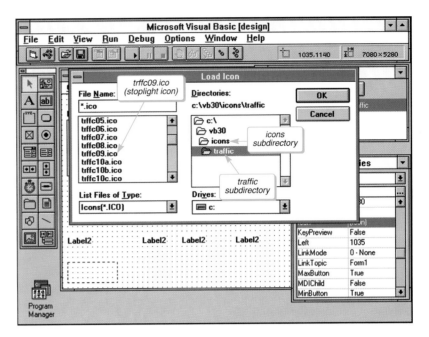

FIGURE 5-37

Setting the Captions of the Label Array Controls

The following steps set the captions of the label controls to reflect the names of the sign containers.

TO SET THE LABELS' CAPTIONS

Step 1: Select the Label2(0) control by clicking its name in the drop-down Object list in the Properties window. Double-click the Caption property. Type `Divided Highway` and press the ENTER key.

Step 2: Select the Label2(1) control by clicking its name in the drop-down Object list in the Properties window. Double-click the Caption property. Type `Stop` and press the ENTER key.

Step 3: Select the Label2(2) control by clicking its name in the drop-down Object list in the Properties window. Double-click the Caption property. Type `Speed Limit` and press the ENTER key.

Step 4: Select the Label2(3) control by clicking its name in the drop-down Object list in the Properties window. Double-click the Caption property. Type `Slippery Road` and press the ENTER key.

Step 5: Select the Label2(4) control by clicking its name in the drop-down Object list in the Properties window. Double-click the Caption property. Type `Do Not Enter` and press the ENTER key.

Step 6: Click the form to place it on top of the Properties window.

The labels' captions appear on the form. If necessary, adjust the location of the labels for even spacing, as shown in Figure 5-38 on the next page.

LECTURE NOTES
■ Emphasize that it is important to select a control by its name in the Properties window when its appearance (Caption) is similar to other controls on the form.
■ Review the methods for correcting typing mistakes made while entering captions in the settings box.

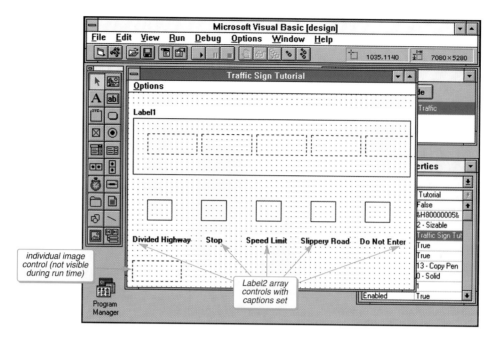

individual image
control (not visible
during run time)

Label2 array
controls with
captions set

FIGURE 5-38

Setting the Properties of the imgSign Array Controls

Controls in an array must have a common value for their Name property. There is no similar restriction on any other properties of controls in an array. The following steps load some of Visual Basic's traffic sign icons into the image controls in the imgSign array by setting the Picture property of each of these image controls.

When dragging is initiated during run time, only an outline of the control is moved across the desktop. An image other than the control's outline can appear as the control is being dragged by setting the control's **DragIcon property**. Double-clicking the DragIcon property in the Properties list opens the Load Icon dialog box that was used to set the form's icon property. In this application, the DragIcon property is set with code statements which will be added later. Perform the following steps to load the traffic icons into the image controls in the imgSign array.

TO SET THE PICTURE PROPERTY OF THE IMGSIGN ARRAY CONTROLS

Step 1: Select the imgSign(0) control from the drop-down Object list in the Properties window. Double-click the Picture property in the Properties list.

Step 2: Double-click the *trffc11.ico* (Divided Highway) icon in the File list box.

Step 3: Select the imgSign(1) control. Double-click the Picture property. Double-click the *trffc14.ico* (Stop) icon in the File list box.

Step 4: Select the imgSign(2) control. Double-click the Picture property. Double-click the *trffc12.ico* (Speed Limit) icon in the File list box.

Step 5: Select the imgSign(3) control. Double-click the Picture property. Double-click the *trffc07.ico* (Slippery Road) icon in the File list box.

Step 6: Select the imgSign(4) control. Double-click the Picture property. Double-click the *trffc13.ico* (Do Not Enter) icon in the File list box. Click the form to move it on top of the Properties window.

The traffic icons are loaded into the controls in the imgSign array, as shown in Figure 5-39.

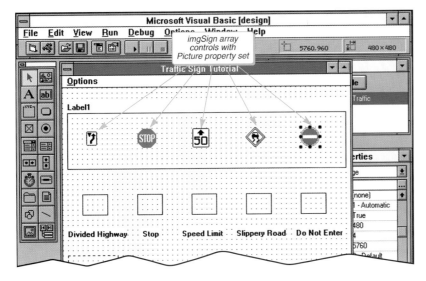

FIGURE 5-39

To load the icons in the previous steps, Visual Basic had to access the .ICO files from the VB3\ICONS\TRAFFIC directory. Once icons are loaded, they are saved as part of the form file, and the .ICO files are not used again.

Setting Properties for the Individual Label and Image Controls

The one label control that is not part of the label array is used to contain the run-time instructions for the Traffic Sign Tutorial. The instructions are centered in the control by setting the Alignment property.

The individual image control (lower left corner of form in Figure 5-38) is not visible at run time. It contains a blank picture that is assigned to other image controls through code statements to make them appear to move. The control is named imgBlank to aid in understanding the functions of the code statements in which its name is used. The following steps set the properties for these two controls.

TO SET THE LABEL AND IMAGE CONTROLS' PROPERTIES

Step 1: Select the label control by clicking it or by clicking its name, Label1, in the drop-down Object list in the Properties window.

Step 2: Double-click the Caption property. Type `Drag And Drop The Signs Into The Correct Boxes` and press the ENTER key.

Step 3: Double-click the Alignment property in the Properties window. Double-click the Alignment property in the Properties window a second time to center the text.

Step 4: Double-click the BorderStyle property in the Properties list to change the value to 1-Fixed Single.

Step 5: Select the Image1 image control by clicking it (located in the bottom left of the Form window) or by clicking its current name, Image1, in the drop-down Object list in the Properties window.

Step 6: Double-click the Name property in the Properties list. Type `imgBlank` and press the ENTER key.

Step 7: Double-click the Visible property in the Properties list to change the value to False.

The new property settings are visible in the Properties window (Figure 5-40).

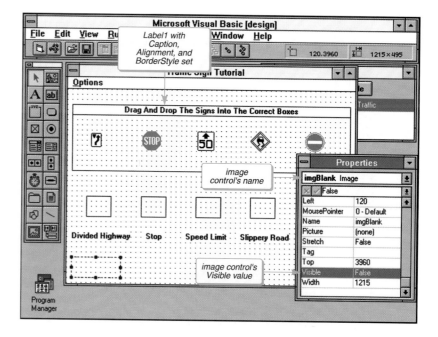

FIGURE 5-40

The design-time property setting is complete. The third phase in application development is to write the code. Before proceeding, save the form using the following steps.

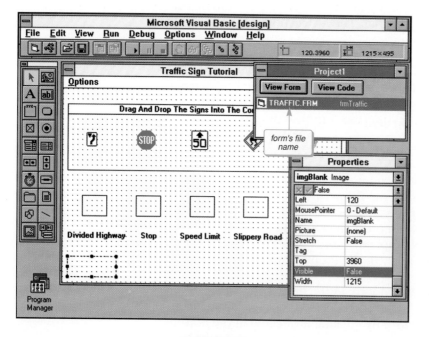

FIGURE 5-41

TO SAVE THE FORM

Step 1: Insert a formatted diskette in drive A.

Step 2: Choose Save File As from the File menu.

Step 3: Type `Traffic` in the File Name box in the Save File As dialog box.

Step 4: Select drive A from the drop-down Drives list in the dialog box.

Step 5: Click the OK button in the Save File As dialog box.

The form is saved as TRAFFIC.FRM. Click the Project window to see the form's file name (Figure 5-41).

▶ WRITING CODE

LECTURE NOTES
▪ Ask students to explain the difference between a source control and a target control during a drag-and-drop operation.
▪ Explain the DragOver event and its arguments.
▪ Emphasize that a drag-and-drop operation begins with a DragOver event.

T he code-writing activities for the Traffic Sign Tutorial include two new events: the DragOver event and the DragDrop event. The **DragOver** event occurs when a drag-and-drop operation is in progress. The mouse pointer position determines which target object receives this event. For example, when an image control (for example, Image1) is dragged over a form (for example, Form1), the Form_DragOver event is initiated. The source is Image1. The target is Form1.

You can write a code statement that applies to any control being dragged over the target by using the word `source` in the code statement. For example, the statement `Source.Visible = False` in a DragOver event subroutine sets the Visible property to False for any control being dragged over the target control. Note that changing the source control's Visible property to False does not affect the source control's DragIcon property. That is, the drag icon is still visible. Changing the source control's visible property to False gives the effect that the source control is being picked up and moved.

Visual Basic automatically adds the following first line to a DragOver subroutine:

```
Sub ctrlName_DragOver (Source As Control, X As Single, Y As Single, State As Integer)
```

The different parts of the DragOver procedure, called **arguments**, are listed in Table 5-1.

TRANSPARENCY
Table 5-1

▸ TABLE 5-1 DRAGOVER PROCEDURE ARGUMENTS

ARGUMENT	DESCRIPTION
ctrlName	The control being dragged over (the target)
Source	The control being dragged
X, Y	The current horizontal (X) and vertical (Y) position of the mouse pointer within the target form or control
State	The transition state of the control being dragged in relation to a target form or control: 0 — Enter (source control is being dragged within the range of a target) 1 — Leave (source control is being dragged out of the range of a target) 2 — Over (source control has moved from one position in the target to another)

LECTURE NOTES
▪ Explain the DragDrop event and its arguments.
▪ Emphasize that a drag-and-drop operation ends with a DragDrop event.

The **DragDrop** event occurs when a drag-and-drop operation is completed as a result of dragging a control over a form or control and then releasing the left mouse button. Visual Basic automatically adds the following first line to a DragDrop subroutine:

```
Sub ctrlName_DragDrop (Source As Control, X As Single, Y As Single)
```

The arguments of the DragDrop procedure are listed in Table 5-2.

▶ **TABLE 5-2 DRAGDROP PROCEDURE ARGUMENTS**

ARGUMENT	DESCRIPTION
ctrlName	The control over which the mouse pointer is located when the left mouse button is released (the target)
Source	The control being dragged. You can refer to properties and methods with this argument. For example, Source.Visible = 0
X, Y	The current horizontal (X) and vertical (Y) position of the mouse pointer within the target form or control

The DragDrop event procedure is used to control what happens after a drag-and-drop operation has been completed. For example, you can use the DragDrop event to move the source control to a new location or change the Visible property of the source control.

Code must be written for eleven events in the Traffic Sign Tutorial application. The control name, procedure, and a description of the action are listed in Table 5-3.

▶ **TABLE 5-3 TRAFFIC SIGN TUTORIAL EVENTS**

CONTROL NAME	PROCEDURE	ACTION
general	Declarations	Declares variables used within the subroutines
frmTraffic	Load	Center the form on the desktop. Sets the DragIcon property for image controls in the imgSign array
frmTraffic	DragOver	Occurs when dragging one of the signs is initiated. Changes the source control's Visible property to False
frmTraffic	DragDrop	Dropping a sign on the form (not in a container) is an incorrect placement of a sign. The source control's Visible property is set to True so the control appears to "snap back" to its original position
imgSign	DragDrop	Dropping a sign on another sign is also an incorrect placement. Same action as the form's DragDrop event.
Label1	DragDrop	Dropping a sign on label is also an incorrect placement. Same action as form's DragDrop event
Label2	DragDrop	Same as Label1_DragDrop event
imgContainer	DragDrop	Evaluates whether placement is correct or not. If correct, sets container's picture; if not, sets source Visible property to True
mnuClear	Click	Clears all pictures from containers; Sets all imgSign( ) Visible properties to True
mnuShow	Click	Sets all imgSign( ) properties to False; Sets imgContainer( ) Picture properties equal to correct signs
mnuQuiz	Click	Hides Traffic form; Displays three questions (one at a time); Keeps displaying question until a correct answer is given; Shows Traffic form

The subroutines for the frmTraffic_DragDrop, imgSign_DragDrop, Label1_DragDrop, and Label2_DragDrop are identical and are written using the same set of steps. The code-writing activities for the Traffic Sign Tutorial are grouped as follows:

▸ General_Declarations subroutine
▸ frmTraffic_Load subroutine
▸ frmTraffic_DragOver subroutine
▸ Label1, Label2, form, and imgSign DragDrop subroutines
▸ imgContainer_DragDrop subroutine
▸ mnuClear_Click subroutine
▸ mnuShow_Click subroutine
▸ mnuQuiz_Click subroutine

LECTURE NOTES
■ Explain what REM statements are and how they are used.

The subroutines written in the sections that follow include remark statements. **Remarks**, also called **comments**, are explanatory statements within a subroutine. A remark can be any text you want to include in your program. Spaces and punctuation are permitted. Comments are used to **document** (provide a written record of) how your code works or to provide any other information with your code. A remark statement must begin with either the word **REM** or an apostrophe (') to indicate to Visual Basic that the statement is not executable. When the application runs, all REM statements are ignored as if they weren't in the subroutine.

Writing the General_Declarations Subroutine

LECTURE NOTES
■ Review the reasons and procedure for declaring variables.
■ Give examples of the different Visual Basic data types.

The Traffic Sign Tutorial keeps a count of the number of correct sign placements by adding the number 1 to a variable named NumCorrect each time a correct placement is made. Since the value of NumCorrect must be available to more than one subroutine, it must be declared. The concept of declaring variables was introduced in Project 2 (page VB95). Recall that variable declarations must include a data type.

Visual Basic allows variables to have a **Variant** data type, so a given variable can store numbers, text, dates, or times. The Variant data type handles all types of data and converts them automatically. Declaring a data type other than Variant restricts the use of the variable but conserves some memory and makes the code run slightly faster. Visual Basic data types are listed in Table 5-4.

TRANSPARENCY
Table 5-4

▸ **TABLE 5-4 VISUAL BASIC DATA TYPES**

TYPE	STORAGE	RANGE OF VALUES
Integer	2 bytes	-32,768 to 32,767
Long	4 bytes	-2,147,483,648 to 2,147,483,647
Single	4 bytes	-3.402823E38 to -1.401298E-45 for negative values; 1.401298E-45 to 3.402823E38 for positive values
Double	8 bytes	-1.79769313486232E308 to -4.94065645841247E-324 for negative values;
Currency	8 bytes	-922,337,203,685,477.5808 to 922,337,203,685,477.5807
String	1 byte/chr	0 to approximately 65,500 bytes (Some storage overhead is required)
Variant	As needed	Any numeric value up to the range of a Double or any character text

For more information about data types, select the Visual Basic Help menu, choose Search, and type `Data Type`

TO WRITE THE GENERAL_DECLARATIONS SUBROUTINE

Step 1: Minimize the Form window.
Step 2: Click the View Code button in the Project window.
Step 3: Enter the following statement in the General_Declarations subroutine:
`Dim NumCorrect As Integer`

The minimized Form window and the Code window appear as shown in Figure 5-42.

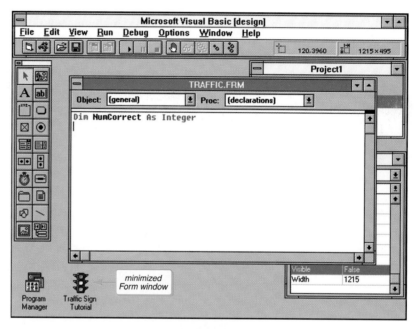

FIGURE 5-42

Writing the frmTraffic_Load Subroutine

The code in this subroutine causes the Traffic form to be centered on the desktop at the beginning of run time. The same code statements used to center the forms in previous projects are used in this project.

This subroutine also assigns a picture to the DragIcon property of each of the controls in the imgSign array. Recall that the default property setting for a drag icon is simply an outline of the control. In the following steps, the DragIcon property for each image is set equal to that image's Picture property. For example, the Picture property for imgSign(0) is the Divided Highway sign. The statement

```
imgSign(0).DragIcon = imgSign(0).Picture
```

sets the drag icon for that control to the Divided Highway icon. Since this assignment must be done for all five signs, the For...Next code structure presented in Project 4 is used. Perform the following steps to write the Load procedure for the frmTraffic control.

TO WRITE THE FRMTRAFFIC_LOAD SUBROUTINE

Step 1: Select the Form control from the drop-down Object list in the Code window.

Step 2: Enter the following statements in the Code window:

```
Rem Center form on desktop
frmTraffic.Top = (Screen.Height - frmTraffic.Height) / 2
frmTraffic.Left = (Screen.Width - frmTraffic.Width) / 2
Rem Set dragicons for signs
For Index = 0 To 4
    imgSign(Index).DragIcon = imgSign(Index).Picture
Next
```

The Code window appears as shown in Figure 5-43.

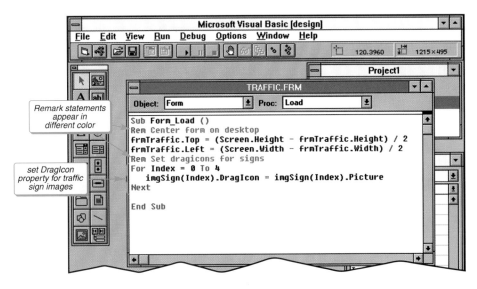

FIGURE 5-43

In the preceding steps, two remarks were added to help clarify the code statements that follow them. Note that when the ENTER key is pressed after a REM statement, Visual Basic changes the color of the statement to further set it apart from executable statements.

Writing the Form_DragOver Subroutine

This subroutine is executed whenever a control is dragged over the form. Since a shape control does not have a DragOver event, this event occurs in the Traffic Sign Tutorial when one of the traffic signs is dragged from its original position. To give the appearance that the sign is being moved, this event is used to change the Visible property of the source control to False. In this way, the source control's drag icon is visible when dragging occurs, but the source control is not visible in its original location.

The steps on the next page write the code statement to set the Visible property to False when the drag-and-drop operation begins.

TO WRITE THE FORM_DRAGOVER EVENT

Step 1: Select the DragOver procedure from the drop-down Procedures list in the Code window.

Step 2: Enter the following statements in the Code window:

```
Rem Set sign to invisible when dragging begins
Source.Visible = False
```

The Code window appears as shown in Figure 5-44.

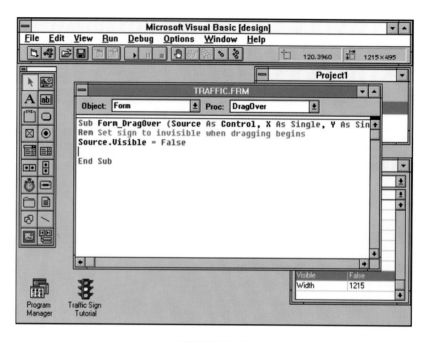

FIGURE 5-44

It is important to note that the Form_DragOver event is the first event to occur during the drag-and-drop operation in this application because the form is the first control that a source is dragged across when dragging is initiated.

Writing the Form, Label1, Label2, and imgSign DragDrop Subroutines

During the drag-and-drop operation in the Traffic Sign Tutorial, a control can be dropped on any of the controls listed above or on one of the controls in the imgContainer array. Recall that the Visible property of the source control (image being dragged) was set to False at the beginning of the drag-and-drop operation in the Form_DragOver event.

The DragDrop event occurs at the end of a drag-and-drop operation when the left mouse button is released. If the control (traffic sign) being dragged is dropped on any control other than an imgContainer, the placement is incorrect. When this error occurs, setting the source control's Visible property back to True makes the control appear to snap back to its original location. The code statements to do this are written in the following steps. The following steps also show how one event applies to all controls in an array.

TO WRITE THE DRAGDROP SUBROUTINES ▼

STEP 1 ►

Select DragDrop from the drop-down Procedures list in the Code window.

The Form_DragDrop subroutine appears in the Code window (Figure 5-45).

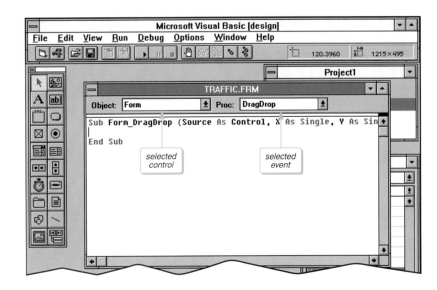

FIGURE 5-45

STEP 2 ►

Enter the following two statements in the Code window:

```
Rem Unallowable drop; return
  sign to original location
Source.Visible = True
```

The Code window appears as shown in Figure 5-46.

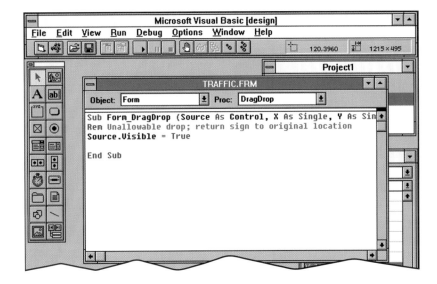

FIGURE 5-46

STEP 3 ►

Move the cursor to the left of the R in Rem. Press and hold the SHIFT key. Press the cursor down arrow key (fl) twice. Release the SHIFT key.

The two code statements written in Step 2 are highlighted (Figure 5-47).

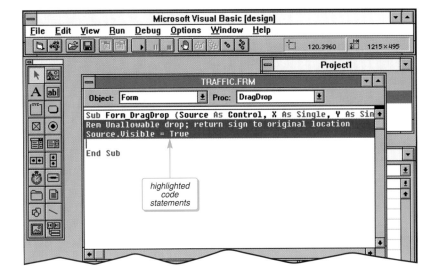

FIGURE 5-47

STEP 4 ▶

Press CTRL+C to copy the highlighted text to the Clipboard. Select the Label1_DragDrop subroutine by clicking Label1 in the drop-down Object list and clicking DragDrop in the drop-down Procedures list. Press CTRL+V to paste the Clipboard's contents inside the active Code window.

The highlighted code statements are copied to the Clipboard and then pasted to the Label1_Drag-Drop subroutine (Figure 5-48).

FIGURE 5-48

STEP 5 ▶

Select the Label2_DragDrop subroutine by clicking Label2() in the drop-down Object list and clicking DragDrop in the drop-down Procedures list. Press CTRL+V to paste the Clipboard's contents inside the active Code window.

The highlighted code statements are pasted to the Label2_Drag-Drop subroutine (Figure 5-49).

FIGURE 5-49

STEP 6 ▶

Select the imgSign_DragDrop subroutine by clicking imgSign() in the drop-down Object list and clicking DragDrop in the drop-down Procedures list. Press CTRL+V to paste the Clipboard's contents inside the active Code window.

The highlighted code statements are pasted to the imgSign_Drag-Drop subroutine (Figure 5-50).

FIGURE 5-50

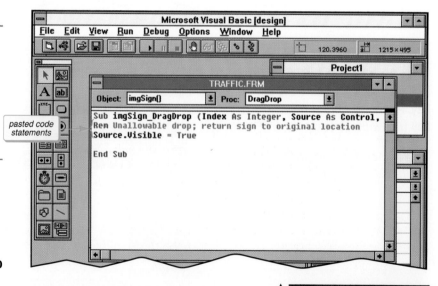

Project 2 presented a method for copying code between subroutines using the mouse and commands in the Edit menu. The preceding steps presented an alternate method for copying code using keyboard commands only. These same keyboard commands were used to copy and paste controls earlier in this project.

Writing the imgContainer_DragDrop Subroutine

Dropping a sign on one of the containers may or may not be a correct placement of the sign. Care was taken to add the controls in the arrays to the form in a certain order and to assign the pictures of the imgSign array and captions of the Label2 array in the same order.

For example, the Picture property of imgSign(0) is the Divided Highway sign. Label2(0) appears on the form below the imgContainer(0) control, and its caption is Divided Highway (Figure 5-51). By maintaining this consistency in array indexes, the "correctness" of dropping one of the imgSign controls on one of the imgContainer controls is determined by whether their indexes match. Recall that Index is a property of the source control when the source control is part of an array, and that Index also is an argument of the DragDrop event that identifies the specific target control when the target control is part of an array. Later, the imgSign controls will be rearranged on the form to make the tutorial more challenging, but this change will not affect their indexes.

LECTURE NOTES
■ Explain why this Drag-Drop subroutine is different than the others in this application.
■ Review the meaning and use of an index.
■ Explain how the code determines whether a sign placement in a container is correct or not.

TRANSPARENCY
Figure 5-51

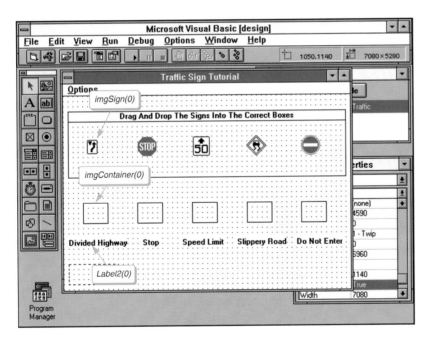

FIGURE 5-51

In the Traffic Sign Tutorial, certain actions occur if the placement is correct, and other actions occur if it is not. This type of logical selection is represented in code with the If...Then...Else structure used in previous projects. One of the actions if the placement is correct is to **increment** (add 1 to) the NumCorrect variable, which is used as a **counter**. Since the number of signs is five, additional actions are initiated if the counter's value = 5. This logic also is structured as an If...Then statement, but the condition NumCorrect = 5 is evaluated only if the current placement is correct. This If...Then structure within an If...Then...Else structure is called **nested**.

LECTURE NOTES
■ Explain the concept and uses of incrementing counters in code statements.
■ Review the If..Then..Else structure.
■ Explain what is meant by nested code structures.

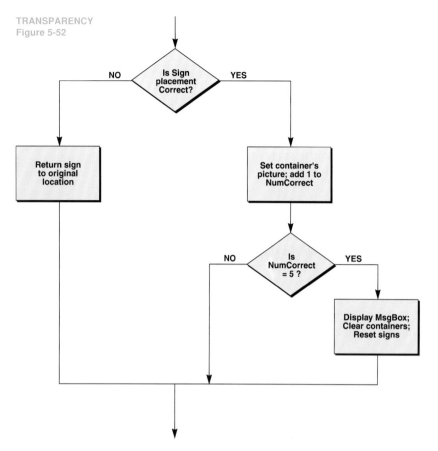

FIGURE 5-52

The logical flow of the nested If..Then structure for the Traffic Sign tutorial is diagrammed in Figure 5-52. The dialog box that indicates all signs have been placed correctly (Figure 5-53) is created using the MsgBox statement.

When the OK button is clicked in the dialog box, the signs are returned to their original positions. This same action occurs when the Clear command is chosen from Options menu in the application. Rather than repeat the code statements in both subroutines, you can execute a second subroutine by **calling** the event procedure for the second subroutine from the first. For example, when Visual Basic encounters the statement `mnuClear_Click` within the imgContainer_DragDrop subroutine, it immediately executes all the code within the mnuClear_Click subroutine and then returns to execute the next code statement in the imgContainer_DragDrop subroutine.

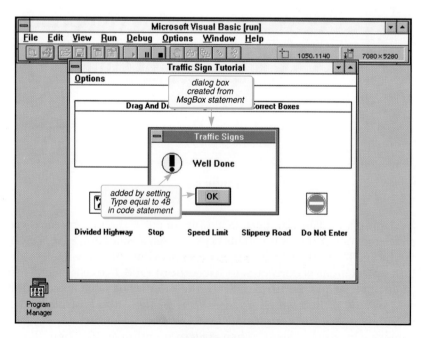

FIGURE 5-53

The following steps write the imgContainer_DragDrop subroutine using the nested If...Then structure.

TO WRITE THE IMGCONTAINER_DRAGDROP SUBROUTINE

Step 1: Select the imgContainer control array from the drop-down Object list in the Code window. Select the DragDrop procedure from the drop-down Procedures list.

Step 2: Enter the following statements in the Code window:

```
Rem Check for correct drop (indexes match)
If Source.Index = Index Then
    Rem Place sign in container; increment NumCorrect
    imgContainer(Index).Picture = Source.Picture
    NumCorrect = NumCorrect + 1
    Rem Check for last sign
    If NumCorrect = 5 Then
        Rem Display message; clear form
        MsgBox "Well Done", 48, "Traffic Signs"
        mnuClear_Click
    End If
Else
    Rem Incorrect drop; return sign to original location
    Source.Visible = True
End If
```

LECTURE NOTES
■ Explain the code statements in the subroutine.

TRANSPARENCY
Figure 5-54

The maximized Code window appears as shown in Figure 5-54.

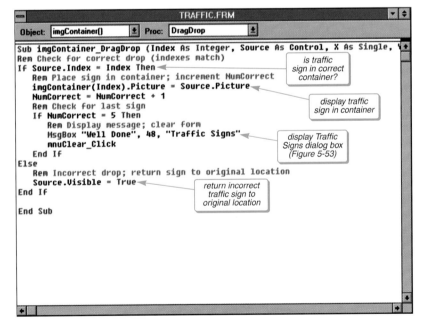

FIGURE 5-54

Writing the mnuClear_Click Subroutine

When the user of the Traffic Sign Tutorial chooses this command, all signs currently in containers are returned to their original locations. This command actually involves two actions: clearing any pictures from the container images and setting the Visible property of the imgSign controls. This subroutine also resets the value of NumCorrect to 0.

Each container is cleared by setting its Picture property equal to the Picture property of the imgBlank control. Each sign appears to return to its original locations by setting the Visible property of the controls in the imgSign array to True.

Because the property setting must be done for each control in the two arrays, the following steps write the subroutine using the For...Next loop presented on page VB229.

TO WRITE THE MNUCLEAR_CLICK SUBROUTINE

Step 1: Select the mnuClear control from the drop-down Object list in the Code window.

Step 2: Enter the following statements in the Code window:

```
Rem Clear containers and reset signs to original locations
For Index = 0 To 4
    imgContainer(Index).Picture = imgBlank.Picture
    imgSign(Index).Visible = True
Next
Rem Reset counter
NumCorrect = 0
```

The Code window appears as shown in Figure 5-55.

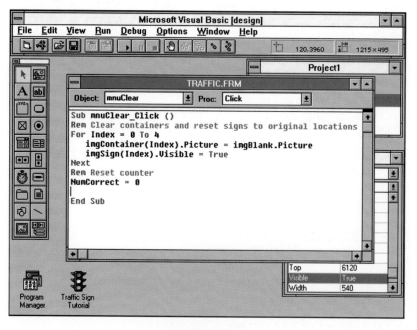

FIGURE 5-55

The mnuShow_Click Subroutine

When the Show command is chosen from the Options menu, all the signs appear to move from their original locations to the correct containers. This move is accomplished by setting the imgSign controls' Visible property to False and by setting each imgContainer's Picture property equal to the Picture property of the imgSign control's corresponding index.

You can choose the Show command any time during run time. Therefore, movements for all controls must be programmed because you don't know which signs have been placed correctly and which ones have not. The following steps use a For...Next loop to perform these tasks.

TO WRITE THE MNUSHOW_CLICK SUBROUTINE

Step 1: Select the mnuShow control from the drop-down Object list in the Code window.

Step 2: Enter the following statements in the Code window:

```
Rem Move all signs to correct containers
For Index = 0 To 4
    imgContainer(Index).Picture = imgSign(Index).Picture
    imgSign(Index).Visible = False
Next
```

The Code window appears as shown in Figure 5-56.

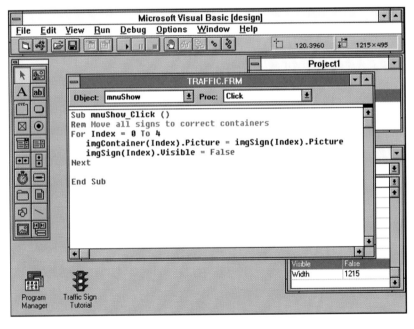

FIGURE 5-56

Writing the mnuQuiz_Click Subroutine

When you choose the Quiz command from the Options menu, you initiate a subroutine that contains several code structures, some of which are nested. The Quiz subroutine presents a series of three questions about the shapes of some signs. A For...Next loop is used to repeat the process of presenting a question and processing an answer.

The questions are displayed using a dialog box (Figure 5-57). An **InputBox function** displays a prompt in a dialog box, waits for the user to input text or to choose a button, and then returns the contents of the text box to the subroutine.

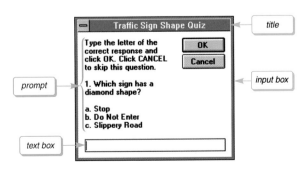

FIGURE 5-57

LECTURE NOTES
■ Explain the InputBox
function and its
arguments.

The syntax of the simplest form of InputBox function is:

InputBox*(prompt, title)*

The arguments of the InputBox function are described in Table 5-5.

TRANSPARENCY
Table 5-5

▶ **TABLE 5-5 ARGUMENTS OF THE INPUTBOX FUNCTION**

ARGUMENT	DESCRIPTION
prompt	String expression displayed as the message in the dialog box. The maximum length is approximately 255 characters depending on the width of the characters used.
title	String expression displayed in the title bar of the dialog box. If the title is omitted, nothing is placed in the title bar.

LECTURE NOTES
■ Explain why the carriage
return and linefeed con-
trol codes are concate-
nated in the code for this
subroutine.
■ Explain the use of the
Select Case statement
and its parts.

The prompt in Figure 5-57 on page VB281 consists of the question and all possible answers. A new line is started for each answer by using the carriage return and linefeed control characters presented on page VB104. This time their use is simplified, however, by creating and using a variable named NL (for new line) that is given the value of the control characters as follows:

```
NL = Chr$(13) & Chr$(10)
```

The variable's name, NL, now can be used in code statements in place of the control code characters themselves.

If the user chooses the OK button or presses the ENTER key, the InputBox function returns whatever is in the text box. If the user chooses the Cancel button, the function returns a zero-length string (" "). More complex InputBox functions are available in Visual Basic. For more information, refer to Visual Basic's online Help facility.

Each time the subroutine loops through the For...Next structure it must select the appropriate question. Project 3 presented the If...Then...Else statement as a method of selection within code. This project uses an additional selection structure, the Select Case statement. The **Select Case statement** executes one of several statement blocks depending on the value of an expression. In its simplest form, its syntax is:

Select Case *testexpression*
Case *expression1*
    statementblock-1
Case *expression2*
    statementblock-2
Case *Else*
    statementblock-n
End *Select*

The parts of the Select Case statement are described in Table 5-6.

▸ **TABLE 5-6 PARTS OF THE SELECT CASE STATEMENT**

PART	DESCRIPTION
Select Case	Begins the Select Case structure. Must appear on a separate line before any other part of the Select Case structure.
testexpression	The name of a variable or any numeric or *string expression* whose value is compared to the *expressions* that follow the word Case in each block (e.g. *expression1, expression2, etc.*). If *testexpression* matches the *expression* associated with a Case clause, the *statementblock* following that Case clause is executed.
Case	Begins a Case clause setting a group of Visual Basic statements to be executed if the *expression* following the word Case matches *testexpression*.
expression	The value of *testexpression* that leads to a different statementblock being executed. Similar to the *condition* in an If...Then statement.
statementblock	Any number of Visual Basic code statements.
Case Else	Optional keyword indicating the *statementblock* to be executed if no match is found between the *testexpression* and an *expression* in any of the other Case selections.
End Select	Ends the Select Case structure. Must appear on a separate line after all other statements in the Select Case structure.

In the Traffic Sign Tutorial, the counter in the For...Next loop is used as the *testexpression*, and the values from 1 to 3 are used in the *expressions* to select the appropriate question. The logical flow is diagrammed in Figure 5-58.

Although the question displayed in the Traffic Tutorial Quiz InputBox changes, the instructions and the set of possible answers remain the same each time. Code writing is simplified by creating three variables, named *inst1, inst2* and *answers*. The *inst1* and *inst2* variables hold the text of the instructions and the codes for new lines. The *answers* variable holds the text of the set of answers. The variables' names then are used in place of all the text. The code statements to create these variables are:

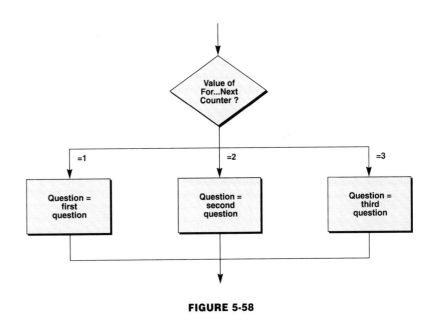

FIGURE 5-58

```
inst1 = "Type the letter of the correct response and click OK. "
inst2 = "Click CANCEL to skip this question." & NL & NL
answers = "a. Stop" & NL & "b. Do Not Enter" & NL & "c. Slippery Road"
```

The code statements and explanatory remarks for the first part of the mnuQuiz subroutine are as follows:

```
Rem Create newline variable
NL = Chr$(13) & Chr$(10)
Rem Create instructions variables
inst1 = "Type the letter of the correct response and click OK. "
inst2 = "Click CANCEL to skip this question." & NL & NL
Rem Create answers variable
answers = "a. Stop" & NL & "b. Do Not Enter" & NL & "c. Slippery Road"
Rem Hide traffic form
frmTraffic.Hide
Rem Loop for three questions
For QuesNum = 1 To 3
    Rem Assign value to variable Question and variable CorrectAnswer
    Select Case QuesNum
      Case Is = 1
          question = "1. Which sign has a diamond shape?" & NL & NL & answers
          CorrectAnswer = "C"
      Case Is = 2
          question = "2. Which sign has an octagonal shape?" & NL & NL & answers
          CorrectAnswer = "A"
      Case Is = 3
          question = "3. Which sign has a round shape?" & NL & NL & answers
          CorrectAnswer = "B"
    End Select
```

LECTURE NOTES
▪ List the remaining actions to be executed in the quiz.
▪ Explain the use of the variable named Response.

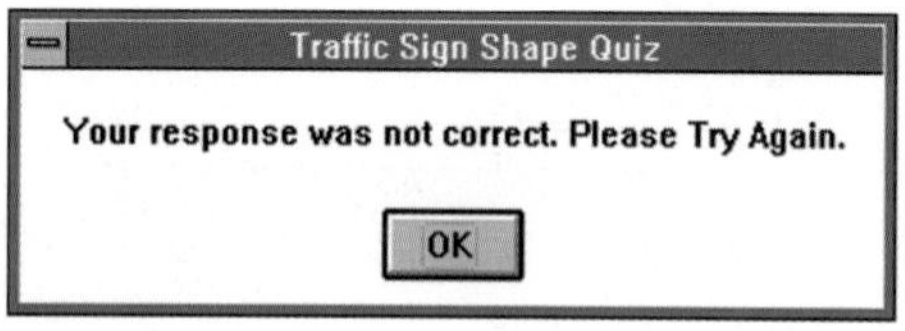

FIGURE 5-59

TRANSPARENCY
Figure 5-59

LECTURE NOTES
▪ Explain the Do Until loop and its parts.

TRANSPARENCY
Table 5-7

At this point in the code's execution during run time, the For...Next loop has begun. The first question has been assigned to the variable Question, and the correct answer to the first question has been assigned to the variable CorrectAnswer.

Next, the question must be displayed and the user's answer processed. An InputBox function is used to display the question and to get the user's answer. Whatever the user has typed in the text box of the dialog box is assigned as the value of a variable when the OK button is clicked. The variable can be given any valid variable name. This variable is named *Response* in the Traffic Sign Tutorial.

If the user has entered an incorrect answer and has clicked the OK button, the value of the variable Response does not match the value of the variable CorrectAnswer. The Traffic Sign Tutorial then displays the message box shown in Figure 5-59.

The application continues to redisplay the message box and the same question until the correct answer is given or until the user clicks the Cancel button. A For...Next loop is not an appropriate structure of repetition for this activity because the number of repetitions is not known in advance. A **Do...Loop** repeats a block of statements while a condition is True or until a condition is met. In this application, the incorrect answer message box and question are displayed until the answer is correct or until the Cancel button has been clicked. One form of the Do...Loop, called a **Do Until loop,** is used. The syntax is as follows:

```
Do Until condition
    statementblock
Loop
```

The parts of the Do Until loop are described in Table 5-7.

▸ **TABLE 5-7 PARTS OF THE DO UNTIL LOOP**

PART	DESCRIPTION
Do	Must be the first statement in a Do...Loop control structure
statementblock	Program lines between the Do and Loop statements that are repeated while or until condition is True
Until	Indicates the loop is executed until condition is True
condition	Numeric or string expression that evaluates to True

The logical flow of this Do Until loop is diagrammed in Figure 5-60. Notice that if the user responds correctly the first time or clicks the Cancel button, the condition is True immediately and the statements inside the loop (statementblock) are not executed. The online Help facility contains information on other variations of Do...Loop statements.

The condition evaluated in the Traffic Shape Quiz is whether the value of the variable Response equals the value of the variable CorrectAnswer or the value "". Recall that the zero length string value (") means the Cancel button was clicked. Notice in the code on page VB284 that the value assigned to the variable CorrectAnswer in Case = 1 is the character uppercase C. If the user enters a lowercase c, the condition will evaluate to False and the loop will continue. A way to account for a user responding in either lower or uppercase is to use the UCase$ function.

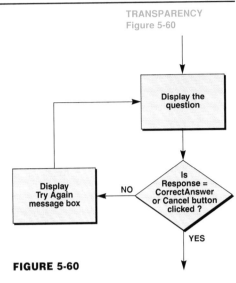

FIGURE 5-60

The **UCase$ function** returns a string with all letters of the argument uppercase. Its syntax is:

UCase$(*stringexpr*)

The argument *stringexpr* can be any string expression. Only lowercase letters are converted to uppercase; all uppercase letters and nonletter characters remain unchanged.

An InputBox statement is placed before the Do Until loop to provide the first opportunity for the user to respond. The loop executes until a correct answer is given *for each question*. That is, the Do...Loop is nested within the For...Next loop, as diagrammed in Figure 5-61. The additional code for the mnuQuiz_Click subroutine is as follows:

```
Rem Display question; assign returned value to
    variable Response
Response = InputBox(inst1 & inst2 & question,
    "Traffic Sign Shape Quiz")
Rem Begin loop for correct answer or Cancel button
Do Until UCase$(Response) = CorrectAnswer Or
    Response = ""
  Rem Create variable to hold text of message box
      for wrong answer
  tryagain = "Your response was not correct.
      Please Try Again."
  Rem Display message box for wrong answer
  MsgBox tryagain, , "Traffic Sign Shape Quiz"
  Rem Display question; assign returned value to
      variable Response
  Response = InputBox(inst1 & inst2 & question,
      "Traffic Sign Shape Quiz")
 Loop
Rem Add 1 to counter in for next loop
Next
Rem Redisplay main form after 3rd question
frmTraffic.Show
```

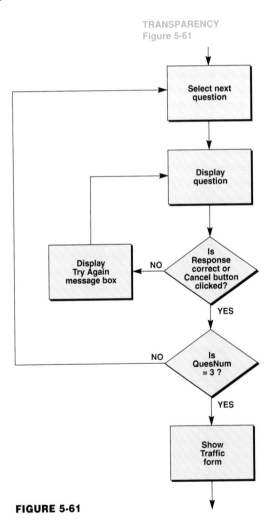

FIGURE 5-61

With the second section of code on page VB285, the mnuQuiz_Click subroutine is complete. In the following steps the mnuQuiz_Click subroutine is entered in the Code window.

TO WRITE THE MNUQUIZ_CLICK SUBROUTINE

Step 1: Select the mnuQuiz control from the drop-down Object list in the Code window.

Step 2: Enter the code for the subroutine, as shown in Figure 5-62.

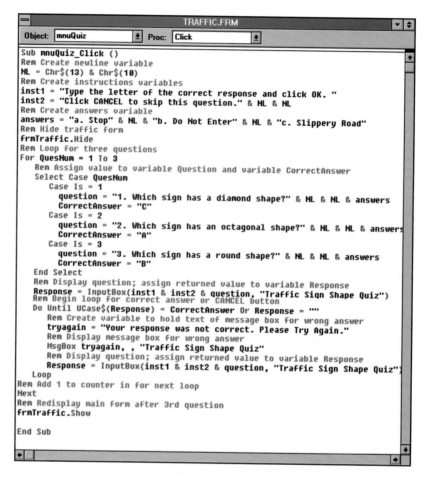

```
Sub mnuQuiz_Click ()
Rem Create newline variable
NL = Chr$(13) & Chr$(10)
Rem Create instructions variables
inst1 = "Type the letter of the correct response and click OK. "
inst2 = "Click CANCEL to skip this question." & NL & NL
Rem Create answers variable
answers = "a. Stop" & NL & "b. Do Not Enter" & NL & "c. Slippery Road"
Rem Hide traffic form
frmTraffic.Hide
Rem Loop for three questions
For QuesNum = 1 To 3
    Rem Assign value to variable Question and variable CorrectAnswer
    Select Case QuesNum
        Case Is = 1
            question = "1. Which sign has a diamond shape?" & NL & NL & answers
            CorrectAnswer = "C"
        Case Is = 2
            question = "2. Which sign has an octagonal shape?" & NL & NL & answers
            CorrectAnswer = "A"
        Case Is = 3
            question = "3. Which sign has a round shape?" & NL & NL & answers
            CorrectAnswer = "B"
    End Select
    Rem Display question; assign returned value to variable Response
    Response = InputBox(inst1 & inst2 & question, "Traffic Sign Shape Quiz")
    Rem Begin loop for correct answer or CANCEL button
    Do Until UCase$(Response) = CorrectAnswer Or Response = ""
        Rem Create variable to hold text of message box for wrong answer
        tryagain = "Your response was not correct. Please Try Again."
        Rem Display message box for wrong answer
        MsgBox tryagain, , "Traffic Sign Shape Quiz"
        Rem Display question; assign returned value to variable Response
        Response = InputBox(inst1 & inst2 & question, "Traffic Sign Shape Quiz")
    Loop
Rem Add 1 to counter in for next loop
Next
Rem Redisplay main form after 3rd question
frmTraffic.Show

End Sub
```

FIGURE 5-62

One last activity must be done before the Traffic Sign Tutorial is complete. In its current state (Figure 5-63), the correct container for each sign is directly below the sign. The following steps rearrange the imgSign controls to make the tutorial more challenging.

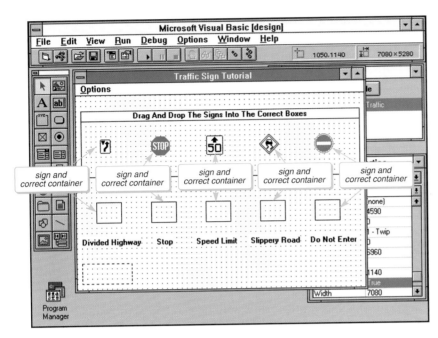

FIGURE 5-63

TO REARRANGE THE IMGSIGN CONTROLS

Step 1: Close the Code window by double-clicking its Control-menu box.

Step 2: Restore the Form window by double-clicking the form's icon.

Step 3: Rearrange the imgSign controls by dragging them to the positions shown in Figure 5-64.

This rearrangement does not affect the controls' indexes and therefore will have no effect on the function of the Tutorial.

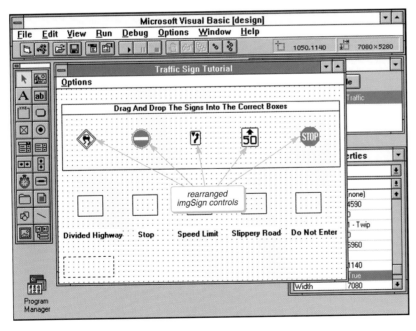

FIGURE 5-64

▶ Saving, Running, Documenting, and Distributing the Application

LECTURE NOTES
▪ Review the steps for saving forms and project files.

The Traffic Sign Tutorial project is complete. Before running the application, the form should be resaved and the project should be saved. The application is documented by generating a written record of the application's form and code. Steps are presented for distributing the application so that persons who don't have Visual Basic can run the application.

Saving the Project

The following steps resave the form file with the added code and save the project file to the diskette in drive A.

TO SAVE THE PROJECT

Step 1: Choose Save Project from the File menu, or click the Save Project tool (🖫) on the toolbar.
Step 2: Type `Traffic` in the File Name box in the Save Project As dialog box.
Step 3: Choose the OK button in the Save Project As dialog box.

The form file is resaved on the diskette in drive A as TRAFFIC.FRM. The project file is saved on the diskette in drive A as TRAFFIC.MAK.

Running the Application

LECTURE NOTES
▪ Demonstrate or discuss the run time features of the Traffic Sign Tutorial application.

With the application saved to a diskette, it can be run and tested. If Visual Basic encounters an error while reading or executing the code, it will halt execution and display and highlight the error in the Code window. The error can be corrected, and the application can be restarted. If you detect and correct any errors in this manner, be certain to resave the project.

When you run an application within Visual Basic, an additional window, the Debug window, is opened on the desktop. The Debug window aids in detecting errors within code in more complex applications. For more information on using the Debug window, consult Visual Basic's online Help facility. The following steps run the Traffic Sign Tutorial and test its functionality.

TO RUN THE APPLICATION ▼

STEP 1 ▶

Double-click the Code window's Control-menu box. Click the Run icon (▣) on the toolbar, or choose Start from the Run menu.

The application appears (Figure 5-65).

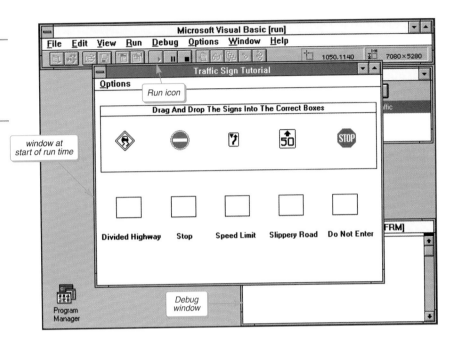

FIGURE 5-65

STEP 2 ▶

Choose Show from the Options menu.

The signs move to the correct containers (Figure 5-66).

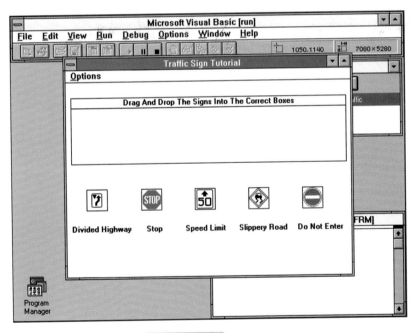

FIGURE 5-66

STEP 3 ▶

Choose Clear from the Options menu to return the signs to their original locations. Drag and drop one of the signs anywhere on the form other than its correct container.

During the drag operation the sign appears to move from its original location (Figure 5-67). When dropped incorrectly, it returns to its original position.

FIGURE 5-67

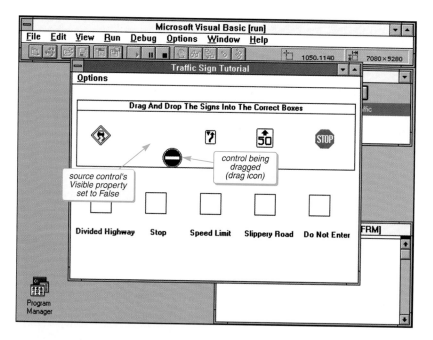

STEP 4 ▶

Choose Quiz from the Options menu. Enter an incorrect answer (a) and then click the OK button. When the dialog box indicating an incorrect response appears, click the OK button.

The question is redisplayed until a correct answer is given (Figure 5-68).

STEP 5 ▶

Complete the quiz, and then test the other features of the application. To end the application, double-click the Tutorial's Control-menu box or click the Stop icon (■) on the toolbar.

Because the dialog box is a modal form, you cannot perform any other function (including stopping the application) until the form is closed by entering the correct answer.

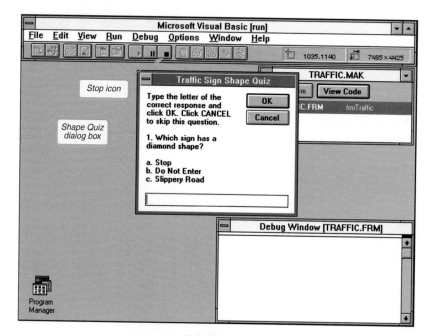

FIGURE 5-68

Documenting the Application

In this project, remarks were added within subroutines to make the code statements more understandable. Also, variable names were chosen that reflected the purpose of the variable, such as QuesNum rather than x or y. Using these methods to aid understanding is called making the code **self-documenting**.

Documenting the application refers to generating a written record of the application. The following steps can be used to print a record of the application when the computer is connected to a printer.

TO PRINT A RECORD OF THE APPLICATION ▼

STEP 1 ▶

Select the File menu from the menu bar.

The File menu opens (Figure 5-69).

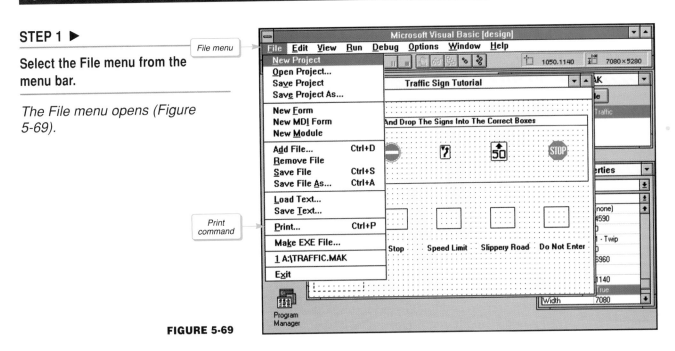

FIGURE 5-69

STEP 2 ▶

Choose the Print command.

The Print dialog box opens (Figure 5-70).

STEP 3 ▶

Click the All option button. Click the Form check box. Click the Code check box. Click the OK button.

The Traffic form and code subroutines are printed.

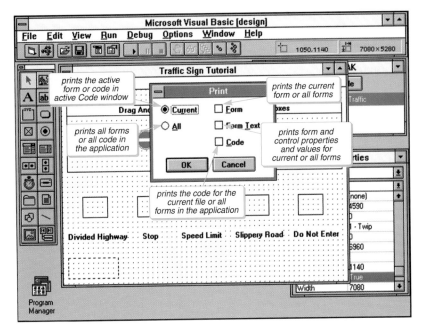

FIGURE 5-70

Making an .EXE File and Distributing Applications

LECTURE NOTES
■ Introduce students to
some of the file manage-
ment issues involved in
distributing Visual Basic
applications.

The Traffic Sign Tutorial can be made executable by following the steps used in Project 3 on page VB174. In that project, the application is saved as an .EXE file and is called stand-alone. However, in Visual Basic, this term is not entirely accurate because at least one other file is required to run a Visual Basic .EXE file.

Many different Windows applications share the use of special files called **dynamic-link libraries**. These files have the **.DLL** file extension. In order for someone who does not have Visual Basic to run your Visual Basic .EXE applications, that person must have the file VBRUN300.DLL in the Windows\System directory. It is legal for you to copy this file and distribute it with your applications.

If your application includes any custom controls, their .VBX files also must be copied to the user's Windows\System directory. They must be distributed with your application regardless of whether the application actually uses the controls. Thus, you should remove unused custom controls from your project, as was done at the beginning of this project.

Finally, if your application itself accesses any .DLL's not already installed on the intended user's PC, they must be distributed as well. For example, the financial function used in Project 3 is part of the MSFINX.DLL, and that file also must be distributed. Visual Basic includes an additional application, called Setup Wizard, that assists in preparing applications for distribution.

▶ PROJECT SUMMARY

In Project 5, the three-step approach was used to build another Windows application. Unused custom controls were removed from the project. The InputBox and UCase$ functions were used in the code statements. More complex code was written using nested structures, the Select Case structure, and the Do...Loop structure. Remarks were added to aid in understanding the code, and a printed record of the application was generated. The file requirements for distributing executable Visual Basic applications were presented.

▶ KEY TERMS

arguments *(VB269)*
AUTOLOAD.MAK *(VB249)*
calling subroutines *(VB278)*
comments *(VB271)*
counter *(VB277)*
custom controls *(VB249)*
.DLL *(VB292)*
Do...Loop *(VB284)*
Do Until loop *(VB284)*
document *(VB271)*

DragDrop event *(VB269)*
DragIcon property *(VB266)*
DragMode property *(VB254)*
DragOver event *(VB269)*
dynamic-link library *(VB292)*
increment *(VB277)*
InputBox function *(VB281)*
nested code *(VB277)*
REM *(VB271)*
remarks *(VB271)*

Select Case block *(VB282)*
self-documenting *(VB291)*
source control *(VB254)*
target control *(VB254)*
UCase$ function *(VB285)*
variant *(VB271)*
.VBX *(VB249)*

In Visual Basic you can accomplish a task in a number of ways. The following table provides a quick reference to each of the major tasks presented for the first time in the project with some of the available options. The commands listed in the Menu column can be executed using either the keyboard or mouse.

Task	Mouse	Menu	Keyboard Shortcuts
Add a Custom Control File		From File menu, choose Add File	Press CTRL+D
Copy Code From the Clipboard to a Selected Code Window		From Edit menu, choose Paste	Press CTRL+V
Copy Highlighted Code to the Clipboard		From Edit menu, choose Copy	Press CTRL+C
Highlight (Select) Code Statements in the Code Window	Drag mouse across code block to be selected		Press SHIFT+arrow keys
Open the Print Dialog Box		From File menu, choose Print	Press CTRL+P
Remove a Selected Custom Control File		From File menu, choose Remove File	Press DELETE
Select a Custom Control File from the Active Project Window	Click on file's name in Project window		

STUDENT ASSIGNMENT 1
True/False

EXERCISE NOTES
■ Use Student Assignments 1 through 6 for classroom discussion or homework exercises

Instructions: Circle T if the statement is true or F if the statement is false.

T (F) 1. The files for custom controls have a .DLL file extension.
T (F) 2. The AUTOLOAD.MAK file is used to make applications executable.
(T) F 3. A control being dragged is called the source control.
T (F) 4. The control over which another control is being dragged is called the object control.
T (F) 5. Run-time dragging of a control automatically changes its location.
(T) F 6. Design-time dragging of a control automatically changes its location.
(T) F 7. CTRL+V can be used to copy a control to the Clipboard.
T (F) 8. After a control is copied to the Clipboard, it can be pasted only once.
(T) F 9. A shape control does not have a DragOver event.

VB293

STUDENT ASSIGNMENT 1 (continued)

T (F) 10. Menus can be selected only during run time.
T (F) 11. The default value of an image control's DragIcon property is the value of its Picture property.
T (F) 12. Only image controls can have DragIcons.
T (F) 13. The different parts of a function or procedure are called arguables.
(T) F 14. A control's DragDrop event is executed when the control is the target during a dragging operation and the left mouse button is released.
T (F) 15. REM statements must begin with the letters REM or with a comma.
T (F) 16. Variables with a Variant data type must be declared.
(T) F 17. Variables used by more than one subroutine must be declared.
(T) F 18. Generally, variables with a data type other than Variant require less memory space.
(T) F 19. Nesting refers to writing one code structure within another.
T (F) 20. One control event cannot be used to initiate other controls' events.

STUDENT ASSIGNMENT 2
Multiple Choice

Instructions: Circle the correct response.

1. The _____ control is not a custom control.
   a. OLE
   b. grid
   c. common dialog
   (d.) scroll bar

✓ 2. To run a Visual Basic .EXE file, a computer must at least have the _____ file.
   a. VB.VBX
   (b.) VBRUN300.DLL
   c. VBX.DLL
   d. all of the above

✗ 3. _____ is the keyboard command to paste a control from the Clipboard to a form.
   (a.) CTRL+C
   b. CTRL+X
   c. CTRL+V
   d. CTRL+P

4. The ability to drag an object during run time is controlled by its _____ property.
   a. DragOver
   b. DragDrop
   c. DragIcon
   (d.) DragMode

5. During a drag-and-drop operation, the DragOver event and DragDrop event belong to the _____ control.
   a. source
   (b.) target
   c. dragged
   d. form

6. Comment statements within code must be preceded by _____.
   a. REM
   b. '
   c. neither a nor b
   (d.) either a or b

7. _____ is not a valid data type.
   a. Integer
   b. Long
   (c.) Short
   d. Double

✓ 8. A variable used in code to keep track of the number of times something has occurred is called a(n) _____.
   a. flag
   b. increment
   c. nest
   (d.) counter

9. The Select Case statement is a code structure used for _____.
   a. repetition
   (b.) selection
   c. sequence
   d. none of the above

✓ 10. An InputBox function always contains a(n) _____.
   a. text box
   b. OK button
   c. Cancel button
   (d.) all of the above

STUDENT ASSIGNMENT 3
Understanding Code Structures

Instructions: Figure SA5-3 shows an interface for an application that calculates the total cost of the purchase of ball point pens. The unit price depends on the quantity ordered, as follows:

QUANTITY	PRICE PER UNIT
< 150	.55
151-250	.48
251-500	.42
> 500	.40

FIGURE SA5-3

Draw a flowchart and write a subroutine to calculate the total price. Use a Select Case statement within the subroutine to select the appropriate unit price before calculating the total price.

STUDENT ASSIGNMENT 4
Understanding Code Structures

Instructions: Figure SA5-4 shows an interface for an application that computes weekly pay, given the number of hours worked and the hourly pay rate. If the number of hours worked exceeds 40, the person is paid an overtime rate of 1.5 times the normal rate. If a person works more than 40 hours and his pay rate is less than $4.50, he receives a $10 bonus for that week in addition to the regular and overtime pay.

Draw a flowchart and write a subroutine to compute the week's pay. Use a nested If...Then structure to determine whether the $10 bonus is added to the pay.

FIGURE SA5-4

STUDENT ASSIGNMENT 5
Understanding Code Structures

Instructions: Draw a flowchart and write a subroutine to perform the following actions:

Display an input box that prompts the user to supply an examination score. After a score is entered, the input box should prompt for another score. After the fifth score is entered, the average of the three scores should be displayed using a MsgBox statement.

STUDENT ASSIGNMENT 6
Understanding Code Structures

Instructions: A bank computes its monthly service charge based on the number of checks written. The service charge is computed as $.25 plus $.09 on the first ten checks plus $.08 on the next ten checks plus $.07 on the next ten checks plus $.06 on any additional checks.

Write two subroutines that calculate the service charge, given the number of checks. The first subroutine should use a Select Case statement. The second subroutine should perform the same calculation using an If...Then...Else block.

C O M P U T E R   L A B O R A T O R Y   E X E R C I S E S

EXERCISE NOTES
■ Exercise 1 provides students with experience using the DragMode and DragIcon properties of controls to ad drag-and-drop operations to applications.

COMPUTER LABORATORY EXERCISE 1
DragMode and DragIcon Properties

Instructions: Start Visual Basic. Open the project CLE5-1 from the subdirectory VB3 on the Student Diskette that accompanies this book. Complete the following tasks.

1. Choose the View Form button. The form contains two image controls, two frames, and five Option buttons, as shown in Figure CLE5-1.
2. Set the Visible property of the Image2 control to False.
3. Set the following captions as shown in the table below.

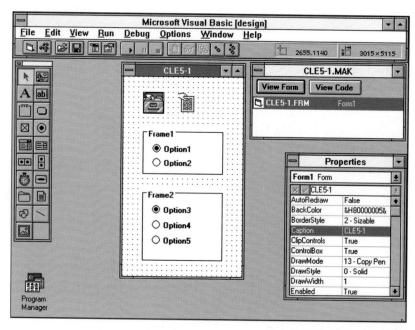

FIGURE CLE5-1

CONTROL	CAPTION
Frame1	DragMode
Frame2	DragIcon
Option1	Manual
Option2	Automatic
Option3	None
Option4	Image1.
Option5	Image2.

4. Enter the subroutines listed in the table to the right for the Option button Click events.
5. Save the form as CLE5-1A.FRM, and save the project as CLE5-1A.MAK. Close the Code window.
6. Run the application. Select the Manual DragMode Option button. Drag the image around the desktop. What happens?

EVENT	SUBROUTINE
Option1_Click	Image1.DragMode = 0
Option2_Click	Image1.DragMode = 1
Option3_Click	Rem Image2.DragIcon is blank Image1.DragIcon = Image2.DragIcon
Option4_Click	Image1.DragIcon = Image1.Picture
Option5_Click	Image1.DragIcon = Image2.Picture

7. Select the Automatic DragMode option button. Drag the image around the desktop. What happens?
8. Select each of the three DragIcon option buttons, and drag the image around the desktop. What happens?
9. To end the application, click the Stop icon on the toolbar, or double-click the form's Control-menu box.
10. Check with your instructor for directions on turning in the exercise.

COMPUTER LABORATORY EXERCISE 2
The DragOver Event

Instructions: Start Visual Basic. Open the project CLE5-2 from the subdirectory VB3 on the Student Diskette that accompanies this book.

Perform the following steps.

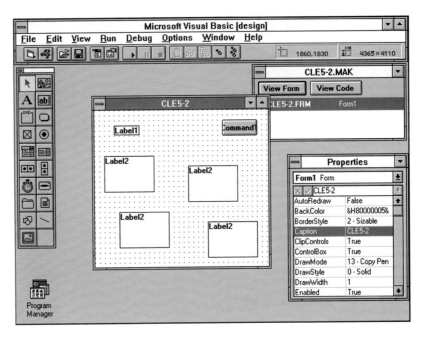

FIGURE CLE5-2

1. Choose the View Form button in the Project window. The form contains one label, one Command button, and one label control array, as shown in Figure CLE5-2.
2. Set the control properties as shown in the table below and to the bottom right.
3. Enter the following Command1_Click subroutine:

```
For Index = 0 To 3
  Label2(Index).Caption = ""
Next
```

4. Write the following Label2_DragOver subroutine:

```
If State = 2 Then
  Label2(Index).Caption = "Target"
Else
  Label2(Index).Caption = ""
End If
```

5. Save the form as CLE5-2A.FRM, and then save the project as CLE5-2A.MAK. Close the Code window.
6. Start the application. Click the Clear button.
7. Drag the Label1 control (with the caption Source) around the form. What happens?
8. Drop the label on the form. Click the Clear button. Drag the label again.
9. To end the application, click the Stop icon on the toolbar, or double-click the form's Control-menu box.
10. Check with your instructor for directions on turning in the exercise.

CONTROL	PROPERTY	VALUE
Label1	Caption	Source
Label1	DragMode	Automatic
Command1	Caption	Clear

EXERCISE NOTES
■ Exercise 3 provides students with experience using DragDrop events in applications.

COMPUTER LABORATORY EXERCISE 3
The DragDrop Event

Instructions: Start Visual Basic. Open the project CLE5-3 from the subdirectory VB3 on the Student Diskette that accompanies this book.

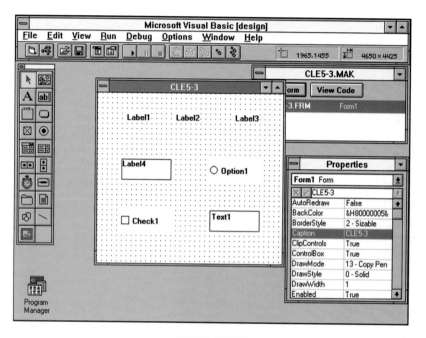

FIGURE CLE5-3

Perform the following steps.

1. Choose the View Form button in the Project window. The form contains four label controls, one text box, one check box, and one option button, as shown in Figure CLE5-3.
2. Double-click Label1's BackColor property in the Properties window. Use the Color dialog box to set Label1's BackColor to red.
3. Repeat Step 2 twice to set Label2's BackColor to yellow and Label3's BackColor to green.
4. Set the DragMode to Automatic for Label1, Label2, and Label3.
5. Write the following subroutine for the Label4_DragDrop event:
   ```
   Label4.BackColor = Source.BackColor
   ```
6. Write the following subroutine for the Text1_DragDrop event:
   ```
   Text1.BackColor = Source.BackColor
   ```
7. Write the following subroutine for the Option1_DragDrop event:
   ```
   Option1.BackColor = Source.BackColor
   ```
8. Write the following subroutine for the Check1_DragDrop event:
   ```
   Check1.BackColor = Source.BackColor
   ```
9. Write the following subroutine for the Form_DragDrop event:
   ```
   Form1.BackColor = Source.BackColor
   ```
10. Save the form as CLE5-3A.FRM, and then save the project as CLE5-3A.MAK. Close the Code window.
11. Run the application. Drag and drop the three labels on the different controls on the form. What happens?
12. Close the application by double-clicking its Control-menu box or by clicking the Stop icon on the toolbar.
13. Check with your instructor for directions on turning in the exercise.

COMPUTER LABORATORY ASSIGNMENT 1
Team Assignment Application

EXERCISE NOTES
■ The four Computer Laboratory Assignments increase in difficulty.

Purpose: To build an application that uses drag-and-drop functionality to add text to list boxes.

Problem: You have been put in charge of organizing the tug-of-war event at the annual company picnic. As people call to let you know they want to participate, you assign them to one of two teams. You would like to have a computer application to keep track of these assignments. You want to be able to type in the name and then drag and drop the person's name on one of two scrollable lists.

Instructions: Perform the following tasks.

1. Start Visual Basic, or open a new project if Visual Basic already is running.
2. Create an interface with three labels, one text box, two simple list boxes, and caption, as shown in Figure CLA5-1.
3. Set the TabStop property of the list boxes to False.
4. Set the appropriate captions for the form and labels.
5. Set the DragMode of the text box to Automatic.
6. Write the DragDrop event for each of the list boxes. Dropping the text box on the list should add the name to that list and clear the name from the text box. Hint: Use the AddItem method to add Text1.Text, and then set Text1.Text equal to " ".

EXERCISE NOTES
■ Assignment 3 and Assignment 4 are suitable for either individual or small group assignments.

7. Save the form as CLA5-1.FRM. Save the project as CLA5-1.MAK.
8. Run the application to test it.
9. Check with your instructor for directions on turning in the assignment.

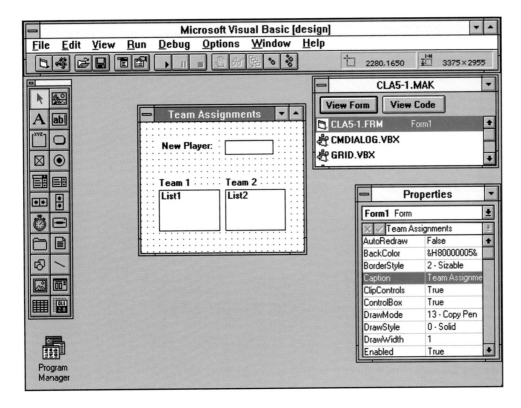

FIGURE CLA5-1

COMPUTER LABORATORY ASSIGNMENT 2
Security Subroutine

Purpose: To build an application that uses InputBox statements, MsgBox statements, and a Do...Loop.

Problem: You want to design a password checking subroutine that will be part of the Form_Load procedure for an application.

Instructions: Perform the following tasks.

1. Start Visual Basic, or open a new project if Visual Basic already is running.
2. Set the form's Caption property to Security Check. All actions for the password check will be part of the Form_Load subroutine, so you needn't do anything else to the form.
3. The subroutine should prompt the user with a dialog box similar to the one shown in Figure CLA5-2a.
4. If the password is correctly entered (it is "pass"), the message box in Figure CLA5-2b should display. Hint: This MsgBox *Type* is 16. If the password is not correct, the message box shown in Figure CLA5-2c should appear. If the user clicks the Cancel button, the application should end.
5. If the user enters an incorrect password a third time, the application should end. Hint: Each time the input box is displayed, a counter variable should be incremented.
6. Use a Do...Loop in the subroutine. Hint: the input box keeps displaying until the password is correct OR the number of incorrect tries is three OR the user clicks the Cancel button.
7. Save the form as CLA5-2.FRM. Save the project as CLA5-2.MAK.
8. Run the application by clicking the Start icon on the toolbar.
9. Check with your instructor for directions on turning in the assignment.

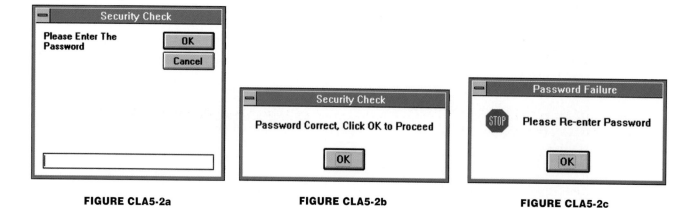

     FIGURE CLA5-2a   **FIGURE CLA5-2b**   **FIGURE CLA5-2c**

COMPUTER LABORATORY ASSIGNMENT 3
Custom Traffic Quiz Input Box

Purpose: To build and use a custom input box.

Problem: In the Traffic Sign Tutorial built in Project 5, the questions in the Shape Quiz were presented to the user by using an InputBox function. You would like to have a customized input box where the input area (text box) is not so wide.

Instructions: Start a new application with a form that has a single command button labeled Quiz. Clicking the Quiz button should initiate the series of three questions and message boxes described in Project 5. However, you should create a second form to display the question and to receive the user's answer rather than using the InputBox function.

Save the main form as CLA5-31.FRM. Save the input form as CLA5-32.FRM. Save the project as CLA5-3.MAK. If you completed the application in Project 5, it can be revised by adding CLA32.FRM to the TRAFFIC.MAK project and replacing the mnuQuiz_Click subroutine with the Command1_Click subroutine written in this assignment. Check with your instructor about revising the TRAFFIC.MAK application and for directions on turning in the assignment.

COMPUTER LABORATORY ASSIGNMENT 4
Currency Exchange

Purpose: To build an application that uses the ListIndex value of a drop-down list box and uses a Select Case structure within code.

Problem: You would like to add some additional sophistication to the currency exchange application that was built and revised in previous assignments. Specifically, you would like the conversion to take place at the same time the type of currency is selected from a drop-down list.

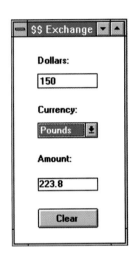

Create an interface similar to the one shown in Figure CLA5-4. The drop-down list should contain the names of the different currencies. Clicking the Clear button should clear all boxes on the form.

Hint: The combo box's Click event is triggered when an item is selected from the drop-down list. The value of the combo box's ListIndex property corresponds to the item selected; the appropriate conversion could be made by selecting different actions based on the value of Combo1.ListIndex. A combo box's text is cleared by setting its ListIndex equal to -1.

FIGURE CLA5-4

Use the following exchange rates. One dollar equals:

    1.4920 pounds
    .54699 guilders
    .61489 marks
    .80160 Canadian dollars

Save the form as CLA5-4.FRM. Save the project as CLA5-4.MAK. Check with your instructor for directions on turning in the assignment.

INDEX